French Cinema

French Cinema

by

Roy Armes

Secker & Warburg
London

000/6131

A1913

791·430944

Luton Sixth Form College
Library

First published in England 1985 by
Martin Secker & Warburg Limited
54 Poland Street, London W1V 3DF

Copyright © 1985 by Roy Armes

British Library Cataloguing in Publication Data

Armes, Roy
    French cinema.
    1. Moving-pictures–France–History
    I. Title
    791.43'0944   PN1993.5.F7

    ISBN 0-436-01804-7
    ISBN 0-436-01805-5 Pbk

Set in Linotron 202 Sabon 11/13 by
Wyvern Typesetting Limited, Bristol

Printed in Great Britain by
Richard Clay (The Chaucer Press) Ltd
Bungay, Suffolk

To Jair

Contents

Acknowledgements   ix

Introduction   1

  1 The Pioneers of a World Industry   7

  2 The Era of Dominance   19

  3 Collapse and Rebirth   34

  4 The Culmination of Silent Cinema   51

  5 The Coming of Sound   67

  6 The Paradoxes of French Realism   86

  7 Four Years in a Bottle   109

  8 A Timid Renewal   125

  9 The Tradition of Quality   146

10 New Wave   169

11 Ebb Tide   194

12 Return to Reality   220

13 The Liberalisation of Cinema   245

Postscript   270

Bibliography   281

Index   291

Acknowledgements

This book would have been impossible without the prior efforts of my many predecessors in the study of French cinema, and the wide range of debts I owe to French critics and film historians, for both factual information and stimulating speculation, is apparent in the select bibliography appended to this volume. Like all London-based students of film I also owe much to the staff of the British Film Institute for their help with screenings and research. I am grateful to Unifrance, the National Film Archive and the various specialist distributors for the provision of stills and must give a special thanks to my publishers for their patience in awaiting a long-delayed manuscript.

Introduction

Scientists are not, of course, the only group that tends to see its
discipline's past developing linearly toward its present vantage.
The temptation to write history backward is both omnipresent
and perennial.

Thomas S. Kuhn, 1962

Any one-volume history of a national cinema is a hazardous undertaking. Limited by its length to the national production of films, it runs the
risk of presenting a very distorted picture of the ordinary spectator's
experience of film going, since from 1914 world screens have been so
dominated by Hollywood that in most cases the national production
represents only a small proportion of what is seen. Perhaps an even
greater hazard is the almost inevitable creation of a false but persuasive developmental pattern based on some unarticulated biological
model: the infant cinema . . . its first tentative steps . . . growth to
maturity . . . decline in face of television. . . . The particular structure
and period division of this book are designed as far as possible to
prevent such a view emerging, but it must be admitted that the very
vocabulary of development and progress is all-pervading.

An additional difficulty of the one-volume history, in the case of
French cinema, is the sheer abundance of interesting work at virtually
all periods of the cinema, from its pre-history to the present day.
France offers examples of every form of production, from the total
industrialisation characteristic of the period prior to 1914 to the
extremes of avant-garde individualism, of which *Un Chien andalou* is
such a striking pioneer example. French cinema is also a very fruitful
area for the application of an auteurist approach. Even when world
economic dominance was lost, French cinema continued to produce a
succession of film makers – Gance and Clair, Renoir and Carné,
Resnais and Godard – who are international figures in a true sense.
Obviously it is impossible here to do full justice to such figures or to

1

treat at length such major works as, say, *Napoléon, La Règle du jeu* or *Hiroshima mon amour*. It is, however, such films and their makers which form the focus of this study. A quite different history of French cinema could be written by considering not those works which have attracted critical attention but those which have proved most popular with French audiences. But here I have deliberately kept to those films which have been seen to have artistic merit, striving as far as possible to put these into an appropriate context.

A project of the kind undertaken here is now frequently regarded with some scepticism. Allen Thiher (1979), for example, doubts 'if it is even possible to write an intelligent history of film'. But rather than surrender to this fashionable rejection of an historical approach, it seems more profitable to seek other models of historical enquiry. The particular approach adopted here owes much to the project for a history of science outlined by Thomas Kuhn in his book, *The Structure of Scientific Revolutions*. Observing that 'a few historians of science have been finding it more and more difficult to fulfil the functions that the concept of development-by-assimilation assigns to them', Kuhn goes on to point out the problem caused by once current but now discarded views, which historians are forced to realise 'were, as a whole, neither less scientific nor more the product of human idiosyncrasy than those current today . . . Out-of-date theories are not in principle unscientific because they have been discarded'. But the inclusion of such material, together with a more precise probing of the nature of scientific discovery, leads to a modification of the whole concept of history:

> Gradually, and often without entirely realising they are doing so, historians of science have begun to ask new sorts of questions and to trace different, and often less than cumulative, developmental lines for the sciences. Rather than seeking the permanent contributions of an older science to our present vantage, they attempt to display the historical integrity of that science in its own time.

In some ways this present book attempts an analogous history of French cinema, setting out to offer a study of the successive styles of film production adopted by groups of film makers in response to changing theoretical conceptions of cinema and differing economic, social and cultural circumstances.

Too often, books claiming to be film histories take a simple paradigm of cinema – some such definition as 'classic Hollywood cinema' – and limit their analysis to those film makers who may be seen to have contributed to it, ignoring or denigrating those whose efforts were directed to other ends. This present history is not concerned with tracing such a development, which equates significant change with progress towards (or echoes of) the eventually dominant Hollywood style. The cinema may have become a narrative art of a particular kind with D. W. Griffith, but it had been an art of another kind since its inception. If we accept the photographs of Eugène Atget as art, then an equally strong case can be made for a work like Louis Lumière's *Barque sortant du port*. The Hollywood industry may have based its world dominance on a particular form of narrative continuity film making, but Pathé controlled the world industry with quite a different form of cinema in the years before 1914. And, as Paul Hammond (1974) rightly observes, Méliès remains an artist, in the same sense as Stan Brakhage, even though his particular form of artisanal production may have been outmoded commercially by 1905. In considering the successive styles of French cinema it is important, therefore, to stress the discontinuities and dissimilarities over time, rather than to attempt to extract a single linear pattern of cause and development. By 'style' is meant something akin to the cluster of attitudes, approaches and assumptions that Kuhn calls a 'paradigm'. For example, the particular circumstances of French international commercial dominance, the approach to film as a commodity by Pathé and Gaumont, the physical organisation of production, the budgeting, the sources of recruitment of film makers, the type of outlet for distribution and the programming pattern, all come together to create a style of film making between 1906 and 1914 which can be defined across a wide range of personal approaches and commercially defined genres. But while scientists, if Kuhn is to be believed, customarily unite after any major scientific revolution, to the extent that anyone who persists in following an outdated and supplanted paradigm is simply regarded as no longer acting as a scientist, this is not the case in the arts. There are always veterans continuing – often with great popular success – with styles which have been in some sense superseded: Louis Feuillade's work after 1914 is a good example of this, and Méliès, of course, continued with an artisanal style of production long after the industrialisation of cinema.

In the elaboration of successive styles, the notion of chronology is crucial: the tracing through of developments as they occur without clouding the issue by bringing in concepts appropriate only for a later period. Film makers in France before 1914 did not find the type of editing style pioneered during that period by Griffith because they were not looking for it: their film making had quite different roots and rationale. It is important, in approaching film history, to remain open to an awareness of the wide range of phenomena contained within the concepts 'film' and 'cinema'. Louis Lumière was quite right when he predicted that the cinematograph, as a novelty, would have a commercial life of only a year or two. In the form in which he conceived the cinematograph this was indeed the case. The Lumière company began to withdraw from production as early as 1898 and Lumière had sold his patents by 1902. The fact that the same term 'cinematograph' – or some variant on it – was subsequently applied to quite other developments in cinema involving film as a theatrical spectacle in no way invalidates Lumière's judgment. Where terminology is concerned, it is useful to bear in mind Apollinaire's 1917 poem:

> If we were artists
> We wouldn't say cinema
> We'd say ciné
> But if we were schoolteachers from the sticks
> We wouldn't say ciné or cinema
> But cinematograph.

The period division adopted here is that determined by the internal economic developments of production, distribution and control in the cinema. On occasion the breakpoints coincide with national or world events, such as the outbreak of war in August 1914, which caused an immediate and catastrophic disruption of production in France, or the Occupation period of 1940 to 1944 during which new forms of organisation and censorship were imposed. But other breakpoints – that between 1905 and 1906, for example – are purely internal ones, related to changes in the film industry itself which do not have external political causes. But there are always overlaps and discrepancies and I should not like the period styles discussed here to be seen in any way as monolithic. While some great film makers produce work which is the summation of a particular dominant style – one thinks of Marcel Carné's embodiment of the very essence of what is generally known as 'poetic realism' in Le Jour se lève – others have a greatness which can be measured by the distance between them and their more prominent contemporaries. A good example of this is the relation of Robert Bresson and Jacques Tati to the dominant film makers of the period after World War II: René Clément, Henri-Georges Clouzot and Claude Autant-Lara.

In adopting this approach I hope that I can in some way counter the recurrent notion of 'progress' which so hampers attempts to see the cinema in its true historical light. Kuhn observes that the years during which painting was regarded essentially as a mode of representation were precisely those during which a sense of progress in the art of painting was strongest. Perhaps it was inevitable therefore in the case of a new medium like the cinema, which is so intimately caught up with questions of reproduction and representation, that its first historians should be equally concerned with tracing progressive development. But growing awareness of the particular qualities of visual organisation, non-narrative structure and notions of spectacle in early cinema allow us to see those years in all their distinctive richness and diversity. Such an approach also serves to validate those developments during the last two decades which, because of their play with the concepts of narrative continuity, are rejected by the more traditionally minded historians as being in some sense 'anti-cinema' (as Francis Courtade (1978), for example, omits Alain Robbe-Grillet and Marguerite Duras from his account of French cinema up to 1978). Here, it is hoped that the infinitude of these links in stylistic conception making up the history of cinema can at least be indicated, as much as those of inspiration between, say, Jasset and Franju, Feuillade and Resnais, or Renoir and Truffaut.

1 The Pioneers of a World Industry 1895–1905

> Last night I was in the Kingdom of Shadows. If you only knew how strange it is to be there. It is a world without sound, without colour. Everything there – the earth, the trees, the people, the water and the air – is dipped in monotonous grey. Grey rays of the sun across the grey sky, grey eyes in grey faces, and the leaves of the trees are ashen grey. It is not life, but its shadow, it is not motion but its soundless spectre . . .
>
> Maxim Gorky, 1896

The contribution of France to the prehistory of cinema is considerable. As is now widely appreciated, the cinema was not invented by any one individual. Though Louis Lumière may rightly claim credit for organising the first public performance of projected films to a paying audience, he was only one of a number of scientists, engineers, inventors and visionaries who contributed to the invention of the cinema in the late 1890s. In the chain of events leading up to 28 December 1895, key roles were played by Frenchmen at all points. The French contribution to the development of photography – the work of Niepce, Daguerre and Bayard – is well known, and of the two scientists who concerned themselves most profitably with the analysis of motion in the 1880s, Muybridge and Marey, the latter was French.

Etienne Marey (1830–1904), a physiologist fascinated by the study of animal locomotion, made his crucial contribution in 1882 with the invention of the 'photographic gun', itself an adaptation of an idea pioneered by another Frenchman, Jules Janssen (1824–1904). Marey's initial 'photographic gun' could record only twelve images but he modified it several times and eventually devised a 'chronophotograph' which used the rolls of photographic paper marketed by Eastman in 1888 and allowing space for one hundred and fifty images. Marey's work contributed much to the eventual emergence of the cinema and his meeting with Edison at the Paris

7

Exhibition of 1889 also helped to stimulate the American inventor's interest in moving pictures. But his specific orientation was quite different from that of subsequent film makers. Far from trying to recreate the illusion of movement – as Lumière was to do successfully in 1895 – Marey was concerned with its analysis and decomposition. To create and project a sequence of images which reproduced movement in real time – and so presented all the same problems of analysis as actual moving birds and animals – would have been a meaningless undertaking for Marey. Moreover, since he was concerned only with movement, he worked progressively to reduce the realism of the image (on which the eventual success of Louis Lumière was to rely so strongly), firstly by posing his subjects in white against black backgrounds and eventually by dressing them totally in black with only gleaming strips and markings on the limbs whose movements he wished to capture.

Another pioneer whose work deserves attention is Emile Reynaud (1844–1918), whose 'pantomimes lumineuses', first shown at the Musée Grévin in October 1892, are the direct ancestor of the animated film. Reynaud's work in developing his praxinoscope projector is in a sense the culmination of the nineteenth-century interest in optical toys and devices which developed quite separately from photography. Reynaud's shows of projected hand-drawn images offered the elements of colour and spectacle to his audiences, but lacked the commercial potential of either Edison's kinetoscope or Lumière's cinematograph.

The key step in the progress towards cinema was taken by the American Thomas Edison (1847–1931) who commissioned his assistant W. K. L. Dickson (1860–1935) to develop the kinetoscope or peepshow which was first marketed in 1894 and proved an instant success. Since he failed to patent his equipment in Europe, the way was open to others to build their own versions of the kinetoscope – as Robert William Paul did in England – or to adapt the idea to embrace the projection of photographic images of movement. Although Louis Lumière was the first to accomplish this successfully, he was only one of many who tackled the problem in the 1890s. As well as Robert Paul and Birt Acres in England and Max Sladanowsky in Germany, there were several other Frenchmen active in the field, among them Louis Leprince, Eugène Lauste and Marey's former assistant Georges Demenÿ.

*

1895 was a crucial year for Louis Lumière (1864–1948) and for his cinematograph. Between the patenting of the cinematograph on 13

February 1895 – though it was not so named until a supplementary document was lodged on 30 March – and the first public showings to a paying public on 28 December 1895 in the so-called 'salon indien' at the Grand Café at 14 boulevard des Capucines, a great deal occurred. The prototype camera, built by Charles Moisson at the beginning of the year, had to be tested, sheets of celluloid imported from New York to serve as a base for the photographic emulsion, and a first film shot and tried out on an audience. This film, a first version of *La Sortie des usines Lumière*, was first shown on 22 March at a meeting of the Society for the Encouragement of National Industry in Paris. Several other films had been made before the next major showing at the Congress of the French Photographic Society on 10 June 1895 in Lyons, when the success of the screenings was enhanced by the two films shot, processed and printed during the sessions. Throughout the spring and summer of 1895, in fact, Louis Lumière shot with the prototype camera most of his best known films: *L'Arroseur arrosé*, *Partie d'écarté*, *Arrivée d'un train à la Ciotat*, *Barque sortant du port*, *Repas de bébé*. All of these were shot to demonstrate the qualities of the Lumière camera and there is no reason to think that at this stage Lumière contemplated an exploitation of the *output* of the cinematograph as a spectacle. It is far more likely that he intended to market the cinematograph itself – which, unlike the Edison kineto-scope camera, was light, portable and easy to operate to the same kind of customers as those to whom he supplied still photographic equipment (the Lumière Brothers' company was at this time the largest supplier of photographic materials in Europe). None of Louis Lumière's experience as a photographer would immediately lead him to the idea of projected moving pictures as a theatrical spectacle.

At some point, however – and it is logical to think that it was through the influence of his father, Antoine, who maintained connec-tions with the Parisian world of spectacle – the idea of public showings was born. Once embarked on this path, the Lumières acted decisively. The first of twenty-five copies of the cinematograph prototype was ready on 20 December and commercial showings began eight days later. With initial success assured, the order for a further two hundred cinematographs was placed on 31 December, and early in 1896, Louis Lumière began to train a team of fifty operators who would take the cinematograph to most of the capitals and major cities of the world, to set up public showings and to shoot local scenes to add to the catalogue.

While it is impossible to define precisely which of the 1,424 little films listed in the Lumière catalogues were made by Louis Lumière himself (he continued shooting films until 1897–98), we do know that virtually all those shot in 1895 and most of those in early 1896 were his own personal work. His brother, Auguste Lumière, shot just one film, *Mauvaises herbes* in 1895, otherwise Louis guarded the camera jealously. Perhaps because of the brevity of the Lumière films few attempts have been made to analyse them. But those analyses which have been made strongly contest the general opinion that these are simple 'slices of life'. Firstly, Lumière himself was a very experienced still photographer, and the organisation of space in these early films is by no means random. Secondly, the handling of time in these short films is also tightly organised, as Marshall Deutelbaum (1979) has demonstrated. From the very first film, *La Sortie des usines Lumière*, which is framed by the opening and closing of the factory gates, a conscious effort has been made to organise the time of the event so that it coincides with the running time of the film. However slight, the event is never unshaped. Thirdly, these little views are in no sense a neutral or objective record of the world. As Vincent Pinel (1974) has aptly observed, they reflect Lumière's position as a prosperous member of the European bourgeoisie, which was then at the height of its powers and confidence, both in their choice of subjects and in their air of certainty in the durability of the social world they depict.

In addition to being, in this way, the first authentic creator in the history of cinema, Louis Lumière was also the first to give it a form of distribution. Although the beginnings in the boulevard des Capucines were modest, he quickly saw the potential of a world market for moving pictures, and as soon as his team of operators was trained, he sent them out, not only to the capitals of Europe, but to major cities in North Africa, Asia, America and Australia. Refusing to sell the cinematograph (which fulfilled the three roles of shooting, printing and projecting), he attempted as far as possible to control the means of production and distribution of moving pictures and leased only the exhibition rights. Since he provided the projectionist, he retained an extraordinary degree of control. It was only the fact that others also constructed and sold viable cameras and projection systems in 1896 which prevented him from obtaining the monopoly which he sought.

Georges Méliès (1861–1938), the son of a self-made businessman who had made a fortune from the manufacture of boots and shoes, was one of the first visitors to the Lumière screenings at the Grand Café. At the time Méliès was working professionally as a conjurer and illusionist at the Robert-Houdin theatre, which he had bought in 1888. Unable to purchase a Lumière cinematograph, he obtained an animatographe projector from R. W. Paul in London and used it to design his own camera. His first films were street scenes in the manner of Lumière, but as early as 1896 he was filming his own stage illusions such as the *Escamotage d'une dame chez Robert Houdin*. The following year he built himself a 'glass house' studio in the garden of his house at Montreuil. The theatrical origins of this are demonstrated by the fact that it adopted the dimensions of the Robert-Houdin stage (fifty-five feet by twenty feet and twenty feet high) and included all the illusionist's theatrical machinery. Whereas Lumière's production experienced a crisis in the late 1890s, Méliès's work grew in inventiveness and assurance. In 1899 he produced a major example of the then favoured genre of the reconstructed newsreel, *L'Affaire Dreyfus*, which ran to 240 metres (or thirteen minutes), and also introduced what was to be his favourite genre, the fairy-tale, with *Cendrillon*. In addition he made short subjects of every kind, from 'stag' films (*Après le bal* (1897), with his future wife, Jehanne d'Alcy), to publicity shorts. In the early 1900s Méliès's Star Film company produced and distributed a number of trick films, including *L'Homme orchestre* (1900), *L'Homme à la tête de caoutchouc* (1901) and *Le Mélomane* (1903), as well as the series of fairy stories, *Barbe Bleue* (1901), *Le Brahmane et le papillon* (1901), *Voyage à la lune* (1902) and *Voyage à travers l'impossible* (1904).

Although Méliès was primarily concerned with making films and running the Robert-Houdin theatre (for which he was responsible until 1914), he had to set up foreign agencies to distribute his films. In London he had links with Charles Urban, who commissioned a reconstruction of *Le Couronnement d'Edouard VII* in 1902. The New York office of Star Films was headed by his brother, Gaston Méliès, and other agencies were opened in Berlin and Barcelona. But the growing industrialisation of film making after 1905 rendered Méliès's own artisanal methods commercially obsolete. Although he was, with Pathé, one of only two European producers invited to join the Motion Picture Patents Company, through which Edison hoped to control world film production in 1910, Méliès's presence was more a tribute to his artistic reputation than to the commercial importance of his output at this time. The films made between 1909 and 1912 in the USA by his brother, Gaston, did little to ease his financial problems and by 1912 Méliès ceased production altogether.

Georges Méliès has a unique status in early French cinema. Producer, writer, director and actor, he had total control over his work and his ouput can be analysed in terms of an individual creation in ways which would be inappropriate for any of his contemporaries employed by Gaumont or Pathé. Méliès's world is one which parodies the pretensions of the present and at the same time brings to the surface basic human fantasies and desires. It combines transformations and humour, nowhere more so than in its treatment of women.

This world is rich – poetic in the full sense of the word – and to say that it was superseded after 1905 is to oversimplify and distort. Méliès's concept of the cinema is a fully rounded one – in which most of the future elements of film style have their place – but it is not one in which narrative continuity plays a part. There is no doubt that Méliès's historical importance derives from the fact that it was he who first introduced to the cinema a notion of spectacle and that this notion owed its definition to his role from 1888 to 1914 as director of the Robert-Houdin theatre. Yet his concept of the function of the camera remains very much in line with that of Lumière. Both wished to record a pre-existing phenomenon organised for the camera: tiny everyday events in the case of Lumière, more elaborately contrived theatrical spectacles in the case of Méliès. This results in the spectacle always being produced *for* the camera instead of the situation in which the camera is itself creatively involved. It is this limitation which condemned Méliès to appear outmoded as cinema developed in its unforeseen way towards the concept of narrative continuity. For Méliès, the only break from the single unifying viewpoint he adopted – the camera placed in 'the best seats in the stalls' – could come when some trick effect was envisaged. Close-ups are present in his work but they are used only for special effects – to indicate giants or monsters – and it was inconceivable that he should introduce them simply to make the narrative flow in a way for which he saw no need.

The single viewpoint, although common in the early years of the cinema, is also very much an element in Méliès's personal style, reflecting his way of viewing the world. As a conjurer he seems always to have wanted to call into question the logic and concreteness of the world by his play with tricks and transformations, and the single viewpoint is a way of emphasising the tension between the playfulness of the film maker and the solidity of the physical world. Even eighty years later his films retain their naive freshness. In this way his style is based on an aesthetic which has a total unity and coherence, even if it could not support a film longer than a single reel (fifteen minutes). The problematic status of Méliès in respect of the development of cinema through the years up to 1914 should not, however, lessen our respect for him as an artist. If we take as our starting point his sense of composition and the work done on a single frame, it is easier to draw him out from his role as a primitive or mere precursor. It then becomes possible to draw comparisons with those more recent artists who have also questioned the primacy of narrative. In this sense we can compare him not only to avant-garde or independent film makers who have consciously manipulated the individual frames (such as Stan Brakhage, who acknowledges that his sense of the life of the isolated frame is derived from Méliès), but also film makers working, like Tati, in the mainstream of commercial production.

*

The two men who succeeded Lumière and Méliès as the leading figures in French, and indeed world, cinema – Charles Pathé and Léon Gaumont – were men of a very different kind. In 1894, when he first became interested in the Edison phonograph, Charles Pathé (1863–1957) had already tried to make his fortune in a number of ways both in France and in South America. Although he began by personally taking a phonograph around the fairs near Paris in the 1890s, he was soon installed in the Cours de Vincennes, selling phonographs and cylinders obtained from London, on which he himself recorded songs and patriotic speeches. In February or March 1895 he bought from R. W. Paul in London several copies of the Edison kinetoscope and began to offer these too to his fairground clientèle, but with the Lumière screenings of December 1895 it was clear that the days of the kinetoscope and its imitations were numbered. Pathé therefore commissioned from Henri Joly the design of a film camera/projector which he marketed under his own name after breaking off his association with Joly. The latter's contribution had been of capital importance, but he was never to get the recognition he deserved. An unfortunate figure in early cinema, Joly was denied credit by Pathé and when he set up his own company with the engineer, Ernest Normandin, the projector he devised was the one which was in use at the time of the disastrous fire at the Bazar de la Charité of 1897, in which one hundred and forty members of the upper bourgeoisie lost their lives.

The initial prosperity of Pathé Frères, founded in 1896, was based largely on the phonograph, which now began to be marketed as a consumer durable for domestic entertainment in well-to-do homes. But although until 1900 the cinematograph contributed no more than a tenth of the company's profits, Pathé's interest in it remained strong. In 1902, after acquiring the Lumière patents, Pathé commissioned a new camera, this time from the engineer, Pierre Victor Continsouza. This was specifically designed for the single function of shooting film and soon dominated the market, to such an extent that it has been estimated that in the period up to 1918, sixty per cent of all films were shot with a Pathé camera. Intially arrangements for the actual production of films were rudimentary in the extreme, just a simple stage some ten metres by eight, open to the weather, and with a very basic set of props stored in a nearby shed. It was not, in fact, until 1902 that the first Pathé studio – on similar lines to that of Méliès – was built at Vincennes.

By this time the production of films at Pathé was under the direction of Ferdinand Zecca (1864–1947), who had joined the company in 1899. Under Zecca output rapidly increased, both in terms of the number of films produced and the length of each individual work. Although Méliès's work served as an inspiration for much of Zecca's, there was none of the former's conscious artistry under the Pathé regime, where film making was seen as an industrial process not markedly different from canning peas. Although other employees joined the company as directors, or were promoted to this role, in the early 1900s – Lucien Nonguet, Laurent Heilbronn and the former conjurer, Gaston Velle – Ferdinand Zecca remained the key figure in all this production. He was a studio head in the sense that the term was later to be used in Hollywood. He was involved in the choice of every subject or script, viewed all the material shot, hired and fired every actor, and generally made his personality very forcibly felt by all those engaged on production at Pathé.

The most ambitious Pathé film of this period was the *Vie et passion de Notre Seigneur Jésus Christ* (1902), directed by Lucien Nonguet under Zecca's supervision, which was originally shot in twelve tableaux but was augmented several times up to 1905 until it eventually comprised thirty-two tableaux and 720 metres. Zecca, however, had his own particular genre with which his name is indissolubly linked: the 'realistic' film. The series began with *L'Histoire d'un crime* (1901), which was based on a series of waxwork tableaux in the Musée Grévin, just as the later *La Vie d'un joueur* (1903) was inspired by an exhibit seen by Charles Pathé at Madame Tussaud's in London. Other notable Zecca films of the same genre were *Les Victimes de l'alcoolisme* (1902), *La Grève* (1904) and *Au pays noir* (1905). Although the latter does contain scenes shot in the open air, the 'realism' of Zecca is far removed from that of Lumière. The impact derives partly from the choice of violent and melodramatic subject matter but also from the theatrical decor and staging. Most of Zecca's collaborators were men with stage experience and a key to the success of these films – like the fairy-tales produced in imitation of Méliès – was the quality of the set designers. In the course of these years there is a gradual development from painted backcloths to more three-dimensional sets (although the use of natural lighting remains constant), but the camera is still used to record a spectacle created in front of it. Only later does the camera play an essential role in the constitution of this spectacle.

While Zecca kept films flowing from the Pathé studios, Charles Pathé himself continued to develop the company, and the profits were enormous. The costs of production were kept to an absolute minimum, so that the investment in any film could be recovered by the sale of just fifteen copies. In fact, an average of 350 copies of each film were sold. As Sadoul points out – with production in 1905 amounting to 12,000 metres of negative per year and sales of up to 12,000 metres of positive film per day – total costs had been recovered by mid-January and every sale after that represented pure profit.

*

Pathé's only serious rival in France was Léon Gaumont (1863–1943) whose company, although small in comparison to Pathé's, was still a major force in the world film industry. Although for many years still photography remained the company's main concern, Léon Gaumont was attracted by the idea of developing the moving picture side of the business. But Gaumont's interest lay essentially in the equipment and he lacked any vision of the educational or entertainment potential of the cinema. The production of films was undertaken only as a necessity – to fill the demands of customers who bought Gaumont's projectors – and it was Gaumont's secretary, the twenty-four-year old Alice Guy (1873–1968), who was entrusted with supervising production in 1897. Occupying this post until 1906, when she left for Berlin to accompany her future husband, Alice Guy was responsible single-handedly for virtually all the Gaumont production in Paris, becoming the first woman film director in the history of cinema. Gaumont's personal attitude towards production was one of indifference. Guy recorded (1976) that she was only allowed to undertake her production role 'on the express condition that it would not hinder my functions as his secretary'.

Alice Guy's importance in the history of French cinema is considerable and Francis Lacassin (1972) has listed some 301 films of all kinds – trick films and fairy-tales, dramas and comedies, a life of Christ and even one or two of the stag films common at the period – made between 1897 and 1906, as well as over 100 'phonoscènes'. The latter, a preoccupation of Gaumont's between 1900 and 1906, were recordings of popular singers and actors which constituted an ancestor of the talking film. Since the synchronous recording of images and sounds was impossible at this time (cameras were still hand-cranked), they were filmed to playback. In 1905 Gaumont built a real studio at La Villette – three times bigger than any owned by Pathé and the largest in Europe – and it was Alice Guy who directed the first production there, *La Esmeralda* (1905). But Gaumont's concept of film production was rudimentary. The open-air filming which characterised the Gaumont style up to 1905 was determined more by economic than aesthetic concerns and, in designing his studio, Gaumont advanced little further than Méliès, merely substituting as his model the stage at the Opéra in place of that at the Théâtre Robert-Houdin.

Between them Gaumont and Pathé totally dominated film production up to 1905 and beyond. They were both men whose initial interest was in equipment rather than film making, so that the film industry was based, not on production, but on the manufacture of cameras and projectors. The people they chose as artistic directors – Guy and Zecca – were both largely without theatrical experience and had initially very limited artistic ambitions. Films were mass-produced without any understanding that they might potentially become works of art. Films were cheap, short and important only in as much as they were profitable. Since profits from the outright sale of prints were so enormous, there was no incentive for change and the world of French film production was – with the exception of Méliès – characterised by a limitation of ambition, by plagiarism rather than inventiveness and by a very modest view of the medium's potential. These limitations were enhanced by the nature of film exhibition. From 1900 onwards an increasingly important role was played by the travelling fairground entertainers who took programmes of films from place to place and in general demanded little more than the crudest farces or action-packed reconstructed news items in the manner of the shows at the Musée Grévin.

*

Having looked, in outline at least, at the developments in French cinema during the first ten years of its existence, it is perhaps appropriate to step back and look in more general terms at the nature of cinema prior to 1906. It would be quite wrong to assume that the subsequent development towards narrative cinema was in any way contained in, or necessitated by, development during this first decade. This period is characterised, indeed, by a wide range of possible directions predicted or planned for the cinema and the pioneers themselves were confused about the nature of the new medium. Many of these confusions derived from the economic context in which the cinema developed. The late nineteenth century was a period in which small businesses predominated in France and the situation of Louis Lumière, a factory-owner who still concerned himself personally with the smallest details of the engineering of a film camera, was in no way exceptional. The businessman of the time operated in a context of unbridled capitalist 'free trade' and 'free enterprise'. There was, of course, no trade unionism to trouble the originators of the cinema and no need for them to concern themselves with payments to authors of the works which they pillaged. At the same time they enjoyed no copyright over the work they produced and were totally vulnerable to plagiarism. As a result, film was generally seen as a product in no way different from a car or a can of beans: produced by employees at a fixed rate and sold outright by the foot or metre to all-comers.

This attitude towards film blocked any development of the cinema in two ways. Firstly, it hindered any move towards more complex, and hence more expensive, works. Since the rate per metre was constant, there was no way of recovering the additional costs of a more elaborate *mise-en-scène*. The longer films of the first decade are rare – limited to those with special subjects – the Passion, for example – and almost always the individual parts were sold separately if required. In addition, the prevalent concept of cinema allowed no real sense or definition of authorship. With the exception of Méliès, none of the film makers of this decade has a marked personality: directing was combined with other roles – production, camerawork, scriptwriting. Responsibility for the handling of camera position and the direction of actors might be split between two people, and even when one person combined both roles, his work might be anonymous and the credit for the film given to a writer or producer.

The definition of the film camera as a simple means of reproduction and nothing more is crucial both to the range of early cinema and its particular impact on its audience. Basically the range of pre-1906 cinema was defined by what could be easily reproduced: street scenes and waves beating on the beach, military parades and visits by foreign dignitaries on the one hand, but also – and indifferently – conjuring tricks and music-hall acts, singers (for Gaumont's 'phonoscènes'), ideas from strip cartoons, fragments of farces, novels, stage plays and operas. There were stag films and scientific films, 'scenes of real life' which did little more than depict situations familiar from the moralising tracts of the period and 'reconstructed newsreels' which drew on the period's natural catastrophes (such as the eruption of Mount Pelée) and scandals (the Dreyfus affair), so as to supplement the action-packed scenes conjured up by a succession of colonialist wars (the Boxer Rebellion, the Boer War, the Spanish-American War) and popular uprisings (the 1905 Russian revolts). The unquestioning acceptance of these reconstructions points very clearly to the nature of the film experience during this first decade. Films were short sequences of often flickering images, totally lacking what would seem to be crucial aspects of reality: sound and colour. But the spectators of the 1890s lacked our experience of the ubiquity of radio and for them reproduced sound was still a fairground attraction (on which the initial fortune of Pathé Frères was based). Colour, as the Lumières discovered to their surprise at the earliest projections to learned

17

societies in 1895, was regarded as less striking or significant than movement: fifty years of black-and-white still photography had accustomed audiences to accepting without question a black-and-white world as 'reality'.

The standards of reference against which pre-1906 films were measured were not those we know today – the newspaper photograph or the television report – but the contemporary media of reporting distant catastrophes: the drawn illustrations of the *Petit journal* or the *Monde illustré* and the waxwork tableaux of the Museé Grévin. To both of these, the cinema could add a crucial element of reality – movement – and this sufficed, for a decade at least, to ensure the acceptability of film reconstructions.

The particular qualities of pre-1906 cinema have been brilliantly accounted for by Tom Gunning (1982) in his concept of 'non-continuous style'. Its roots lie in such nineteenth-century phenomena as the comic strip and the caricature, the magic-lantern show, the popular song and the vaudeville act. It is a cinema for which the basic unit is the simple autonomous shot. The amount of work done on and by this individual shot is often considerable: some of Méliès's trick films – such as *Le Mélomane* – needed half-a-dozen or more exposures. Aspects of time subsequently placed consecutively in separate shots in narrative continuity cinema (flashbacks, for example) are at this period still contained within the single image, as in Ferdinand Zecca's *L'Histoire d'un crime*, where the present (the prisoner in jail) and the past (the stages of his path to conviction) are enacted simultaneously. The fundamental aesthetic is one of simple reproduction, whether the camera captures real events or stage happenings, and is theatrical only in the manner in which the staging occurs, or in the style of the painted decor. It is not a consciously organised style, with its own tight rules and conventions of the kind that narrative continuity cinema was later to develop, but rather a potential field for a number of quite contrary – even contradictory – approaches. The visual world of pre-1906 cinema is not a closed one – the baby in Lumière's *Repas de bébé* reaches out to us and the performers in Méliès's films act, even bow, towards us – but it is organised either in depth on the lines of conventional late nineteenth-century photography or in tableau form following current theatrical practice. Within this context, fiction and documentary, the artificial and the real, can cohabit – even within the same shot.

2   The Era of Dominance
1906–13

En 1908, un metteur en scène employé chez Zecca tournait dans les studios *Pathé* et sur de la pellicule *Pathé*, avec une caméra *Pathé*, des films développés et tirés dans les usines *Pathé*, exploités en France dans des salles contrôlées par *Pathé* et munies de projecteurs *Pathé*. Ils étaient en outre vendus à l'étranger par l'entremise des agences ou succursales *Pathé*. Le cycle bouclé, l'argent revenait à sa source grossi de tous les gains réalisés en cours de route.

Jean Mitry, 1967

The years 1906 to 1913 are those of French dominance over world cinema, during which Pathé exercised a hegemony unequalled by any single company since. In 1908, at the height of its power, the company controlled an estimated one-third of the world film business. This dominance was the direct result of the industrialisation of the cinema undertaken by Pathé and, on a smaller scale, by Gaumont in the mid-1900s. Neither company could now function on the artisanal level at which one person – Zecca or Alice Guy – was personally responsible for the bulk of production. Pathé opened no less than five studios in Paris and at Gaumont's single, but much larger, studio four directors could work simultaneously. The expansion was on every level: the number of films produced, the length of the average film, the number of copies printed of each. Foreign agencies now became production companies in their own right, as well as distributors of French products. Although Pathé began the move towards the rental of films in place of their outright sale as early as 1907 – thereby opening the way to more complex and expensive productions – the product on which French dominance was based was a standardised one. Around 1908 Pathé films were normally 300 metres long at most – that is, with a running time of around fifteen minutes – and comic films would be shorter, perhaps half that length. Dramatic films would be preceded by an introductory title, the action arranged in a series of tableaux each shot from a static camera position. Titles within the film would introduce characters and action (dialogue titles were introduced only later). Exteriors would be shot on location and interiors in a simple studio open to the light, with fairly rudimentary sets and a standard range of props. The camera would not normally come close to the action but would photograph it largely in long shot or in 'French foreground', that is, framing the actors from head to shins.

Certain traditional genres, such as the reconstructed newsreel, went out of fashion at this period, as the demand for longer and more dramatically structured films increased. In a similar way the trick film was gradually discarded, although Méliès continued in production and a number of remarkable films in the Méliès tradition were produced for Pathé by Gaston Velle and the Spaniard Segundo De Chomon. Méliès indeed made an enormous effort to keep pace with his rivals, personally making sixty-eight films (with a running time of some ten hours) in 1908, but the basis of his production methods remained artisanal and by 1912, when he produced the last of his films, now for the Pathé company, he was a virtually forgotten figure (totally unknown, for example, to Henri Fescourt who began his directing career in 1911). One new genre which did come into being to replace the trick film was the animated film, of which Emile Cohl (1857–1938) was a pioneer. Working for Gaumont from 1908, his films included examples of drawn animation (*Fantasmagorie* and *Un Drame chez les fantoches*, both 1908, and *Les Joyeux microbes*, 1909) and puppet films (*Les Frères Boutdebois*, 1908). At the height of the Disney era, Cohl was disregarded as a 'primitive' but now the true value of his work can be appreciated. The little outline figures retain their charm and, despite their simplicity, are full of expression. The pacing is good and the action has all the flights of fantasy, transformations and sheer impossibilities of a good cartoon.

In this period of industrialised production the role of the production companies is a key to the understanding and appreciation of the films produced. The newly founded companies of the mid-1900s – Eclipse (founded 1906), Lux (founded 1907) and Lion (founded 1908) – mostly made little impact compared to the two industrial giants, but Eclair (established in 1907 and soon dominated by Victorin Jasset) did make its mark and achieved considerable commercial success. The company which was in some ways most influential in setting a new direction for French production, the Film d'Art, which began work in 1908, was not a commercial success, perhaps because its output was initially distributed by Pathé, who seems to have been intent on stifling it in favour of his own productions. But all the Film d'Art's rivals had to produce work of the same kind in imitation. Central to the notion of film production at this time are the genres developed – usually in mutual imitation – by all the major companies. The period up to 1914 saw a first burst of creativity in film comedy – from André Deed to Max Linder (who became the first real internationally recognised film star) – and the establishment of a particularly French form of crime melodrama which flourished from Jasset's *Nick Carter – Le Roi des détectives* (1908), made for Eclair, to Louis Feuillade's *Fantômas* series (1913–14). The key feature of French production at this period is the theatrical film developed under the impulse of the Film d'Art, which began with the production by André Calmettes and Le Bargy, together with the latter's colleagues from the Comédie Française, of *L'Assassinat du Duc de Guise*. In terms of the French context of 1908 this represented a considerable advance in terms of the ambition it displayed, the care shown for detail in every aspect of decor and costume, and above all, the restraint of the acting. While still essentially theatrical in conception and with the basic unit of narration remaining the scene taken in a single long-held shot and not broken down into smaller units, it does possess its own particular style. The film covers little more than a single incident: the Duc de Guise, although warned of the king's evil intentions, pays no heed and is murdered by the king's men. Most of the scenes comprise just a single shot (with the occasional insert of, say, a letter) but the murder itself is developed more elaborately. The characters move diagonally across the stage to use the foreground for significant action, and situations in the background are revealed or concealed by the movement of extras, not by that of the camera. The sets themselves are solidly built and the action unfolds in a clear and ordered way. In the five-shot sequence depicting Guise's death, the action flows fairly smoothly from shot to shot (although without precise matching of screen positions in successive shots), following Guise from the anti-chamber to a second and a third room and then back again. Characterisation is very theatrical and the poses struck look declamatory to modern eyes, but in the context of 1908 French cinema it is comparatively restrained and compares favourably with similar reconstructions of historical scenes made subsequently in the years up to 1914. André Calmettes (1861–1925), who achieved no comparable success with his subsequent versions of stage drama, continued as artistic director of the Film d'Art until 1913, retiring from direction when he was replaced by Henri Pouctal.

During the period up to 1914 a number of other directors – all of them with theatrical backgrounds and training – were also involved in film adaptations of the classics which, whether novels or plays, were transferred to the screen according to the model of the Film d'Art.

These were the men who pioneered the move towards longer films – up to an hour or more – and among them the most significant was perhaps Albert Capellani (1870–1931). Capellani, who had worked with André Antoine in the theatre, made his debut with Pathé as early as 1905. His early work – culminating in *L'Homme aux gants blancs* (1908) – was in a large range of genres, but after becoming artistic director of SCAGL he soon became best known for his adaptations of the classics, such as Zola's *L'Assommoir* (1909) and *Germinal* (1913), and Hugo's *Notre-Dame de Paris* (1911). His masterpiece is a two-part version of Hugo's *Les Misérables* (1912), which is the longest film to be made in France before 1914 (with a combined running time of some three and a half hours).

The lack of progression in French cinema after 1908 is borne out by the most celebrated of all the theatrical dramas of the period, Louis Mercanton's *Les Amours de la Reine Elisabeth/Queen Elizabeth* (1912). Shot in London, this film is nevertheless very much in the French tradition and, anticipating the formula of 'famous players in famous plays' later taken up by Adolph Zukor, who imported the film into the USA, it starred Sarah Bernhardt, then in extreme old age. Although the four years that separate it from *L'Assassinat du Duc de Guise* are those in which film was undergoing a revolutionary development elsewhere – in Denmark and the United States in particular – *Queen Elizabeth* shows no technical advance. If anything the film marks a retreat compared to *L'Assassinat*: the sets are clearly painted canvas rather than authentically three-dimensional constructions, and there is no cluster of shots with the dramatic impact of those depicting Guise's death. There is no separation of the stage into planes of action, and often the movement of extras in the background clutters or obscures the significant events in the foreground. Even the use of depth – as when Elizabeth watches through a window as Leicester is led off to the Tower – is handled in a theatrical way. Despite Bernhardt's presence, there is no way in which the film is structured to engage sympathy or create identification.

*

The hold which Pathé exercised over theatrical drama was echoed in the various forms of comedy too. Of the fifty-eight new comic series begun between 1906 and 1914, Francis Lacassin (1972) notes that twenty were launched by Pathé, compared to eight each by Gaumont and Eclipse and seven by Eclair. Moreover, during the latter part of this period Pathé had the services of the greatest and most popular comedian of the time, Max Linder, who by 1914 had become both the highest paid actor in the world and the first film star to achieve a truly

1. Louis Lumière: Barque sortant du port (1895)

2. Georges Méliès: Les Quatre cent farces du diable (1906)

3. Louis Feuillade: Juve contre Fantômas (1913)

4. Max Linder: Max pédicure (1914)

5. Abel Gance: La Roue (1922)

6. Jean Renoir: Charleston (1927)

7. Abel Gance: Napoléon vu par Abel Gance (1927)

international reputation. In the period up to 1905 comedy had not been a function of specialised directors: Zecca and Alice Guy made comedies just as they tackled every other genre, and there were no comic stars. But 1905 saw the arrival of the prolific and inventive writer, André Heuzé, at Pathé and the actor, Roméo Bosetti, and writer-director, Louis Feuillade, at Gaumont, and immediately, in both companies, a new genre of chase films was developed, with a fresh note of absurd and surreal comedy. A further stage was marked by the appearance of the first of the series starring the clown, André Deed as Boireau (from 1906 to 1908). While Deed was soon lured to Italy – where he starred as Cretinetti – in Paris a whole range of successors had made their appearance before the end of 1910, among them Roméo (Roméo Bosetti, Gaumont), Rigardin (Charles Prince, Pathé), Calino (Clément Mégé, Gaumont), Gontran (René Gréhan, Pathé), Little Moritz (Maurice Schwartz, Pathé).

The most important and talented of the new comedians, Max Linder (1883–1925) had begun as an extra at the Pathé studios in 1905. He established himself only slowly there, and it was not until 1910, working first with the director, Georges Monca, and then with Lucien Nonguet, that he created the comic persona with which he will always be associated: the elegant, debonair man-about-town Max, complete with stick, gloves and silk hat. Whereas his predecessors were largely clowns and slapstick artists, Linder was an actor and a much more restrained figure. Although Linder continued to use collaborators in the elaboration of his situations and scripts, he took over the direction of his films in 1911 and continued in this dual role of actor-director until his departure for the United States. By 1912 his salary from Pathé had reached the mythic figure of a million francs a year and it was during this and the subsequent two years that he made the bulk of the films which made him a dominant influence on the development of screen comedy in both France and America.

Linder's comedies share many of the same qualities as the contemporary historical dramas. Although his comic inventiveness may be more to our taste than the rhetorical gesticulating of the tragedians from the Comédie Française, the relation of the camera to this performance remains essentially the same. It is used simply as a recording device for the performance viewed in its entirety. Occasionally, as in *Max pédicure* (1914), this is a virtuoso set of elaborations on a single situation. But generally the gags are just sketched in. Just as D. W. Griffith never mastered continuity cutting because he always changed the action slightly each time he did a retake (making smooth intercutting of the two impossible), so too Linder was unable to go beyond the first sketch of an interesting idea. Like Griffith too –

although this was less of a handicap in comedy – Linder played all the action of his films towards an audience, as in the theatre, winking and gesturing to the spectators as he set off in pursuit of a young lady or organised a prank to be played on his mother-in-law. The character he creates in these little films is a consistent one – always at the mercy of his emotions, often the butt of the action, but never vicious or savagely aggressive. He never departs from the plane of comedy – into sentimentality, for example, or real drama – and his comic touch remains sure throughout.

Linder is one of the tragic figures of cinema history. The peak of his career lasted just four or five years and he was caught up in the collapse of the Pathé empire around 1914. Used to working for a big company, he was never to master the art of being an independent producer. In 1925 he killed himself in a suicide pact with his young wife.

*

With his dominant position in production paralleled by his control in other aspects of the industry, Pathé reached his peak around 1908, at which point the company owned a number of important cinemas (including the first luxury cinema, the Omnia-Pathé, opened in 1906), factories at Vincennes, Joinville and Chatou, Continsouza's workshops for the production of equipment, and five studios: two at Vincennes, two at Joinville and one at Montreuil. Abroad it had not only the agencies set up between 1904 and 1906, but also foreign-based production companies: Hispano Film (1906), Film d'Arte Italiano (1909), Pathé-Rouss in Moscow (1907), Pathé-Britannia in London (1909) and, most important of all, Pathé-America (1910). Despite the monopolistic ambitions of Edison and Eastman, Pathé was able to maintain his position in both Europe and the United States until 1910 but already by this time half of his profits came from distribution in the American market. The length and cost of films continued to increase in the years up to 1914, but this growth of production was not accompanied by a similar growth in the French domestic market for film exhibition and by 1912 only ten per cent of Pathé's profits came from France, as against seventy per cent from the United States. But when Pathé tried to develop the American part of his business by increasing production and opening his own distribution company, he ran into conflict with the other members of Patents Trust and even before the outbreak of war in 1914 the highly profitable American operation was in difficulties, although these were to some extent masked by the enormous success of the serials beginning with *The Perils of Pauline (Les Exploits d'Elaine)*. But it was films like these – produced abroad by the Pathé company itself – which led the Hollywood invasion of French screens during the period of the war.

Alongside the theatrical production inspired by the Film d'Art and the comedies in which Max Linder excelled, there emerged a new genre of popular drama in which Pathé did not have so predominant a role. This was the episodic crime fiction, based on popular newspaper serials, whose originator in France was Victorin Jasset (1862–1913). Jasset, who had already assisted Alice Guy in 1906 on *La Vie du Christ* and *Descente dans les mines de Fumay*, was engaged by the Eclair company in 1908. At this time Jasset was already forty-six years old, with a long theatrical experience as a stage designer behind him, but in the five years before his early death in 1913 he made a distinctive mark on French production. In 1908, working with Georges Hatot, Jasset made *Le Guet-apens*, the first of a series entitled *Nick Carter – Le Roi des détectives* and adapted from the American dime novels concerning the great detective which had begun appearing in French translation the previous year. This first film was followed at roughly fortnightly intervals in the latter part of the year by five others: *L'Affaire des bijoux*, *Les Faux monnayeurs*, *Les Dévaliseurs de banque*, *Les Empreintes*, and *Les Bandits en noir*. Running less than two hundred metres, *Le Guet-apens* tells its simple action story in just seventeen shots, with no real need of titles and largely in long shot, mixing real exteriors with fairly rudimentary interior sets, and moving the camera in closer only in the shot in which Nick Carter dons his disguise. It is stylistically unremarkable, recounting the story of a doctor kidnapped by bandits and rescued by Nick Carter, who disguises himself as an old beggar-woman to achieve this feat. The choice of a detective hero who shows superhuman perception and infinite skill in disguise sets the pattern for a whole area of French popular cinema in the years up to World War I, and not surprisingly Nick Carter's exploits were also brought to the Parisian stage the following year.

In addition to his administrative responsibilities at Eclair, Jasset was also able to make three episodic films during 1911–13 in which he switched his attention from the master detective, Nick Carter, to the master criminal, Zigomar. Each of these films, sometimes wrongly described as serials, runs to some one thousand metres (forty-five minutes) and is designed to be seen, with intervals, at a single showing. The first of the three, called simply *Zigomar* (1911) is made up of three quite distinct episodes and sets the master criminal (played by Alexandre Arquillère) against the patient but hapless detective, Paulin Broquet (played by André Liabel). The subject matter – kidnappings, daring robberies, disguises, fights to the death and so on – sets a pattern for this whole area of French production and leads, in

Zigomar, to a spectacular ending in which the master criminal is apparently killed when his underground retreat is blown up. The success of *Zigomar*, in which Josette Andriot appeared for the first time, was considerable and prompted the Eclair company to extend its activities and set up its equivalent to the Film d'Art, the Association Cinématographique des Auteurs Dramatiques (ACAD). The sequel, *Zigomar contre Nick Carter* (1912), began with the resuscitation of the bandit, now confronted by his arch enemy, Nick Carter, whom he deceives through his diabolical ingenuity and mastery of disguise for four successive episodes until he again apparently meets his death with a self-inflicted dose of poison when imprisonment seems imminent. The third film in the series, *Zigomar, Peau d'anguille* (1913), again comprised three equally diverse episodes. All three Zigomar films, although relying on action and swift-moving transformations, are very much in the French pre-World War I style, with a good deal of theatrical grouping, frontal acting and absolutely no interest in the lessons of the narrative continuity cinema developing at this time in the United States. Although Jasset was able to complete the first film in a new series, *Protéa* (1913), this time with a woman (Josette Andriot) as the central character, he died suddenly that same year, at the age of fifty-one. Within the Eclair company the traditions he had established during his four years as artistic director were continued, and four further films in the *Protéa* series were completed between 1914 and 1919. But Jasset's real heir was the artistic director of the rival Gaumont company, Louis Feuillade (1873–1925).

Although overshadowed by Pathé and barely a quarter of its size, Gaumont at this period was still a very large company operating on a world scale whose profits trebled between 1906 and 1907. The Gaumont studio at La Villette, expanded in 1908, was the largest in the world up to 1914, just as the company's showpiece, the Gaumont Palace (formerly the Hippodrome), was the world's largest cinema when it opened in 1912. Lacking the entry into the United States market which Pathé's industrial power had gained him, Gaumont used other strategies to maintain its considerable output at a profitable level. The keynote of the Gaumont production under Feuillade was efficiency, originality (literary adaptations were barred), and careful lighting and composition, which had to take the place of expensive sets and large casts of extras. Feuillade's work is only understandable in this context and the later celebration of his work by the young surrealists should not lead one to imagine him to be any sort of frustrated artist or poet of cinema, suffocating in a world dominated by business decisions. Quite the contrary. Feuillade, a man of enormous vitality and Southern temperament, was the archetypal family man whose personal life was conducted on strictly ordered bourgeois principles. In no way an innovator in terms of either form or content, he took the popular forms of the cinema of his day to their highest level of expressiveness. But all his work is shaped by a concept of cinema as a commercial medium, a means of making money, and it was inconceivable for him to adopt aesthetic strategies which were not rooted in sound commercial practices or to make films which were not aimed at the widest possible popular audience.

Before reaching the level of mastery visible in the *Fantômas* series (1913–14) and its successors of the World War I and immediate post-war period, Feuillade had an extremely long and solid apprenticeship. He worked virtually without a break from the time he took charge of production at Gaumont in 1906 up until his death in 1925, producing perhaps six hundred films of every conceivable type and genre, from tiny comic sketches to massive series with a running time of nine or ten hours. In his early years at Gaumont he was making two films a week, many of them little comedies. Humour is a constant feature of his work from the first scripts sold to Alice Guy in 1905 up to the thirty films of the *La Vie drôle* series in 1913, but dramas and melodramas also abound from the late 1900s. Feuillade grouped a number of his more serious works, in which his interest in religious subjects and concern with the quality of the pictorial image are most apparent, under the banner of the *Film esthétique* from 1910 onwards. The commercial underpinning of Feuillade's aesthetics is very apparent in this series, for uplifting, non-contentious stories told with a clear pictorial sense were a highly marketable commodity at this time. Similarly the subsequent *La Vie telle qu'elle est* series (1911–12) can be seen as reflecting the need to make an inexpensive response to the Vitagraph films beginning to make their appearance on the French market, as much as any kind of socially motivated quest for 'realism'. As Francis Lacassin (1966) points out, this rather drab series is in many ways less interesting than the manifesto which Feuillade composed to accompany and justify it. Most of Feuillade's major work forms part of a series of some kind and it is clear that he saw films in generic terms rather than as individually sculpted works. Thus his major output of comedy in the pre-war period comprises the seventy-six films in the *Bébé* series (1910–12), with a four-year-old child star (who eventually became the adult actor René Dary, Gabin's co-star in Becker's *Touchez pas au grisbi*), and the subsequent fifty-three films featuring the urchin *Bout-de-zan* (1912–16). The Gaumont company needed not only a response to Pathé's comedy output, but also an answer to the innovative work of Jasset at Eclair. It was in this light that Feuillade conceived his own *Détective Dervieux* series of 1912–

13 and then began the first of the series with which his name will always be associated, *Fantômas* (1913–14).

Although *Fantômas* is often described as a serial and given showings as if it were a single continuous work, it in fact comprises five separate films of about an hour's length each, which were individually made and released at irregular intervals over a period of some twelve months (from May 1913 to April 1914). But though the five *Fantômas* films are quite separate, they are all in the same style and derive from the same source, the stream of feuilletonesque novels which Pierre Souvestre and Marcel Allain had begun publishing in Paris a few years earlier. The first of the series, called simply *Fantômas* (1913), begins by presenting the master criminal (played by René Navarre) and showing him in some of his many disguises. The action is packed with events, leading from the initial daring robbery to Fantômas's seduction of Lady Beltham (Renée Carl) and the murder of her husband. *Fantômas*, like its successors, is typical of French production of the period, in that it is a work conceived in terms of long-held sequences, rather than clusters of shots. The published breakdown of the film lists only eighty shots in a work running almost fifty minutes at silent speed.

The second instalment, *Juve contre Fantômas* (1913) contains some of the most celebrated sequences in Feuillade's work – the gun battle among the barrels on the quai de Bercy, and the scene of Inspector Juve donning a spiked belt over his pyjamas as he settles down to await the boa constrictor which he expects Fantômas to send against him. The spectral image of the man in black, gloved and hooded so that only his eyes and mouth are visible, is also very much in evidence. In *Le Mort qui tue* (1913) Fantômas sets the police a puzzle when he kills the sculptor Jacques Dollon, cuts off his hand and uses a glove made out of the skin to leave confusing fingerprints. *Fantômas contre Fantômas* (1914) begins with the unfortunate Juve under arrest and suspected of himself being Fantômas. The latter, however, enjoys his freedom and a number of simultaneous identities, including Père Moche, leader of a gang of ruffians, and Tom Bob, a New York detective who shows uncanny understanding of Fantômas's crimes. *Le Faux Magistrat* (1914) begins with yet another jewel robbery and then proceeds to chronicle the misdeeds of Fantômas when he takes the identity of a magistrate whom he murders on a train. Perhaps the best-known sequence is that in which a rain of blood and pearls falls onto the congregation from a church tower where Fantômas has suspended the body of yet another victim from the bell rope. With its intertwined worlds of criminals and police, its susceptible aristocratic ladies and corrupt gaolers, its succession of false bankers and phoney magistrates, *Fantômas* can easily be read as an anarchistic celebration of revolt. After all, it celebrates the triumph of the master criminal over the bourgeois order, shows a succession of outwardly worthy gentry coldly murdered and presents a world where logic is continually overturned. These are undoubtedly the qualities – the derisory picture of the bourgeois world and the reversal of order and logic – which served to endear *Fantômas* to the group of young poets and artists grouped around the surrealists and whose praise gave the solidly middle-class Feuillade his paradoxical fame.

The other side of the coin – the blithe acceptance of the unchallenged stylistic conventions of a cinema based on the minimal unit of the sequence shot and of a purely commercial role for the film director – weigh as heavily on Feuillade as on his contemporaries. Perhaps the greatest freedom at this period is shown by another Gaumont director, Léonce Perret (1880–1935), whose work has been noted by both Mitry and Sadoul. Perret was simultaneously an actor in rather crude slapstick farce – the *Léonce* series of 1913–14 – and a director with a taste for heavily melodramatic plots. But in films like *Le Roman d'un mousse* (1912) and *L'Enfant de Paris* (1913) he was one of the first French directors to explore the potential of narrative continuity cinema. But the weight of the French style is apparent in his work too. The opening reels of *Le Roman d'un mousse*, for example, follow the somewhat ponderous style perfected by Feuillade, with action organised in depth and shot in long static takes, lasting a minute or more and broken only occasionally by an insert (for example, a letter) or a dialogue title. But when the film begins to show the kidnapped boy on board ship, we find continuity sequences of a kind not attempted elsewhere in French cinema at this time. Perret was also clearly very conscious of the possibilities offered by lighting. Several scenes include a moment where a character switches on the lights, and in his exteriors and balcony scenes Perret shows a penchant for silhouette effects. There is even a primitive point of view sequence, when he cuts from a couple on the balcony looking out to sea, to the sun setting, and then back to them as they turn away and go into the house. But the overall effect of *Le Roman d'un mousse* is of a conventionally moralising melodrama.

*

Audacities such as those of Perret are rare in French cinema of the pre-World War I period, which can only be understood in retrospect if the nature of production and exhibition at the period are borne in mind. It was the fairground operators who dominated the exploitation of films in France in the early 1900s and, although fixed cinemas came into being after 1905, there was nothing like the explosion occasioned by the appearance of the nickelodeon in the USA. The minimal demands made by fairground audiences account both for the low standards of the films produced and the failure of the cinema to widen its audience in France. Pathé's decision to move in 1907 from the direct sale of films to a system of rental was therefore taken before the alternative market which such a system required had come into existence in France. Pathé's actions were motivated by developments in the American market of which he had so considerable a share, and in France he had to set up a separate company which continued to sell films outright, since the other French companies such as Gaumont, Eclipse, Lux and Méliès refused to follow his lead and continued to sell their productions.

From this point on there is a fundamental contradition in Pathé's production strategy. Following the success – within the industry in particular – of the quality production exemplified by the Film d'Art, Pathé supported the making of theatrical films suited to the tastes of the lower-middle-class French audience which began to frequent the new fixed cinemas that were set up after 1908. But although this audience came to define the nature of the product, it could not of itself assure its profitability. The number of cinemas and the size of audiences in France continued to lag behind those elsewhere in Europe, constituting little more than half those in Germany and a quarter of those in Britain. In these circumstances Pathé drew between eighty per cent or more of his profits from abroad and the audiences there were of a very different social composition from those in France. The gap widened between the Parisian product which Pathé offered and the actual needs of the American audience from which his company drew most of its revenue, and Pathé, concerned with his foreign markets, neglected to pour equal energy into the creation of a wider audience in France. Whereas the American companies which rose to dominance during and after World War I based their product on the tastes of their local audience and their costings on the local market which they could control, Pathé continued with a strategy of imposing on the whole international audience a product shaped by the values of only one tiny (French) section of this audience. For a while the company's power as a distributor and the fact that so much foreign production (in the USA, Britain, Russia etc.) was initiated by its subsidiaries (and by those of Gaumont) masked the precariousness of the French hold on world cinema, and profits continued to rise through the early 1910s. Eventually, however, the contradiction was to be brought home to Pathé, as the foreign subsidiaries became not branches of the parent company, but rivals to the production carried on in France.

French cinema during its period of world dominance from 1906 to 1913 offers a remarkable example of industrial organisation which – despite the total disparity of style – has marked similarities with the structure which was later to emerge in Hollywood. Like the latter in its 'Golden Age', French cinema of this period was largely a closed world, on which developments elsewhere – in Denmark, Italy, the USA – had comparatively little influence. For the vast majority of French film makers the lessons of the narrative continuity cinema which Griffith and others were developing during these years went largely unheeded. What French film companies were concerned with was copying each other's successes and adapting each other's innovations, as the flood of literary adaptations after *L'Assassinat du Duc de Guise* and of thrillers after Jasset shows. As a result the French production of the years preceding World War I has an enormous homogeneity.

The organisation of production was such that the tastes and prejudices of men like Pathé and Gaumont were apparent in the films produced by their companies. Henri Fescourt (1959), who made his first films between 1911 and 1913, is an admirable guide to the attitudes and assumptions of the period and gives us a clear picture of Léon Gaumont's priorities: a preoccupation with decency, a concern with middle-class proprieties, and an avoidance of dirt or squalor in a scene, whether in the studio or on location. Such attitudes are important in any analysis of the 'realism' that might be expected to follow from Gaumont's well-known espousal of location shooting. The key figure in the day-to-day realisation of the house style – at Gaumont as elsewhere – was the artistic director Louis Feuillade. As Francis Lacassin notes, the contact between the austerely correct Gaumont and the jovially expansive Feuillade was totally harmonious for over twenty years. Gaumont would set the tone, appearing at the viewing sessions (at eight o'clock each Tuesday morning) to see the whole of the week's output, to praise, criticise or, in exceptional cases, fire the relevant director (with the words, 'You really must try your hand at something else'). But Feuillade was the one in everyday control and the same pattern was followed at the new companies which came into being after 1906: Calmettes, until 1913, at the Film d'Art; Capellani at SCAGL; Jasset at Eclair. It was on the strengths and weaknesses of these men, who were generally practising directors of great versatility, that the quality of the product would depend, although many of their contract directors, even at this early period, would be specialists: Cohl for animation, Bosetti for farce, Velle for trick films etc. Certainly pre-1914 cinema was a form in which genres were well-defined and strictly adhered to.

The first priority of the production companies was the maintenance of output and a rate of one film per week for a director – six days for shooting and one for assembling the print – was common. The effect of this flood of commercial production on the thinking of directors was considerable and Henri Fescourt emphasises the fact that even for a young man with an artistic background like himself the only point of view that counted was that of commerce. His confession of his attitudes in the period up to 1914 is worth quoting as symptomatic of the times:

> It would never have crossed my mind to strike the slightest blow against the commercial weight, which I accepted as a law of nature, or even to dream of escaping into a world of art for art's sake. The constant problem was to succeed in the difficult task of reconciling conformism and novelty, in such a way that nothing stood in the way of the largest possible sales.

Within this strictly controlled ideological framework, it would seem that artistic directors and their principal *metteurs en scène* had considerable practical control over their productions. Most directors wrote their own scripts (or chose the writer or scenario), selected actors, organised sets (usually from the limited range of material at hand) and even determined locations for shooting. The key requirement placed on them was to produce regularly and within budget. The latter, during Fescourt's time at Gaumont before the outbreak of war, was basically eight francs per metre of negative, although this figure could be increased and even, on occasion, doubled, if suitable justification could be produced. Tendencies towards inappropriate self-expression were thus limited financially, for French productions were under-financed in comparison to their Italian or American contemporaries. But they were also hindered by the fact that film directing, although a well-paid and responsible job, was not one to which any mystique was attached. Any successful writer or actor might be invited to try his hand, as Fescourt was in 1911.

Despite the apparent diversity of genres, the ease with which Feuillade or Jasset as writer-directors moved from one to another indicates that in France between 1906 and 1913 – as later in Hollywood – there exists a basic style common to all. Mitry's crucial point with regard to Lumière and Méliès – that despite all the differences of style and subject matter the same conception of the role of the camera is common to both – is valid too for the period from 1906 to 1913. If we disregard the surface differences between a version of *L'Assassinat du Duc de Guise* with its actors drawn from the Comédie Française and a popular melodrama series like Jasset's *Zigomar*, a unity of stylistic concerns can be discerned. Indeed, where later critics like

Louis Delluc were hostile to the whole Film d'Art movement, Jasset was one of its warmest admirers. Regardless of whether the product was a literary adaptation or an original thriller, whether it was filmed on location or in the studio, it was treated without concern for any cinematic specificity, for the basis of the common style was theatrical. The classic virtues sought by heads of studios and their artistic directors were clarity in the photography, sensitive choice of detail in the treatment of sets and, above all, restraint in the acting. There was no space in this dominant style for any pretension to art, and pre-1914 French cinema was fundamentally philistine in a way that no subsequent period of film making was to be. The fact that Louis Feuillade shared the assumptions of his contemporaries needs to be remembered when we consider his work today. From the surrealists down to Franju and Resnais it has been a reading at a second degree, a delight in unconsciously contrived incongruity and unintended poetry, which has been the secret of his appeal. Such an approach is far removed, however, from the attitudes and assumptions of Feuillade himself, who saw his role as that of a popular entertainer and whose work, like his life, was unencumbered by aspirations towards art.

But just as art can be found in Feuillade, so too can messages. We can talk of a dominant style because the only opposition is to be found in the archaic remnants of an earlier period, such as Méliès. Virtually all directors – even newcomers fresh from the world of Parisian culture outside the industry – accepted the norms set by Gaumont and Pathé without question. But in doing so they were also accepting a set of values – implicit if not explicit – with which they would perhaps have had less sympathy had they realised their position. It is not simply a matter of the omnipresent moralising whereby sinners got their deserts, or the social stereotyping and caricature whereby strikers were mere idlers or women in revolt would be depicted as drunken harridans. Or even the calculated shift in relation to pressures from outside, so that the master criminals of *Zigomar* and *Fantômas* were replaced as heroes by valiant detectives fighting to preserve middle-class values (a shift anticipating that from gangsters to G-men heroes in early 1930s Hollywood). Rather it is the extent to which experience is trivialised by being seen not in universal terms, but simply in relation to the inadequate social norms of a self-satisfied commercial bourgeoisie. Only the French cinema's dominant economic position in distribution allowed it to continue for so long with a form of cinema that had so little connection with the basic needs and desires of the bulk of its audience.

3   Collapse and Rebirth
1914–22

> Il y aura un cinéma français. L'imitation exaspérée, alternée ou
> simultanée, des Américains ou des Italiens, apprend peu à peu à
> modifier une technique défectueuse ... Je crois que, dans six
> mois ou dans six ans, nous pourrons voir des films français où il
> n'y ait absolument rien d'idiot: cela nécessite la suppression
> totale des scénarios actuels, la suppression presque totale des
> acteurs et actrices de ciné – nous en garderons une douzaine – la
> suppression presque totale des metteurs en scène actuels – nous
> en garderons une demi-douzaine, et encore ce chiffre est-il très
> exagéré.
>
> Louis Delluc, 1918

The declaration of war in August 1914 had an immediate and
catastrophic effect on French film production. Within a month many
leading film makers and much of the labour force in the industry had
been mobilised, buildings requisitioned and the chemicals needed for
the manufacture of film stock diverted to the armaments industry. The
film industry in France was never to be the same again and Pathé, who
failed in his attempt to develop a unified distribution system, virtually
abandoned production altogether. Elsewhere there was some resumption in 1915 and a number of established directors made patriotic
features, but for many 1914 saw the end of their careers. Among the
key artistic directors of production companies, Jasset had died in 1913
and Calmettes had abandoned film making the same year, when
replaced at the Film d'Art. Now, in 1914, both Zecca and Capellani
went to the USA – to be followed in 1917 by Linder – and though all
three returned to France in the 1920s, none was again to become a
leading film maker. Velle too abandoned film making around 1914
and, of those who continued, most – Durand, Feuillade, Fescourt and
Poirier – had their careers disrupted, although some were able to work
in the army film service.

By the time French production resumed hesitantly in 1915 the

American invasion of French screens had begun, spearheaded ironically by serials produced in New York by a Frenchman, Louis Gasnier, for a French producer, Pathé. 1915 saw *The Exploits of Elaine*, released under the title, *Les Mystères de New York*, and to be followed, confusingly enough, by the earlier *Perils of Pauline*, shown in France as *Les Exploits d'Elaine*. 1915 also saw the first Chaplins released in Paris, and in 1916 came the event which marked a whole generation of French critics and film makers, the screening of Cecil B. De Mille's *The Cheat*, under the title *Forfaiture*. Although the impact of this film was felt more strongly within the industry than by the general public, there were soon other important films to capture the imagination, including *Intolerance* and some of the major productions of Thomas Ince. In 1919, before the American impact had been fully absorbed, it was supplemented by the first showings of productions from the emergent Swedish film industry.

Of course the break between the cinema before 1914 and the cinema after 1914 was not absolute, and a few film makers continued imperturbably in the old styles. The period from 1915 to 1922 is one of transition, symbolised by the situation at Gaumont in 1919, where one finds the forty-six-year-old veteran Louis Feuillade, dressed in his grey 'chemist's overalls', directing alongside a twenty-nine-year-old beginner, the ex-littérateur Marcel L'Herbier, resplendent in a monocle and white gloves. Even here though there are secret affinities, since it was the actress, Musidora, star of Feuillade's *Les Vampires*, who had convinced the reluctant L'Herbier to take the cinema seriously. But within this temporary cohabitation of opposites there was only one direction in which French cinema was moving. If *Les Vampires* can stand for much of what was best in French cinema in 1915–16, it is to Abel Gance's very different masterpiece, *La Roue*, that we must turn to find a work which can similarly represent the state of French film making in 1922, when silent cinema stood poised on the brink of its period of greatest achievement.

In the new taste for American films one element was undoubtedly the exotic: Hollywood showed aspects of life, landscapes, characters, of a kind absent from pre-1914 French cinema. But essentially the style represented by *The Cheat* or Ince's *Civilisation*, to which the younger generation of film makers responded, was the narrative continuity cinema which had developed over the previous five years or so in the United States. One characteristic of this style to which all could respond was the restraint of the acting – an ideal before 1914 for both Jasset and the founders of the Film d'Art – and all commentators praised the performance of Sessue Hayakawa in *The Cheat*. But this marvellously controlled style of acting was highlighted in the American films by a quite novel sense of closeness to life, which derived from new techniques of camerawork and cutting. The basis of this new style was not the scene recorded in a single shot but the scene broken down into a number of shots. Now perhaps a dozen or more individual shots would be needed to capture what, before 1914, would have been conveyed in just a single, long-held take. With the scene thus fragmented, the camera could move in closer to the action, since it was possible to cut alternately between a number of characters instead of keeping at a distance so as to hold them in the single frame. Film was given a whole new rhythmic expressiveness now that shots from various distances and angles could be alternated, and close-ups too could be used for expressive purposes instead of simply being retained for inserts (of letters, clock faces etc). It is the exploration of this new rhythm – the poetry or music of images, to use the kind of analogy favoured at the time – which unites a number of the younger film makers who are otherwise thematically and stylistically disparate.

*

Although a considerable number of new film makers emerged during 1915–22 and the basis for an important vein of avant-garde cinema was created, the bulk of commercial production continued in a solid and unadventurous way. Foremost among the old guard was Louis Feuillade, who resumed his role as artistic director of Gaumont on his release from army service in 1915 and who made some of his most successful and lasting work during this period. In addition to the almost obligatory patriotic films and meditations on the horrors of war – of which *Vendémiaire* (1919) is the most significant – Feuillade plunged his energies into the crime series, echoing the success of *Fantômas* and facing up to the US competition led by *Les Mystères de New York*. The years 1915–20 saw the appearance of five successive series, of which the first and greatest was *Les Vampires* (1915–16), which appeared at irregular intervals in ten parts, each of which constituted a self-contained story. *Les Vampires* is strongly conditioned by the circumstances of its shooting. Forced to work quickly and without a smoothly operating studio machine behind him in face of US competition, Feuillade had no time to polish his scenarios or even to establish a conventional script. The stories pitted an intrepid reporter (Edouard Mathé) and his comic side-kick (Marcel Levesque) against ever more bizarre and audacious exploits perpetrated by a gang of criminals led by a ruthless killer who was a master of disguise. In contrast to the American serials, *Les Vampires* had not a blonde-haired victim as heroine, but a dark-haired villainess, Irma Vep (an anagram of 'vampire') played with great relish by Musidora. Many of the stories, which were increasingly improvised on the streets around the studio, give the impression of having been begun without any clear idea of how they will end, and the pressures of a changing cast of players meant that from time to time a seemingly indestructible villain was inexplicably killed off. The death of the Chief Vampire was apparently as great a surprise to Jean Aymé, who played the role, as it is to us, since Feuillade, exasperated by his continual lateness, decided on the spur of the moment to kill him off. But his successor, Satanas, had to die a couple of episodes later, when the actor, Louis Leubas, was recalled to active service. It is the improvisation and incoherence which gives *Les Vampires* its power. Continually we are confronted by moments of total incongruity – a huge cannon is wheeled out, a whole party of socialites is gassed, an actress is killed on stage or a character is kidnapped by being lured to the window and lassoed from below. Unexpected deaths and resurrections, sudden car chases or rooftop pursuits, secret panels and catacombs follow in a vivid pattern which has clearly been orchestrated by a director who, continuing in the traditional style, still organises his action in depth and with the players turned to face the audience in theatrical style. It was the anarchistic view of society, the supreme disregard of logic – so appropriate at a time when the old social order of Europe was crumbling under the impact of World War I – which led André Breton and Louis Aragon to see in *Les Vampires* 'the reality of this century. Beyond fashion. Beyond taste'.

Those same reasons which drew the surrealists to *Les Vampires* led the chief of police in Paris to ban the film for two months – until Musidora's charm made him change his mind – and subsequently Feuillade's work becomes more ordered and socially responsible. It also becomes more carefully organised in terms of production. *Judex* (1917), for example, was totally pre-scripted in collaboration with the popular novelist Arthur Bernède before its five weeks' continuous shooting. Its release in twelve weekly instalments was accompanied by the newspaper serialisation which had contributed so much to the success of *Les Mystères de New York* and became the standard French practice at this period. The subject of *Judex* continued to be a manichean struggle between good and evil, but now the emphasis is on the honourable caped avenger, Judex (René Cresté), who confronts the evil banker Favraux (Louis Leubas) and the wicked Diana Monti (Musidora). Judex's efforts to clear his dead father's name from his base in an underground laboratory beneath a ruined castle are complicated by his love for Favraux's beautiful, innocent daughter, Jacqueline (Yvette Andreyor), but he eventually triumphs thanks to the help of his comic servant Cocantin (Marcel Levesque) and a resourceful urchin (Bout de Ian). This formula was an enormous commercial success and Feuillade repeated it in *La Nouvelle mission de Judex* (1918), a more logical and explicitly moralising series which is generally regarded as being among this weakest work. By contrast *Tih Minh* (1919) contains some of Feuillade's most memorable scenes organised around the sufferings of its Indo-Chinese heroine (played by English actress Mary Harald). Hypnotism, drugs and madness, deaths and resurrections, mysterious oriental forces and miraculous escapes are all contained in a narrative which surrounds its melodramatic plot with an aura of mystery, and a wealth of both comic and dreamlike detail. Many of Feuillade's best qualities are also to be found in *Barrabas* (1920), shot like *Tih Minh* on the Côte d'Azur, and in which the familiar figures of the wicked banker and the evil secret society re-emerge to threaten the social order. Feuillade continued to direct until the eve of his death in 1925, but his later series lack the forcefulness of his earlier work. He remained a pillar of the industry, but his work was now attacked by a new generation of critics, led by Louis Delluc, and it was not until the 1960s that his films were rediscovered and his reputation rehabilitated.

The pre-1923 work of Feuillade's contemporaries has not benefited from a similar reappraisal. In general few of those prominent before 1914 remained so afterwards, but two who succeeded were Louis Mercanton (1879–1932), artistic director of Eclipse, and Henri Pouctal (1859–1922), since 1913 artistic director of the Film d'Art. Both made patriotic dramas in the early years of the war. Subsequently Mercanton who had directed Sarah Bernhardt in the celebrated *Queen Elizabeth* in 1912 continued with theatrical subjects starring Suzanne Grandais, Réjane and, in *Un Roman d'amour et d'aventures*, the young Sacha Guitry. Pouctal, who died in 1922, had a more solid output which included two widely praised features, *Monte-Cristo* (1918) and *Travail* (1919). Some of those who were mobilised did not resume their film careers for four or five years. Thus Léon Poirier (1884–1968) returned to film making only in 1919, when, as director of the prestigious Pax series at Gaumont, he began a series of half-a-dozen films from *Ames d'orient* (1919) to the great popular success, *Jocelyn* (1922). One of the key commercial organisations of the decade leading up to the arrival of sound was the Société des Ciné-romans, originally founded in Nice in 1916 by René Navarre, star of *Fantômas*. Taken over by the newspaper tycoon, Jean Sapène, it became a powerful force on the industry with Louis Nalpas as director of production and Arthur Bernède, author of *Judex*, as head of the script department. It was Nalpas who gave the necessary encouragement and opportunity to two young directors whose careers had begun at Gaumont before 1914 but whose health had been seriously affected by their experiences at the front: Henri Fescourt (1880–1966) and René Le Somptier (1884–1950).

*

Another group of talented film makers with pre-1914 experience was that led by the producer, Joseph Ermoliev, which left Russia in the aftermath of the Revolution and reached Marseilles via Istanbul and Athens in 1919. The energy of this group, which contained many of the key figures from the brilliant burst of film making which marked the end of the pre-Soviet era, is typified by the fact that en route for France they shot a feature film which used the ship and the various ports they visited as its background. *L'Angoissante aventure*, directed by Yakov Protozanov (1881–1946) from a script written with Alexandre Volkov and starring the great actor Ivan Mosjoukine, was completed by October 1919. In Paris Ermoliev founded his own production company, arranged distribution through Pathé-Consortium and hired the old Pathé studios at Montreuil. When Ermoliev himself moved to Berlin in 1922, the company was reformed as the Société des Films Albatros, under the direction of Alexandre Kamenka. This company was to play a key role in 1920s French film making which far exceeds the intrinsic merits of the films made by its Russian directors.

Another newcomer to the French film making scene after 1914 was the great theatrical director, André Antoine (1858–1943) who, after thirty years as a key figure on the French stage, signed a contract with Pathé. During his years of theatrical work, Antoine had shaped and influenced a number of younger directors who had subsequently turned to the cinema and it was one of these, Albert Capellani, whom he assisted in the direction of *Quatre-vingt-treize*. Begun on the very eve of the outbreak of war, this first film project was not finished or released until 1921. By this time Antoine's own film making career was virtually over, but between 1916 and 1922 he completed seven features. All these films were adaptations, from Dumas's *Les Frères corses* (1916), to Daudet's *L'Arlésienne* (1922). Although the scripting has been widely criticised, the principles on which Antoine based his directing style have a wide validity. Approaching film from a quite different background from that of the American directors of the period, he nevertheless stressed many of the same elements. Because of his long and innovatory theatrical experience Antoine was particularly scornful of films which aped tired theatrical conventions or used sets which would have been rejected out of hand by any self-respecting stage producer. He stressed the absurdity of the frontal style of playing still utilised by Feuillade and many of his contemporaries, and argued for a more flexible camera style which would follow the action. Above all, he emphasised the importance of shooting on location, a procedure he invariably utilised in his own productions. Antoine failed to achieve an impact in the cinema akin to that which he had had in the theatre, but his undoubted influence – like that of the Albatros company in the 1920s – has yet to be adequately explored. For example, it was with Antoine that Julien Duvivier (1896–1967) began his film career as assistant director.

Perhaps the most significant film director to make his debut in France during the war years was the Belgian-born Jacques Feyder (1888–1948). After several years of small acting roles on stage and in films, Feyder became the assistant of the prolific Gaston Ravel at Gaumont in 1914. Two years later, when Ravel was mobilised, Feyder completed his first film, *Monsieur Pinson, policier* (1916). After half-a-dozen similar short films he was given the task of directing the comic scripts regularly provided by the dramatist, Tristan Bernard. Late in 1917, when he had made a further ten or so short films, none of which exceeded six hundred metres in length, Feyder in turn was required for military service. On his return to Paris in 1919 he made the first film on the credits of which his name appears, yet another comedy for Gaumont, *La Faute d'orthographe*, and then plunged into an enormously ambitious undertaking, the adaptation of Pierre Benoît's best-selling novel *L'Atlantide* (1921). This project, produced by Louis Aubert and backed by the Thalmann Bank, required extensive location shooting in the Algerian desert and a budget approaching two million francs. Although it has not lasted particularly well, the film was enormously popular with audiences in the 1920s, and the subject was to be remade by Pabst in 1932. Despite the fact that Stacia Napierkowska hardly possessed the qualities of a ravishingly attractive *femme fatale* capable of driving men to their deaths, the use of North African locations, the camerawork of the team led by Georges Specht and a melodramatic story with all the elements required to exploit the current fashion for orientalism ensured the film's success.

Feyder confirmed his status as a major director the following year with a very different project, *Crainquebille* (1922), adapted from a story by Anatole France, then at the height of his fame. In this simple tale of an old market trader imprisoned for a trivial offence but saved from despair by the friendship of a small boy, Feyder drew masterly performances from the old stage actor Maurice de Féraudy and the young Jean Forest, who was to star in several of his later films. In this work the director was able both to give a vivid portrait of the poorest districts of Paris through his location shooting and also offer insight into Crainquebille's mental world through a subtle use of subjective camerawork, distortion and cutting, especially in the celebrated court scene. These two varied and successful features saw Feyder poised on the brink of a brilliant career.

*

The impulse for a radically new cinema came not from Feyder but from a loosely knit group of film makers who came to prominence in the period immediately following the war, although one of them, Abel Gance, had been directing since 1911. A key figure – although not in any sense the leader of a movement or faction – is the critic and subsequently film maker, Louis Delluc (1890–1924). Like Raymond Bernard and Marcel L'Herbier, Delluc began to interest himself seriously in the cinema under the impact of *The Cheat*, a film whose limitations he could appreciate but whose form opened his eyes to the possibilities of a new art. Prior to this his ambitions had been literary and theatrical. Abandoning his studies for a career in journalism, Delluc had written poetry, plays, novels and dramatic criticism. He continued to write even after he had turned to film making and in all – despite his early death – published over a dozen literary works of various kinds, in addition to three collections of film criticism (*Cinéma et cie*, 1919; *Photogénie*, 1920; and *Charlot*, 1921) and a volume of screenplays, *Drames de cinéma* (1923).

Delluc was not the first critic to treat the cinema seriously; René Jeanne had written in the daily press as early as 1912 and the Italian critic, Riciotto Canudo, based in Paris from 1908, began publishing a number of important theoretical articles at about the same time. Similarly the important magazine, *Ciné pour tous*, was founded by Pierre Henry in 1919, two years before Delluc's own journal, *Cinéa*. But none of this detracts from the importance of Delluc's stance. Like André Bazin some thirty years later, Delluc developed his ideas in relation to specific films – attacking the Feuillade of *La Nouvelle mission de Judex*, while offering a keen appreciation of examples of American and Swedish cinema and the works of Antoine, L'Herbier, and Gance. Delluc does not offer a worked-out theory of cinema but a number of key ideas recur. He emphasised the importance of cinema as a popular art, attacking the influence of the bourgeois theatre and stressing the crucial importance of rhythm and pacing. Although he took many of his examples from American cinema, he did not place emphasis on physical action, and totally rejected the incident-packed serial or *ciné-roman*. He sought instead a cinema which would be truly the expression of its author and put stress on the inner life of its characters. This, he felt, could be best achieved through a poetic, lyrical use of images, reinforced by the choice of apt, concrete detail and use of carefully selected natural settings. Going beyond the customary call for restraint in acting, Delluc advocated a masklike impassivity, of which Sessue Hayakawa furnishes a key example.

Between 1919 and 1923 Delluc was involved in the production of nine films, all but one of which starred his wife, Eve Francis. *La Fête espagnol* (1919), his first script, was directed by Germaine Dulac, who had directed Eve Francis in *Ames de fous* the previous year. As was so often the case at this period, the crucial production support came from Louis Nalpas. Unlike the majority of melodramas of the period, *La Fête espagnol* was conceived directly for the screen. It concentrated on a single incident: a beautiful woman, Soledad (Eve Francis), drives the two rivals for her love to kill each other in a duel, then allows herself to be carried off by a third young man, indifferent amid the dancers to the destruction she has caused. With its physical action reduced, as always with Delluc, to a minimum, the film desperately needed the real Spanish settings which the production budget would not allow and it has generally had a mixed reception from critics and historians. This film set the pattern for Delluc's subsequent eight films, all of which he directed himself. Except for the comedy, *Le Tonnerre* (1921), which was adapted from a story by Mark Twain, all were made from his own original scripts and involve an intense interaction between just a handful of characters. For none of this work did Delluc have truly adequate resources and he was never to find the popular success which would have allowed him bigger budgets. In part his lack of success derives from his concentration on the inner world of his characters to the detriment of his own directional style. Unlike Gance and L'Herbier he did not, it seems, have an instinctive flair for images and the interest of his films lies more in their construction than in their realisation. Almost all of them, from *Fumée noire* (1920) to *L'Inondation* (1923), contain some noteworthy stylistic exploration or innovation: interaction of past and present in *Le Silence* (1920), concentration on the atmosphere of a single setting in *Fièvres* (1921), the use of landscape in *Le Chemin d'Ernoa* (1921). Delluc's generally recognised masterpiece is *La Femme de nulle part* (1922) in which a woman returns to a villa where, thirty years before, she had abandoned her husband. Now she finds the same pattern repeating itself with the present occupant and so, before setting out again, she persuades the young woman to stay loyal to her marriage. Here Dulluc was able to give full expression to his interest in time and memory, to the interaction of character and setting, and to the development of a novel plot structure. Louis Delluc is a figure apart in French cinema and his death at the age of just thirty-four means that his career is in striking contrast to that of his two contemporaries, Gance and L'Herbier, both of whom survived into their nineties, but his place in French film history is assured.

Germaine Dulac (1882–1942), who directed Delluc's script for *La Fête espagnol*, was centrally involved in the attempts to create a renaissance of French cinema after 1914. An ardent socialist and feminist, she was not the first woman film maker in France, but her personality was much more forceful than that of Alice Guy and she made no attempt to hide her strongly held opinions. After a career as a journalist and a visit to Rome with the actress and dancer Stacia Napierkowska, she made her debut as a director with *Les Soeurs ennemies* (1915). Three further films followed before she made the serial *Ames de fous* (1917), starring Eve Francis, celebrated for her performance in Paul Claudel's plays, who introduced her to Louis Delluc. Their collaboration on *La Fête espagnol*, made in 1919, marks the high point of Dulac's early career, although, as is the case with the films directed by Delluc himself, critics have found more to praise in the writing than in the directing of the work. Although she continued experimenting in four further films made between 1919 and 1921, real success eluded her. But with *La Souriante Madame Beudet* (1923), she was to achieve a success which would put her in the forefront of French avant-garde film making.

Another film maker who was to emerge brilliantly in 1923 was the somewhat younger Jean Epstein (1897–1953) who abandoned his studies of medicine in 1921 and moved to Paris. Asked later about his discovery of cinema, Epstein mentioned the viewing of some early Chaplin shorts in London in 1914 and a 1918 Thomas Ince production, *Selfish Yates (L'Etincelle)*. Epstein's other first loves were literature and philosophy and while still in his early twenties he published three books in quick succession, one on literature (*La Poésie d'aujourd'hui: un nouvel état d'intelligence*, 1921), one on philosophy (*La Lyrosophie*, 1922) and, in between, an aptly titled initial collection of thoughts on film, *Bonjour cinéma* (1921). Epstein had already established contact with the poet, Blaise Cendrars, Gance's collaborator on *La Roue*, and with Germaine Dulac, and had assisted Louis Delluc on *Le Tonnerre*, when in 1922 he was given his first chance to direct by Jean Bénoît-Lévy, who had been commissioned to produce a film commemorating the centenary of *Pasteur*.

*

If Epstein's career did not get properly under way until 1923 and Delluc and Dulac, for all their qualities, were perhaps ultimately more important for their new conceptions of cinema than for their actual realisations, there were nonetheless two young film makers active in the immediate post-war years whose ambitions were matched by their skill in the handling of actors and images: Abel Gance and Marcel

L'Herbier. L'Herbier (1890–1979) had initially hoped to make his name in either literature or music, and his theatrical ambitions overlap with his beginnings as a film maker. After a first book, *Au jardin des jeux secrets*, published in 1914, he had two plays performed in Paris. L'Herbier's idols were Wilde, Claudel, Debussy, when the impact of *The Cheat* led him to turn his attention to the cinema. He wrote two scenarios for Mercanton and Hervil, *Le Torrent* and *Bouclette* (which he had wanted to call *L'Ange de minuit*), and then published his views on cinema in a long essay with a typically literary title, 'Hermès et le silence' (1917). Although a first personal film project, *Phantasmes* (1918), remained incomplete, he quickly wrote and directed, at his own expense, for the propaganda ministry, a new experimental piece *Rose France* (1919). But this visual essay appeared only after the end of the hostilities and was a commercial failure both for L'Herbier and his co-producer, Léon Gaumont. Undeterred – or perhaps in order to recover his initial investment – Gaumont commissioned L'Herbier to make a work of purely commercial ambitions, the adaptation of Bernstein's play, *Le Bercail* (1919), and then – within the context of his 'Pax' series – allowed him full liberty to make a series of five strikingly diverse and original films.

In his autobiography L'Herbier refers to the period 1919–22 as his 'years of initiation'. For the first of the series, *Le Carnaval des vérités* (1919), shot partly at Biarritz and partly in the Gaumont studios, he had the collaboration of a number of close associates who figure in many of his films of the period: Jaque Catelain and Marcelle Pradot among the cast and the eighteen-year-old Claude Autant-Lara (whose parents had produced L'Herbier's first play at their Art et Action workshop) as one of the designers. With *Le Carnaval des vérités* enthusiastically accepted by Gaumont, L'Herbier went on to a more ambitious project, inspired by a Balzac story. The resulting film, *L'Homme du large* (1920), was shot largely on location on the Britanny coast and introduced the sea as a major element in the drama. Although the plot had, as so often with L'Herbier, elements of melodrama (the conflict of father and son, the opposition of town and country etc.), the director's visual command, his interest in audacities of framing and superimposition and concern with the rhythm of the editing are very apparent. In its mixture of symbolism and reality, documentary force and contrivance, *L'Homme du large* points to what will be the specific interests of the new French avant-garde cinema. After this solemn drama, L'Herbier turned to comedy, directing first a parody of the excesses of the contemporary crime film, *Villa Destin* (1920), for Gaumont and then, at his own expense, a humorous sketch, *Prométhée . . . banquier* (1921), to form part of the performance of his one-act play at the Colisée theatre.

With *El Dorado* (1921), he returned to a more serious vein and produced his major film of the pre-1923 period. *El Dorado* is, on one level, a simple melodrama, set in a Spain seen through the novels of Maurice Barrès (who was, coincidentally, scorned by the dadaists in a mock trial that same year). The world shatters for a young dancer, Sybilla (Eve Francis) when, already deserted by her husband and in charge of a sick child, she sees the painter she loves (Jaque Catelain) stolen by a rival. Overcome with despair she kills herself in the very cabaret where she dances nightly. The emotional force of this story was reinforced both by an original musical score by Marius-François Gaillard and by a photographic style which takes L'Herbier's visual concerns to fresh heights. Throughout, he is intent to give, through blurred focus and a range of optical masks and devices, a visual effect which reflects the mental and psychological state of his characters. L'Herbier does not stylise the decor as was done at this period in Germany, but uses location shooting (much of the filming was done in Spain) combined with camera and lighting effects. Thus the heroine's indifference to her surroundings is conveyed through subjective imagery, just as her death at the El Dorado is accompanied by a grotesque shadow play on the curtain behind her. It is ironical that such a film should have been produced by Gaumont who throughout his career as a producer had argued so forcibly for clear, sharp images, but even he had to admit the film's power. From its first showing it was a commercial and artistic success to match Gance's *La Roue* the following year. L'Herbier was unable to repeat this success in a second Spanish extravaganza, a heterogeneous account of *Don Juan et Faust* (1922) in which stylised costumes designed by Autant-Lara clashed with real Spanish landscapes and, as the director puts it, Velasquez is set against the Gothic. The shooting proved difficult and the film went over budget (although still costing perhaps half as much as Feyder's *L'Atlantide*). It was released without being properly finished and ended L'Herbier's collaboration with Gaumont. Later in 1922 the director set up his own company, Cinégraphic, through which he was to produce his subsequent silent films.

An even longer and more flamboyant directorial career is that of Abel Gance (1889–1981), who wrote his first film script in 1909 and directed his last feature, *Cyrano et d'Artagnan*, in 1964. Like L'Herbier, he began with theatrical aspirations, attempting vainly to gain admission to the Conservatoire. It was as an actor that he first came into contact with the cinema, but even when he had graduated to providing scripts for Gaumont, Gance still sought to make his name as a playwright. A first drama in 1909 was followed four years later by a verse tragedy for Sarah Bernhardt, *La Victoire de Samothrace*. Introduced to the great actress by Edouard de Max, whom he had met through his film work, Gance obtained her agreement to appear in the play. But the outbreak of war in 1914 put an end to these plans and the play was never produced. Meanwhile Gance had turned to film direction and founded his own production company. After making four independently produced films in 1911–12, Gance was invited to join the Film d'Art. A first drama, *Un Drame au Château d'Acre*, was followed by the first of the films by which Gance is remembered today, *La Folie du Docteur Tube* (1916). This story of a mad scientist allowed the director to play with distorting lenses and optical effects with all the inventiveness of Méliès.

Although *La Folie du Docteur Tube* was held back from release, Gance was undeterred and made a further fifteen films in the years 1916–18. These established him as the leading young director of the period. His range was wide and his work shows an increasing command and complexity, while remaining within the conventions of melodrama. Gance's cinematographer throughout this series of films was the talented Léonce-Henry Burel (later to work with Robert Bresson) and one of their most striking characteristics is the growing visual sophistication. Both *Les Gaz mortels* and *Barberousse*, made in 1916, are exploratory features. While the narrative is laboriously told, the individual detail is striking if repetitive: poison snakes as well as poison gas in the first film; poisoned cigars and a dreamlike dual identity for the bandit-cum-newspaper proprietor (whose circulation benefits from the criminal's exploits) in *Barberousse*. If very little emotion is generated in these slow but overacted films, a real advance is made with *Mater dolorosa* (1917). This celebration of the sufferings of a guilty woman starred Emmy Lynn as a wife who has an affair with her brother-in-law. Ending with forgiveness and reconciliation, this tearful bourgeois drama reached a wide audience and Gance was encouraged to show fresh ambition in his subsequent work.

La Dixième symphonie (1918) has a familiar melodramatic story line. This time the husband (Séverin-Mars) is a composer and the sufferings Emmy Lynn gives him serve as the material for his greatest symphony. Burel's photography here is quite remarkable and the film contains a mass of visual metaphors to match the literary quotations with which Gance studs the inter-titles. Gance's eclectic approach leads him to bring together pathos, comedy and symbolism (repeated shots of an impassive idol) to flesh out the simple-minded melodrama. There are experiments with thought images and an ambitious attempt to visualise the hero's symphony, and even if not all of this is wholly successful, there is a constant interest to be found in Gance's use of masking and the play of silhouettes and shadows to create mood and his evident awareness of the ability of faces, movement and lighting to convey emotion. *J'accuse* (1918), the most celebrated of these early films, reflects Gance's own brief experience of the battle-front and constitutes a forceful if rhetorical plea for peace. The film begins as a conventional romantic melodrama, concerning the rivalry of two men in love with the same woman. But Gance's emotional involvement with his subject breaks the bonds imposed by this structure, and the latter part of the film becomes a vast denunciation of war. Gance's visionary hero, the crazed poet Jean Diaz (Romuald Joubé), conjures up visions of the battlefield and summons the dead from their graves to bear witness to the need to preserve peace (the film was released shortly after the Armistice). Grandiose and banal, naive and impressively baroque, *J'accuse* is quite the opposite of a sober documentary record. Gance's approach is resolutely apolitical, but the film constitutes an eloquent denunciation of the horrors of the war which had torn Europe in two, told with some of the most strikingly audacious imagery as yet created in French cinema.

Since the ambitious *J'accuse* did not achieve the audience response which he had sought, Gance abandoned the second two parts of his planned triptych and chose a simpler and more accessible subject. This was *La Rose du rail*, a conventional melodramatic story of the rivalry of three men – including a father and his son – in love with a waif whom the older man has adopted and brought up as his daughter. But Gance's towering imagination could not be contained within the conventional limits of this story and by the end of shooting the project had been renamed *La Roue* and taken on quite new dimensions. Gance spent six months drafting the script and assuring himself of the backing of Charles Pathé, who had previously financed *J'accuse*. Then, for this, his most ambitious project to date, he spent virtually the whole of 1920 shooting on location, at the railway yards near Nice, on the Côte d'Azur and around the funicular railway on Mont Blanc. During this time he developed his subject in two fundamentally incompatible ways. On the one hand he attempted to turn his hero, played by the tragedian Séverin-Mars and now called Sisif, into a figure of stature to equal those found in Greek tragedy. This particular ambition is very apparent in all versions of *La Roue*, and one of the most controversial aspects of the film both for contemporary critics and for subsequent historians has been this conception of a figure who is an amalgam of Oedipus (in his blindness and devotion to his daughter), Sisyphus (in his life of unremitting struggle) and Lear (in his loss and madness). The second line of development stemmed from Gance's decision to shoot on location. This led him, it would seem, to develop a ferocious social satire worthy of Zola and thereby provoke the railway unions to demand cuts and modifications to the released version. When complete *La Roue* was three times the planned length and this social aspect of the work, which in any case clashed with the theatricality of Séverin-Mars's central performance, was largely sacrificed to allow the retention of passages dealing with the central conflicts and others containing sequences of particular visual excitement.

Gance's early work was conceived in reaction to the limitations of pre-1914 French cinema but it largely retained the conception of a film as a series of long takes, each of which presented in its entirety a significant stage of the action. All the evidence points to Gance having shot *La Roue* in similar fashion. Certainly many of the juxtapositions from which the particular poetry of the work flows are thematic rather than stylistic – the setting of roses against railway engines, aspiration against disaster, a joyful dance against the horror of death, mountains, violins and high society against the life and work of a poor railwayman. These are patterns which Gance had developed in *La Dixième symphonie* and before, just as there is a considerable continuity in the concept of Sisif, the visionary hero, who echoes the composer in *La Dixième symphonie* and Jean Diaz in *J'accuse*. Later this same love for the lonely tragic figure will determine Gance's choice of historical heroes: Napoleon, of course, but also Savaronola (in *Lucrèce Borgia*) and Beethoven (in *Un Grand amour de Beethoven*). The version which Gance assembled in the early months of 1921 presumably reflected these preoccupations in ways not dissimilar to those employed in *J'accuse*. But the final decisions were not taken on what precise form was to be given to a project which had by now cost some two and a half million francs (making it the most expensive project of the period, surpassing even Feyder's *L'Atlantide*). In April 1921 Gance's wife died and to recuperate he took a five-month trip to the United States. There he met D. W. Griffith and saw many of the latest examples of Hollywood cinema. Returning to France he spent the whole of 1922 re-editing his film in the light of what he had learned, so that *La Roue* stands out in the history of French cinema not only because of its towering ambition but also as a crucial example of the impact of Hollywood conceptions of narrative continuity cutting on a European film maker.

In an invaluable piece of research, Roger Icart (1981), whose work on *La Roue* is fundamental to an understanding of the film, has shown that in the re-editing almost every shot was cut in a manner not anticipated in the shooting script. Most long takes were divided into two or more sections and intercut with neighbouring shots, doubling or tripling the number of edits. In this way a quite new spatial and dramatic effect was created and Gance was able to shape the vivid rhythmic style for which the film is renowned. But even after a year of re-editing Gance was left with a monstrosity of the dimensions of Stroheim's first version of *Greed*. Inevitably compromises had to be made in the attempt to obtain a commercially viable product and the long series of shortened versions chronicled by Icart begins. The length of the version shown at the initial presentations at the Gaumont-Palace on 14, 21 and 28 December 1922, when the film created a furore in the profession, is not known. The version announced for release in Paris in 1923 was thirty-six reels (some nine hours) and comprised a prologue and six chapters, each of full feature length. But this seems to have been shown only in the provinces and the actual version released in Paris, beginning in February 1923, was five reels shorter and arranged as a prologue and four chapters, shown at fortnightly intervals. This is the version which Gance regards as the sole authentic one. But for showing abroad a truncated fourteen-reel version (running three and a half hours) was made and this is the form in which the film has survived. Still shorter versions were made for the film's release in 1928. But despite this mutilation, *La Roue* remains a quite remarkable work, a unique fusion of French and Hollywood styles and the fitting climax to a period of intense change and development in French cinema.

*

Cinema acquired a quite new artistic status in France during the period 1915–22, even if the number of lasting filmic masterpieces produced during these years is small. Any notion of art had been rigorously excluded from pre-1914 cinema, in which commercial values were all-persuasive. The overemphasis of Gance and L'Herbier on occasion can be partially explained as a reaction against this earlier philistinism on the part of two intellectuals who refused to lower their sights and abandon their artistic pretensions when they turned from theatre and literature to the cinema. One small indication of the new approach introduced after World War I lies in the attitude of directors to the signing of their work. Jacques Feyder, making his debut during the war, worked anonymously without complaint or apparent strain and saw his ability to put his name to *La Faute d'orthographe* as a step towards professional recognition, although this was no more than a routine Gaumont comedy. Marcel L'Herbier started from a very different premise. Signing his first work, he then refused to put his name to *Le Bercail* as a way of indicating that this was not a work which had engaged his full creative sensibilities and was surprised

Luton Sixth Form College
Library

49

when Léon Gaumont raised no objection to his anonymity. Other indications of the shift in attitude are furnished by the complex essays on cinema produced by L'Herbier and the young Jean Epstein and by the effusions of Gance. Louis Delluc similarly took the cinema seriously enough to publish a collection of his scripts in the year before his death – a gesture inconceivable before 1914.

It is perhaps wrong to describe the new attitudes introduced by Gance, L'Herbier and Delluc as a movement: the newcomers issued no collective manifesto and pursued resolutely individual lines of development. But they do offer a quite new set of approaches to all aspects of the cinema, which owe nothing to the prior traditions of French film making. Moreover the change they introduced was accomplished in the mainstream of the industry. If Delluc was a marginalised director, L'Herbier made his films before 1922 as part of Gaumont's prestigious 'Pax' series, while Gance's most innovative work had the financial backing of Pathé. The roots of their approach may lie in their openness to foreign influences – particularly films from the United States and Sweden – but their work constitutes an attempt at the creation of a specifically French mode of expression based on neither action nor landscape. Ultimately, their lack of interest in narrative meant that these film makers were to be marginalised in terms of world cinema, but recent research has shown the genuine richness of their explorations of visual expressiveness.

4 The Culmination of Silent Cinema
1923–29

Un grand film?
Musique par le cristal des âmes qui se heurtent ou se cherchent,
par l'harmonie des retours visuels, par la qualité même des
silences.
Peinture et sculpture par la composition.
Architecture par la construction et l'ordonnancement.
Póesie par les bouffes de rêve volées à l'âme des êtres et des
choses.
Et danse par le rhythme intérieur qui se communique à l'âme et
qui fait sortir de vous et se mêler aux acteurs du drame.
Tout y arrive.
Un grand film? Carrefour des arts ne se reconnaissant plus au
sortir du creuset de lumière et qui renient en vain leurs orgines.
Un grand film? Evangile de demain. Pont de rêve jeté d'une
époque à une autre. Art d'alchimiste, grand oeuvre pour les
yeux.
Le Temps de l'Image est venu!

Abel Gance, 1926

The separation made here between French silent cinema before 1922–
23 and what follows should not be taken as implying a break of the
kind found in 1914 and again – with the coming of sound – in 1929. It
is true there are a number of film makers whose careers do not
continue into the second half of the 1920s. Antoine's directing career
ended in 1921, Pouctal died in 1922, followed by Delluc in 1924 and
Feuillade in 1925. Equally the years from 1923 to 1929 saw the
emergence of a number of new directors: René Clair, Jean Grémillon
and Claude Autant-Lara in 1923, Jean Renoir and Dimitri Kirsanoff
in 1924, Alberto Cavalcanti in 1926 and Luis Buñuel in 1929. But the
context in which these newcomers made their appearance had already
been partially formed before 1923, and for the major directing talents
of the early post-war years, the middle and late 1920s were a period of
supreme achievement. Abel Gance and Marcel L'Herbier both built on
the solid foundations of their pre-1923 work to produce strikingly

different masterpieces, while Jean Epstein emerged as a major director. L'Herbier's initiative in founding his own Cinégraphic company in 1922 pointed a way forward, and after 1922 the Albatros company under the direction of Alexandre Kamenka came to play a considerable role in French production. All this work was based on the new artistic status which French cinema had acquired after 1918, and indeed during the latter part of the 1920s Paris became the focal point of experiment in the film. Film historians customarily distinguish three separate avant-gardes in this period, but although the impulses behind these were various and contradictory, the movements overlapped in time and were never rigidly defined. Rather than attempt precise definitions which would cut across the careers of many of the leading film makers, it is perhaps better to stress the continuities and overlaps. Certainly the late 1920s were a period of French cinema characterised by the intermeshing of commercial and experimental impulses. If cinema never became a popular form in a way that it developed in Hollywood, it is equally true that its experimental artists were not marginalised as is customary in most periods of film history. The direction of much of this experiment was contrary to the stress on narrative dominant elsewhere, with the result that until recently this period of French cinema has been wrongly regarded as marginal in terms of the overall development of the medium. Only with the breaking of the firm hold of narrative in the 1970s could this rich era of film making begin to receive the attention it demands.

The Société des Ciné-romans under the artistic direction of Louis Nalpas remained a cornerstone of commercial production with solid, if unadventurous works like Henri Fescourt's massive four-part (thirty-two-reel) version of *Les Misérables* (1925). But more crucial for the artistic development of French cinema after 1922 was the Albatros company. The core of the output produced there by Alexandre Kamenka was initially the work of the émigré directors who had accompanied him from their native Russia and a key commercial factor was his contract with Ivan Mosjoukine, one of the most striking actors of silent cinema. The work of the Russian émigrés has been largely ignored by critics and historians; it was totally absent, for example, from the huge 'Paris-Moscou' exhibition staged at the Pompidou centre in Paris in 1981, but it is clear that films of considerable merit were made in the period 1923–29. Among these one would include Mosjoukine's own *Le Brasier ardent*, co-directed with Alexandre Volkov in 1923, and Volkov's *Kean* (1924), an adaptation of Alexandre Dumas's play in which Mosjoukine again played the lead. When Kamenka's associate, Noé Bloch, left to form his own company, he too was responsible for the making of a number of ambitious films, including such international co-productions as Viatcheslaw Tourjansky's *Michel Strogoff* (1926) and Volkov's *Casanova* (1927). All these films – through their ambition, choice of subjects and skill in direction and interpretation – had a wide impact on French cinema of the period. In addition the Albatros company was involved as producer or co-producer on a significant number of major films directed by French film makers: Marcel L'Herbier's *Feu Matthias Pascal* (1925) and four films by Jean Epstein, three Jacques Feyder films and all of René Clair's silent films after 1926.

In considering the foreign presence in France during the 1920s there are two other directors who cannot be ignored. Dmitri Kirsanoff (1899–1957) was a Russian exile whose background and approach set him apart from the émigré community grouped around Alexandre Kamenka. His highly individual style found perfect expression in a handful of sensitive low-budget impressionistic studies: *L'Ironie du destin* (1924), *Ménilmontant* (1925) and *Brumes d'automne* (1929). Equally original but on a quite different level is the sole French film of the great Danish-born director, Carl Theodor Dreyer (1889–1968), whose earlier eight films had been variously made in Denmark, Sweden, Norway and Germany.

Dreyer's *La Passion de Jeanne d'Arc* (1928) is one of the most controversial masterpieces of the silent era. There is no question about the rigour of Dreyer's approach, the skill of his production team led by the cinematographer (and later Hollywood director) Rudolf Maté and designers Hermann Warm and Jean Hugo, or the commitment of the cast headed by Renée Falconetti, who gives a performance of stunning authenticity. The intensity which Dreyer sought is totally realised in a script which is based on the records of the trial but which compresses the five months of captivity into a single day and the twenty-nine long interrogations into five short confrontations. The film is not narrowly French and all question of nationalism and patriotism is left aside in this study of sainthood, but the compression of the time scale, combined with the reduction of the physical action and the abstraction of the brilliant white sets, roots *La Passion de Jeanne d'Arc* firmly in the French conception of tragedy as exemplified by the work of Jean Racine. The difficulty with which the film confronts the spectator is its paradoxical nature. On the one hand, it is an example of the art of the image to an extent that few films are. On the other, words play a quite crucial role in so far as the bulk of the film comprises the various verbal interrogations of Joan, so that the rhythm and pattern of the images has to be constantly interrupted by written titles. Although the conflict between Joan and her tormentors builds up throughout the film until we can feel the inevitability of her execution, this confrontation is itself totally stylised in terms of close-up compositions and presented in sets of linked images which convey clearly the battle of wills while in no way reproducing the actual points of view of either party. Although Dreyer's *La Passion de Jeanne d'Arc* has received denigration almost in proportion to the praise accorded to it, its status as a monument of silent cinema cannot be seriously called into doubt.

*

As international a director as Dreyer is the Belgian-born Jacques Feyder, who had first come to Paris in 1910 at the age of twenty-five. Paris was the home of Feyder and his actress wife François Rosay, whom he married in 1917 and who remained his constant companion till his death over thirty years later, but the director travelled incessantly. His restlessness was combined with a totally eclectic set of styles and themes. He had already shown his professionalism and versatility as a film maker with the contrasting but highly successful *L'Atlantide* and *Crainquebille* before 1923. That year he shot his only feature film from an original script which he had written himself, *Visages d'enfants*, again starring the young Jean Forest and set this time in Switzerland. Feyder saw himself as a film craftsman, a director rather than an author, an adaptor of given literary material rather than an original creator. This sensitive study of children growing up was based – as Françoise Rosay has made clear – on his own experiences as a father of young people and tells of a young boy's difficulty in coping with the arrival of a step-mother. *Visages d'enfants* has won high critical praise for its psychological exactness and its use of landscape, and Jean Mitry (1973) ranks it among the half-dozen best French films of the 1920s, but Feyder seems to have been hesitant. Although the film was fully shot in 1923, a year passed before the work of editing was begun and the film was not presented in public until 1925. Meanwhile Feyder had shot a new feature which, like *L'Atlantide*, was a study of the *femme fatale*. *L'Image* (1925) was based on an original scenario by the novelist Jules Romains and was shot in Austria and the Hungarian plains for a Vienna-based company. Although Feyder throughout his life remained deeply fond of this story of four men who fall in love with a woman (Arlette Marchal) known to them only through her photograph and whom they fail to recognise in real life, the film was a total commercial disaster.

Feyder's third film released in 1925, *Gribiche*, was made for Albatros and, although it marked a return to the world of childhood, the director was here given a more commercial story concerning a young boy from a poor home (again Jean Forest) who is adopted and educated by a rich American woman. Only when he runs away to

54

8. René Clair: Un Chapeau de paille d'Italie (1927)

9. Luis Buñuel: Un Chien andalou (1929)

10. Jean Cocteau: Le Sang d'un poète (1930)

11. René Clair: Sous les toits de Paris (1930)

12. Jean Renoir: Boudu sauvé des eaux (1932)

13. Jean Vigo: L'Atalante (1934)

14. Jacques Feyder: La Kermesse héroique (1935)

rejoin his family does the woman realise his unhappiness and contrive a happy ending. In retrospect the film is most notable for the emergence of Françoise Rosay – hitherto unnoticed as an actress – in the starring role of the rich American. For Albatros Feyder also made a new story of a *femme fatale, Carmen* (1926), shot in Spain and featuring Raquel Meller. This was an ill-fated venture since Feyder allowed himself to be dominated by his star (as was to happen later with Marlene Dietrich in *Knight Without Armour*) and Carmen emerged as an improbably virtuous victim of men's insensitivity. The following year saw an even greater disappointment. Feyder was on the point of shooting *Le Roi lépreux*, a new adaptation of a novel by Pierre Benoît (author of *L'Atlantide*), when the production collapsed and the only fruit of three months' research in Indo-China was the short documentary, *Au pays du roi lépreux* (1927).

Recovering from these disappointments Feyder went on to produce some of his finest work before his departure for the United States. *Thérèse Raquin* (1928), a heavily dramatic adaptation of Zola's novel produced by Friedrich Zelnick's company DEFU in Berlin and starring Gina Manès, seems to have been one of Feyder's most artistically successful films, but unfortunately all copies have been lost. Contemporary critics speak of the director's precise creation of atmosphere and concentration on the psychological development of the adulterous couple who vainly seek happiness through the murder of Thérèse's husband. On his return to Paris, Feyder changed his style and approach once more to make a highly successful satire in the manner of René Clair, *Les Nouveaux messieurs* (1928). Against all expectation, this lighthearted view of political pretention and connivance adapted from a comedy by Robert de Flers and Francis de Croisset was banned by the censor. To ensure its release, the production company, Albatros, had to agree to significant cuts, but by the time of the film's appearance Feyder was already in Hollywood where he was to direct Greta Garbo's last silent film, the MGM production, *The Kiss* (1929). As a master of narrative cinema, Jacques Feyder stands apart from the occasional experimental excesses of the 1920s. Although concerned to use the full resources of landscape and to probe the psychology of his characters, he never indulges in gratuitous visual effects. For him the story is the crucial element in a film, to be built up through characterisation and the creation of atmosphere, not merely to serve as a pretext for artistic experiment with imagery. With such films as *Visages d'enfants* and the lost *Thérèse Raquin* he set standards against which the achievements of his contemporaries can be measured.

One director whose work can stand comparison with that of

Feyder, both in the 1920s and in the early 1930s, is a newcomer who made his debut in 1923, René Clair (1898–1980). Clair, like Gance and L'Herbier, originally nourished literary ambitions and worked for a while as a journalist while in his early twenties. His first novel, *Adams*, was written the year after his film-directing debut and published in 1926, and his devotion to the traditions of French literature, very apparent in his commentaries on his own published scripts, eventually led him to be the first film maker elected to the French Academy. Beginning his career during the artistic ferment which followed World War I, Clair had connections with many members of the avant-garde and made his second film, the twenty-two-minute short, *Entr'acte*, for Jean Borlin's Ballets suédois. Shot from a script by the dadaist Francis Picabia and with original music by Erik Satie, the film formed part of the ballet, *Relâche*, staged in 1924. But Clair's earlier *Paris qui dort* (1923), a fantastic comedy about a group of people wandering through a Paris which has been immobilised by a mad scientist with his ray gun, shows more clearly the basis of Clair's subsequent career: a keen comic sense, a taste for trickery in the style of Méliès, and a willingness to subordinate play with imagery to the demands of a narrative capable of reaching a wide public. It is not surprising therefore that Clair should have written appreciatively of Feyder's pioneering work in creating a path between the extremes of the avant-garde on the one hand and the ciné-romans (in which Clair had made early acting appearances) on the other.

Clair proved himself to be a world-class director with two films adapted from comedies by Eugène Labiche and Marc Michel which he made in 1927–28 for Albatros. *Un Chapeau de paille d'Italie* (1927) is a classic piece of film making, a silent masterpiece that is so beautifully structured that it has hardly any need for inter-titles. From the opening incident, in which the horse belonging to the hero (Albert Préjean) eats the hat of a young married woman who is dallying in the Bois de Boulogne with a cavalry officer, to the final resolution, *Un Chapeau de paille d'Italie* interweaves a double plot. The hero's prime concern is to get through his wedding and the ensuing festivities and install his bride in the new apartment he has prepared for her. But at the same time he has to satisfy the angry cavalry officer who threatens to destroy every stick of furniture in the flat unless a replacement hat is produced. The film combines a keen satire on bourgeois pretension – it is set in 1895 – with a fast-moving pace, for the film is virtually a single long and complicated chase after a hat which the hero could have had from the beginning if he had opened the present offered by old Uncle Vézinet (Paul Olivier). The flow of the action is constant, with the characters always either arriving late or having to rush off again, whipped along by reasons which the deaf old uncle never begins to understand.

The film is full of brilliantly memorable scenes and moments, as when the hero realises that the man to whom he has just told his story is the young woman's husband or when the cavalry officer, now appeased and offering friendship, advances knowingly and lecherously upon the young bride. But the film is most remarkable for its use of objects. Not only does the plot revolve around the pursuit of a hat, but all the characters are defined by their possessions or items of dress: the old uncle's blocked ear trumpet, one cousin's missing glove and another's slipping tie, the swopped boots that link the bride's father and the deceived husband, and so on. But above all, the film plays on its characters' attitude to their possessions: the hat that 'proves' the wife's innocence, the presents hurled from the window which signify the hero's social shame, the reclaimed presents which convey the guests' refusal of the groom and above all, of course, the threatened furniture which drives the hero to ever more frantic efforts. The following year, after a ten-minute documentary, *La Tour*, Clair repeated his success with *Les Deux timides* (1928), in which he showed his supreme technical command of screen trickery and multiple image split-screen effects to show the divergent worlds of dream and reality and, in the film's celebrated opening scene, to illustrate the contrasting testimony of two lawyers pleading a case in court.

Together with Feyder, Clair was able to continue his career with even greater success after the coming of sound, but not all the younger film makers could make the same double impact. Two other future masters of sound cinema – Jean Renoir (1894–1979) and Jean Grémillon (1901–1959) – both made their debuts in 1923–24 but were unable to achieve real success with their silent films, although they too trod the path between the extremes of the avant-garde and the routine of commercial production. Renoir, son of the great Impressionist painter, came to the cinema as a wealthy amateur, making films with his wife, Catherine Hessling, and a group of friends. After scripting a fairly insignificant melodrama, *Une Vie sans joie* (1924), Renoir turned to directing to make *La Fille de l'eau* (1924), again with Hessling. This tale of an orphan fleeing from her drunken uncle has a strong narrative line and a striking performance by its leading actress. A style characterised by eclectic borrowings cannot disguise the typical Renoir themes of nature, love and life seen as an intermixing of joy and tragedy. Renoir's major silent film, the Zola adaptation, *Nana* (1926), was made under the influence of Stroheim's *Foolish Wives*. This expensive production again featured Renoir's wife, this time partnered by the international stars, Werner Krauss and Jean Angelo. With its complex shooting style, its extravagant decors (designed by Claude Autant-Lara) and its oddly jarring acting styles, this million-franc production failed to find a public and its total lack of success with audience and critics points to Renoir's independence from the dominant styles of the period (a situation repeated with *La Règle du jeu* in 1939). Only fifty years later did *Nana* find serious appreciation, and Renoir's 1920s' career did not fully recover from the failure. 1927 saw a further personal work, *Charleston*, shot with Catherine Hessling and the negro dancer Johnny Higgins in just three days, and a first purely commercial production, *Marquitta*, which is now lost. A low-budget version of Hans Christian Andersen's fairy-tale, *La Petite marchande d'allumettes* (1928), made in collaboration with Jean Tedesco at the Théâtre du Vieux-Colombier, was Renoir's last film with his wife and last personal film in the 1920s. It is a charming fantasy, mixing reality and dream and echoing Chaplin in its naivety and its chase sequences. Subsequently Renoir's career is the routine one of a commercial director. If the military farce *Tire au flanc* (1928) recalls Clair in its best moments, there is little to be said for either the historical drama *Le Tournoi* (1929) or *Le Bled* (1929) made to commemorate the French invasion of Algeria. Both are films which are totally conventional in thought, staging and performance.

Jean Grémillon graduated from playing the violin in a cinema orchestra accompanying silent films to making documentaries with the cinematographer Georges Périnal (himself previously a cinema projectionist), beginning in 1923 with a short on *Chartres*. In 1924 he edited a 'visual poem' from a number of these documentaries. Given a title characteristic of the period, *La Photogénie méchanique*, this short was shown at the Vieux-Colombier, as was a later exercise of the same visually experimental kind, *Tour au large* (1926). During the following two years, again working with Périnal, he made two feature films, *Maldone* (1928) and *Gardiens de phare* (1929). Both were melodramatic stories, the first proposed by the actor Charles Dullin and the second from a script by Jacques Feyder, for whom Grémillon had a profound admiration. Although neither film was wholly success-ful, Grémillon's enormous talent was intermittently apparent and he was able to show his keen sensitivity to landscape in his handling of the canals and fields of *Maldone* and the sea in *Gardiens de phare*.

*

This mainstream of solidly professional film making by directors seeking a wide audience and retaining the primacy of narrative, while not wholly abandoning visual experimentation, gave French cinema some worthwhile achievements and a basis for growth in the 1930s. The continuity in the careers of these men refutes the common assumption that sound constituted a total break in film-making styles, but the number of their silent masterpieces is limited. Only a handful of works – *Visages d'enfants* and the lost *Thérèse Raquin, Nana, Un Chapeau de paille d'Italie* – have been singled out by critics and historians. Far greater impact was made at the time by the controversial but visually more exciting and experimental work of the group which had formed around Louis Delluc after 1918. The labels 'First French Avant-garde' and 'French Impressionist School' have been attached to this loosely connected group, but neither is wholly satisfactory, since the first underplays the commercial importance of the group, while the second – coined by Henri Langlois – implies a wholly spurious relationship with the school of nineteenth-century painting. Still there are common visual concerns linking Dulac, L'Herbier, Epstein and Gance at this period and significantly all held a position of pre-eminence in the silent cinema of the 1920s which was not maintained in the post-1930 sound era.

Germaine Dulac, like Gance, had visited the United States in 1921 and met D. W. Griffith, and her work in the 1920s shows a desire to explore all aspects of the potential of cinema, from the mass art of the ciné-romans to the more esoteric concerns of the avant-garde. In 1923 she made a major contribution with *La Souriante Madame Beudet*, adapted from a play by André Obey staged some two years earlier in Paris. Here, while paying less attention to the development of narrative, she took further the search for a visual style of psychological realism which Feyder had begun in *Crainquebille*. *La Souriante Madame Beudet* uses all the resources dear to French cinema of the period – superimposition, slow motion, distortion of the image – to convey the dreams of her heroine, trapped like Madame Bovary in a provincial life which does not correspond to her imagination. The film had a considerable impact at the time, but Dulac turned to commercial production of episodic melodramas before returning to direct one of the most controversial films of the 'Second Avant-garde'.

A central figure in French 1920s cinema was Marcel L'Herbier, whose own production company Cinégraphic was set up in 1922. L'Herbier launched it with an overambitious programme of productions and many of these, such as his adaptation of Tolstoi's *Resurrection* and a version of *Phèdre* with Ida Rubenstein, were never realised. But he was able to produce the debut films of a number of young film makers, among them the actor, Jaque Catelain, with *Le Marchand de plaisir* (1922) and *La Galerie des monstres* (1923) and the young designer, Claude Autant-Lara, with *Fait-divers* (1924), in addition to financing the last film of Louis Delluc, *L'Inondation* (1924). None of these projects was commercially successful and the same is true of L'Herbier's own first film for Cinégraphic, the celebrated but controversial *L'Inhumaine* (1924). This curious film, part financed by its star, the singer, Georgette Leblanc, wife of Maurice Maeterlinck, is best understood if the nature of its authors' intentions are appreciated. Far from being intended as an avant-garde narrative, *L'Inhumaine* was conceived, in L'Herbier's term, as 'a great mosaic' of the decorative modern art of 1925 which Leblanc proposed to use to introduce the French culture of the period to audiences in New York. The incoherence stemming from the fact that all the settings were produced by different and strikingly individual designers – Fernand Léger, Robert Mallet-Stevens, Claude Autant-Lara and Alberto Cavalcanti – was therefore intended. The mixture of discordant styles is systematic, but as Burch (1973) observes, the film's crucial weakness stems not from this stylistic *parti-pris* or from its parodistic plot, but from the quality of performances by an ageing Georgette Leblanc, whose style is totally unsuited to film, and an insipid Jaque Catelain. In contrast, it is precisely the exceptional quality of Ivan Mosjoukine's performance in L'Herbier's adaptation of the Pirandello novel, *Feu Mathias Pascal* (1925), co-produced with Albatros, which has drawn most attention and made this film L'Herbier's most approachable work of the period. Here L'Herbier was centrally concerned with the creation of a narrative remarkable for its shifts and reversals. Mosjoukine's riveting personality and remarkably flexible acting are set against a virtuoso mixture of stylistic approaches to shooting (superimpositions, play with shadows in expressionist style, location filming of an almost documentary kind etc.).

After two features of a purely commercial ambition co-produced with the Société des Ciné-romans – the enormously successful *Le Vertige* (1926), which anticipates L'Herbier's 1930s work in its smooth theatrical adaptation, and *Le Diable au coeur* (1927) which starred Betty Balfour and was dogged by every sort of misfortune – L'Herbier began work on his major film of the 1920s, a modernisation of Emile Zola's *L'Argent* (1929). The scope of this work was inspired by Gance's *Napoléon*, but rather than talk of his heroes, L'Herbier chose to attack what he hated most, the power of money. Although he took Zola's novel as his starting point, he retained little beyond the title and the outline of the plot. The film's action is transferred to the 1920s and unfolds within opulent, oversized sets built by Lazare Meerson and André Barsacq. The film's largest set, however, is an actual location, the Paris Stock Exchange borrowed for three days over Easter and filmed in a complex multi-camera style by Jules

Kruger, who had earlier worked on *Napoléon*. The visual style's echoes of the major spectacles of 1920s German cinema are enhanced by the presence, as the villains of L'Herbier's cast, of Brigitte Helm and Alfred Abel. Despite the enormous resources deployed – the film cost over three million francs – *L'Argent*'s plot line is straightforward: a young aviator and his wife (Mary Glory) become involved in a dubious financial scheme set up by the lecherous and unscrupulous Saccard (Pierre Alcover).

Jean Epstein's film work of the 1920s is much more accessible than his theoretical writings and contains films of considerable richness and complexity. His work between 1923 and the coming of sound divides into three successive stages. The success of his first documentary, *Pasteur* (1922), resulted in a ten-year contract from Pathé-Consortium which was, however, dissolved after just one year. This period was remarkably fruitful for Epstein who made three fictional films which put him in the forefront of French avant-garde film making, as well as a short documentary on the eruption of Etna, *La Montagne infidèle* (1923). The first and third of Epstein's features, *L'Auberge rouge* (1923) and *La Belle Nivernaise* (1923), were literary adaptations from Balzac and Daudet respectively, but *Coeur fidèle* (1923) which was made from an original script made the most impact. It remains a key work of 1920s French cinema, containing a fairground sequence that, with Gance's railway engine sequences in *La Roue*, can stand as one of the best examples of cutting in the period.

La Glace à trois faces (1927), a medium-length film adapted from a short story by Paul Morand, is remarkable above all for its formal pattern which looks forward to experiments in narrative structure of a kind which were still striking for audiences thirty years later when Alain Resnais made *Hiroshima mon amour*. Its hero is a feckless young man killed in a car crash of whom three contrasting and contradictory images are given through the stories of three women who have loved him. Its mixture of memories and present experiences to create a new flow of time remains remarkably modern. Even more accomplished in terms of acting and setting, and as intriguing in terms of narrative, is Epstein's best-known film, an atmospheric evocation of the dark world of Edgar Allan Poe, *La Chute de la maison Usher* (1928). The film's story of love and madness and its pondering on the relation of the work of art to its author and its subject are told with a marvellously controlled visual style, based on extensive use of slow motion and multiple superimposition and even occasional use of intercut negative images. Just as its hero refuses to accept the division of life and death and summons back, through an effort of will, the woman he has killed through devotion to his art, so too Epstein's film creates a universe where castle and forest, interior and exterior interpenetrate. This masterly evocation of a world of Northern imagination, which can be ranked with Dreyer's *Vampyr*, is a reminder of Epstein's half-Polish origins. These independent works of Epstein were shown largely at the new art cinemas – such as the Vieux-Colombier and Studio 28 – which grew up in the late 1920s and as such they look forward to a new relation between audience and film and a new artistic status for a form which, a decade and a half before, had been a fairground novelty. Epstein was, however, unable to maintain his own company and with just one more commercial effort, *Sa tête* (1929), withdrew from the world of Parisian film production. But his originality remained undimmed and with the masterly *Finis terrae* (1929) he began a trio of low-budget studies of the Breton coast – half-documentary, half-poetic – which would be completed only after the coming of sound.

While Epstein created more than a dozen works between 1923 and 1929, Abel Gance made only two films. One, most improbably, was a short comedy with Max Linder, *Au secours!* (1923), and the other, the towering masterpiece of the period, *Napoléon vu par Abel Gance* (1927). Gance worked for three years on this film which was originally conceived as a massive six-part work to cover the whole of Napoleon's life. Since the eventual six hours of edited footage covers only a portion of part one of this project, the scale of Gance's imagination is immediately apparent. It is the technical aspects of *Napoléon* which have always received the most attention. The film was the end product of ten years' exploration of the visual potential of cinema carried on by a man of almost boundless imagination in the context of a national cinema obsessed with just this aspect of the medium. With a dozen assistants (including his fellow directors, Henry Krauss, André Andréani, Volkov and Tourjansky) and a team of cinematographers led by Jules Kruger, Léonce-Henry Burel and Jean-Paul Mundwiller, Gance deployed extras by the thousand and moved his camera in every conceivable manner, attaching it to a giant pendulum for the Convention scenes, to the back of a galloping horse and even contriving to recreate the trajectory of a snowball. As if this welter of visual effects was not enough, Gance arranged for the screen width to be tripled at the end, so that Napoleon's entry into Italy became a unique visual experience.

There was nothing in French 1920s thinking about narrative which could restrain Gance's imagination. The most successful films of the decade were superproductions with an exotic, historical or literary flavour and in the absence of a strong production system of the kind that had emerged in Hollywood, the director was the undisputed master of film making who, although often pushed into making commercial concessions, was never constrained by a tight studio system. Thus in *Napoléon* Gance was able to combine breathtaking technical virtuosity with a wholly personal conception of his film. Not until the 1970s masterpieces of Coppola and Spielberg do we find the same harnessing of the whole resources of an industry to an unfettered personal vision. Central to Gance's conception was a very nineteenth-century Romantic view of the artist as hero and it is clear that, although he himself played the role of Saint Just, he identified himself as creator of the film with Napoleon (played by Albert Dieudonné) as creator of a new France and master of the forces of history. Napoleon, the man of action, the politician and military genius, becomes a passive figure, a pensive visionary constantly striking attitudes and equipped as a child with an all-too-symbolic pet eagle. The sheer scope of the work makes some unevenness inevitable, but what is remarkable about *Napoléon* is that the most successful moments are in very different registers, not only in the celebrated intercut scenes of Napoleon at sea in a storm and the corresponding storm within the Convention, but also in the quieter schoolday scenes with their occasional prefiguring of Vigo.

Napoléon has become, in the early 1980s, the most celebrated of all silent masterpieces, but Kevin Brownlow's twenty-year self-imposed task of bringing together all the extant footage raises a whole host of questions about authenticity and authorship. Even if we ignore the mutilated and distorted version distributed with great commercial success in the United States by Francis Ford Coppola (cut, run at twenty-four frames a second instead of eighteen or twenty, and equipped with an inappropriate score by Coppola's father, Carmine), we are still left with a paradoxical work. Far from simply constituting a restoration of a mutilated film and recreation of the conditions of the viewing conditions of silent cinema, Brownlow's five-hour version is as much a modern interpretation and distortion as Henri Langlois's seven-hour compilations of episodes from *Judex* or *Les Vampires*. These led to Feuillade's rediscovery, but by compressing into a single viewing half-a-dozen or more episodes meant to be seen at weekly intervals, Langlois set up relationships between the film's narrative and time-span and its spectators which owe nothing to the 1920s, but can have an immediate, 'modern' impact as the films of Jacques Rivette, one of the Cinémathèque's most faithful habitués, show. Similarly, Brownlow's 'original' version corresponds to none that was ever shown in Paris in the 1920s, or would have been deemed feasible then. The actual *Napoléon*, like so many major silent films, existed in several versions and the 1927 showings were either of a shortened version with triptych effects (as at the première at the Paris Opera) or a four/six-episode version shown over a period of weeks. Despite such paradoxes, the great virtue of Brownlow's version – in addition to its revival of interest in silent cinema – is surely to have created a work of self-evident aesthetic complexity, whereas Gance's own reworkings of the material – from his sound version in 1927 to his re-edited *Bonaparte et la révolution* in 1971 – had all tended to simplify and even trivialise what was undoubtedly one of the 1920s' most remarkable achievements.

*

Compared to the audacities of Gance and his contemporaries in the commercially financed feature film, the experimental work of the so-called Second and Third Avant-gardes is somewhat pale and limited. The gulf can be measured, in the career of René Clair, by setting the clever, agreeable but ultimately insignificant dadaist short *Entr'acte* against the formal complexities and thought-out stylisation of his feature-length masterpiece, *Un Chapeau de paille d'Italie*, or, in the case of Renoir, by weighing the experimental *Charleston* (1927) against *Nana*, made the previous year. But the involvement of practising artists in the medium of film did make an important contribution to the climate of French cinema of the period. Since the material costs of a ten-minute silent film were small and an audience for such work was beginning to come into being thanks to the first art cinemas and ciné-clubs, there was every incentive to make films which would be, as it were, the equivalent of a gallery installation. In this style we find the photographer, Man Ray, making a number of short pieces of a visually provocative kind: *Le Retour à la raison* (1923), *Emak Bakia* (1926) and *L'Etoile de mer* (1929), from a poem by Robert Desnos. Similarly, in 1925, Marcel Duchamp made *Anémic cinéma* and Fernand Léger his more celebrated *Le Ballet méchanique*.

The films which have lasted best from among the purely non-narrative films of the period are those inspired by surrealism. Antonin Artaud (1896–1948) was a surrealist poet, a crucially influential theorist of the theatre and a professional actor of considerable magnetism whose unequalled screen credits include works as divergent as *Napoléon*, *La Passion de Jeanne d'Arc* and *L'Argent*. Using the surrealist method of semi-conscious writing to recover 'the sombre and secret logic of a dream', he composed a number of scenarios which have been published. Cinema, he felt, was 'a poison, a subcutaneous injection of morphine' whose images should have a dramatic force which would spring from a shock to the eyes. The only one of his scenarios to be filmed, by the ubiquitous Germaine Dulac, was *La Coquille et le clergyman* (1928), which caused an uproar when screened at the Studio des Ursulines, provoking the surrealists to insult Dulac publicly. A second and more celebrated surrealist short is *Un Chien andalou* (1929), made jointly by Luis Buñuel and Salvador Dali. Again the initially harmonious collaboration was destroyed by feuding and bitter denunciations, although with the passing of the years the internal politics of the surrealist movement and even the distance separating Buñuel in this film and its 1930 successor, *L'Age d'or*, from Jean Cocteau and *Le Sang d'un poète* (1932) seem of little account, compared to the common avant-garde spirit which unites them. Certainly Artaud, Buñuel and Cocteau all form part of a common ancestry for later experimental film makers. *Un Chien andalou* is a remarkable work that prefigures much of Buñuel's mature production and remains as unfathomable as ever in its paralogic. The opening in particular, with its eye-slitting sequence, remains startling even now for the unwary and the coherence of the film's systematic illogicality and heavily Freudian symbolism still retains its impact.

But just as the feature-film making of the period combined visual experimentation with a fondness for location shooting, so too this 'Second Avant-garde' was accompanied by a third, which comprised the tentative beginnings of a documentary school. To this tendency one may link some of Jean Grémillon's early documentaries, such as *Tour au large*, Clair's study of the Eiffel Tower, the ten-minute *La Tour* (1928) and Georges Lacombe's *La Zone* (1928). The trend continued into the 1930s with such films as Marcel Carné's *Nogent, Eldorado du dimanche* and Buñuel's *Las Hurdes*, shot in Spain. Perhaps the most interesting work in this area is that of the designer and future stalwart of the GPO Film Unit, the Brazilian-born Alberto Cavalcanti, who followed a study of the city, *Rien que les heures* (1926) with a short film mixing drama and documentary, *En rade* (1927).

*

French 1920s cinema has generally been little prized by critics and historians. A key to the difficulty is René Clair's apt definition of the principal task of a 1920s director as being 'to introduce, by any kind of ruse, the largest possible number of purely visual themes into a script designed to please everybody'. How indeed are we to evaluate a cinema which combines subjects that are bourgeois, pretentious and literary in the worst sense of the word, with a visual style that proclaims itself as original, experimental and avant-garde? As we have seen, the avant-garde did not allow itself to be marginalised and film makers like Gance and L'Herbier seized the opportunities for individual expression offered by the disorganisation of the film industry. But this individuality often rested on very nineteenth-century conceptions of the artist as creative genius and was buttressed by a reliance on the titles, if not the substance, of earlier literature. This was a cinema in which the director retained the upper hand over his writers and in which the contribution of key designers was set against a concern with location filming. Studio personnel were very important, but, as a film like L'Argent shows, a preoccupation with visual effects – decor and movement, masking and superimpositions, slow-motion photography, symbolic lighting, and so on – did not imply any turning away from the real social world or from nature.

French film makers of the 1920s refused to subordinate the visual style of their film making to the demands of narrative continuity which was already dominant in the United States and elsewhere. This cinema can only be understood if the claims to primacy of narrative are discarded and film is accepted as a mode of expression which may legitimately captivate its audience by other means. In this sense it forces upon us a widening of the conception of cinema to take in forms alien to the Hollywood tradition. But the question of what value is to be attached to this alternative approach, this refusal to submit rhythm and visuals to the demands of narrative, is more complex. Noel Burch and others have claimed that since this cinema breaks the conventional codes of Hollywood, it is therefore to be prized as a vitally important modernist cinema. While this is a refreshing alternative to the traditional denigration of French 1920s cinema, it is still open to objections of two kinds. Firstly, in historical terms, it overestimates – or at least distorts – the achievement of Gance and L'Herbier, since the conventions they disregarded were not fully established in France at this time and the Hollywood-style production practices which would have supported them were totally lacking. Only after 1930 did what can be crudely called the Hollywood style and mode of production become dominant in France, and then these film makers were marginalised. From another angle, while it is true that these films – like the primitive cinema before 1905 and the 1970s work of, say, Marguerite Duras and Alain Robbe-Grillet – demand to be judged by criteria other than those underlying the Hollywood aesthetic, their rejection of these codes does not, of itself, make them modernist or genuinely revolutionary. The weight of nineteenth-century traditions of art and literature, weighing on Gance and L'Herbier as much as on Feyder and Clair, cannot be easily put aside, and a true evaluation will have to take into account the conventional content, subject matter and ideological assumptions, as well as the visual and rhythmical audacities. Happily, thanks to the new availability of Gance's masterpiece, the publication of Epstein's collected works and the pioneering studies of Noel Burch, such a re-evaluation can now begin.

5 The Coming of Sound
1930–34

Le cinéma français entre 1930 et 1939, c'est . . . un cinéma
d'essence théâtrale, qui ne prétend guère au réalisme, même s'il
vise souvent la justesse de la psychologie. Ses procédés favoris
sont l'enflure, l'emphase, la caricature et la fantaisie la plus
débridée.

Christian Viviani, 1977

Barely ten years after it had begun its recovery following World War I
and the collapse of its world dominance, the French film industry was
again plunged into chaos, this time by the advent of sound. The end of
an era was marked symbolically, when Marcel L'Herbier's silent
masterpiece, *L'Argent*, which had opened on 9 January 1929, was
followed at the Aubert-Palace seventeen days later by *The Jazz Singer*,
which was seen by half a million spectators during its forty-eight week
first-run screening. Experiments with sound in France date back to
the earliest years. Even before the commercial opening of the
cinematograph, Louis Lumière had shot a conversation between M.
Janssen and M. Lagrange and shown it at the Congress of French
Photographic Societies at Lyons in June 1895 with a primitive form of
synchronous dialogue, when the two participants positioned themselves behind the screen and repeated the words they had spoken while
being filmed. Léon Gaumont had persistently experimented with
forms of sound film, from the early 'phonoscènes' shot by Alice Guy at
the turn of the century. But when Hollywood made its decisive
conversion to sound, there was no viable French system which could
enter into competition. Indeed in the whole of Europe only the
German Tri-Ergon system adopted by Tobis-Klangfilm could rival the
patented systems developed by Western Electric and RCA, so that
when the battle for supremacy was fought out in France, it was a
struggle between foreign interests in which the French themselves
could play only a small role.

This was a period of intense activity. Production virtually doubled between 1929 and 1930 (rising from 52 to 94 features) and from 1931 onwards remained comfortably above one hundred films a year until 1939, when it fell to around ninety. But the organisation of this great mass of production – some twelve hundred films were completed in France during the 1930s – differed markedly from that of earlier periods. With sound production, costs tripled and it was no longer possible for film makers themselves to finance and so control their own work. The two huge vertically integrated companies – Pathé-Natan, taken over in 1929 by Natan Tanenzapf, who later took the name Bernard Natan, and Gaumont-Franco-Film-Aubert (GFFA), fused by Louis Aubert in 1930 – were both brought by bad management – and in some cases, fraud – to virtual bankrupcy during this period (the Gaumont crash coming in 1934 and the Pathé-Natan one in 1936). As a result, film making became an intensely speculative activity indulged in by a myriad of tiny, undercapitalised companies. Each year fifty or more companies would go into liquidation and a hundred or more new ones would be founded, many of which never succeeded in making a single film. The confusions of the organisation of production were equalled by those surrounding the definition of the product itself. The costs of the change-over to sound were enormous and for a considerable time there were doubts as to which system would be successful: sound on film or sound on discs, the latter being initially the more successful commercially. Silent cinema persisted in France therefore until well into the 1930s, and even towards the end of 1931 it has been estimated that less than a quarter of France's 4,500 cinemas had been converted to sound. As for the sound film itself, all attempts at production involved choices between radically divergent and often highly limited forms of equipment amid a hubbub of strident and misleading publicity and a ruthlessly fought patents war. While virtually every 1930 film claimed to be '100% talking', many were no more than works conceived silent and modified by a quickly recorded musical score and effects, or would-be comedies and dramas weighed down with static recordings of inappropriate songs. Location shooting was taboo and camera movement within the studio often very difficult. Moreover, after the first novelty of synchronous sound had worn off, French audiences proved themselves hostile to both dialogue in foreign languages and to subtitled prints. Since the techniques of dubbing were not perfected for several years, the early 1930s were a period when films were made in multiple-language versions, either using the same sets and shooting script with a succession of casts of different nationalities or even, on occasion, with a single cast mouthing languages they did not speak, while the dialogue was recorded simultaneously by the appropriate foreign-language speakers crouching on the set but out of camera range.

The extent of the transformation of French cinema can be gauged by a brief consideration of the careers during the early 1930s of some of the great figures of French silent cinema. Henri Fescourt shot *La Maison de la flèche* in 1930 at Twickenham for a small French company, then went to Sweden to shoot the French-language versions of films made by Gustav Molander and Gustav Edgren. Five years of inactivity followed before he was able to direct again, and then it was merely to remake his 1928 success, *L'Occident*. Marcel L'Herbier made 'the first 100% talkie shot in a French studio', *L'Enfant de l'amour* (1930) and a triple-language film, *La Femme d'une nuit* (1930), in Berlin. Although he was able to show glimpses of his old talent in two lively adaptations of Gaston Leroux thrillers, *Le Mystère de la chambre jaune* (1930) and *Le Parfum de la dame en noir* (1931), he was subsequently typecast as a maker of filmed stage plays. Abel Gance conceived *La Fin du monde* (1930) as a silent film and, even with the addition of a sound track in which he attempted characteristic experiments with sound perspective and distortion, he could not avoid a commercial failure. Between a second failure – a remake of *Mater dolorosa* (1932) – and a sound version of *Napoléon Bonaparte* (1934) Gance too was reduced to filming imposed subjects in a theatrical style. Jean Epstein was at least able to complete the Breton 'trilogy' begun with the silent *Finis terrae* (1929) by shooting the short *Mor Vran* (1931) and the feature-length *L'Or des mers* (1932). But these two experiments with the poetic fusion of image and sound, which rank among his best works, passed unnoticed in the contemporary enthusiasm for theatrically dialogued studio features.

In the new atmosphere of the 1930s one might have anticipated the extinction of avant-garde film making. But in fact a few memorable works were completed in the early 1930s, including two of virtual feature length commissioned and financed by a wealthy amateur, the Vicomte de Noailles. The first of these, Luis Buñuel's *L'Age d'or* (1930), was made with the same freedom and audacity as the director's earlier short, *Un Chien andalou*. Hailed by the surrealists, its showing provoked reactionary thugs to smash the cinema and the prefect of police to ban the film. Indeed *L'Age d'or* received its first public distribution in France only fifty-one years later, in 1981, when it was put out by Gaumont. Buñuel proclaimed the cinema as 'a magnificent and perilous weapon', ideal for expressing the world of dream, emotion and instinct, and most early critics concerned themselves with the film's content: its hymn to *amour fou*, its blasphemy and its open hatred of state and army. If its once shocking images and incidents – a blind man being deliberately knocked down, a girl finding a cow in her bed, lovers grappling desperately in the mud, a gamekeeper casually shooting his own child, images implying masturbation and mutilation – have now lost something of their bite, the film's formal aspects remain fascinating. *L'Age d'or* began as a second collaboration of Buñuel and Salvador Dali, who quarrelled during the making, after some location footage had been shot at Dali's home at Cadaqués. This, combined with fragments of documentary and newsreel, location footage from the Parisian suburbs and studio material shot at the Billancourt studios in Paris, served to make a unique collage. While individual sequences are edited in fairly conventional if fragmentary ways, the film moves without overall narrative coherence to link anachronistic and discordant titles, a documentary on scorpions, shots of bishops and bandits, street scenes, upper-class parties and parodistic images of Jesus Christ as leader of a band of unprincipled libertines. The use made of sound is particularly original for the period: classical music is used to counterpoint the violent or aggressive images, voice-over commentary reduced to meaninglessness, dialogues split and juxtaposed, and sound effects allowed their full poetic and allusive power.

Also commissioned by Noailles and shot in 1930, but not given a public screening until two years later, was *Le Sang d'un poète*, the first film by Jean Cocteau (1889–1963). It was received with contempt by the surrealists, but time has shown it to contain images of an equal poetic power, if less intensity. Where Buñuel is provocative and aggressive, Cocteau borrows the mechanism of the dream only so as to allow memories to 'entwine, move and express themselves freely'. Working closely with his cameraman, Georges Périnal, and composer, Georges Auric, Cocteau has set out to make 'a realistic documentary of unreal events', a narcissistic self-portrait in which imagined images – such as those seen through keyholes in the Hôtel des Folies-Dramatiques – mingle with authentic personal memories, like the snowball fight and death of a fellow pupil at the Lycée Condorcet. With its toying with basic film trickery, its confusion of statues and women, human beings and collage-style paintings, its symbolic imagery of a mouth trapped in the palm of a hand or a black guardian angel, *Le Sang d'un poète* is a rich repository of the obsessive themes and images out of which Cocteau was to build his personal oeuvre. Although Buñuel was able to make the documentary, *Las Hurdes*, in Spain in 1932, neither he nor Cocteau was to direct a further feature film until after World War II (when Cocteau made *La Belle et la bête* and Buñuel the first of his Mexican films, *Gran Casino*).

*

It is fascinating to contrast the lasting quality of these innovative and independent works – which have become staple fare for film societies and ciné-clubs – with the total expendability of the bulk of early sound production in France. The battle for supremacy between Hollywood and the German film industry dominated all production activities, although interesting work was done from the earliest years of sound by the smaller French producers who often had to struggle with inadequate equipment and financial backing. What is particularly striking is the contrast in tactics adopted by the two giants: the one seeking supremacy through the sheer quantity of films produced for immediate local consumption, while the other sought successfully to create a prestige product that could be marketed worldwide.

At the Joinville studios in Paris re-equipped by Paramount and under the supervision of Robert Kane – who, it seems, spoke no French – the stress was unambiguously on quantity. The tone was set by Paramount's first production, an insignificant comedy called *Un Trou dans le mur* (1930), directed by René Barberis, of which a reputed thirteen different-language versions were made. Since the aim was the colonisation of the whole European market, not just the dominance of French screens, a mere twelve days of studio shooting were allowed for each production, which would be immediately remade in at least four or five other languages. By 1932 – the year in which the parent company in Hollywood, which had suffered huge losses during the Depression, halved its production budget – the output of French films alone at Joinville had reached twenty-four films a year, that is, two a month. The basis of this enormous output was the adaptation of existing works, especially stage plays, so that almost overnight the lessons of the complex and visually sophisticated art of silent cinema were forgotten. At Joinville, French cinema returned to an equivalent of the stylistically anonymous canned theatre of pre-1914, with spoken dialogue replacing the inter-titles. The sole difference was that the new products of the early 1930s lacked any pretence of a national identity. In so far as one can speak of an 'original' version in these circumstances, this had to be basic and uncomplicated, since the directors of the foreign versions would be required to copy it slavishly, shot by shot. The arrival of the sound film was a bleak time for European cinema, now at the mercy of foreign patent-holders and suppliers of equipment. And, just as foreign-language films were made at Joinville, so too French-language versions were made in the studios of Hollywood and Berlin, so that in the early 1930s perhaps twenty to twenty-five per cent of all French-language films released in France were actually made abroad. It is a reflection of the difficulties of the times that even as gifted a director as Jacques Feyder, who had gone to

Hollywood to direct Greta Garbo in *The Kiss*, found himself reduced in 1930 to making such foreign-language copies for MGM's drive into the European market: the German and Swedish versions of Clarence Brown's *Anna Christie*, the French version of *The Unholy Night*, the French and German versions of Lionel Barrymore's *His Glorious Night*.

Out of all the frenzied activity of Joinville, where production was abandoned in 1933 in favour of post-synchronised dubbing in the modern sense, virtually nothing remains of interest beyond the first involvement in film making of Marcel Pagnol (1895–1974). Born near Marseilles and drawing his inspiration from this great port and its surrounding countryside, Pagnol was a former schoolmaster who had achieved enormous success as a playwright in the late 1920s. With the advent of sound his work was inevitably sought out by producers and within three years all three of his big stage hits had been filmed: *Marius* by Alexander Korda for Paramount in 1931, *Fanny* by Marc Allégret in 1932 and *Topaze* by Louis Gasnier (the veteran director of *The Perils of Pauline*) in 1933. While Pagnol had nothing directly to do with the making of the latter film, the screen adaption of which was signed by Léopold Marchand, the other two contributed greatly to his subsequent career. Learning the basic techniques of film making from the talented Hungarian-born Korda, who already had an international career behind him and was to go to London, the scene of still greater triumphs, later in 1931, Pagnol became the most articulate advocate of the talking picture in France. Quite unimpressed by the glories of the silent cinema, Pagnol proclaimed that while it was merely the art of printing and distributing pantomime, the sound film was the art of printing and distributing theatre. Dependence on dialogue was the criterion of value for the new form and a film comprehensible if projected silent was, quite simply, a bad film. However adequate this stance is as a description of assumptions at Joinville, it is, as we shall see, refuted by Pagnol's own achievements in the late 1930s.

Pagnol's Marseilles trilogy – *Marius, Fanny* and *César*, which he directed himself in a 1936 screen version which reunited the original cast – represents one of his most popular and lasting achievements. The remarkable unity of tone and manner of the three films – with all the central themes established in *Marius* – makes it appropriate to speak of the trilogy as Pagnol's work, despite the skilled direction of Korda and Allégret in the first two episodes. Pagnol has succeeded in creating a vitally engaging set of characters, particularly the older generation of César (Raimu), Panisse (Charpin) and Honorine (Alida Rouffe), who remain convincing even while they are clearly conceived as virtuoso acting pieces. The younger characters are less riveting, although Pierre Fresnay is suitably intense as Marius and Orane Demazis makes a touching Fanny. On one level the trilogy is the record of a certain aspect of traditional Marseilles life which, thanks to the evocative vividness of the language, needs no more than a hint of physical existence in terms of images and sound effects. It is also, initially at least, a celebration of the values of family, honour, possessions and idleness, but the mood darkens through the trilogy, so that *César*, set eighteen years after the earlier films, becomes almost a lament for these values, with the role of the family, for example, subjected to real questioning. But above all the trilogy thrives because of the strength of the characterisation – with Raimu's forcefulness balanced by Charpin and Alida Rouffe – and the sheer skill and wit with which the set-piece scenes – the card game in *Marius*, the wedding in *Fanny*, for example – are written. Pagnol's trilogy moves easily between almost farcical comedy and underplayed melodrama, delighting in verbal felicities but always aware of the gap between words and actions and, finally, of the inadequacy of gestures to cover the damage caused by human frailty.

In the years following *Fanny* Pagnol worked as scriptwriter for a number of other directors. But the success of his work had given him his creative independence and when he put forward his theory of cinema in 1933 it was in his own film journal, the *Cahiers du film*.

*

If the purely exploitative nature of Hollywood's concern with the French film market is all too crudely apparent, the links between France and Germany are both subtler and more ambiguous. The full story of the relations between the French film industry and the German occupying forces between 1940 and 1944, for instance, would have to take into account the constant interaction during the 1930s, when the French need for capital investment met up with the German search to earn foreign currency. It is this latter commercial need which leads to the Germans' conception of cinema in purely entertainment terms. This in turn allows even committed anti-fascists like Jean Grémillon and his 1930s assistant Louis Daquin to work without qualms in the Berlin studios, and permits René Clair to create some of his most Parisian films thanks to German capital investment. Many leading figures in the French film industry apparently saw nothing questionable about close involvement with Hitler's Germany – so long as it was profitable – and began work before Hitler's accession to power in 1933. Indeed the latter paradoxically created a German émigré cinema in France to parallel the growing importance of French film making in Berlin. The first German involvement came from the

Tobis company, which had taken over the Tri-Ergon sound film patents previously held by UFA and in 1929 strengthened its position by merging with Klangfilm, a subsidiary of the electrical giants, AEG and Siemens. Seeking to confront growing Hollywood dominance and exploit its patents in the international market, Tobis-Klangfilm moved into France, setting up its own sound studios at Epinay and equipping the French studios of Pathé and Eclair. At Epinay the emphasis was on prestige production and it was here that René Clair in 1930–32 made the four sound films which put him in the forefront of European production.

If Pagnol's Marseilles trilogy draws its strength from its uninhibited use of language, Clair's first sound films are marked by a reluctance to use dialogue or effects naturalistically. This is hardly surprising since already in his silent films Clair had been concerned to shape his materials, never simply to record a pre-existing reality. Before beginning work on *Sous les toits de Paris* (1930), Clair had made clear his conviction that 'the alternate use of the image of the subject and of the sound produced by it – not their *simultaneous* use – creates the best effects', and his film was designed to illustrate this concern with the counterpointing of images and sounds. Seen today, one of the most striking aspects of the film is the way it constitutes almost a textbook collection of ways in which to avoid synchronisation, either by obliterating the visuals (with smoke from a passing train or by having the light switched off) or by cutting off the sound (by closing a glass door, for example) so that communication with the audience is made through mime in the traditional style. *Sous les toits de Paris* is set in a Paris meticulously designed in the studio by Lazare Meerson and expertly photographed by Georges Périnal. It makes extensive use of songs of Moretti and Nazelles to link the action involving a group of characters living on the fringes of crime and violence. But Clair's attention is never on the sordid, and here he concentrates on the manner in which the friendship of two men, played by Albert Préjean and Gaston Modot, triumphs over their rivalry for a pretty but flirtatious girl (Pola Illery). *Sous les toits de Paris* established Clair as an internationally successful film maker even before he had received full recognition in France, and his film was particularly well received in Berlin, where his style proved particularly influential.

René Clair's masterpiece of the period is *Le Million* (1931), made with largely the same crew and a cast which this time starred René Lefèvre and Annabella. Adapting a comedy of the kind which had served as basis for the silent *Un Chapeau de paille d'Italie*, Clair replaced virtually all the dialogue with songs, introduced a chorus of tradespeople to comment on the action, and amused himself by setting the film's climax on stage during a parodied performance at the Opéra Lyrique. Again Meerson's setting is a studio-built Paris, but this time it serves as a fantastic setting for a huge and intricate chase – the pursuit from one end of the film to the other of a winning lottery ticket inadvertently left in the pocket of a jacket which has been disposed of. The plot has all the precision and intricacy of a watch mechanism and the pace never flags. As usual with Clair the characters are to some extent marionettes and issues such as the opposition of police and crooks are treated as pretexts for songs and for comedy which has only the slightest hint of any social critique. Throughout, the film is packed with striking parallel actions (as in the many double chase sequences), ironic interplay (the lovers miming their love to the singing of the grotesquely fat opera stars) and moments when life itself becomes a ballet (like the battle on stage for the jacket which is given the choreography and the soundtrack of a rugby scrum). While individual sequences in subsequent films reach similar heights of fantasy, no later Clair film sustains its magical mood with the same sureness of touch.

Still working for Tobis and with much the same crew and collaborators, Clair followed *Le Million* with two further striking films, one of which pleased critics rather than audiences, while the other was commercially more successful but has been largely ignored since the 1930s. *A nous la liberté* (1931) was by intention a more serious comedy, which sets out to demolish the notion that work is freedom. Many of the ideas – such as the initial linking of classroom drill, factory production line and prison workshop – are excellent and the use made of Georges Van Parys's music is always apt. But Clair shows himself more skilled at attacking the whole notion of work than at offering a precisely focused criticism of a specific system. The film is imbued with sympathy for the poor and the workers, opposition to the powerful and scorn for the pretentious (like the top-hatted bourgeois whom Clair wickedly shows racing in all directions in pursuit of banknotes blowing in the wind at the end of the film), yet it can offer no positive solutions. Beauty for Clair is sentimental picture-postcard charm, culture is equated with pretension, and at the end the workers enjoy a permanent holiday without any hint that prolonged leisure might provide problems. At the heart of the film is a deeper relationship than that in any earlier Clair film – the friendship of two convicts, one of whom becomes the factory owner, while the other remains a penniless employee. Significantly, although this relationship can survive separation and surmount social difference, it cannot lead to social integration. At the end the pair can only abandon everything and set off like tramps to savour the world from outside society. This anarchistic evasion is characteristic of French cinema of the early

75

1930s and finds its echoes – albeit in very different stylistic contexts – in the work of Vigo and Renoir.

Quatorze juillet (1932) re-established the Parisian poetry absent from *A nous la liberté* but retained the emphasis on personal relations. Here the focus was the love of a young florist (Annabella) for a taxi-driver (Georges Rigaud), which is troubled when his former mistress (Pola Illery) intrudes into his life again. If anything, the importance which Clair attaches to this slight story unbalances the film, which elsewhere contains sequences in which his love for Paris is more apparent than ever. The film's mixture of sadness and festivity, tenderness and betrayal, is perfectly suited to its Fourteenth of July setting. But the marvellous sense of overall shape and consistent sureness of touch which characterised *Le Million* are missing here. While some moments are more touching than anything in the earlier film, the tone is uneven, so that one of Clair's finest creations, the rich drunkard Monsieur Imaque (Paul Olivier), seems to have strayed into the action from some other, more openly comic film. After a break of over a year and a dispute with Tobis which robbed him of his customary team of collaborators, Clair made his fifth sound film, *Le Dernier milliardaire* (1934). This satire on the pretensions of petty monarchies pleased no one and had the misfortune to open just a few weeks after the assassination of King Alexander of Yugoslavia in Marseilles. Here, in *Le Dernier milliardaire*, Clair's sense of human futility is given free reign, as is the constant underlying tendency towards caricature. The resulting film again contains memorable individual sequences, but as a whole it is awkward and ultimately unsatisfying. After this commercial failure Clair went to London to make *The Ghost Goes West* (1935) for Alexander Korda and stayed on to make the less successful *Break the News* in 1937. Two years later he began a new film, *Air pur*, in France, but shooting was interrupted after only a few weeks by the outbreak of war and the project was abandoned. Clair spent the war years in Hollywood and it was not until 1947 that he was to make a new film in France.

If Clair's work between 1930 and 1932 can be said to mark a first high point in Franco-German collaboration, he was by no means alone. Julien Duvivier in the early 1930s and Jean Grémillon towards the end of the decade both worked successfully in Berlin, and some of Jacques Feyder's best work of the mid-1930s was shot, like Clair's, at the Tobis studios at Epinay on the outskirts of Paris. It is clear that the Germans were also very concerned to obtain entry to the French market for their own films. Highly successful French versions were made of the early German musical comedies which followed the paths opened up by Clair with *Sous les toits de Paris*. On a somewhat more serious artistic level French versions were made of G. W. Pabst films and the Franco-German co-production, *Kameradschaft* (*La Tragédie de la mine*, 1931), in which the German and French characters each speak their own language, is no doubt a second high point in the collaboration between the two countries.

In view of these links, it is hardly surprising that when the advent of Hitler in 1933 drove most of the great German directors and a large number of technicians into exile, their first stopping point was Paris. None of the work of the expatriate film makers such as G. W. Pabst, Max Ophuls and Fritz Lang during this period is of particular lasting interest, but the flood of producers, directors and technicians reached such a level that it has been estimated that in 1934, while some twenty per cent of all 'French' films released were French-language versions made abroad, a further twenty per cent were made in France but totally without local roots by foreign directors and crews who were merely in transit.

*

Though both bulk of output and prestige productions were so largely the result of foreign-financed companies, considerable efforts were made by French producers from 1929 onwards. The title of 'first French talking picture' is disputed between André Hugon's *Les Trois masques* (1929), shot at Twickenham for Pathé-Cinema, and a film which opened a day or two earlier, Gaumont's *Le Collier de la reine* (1929), made by Gaston Ravel and Tony Lekain – though in truth neither work contained more than snatches of dialogue and songs to supplement the ubiquitous music. It is really only in 1930 that films of lasting value begin to be produced: *Sous les toits de Paris*, *L'Age d'or* and the first sound films of Grémillon and Duvivier. The career of Julien Duvivier, one of the imperturbable professionals of French cinema who was to shoot some eighteen films during the 1930s, gives a good indication of the diversity and limitations of French commercial production in these early years of sound. Of the nine films he made between *David Golder* (1930) and the ambitious but academic *Maria Chapdelaine* (1934), only *Poil de Carotte* (1932), a sensitive study of a child's world, is remembered today.

Although Dudley Andrew (1980) has claimed that Jean Grémillon's first sound film, *La Petite Lise* (1930), predicts the poetic realist school, in which Duvivier was to excel, 'in its rhythm, tone and dramaturgy', Grémillon's career has none of Duvivier's satisfying continuity and commercial success. Like Grémillon's two silent features, *La Petite Lise* is an unashamed melodrama, although perhaps better written than most, since the screenplay is by Charles

Spaak, another key figure of the 1930s. The film's pace is kept deliberately slow, as in the opening scenes in the tropical prison at Cayenne. Although the staginess of the plot is accentuated at times by Alcover's heavy performance, *La Petite Lise* is full of strikingly devised effects: a sensitive employment of sound and music (by Roland Manuel, a lifelong friend and collaborator), a use of light effects for dramatic impact, and a very conscious interplay of locations – setting the sordid nightclub against the heavy gloom of the Cayenne prison, for example. As remarkable as the work with sound is the role accorded to the camera, which at times is used in ways which are strikingly modern: filming a conversation from behind, or holding the image of a setting after the hero has moved on, so that the action is conveyed solely through the overheard sounds. *La Petite Lise* was produced by Emile Natan (brother of Bernard), who hated the film. When it proved a commercial failure, Grémillon's career in the French industry was virtually finished for a decade.

Grémillon was not the only film maker whose career was destroyed in the early 1930s. Pierre Prévert (b.1906), together with his brother, the poet and future screenwriter, Jacques Prévert, and a group of friends, made his first film, the fifty-minute *L'Affaire est dans le sac* in 1932. The circumstances could hardly have been less propitious: a mere week for scripting and another week's night-time shooting, using an existing street set in the Pathé-Natan studios, plus one day for exteriors. The film reflects the limitations of this mode of production, but is marked too by a youthful invention and unbridled enthusiasm. Nonetheless it was a total commercial failure, and Pathé apparently ordered all copies to be destroyed. Copies of the film do still exist, but it was not until 1943 that Pierre Prévert was able to direct a full-length feature film.

Perhaps the most tragic figure of the early sound era is Jean Vigo (1905–34) whose total output represents less than an evening's viewing. When he died at the age of twenty-nine, he left a forty-seven-minute film banned by the French censors until 1945 and a first feature which was being re-edited to include a popular song as he lay on his death-bed. Vigo had been one of the pioneers of the ciné-club movement in France and he learned his film making from his viewing as much as from the very minor assistant roles in various professional productions which he occupied in the late 1920s. Like all his later work, Vigo's *A propos de Nice* (1930) was shot by Boris Kaufman, brother of Dziga-Vertov and later Hollywood cinematographer (working for instance on Elia Kazan's *On the Waterfront*). This forty-minute essay in documentary shows the influence of the Soviet film makers and theorists, of René Clair's *Entr'acte* and Erich von Stroheim's *Foolish Wives*, a film which also had a deep influence on Jean Renoir. *A propos de Nice* was shot with Vigo's own Debrie camera, without a clearly defined shooting script or strong commitment to any abstract notion of the social application of documentary film making. This is a piece of personal film making and in these terms Vigo's commitment is strong. His childhood had been marked by the death in prison – under very suspicious circumstances – of his father, a leading figure in the anarchist movement, who later became a socialist newspaper editor using the pseudonym Miguel Almereyda. Vigo was twelve at the time of his father's probable murder, and in this first film he depicts Nice as a city of death, filled with the old, the ugly and the gamblers. Its monuments and hideously elaborate cemeteries are stressed and the annual carnival filmed with a fascinated horror. Vigo himself described *A propos de Nice* as 'a documented point of view'. It is full of striking imagery and startling juxtapositions and its densely packed texture makes it a work of considerable value in its own right, beyond its significance as the first expression of many characteristic Vigo themes and concerns.

A propos de Nice, shown at the Vieux-Colombier cinema in Paris in May 1930, was essentially an amateur film, funded with money provided by Vigo's father-in-law. He followed it with a commissioned work, a ten-minute documentary on a champion swimmer, *Taris* (1931). Towards the end of the following year the shooting of *Zéro de conduite* (1933), independently produced at the GFFA studios, was begun, to be interrupted several times because of Vigo's illness. The technical quality of both image and sound in this forty-five-minute fictional study of school life is poor and the narrative is often difficult to follow. Rather than a rounded and polished work, *Zéro de conduite* is a marvellously sensitive and evocative series of fragmented impressions of life at a boarding school, with most of the linking and bridging shots missing. The sense of personal involvement is total and Vigo has even used the names of his own schoolfriends for the central characters. Caussat, Colin, Bruel, together with the delicate but rebellious Tabard, move – as no doubt Vigo and his companions would have liked to move – from childish games to revolt against the school system. The adults who represent this system are all caricatured – a supervisor reminiscent of Caligari who steals from the children, a dwarf as headmaster, a fat pederastic science teacher, and one solitary sympathetic figure, Huguet, who does Chaplin imitations and headstands. Vigo's attitude is clear in the final scenes in which the masters and visiting dignitaries watch the meaningless founder's-day celebrations in front of – and hardly distinguishable from – a set of fairground dummies. Vigo was marked by an unhappy childhood – illegitimate, often in poor health, forced to live under a pseudonym, he was hardly likely to see childhood as a golden age. Indeed *Zéro de conduite* is one of the rare films to capture the awkward mixture of charm and ugliness, scatology and innocence, close friendship and burgeoning sexuality to be found in a boys' boarding school. But Vigo's approach is incredibly delicate, and material that could have been merely crude or embarrassingly personal is here presented with a sure lightness of touch, so that the film stays in the memory as a series of flashes of insight into childhood: the return after the holidays, the classroom and punishments, the playground and loneliness, the dormitory at night, the longing for revolt and escape. In the circumstances, and despite its final celebration in image and song of the boys' revolt, *Zéro de conduite* seems an unlikely film to have been banned for some twelve years by the censor. But after its first showing in 1933 it was not released again in France until 1945, when it was shown with Malraux's *L'Espoir*.

Vigo's ability to move effortlessly between reality and fantasy and thereby create a unique poetry is even more notable in the feature-length *L'Atalante* (1934), shot largely on location and with studio interiors designed to offer the same constrictions as location work. Vigo's tuberculosis was becoming worse and worse, and he was in fact too ill to supervise the last shot taken – the marvellous helicopter image of the barge with which the film concludes. But his impending death is never apparent in *L'Atalante*, which is a hymn to life. Having purged his nightmare memories of childhood in *Zéro de conduite*, Vigo here celebrates a mature relationship, the survival of a new marriage in the face of initial difficulties and quarrels. To accompany the newly-weds – Jean (Jean Dasté, the Huguet of the earlier film) and Juliette (Dita Parlo) – Vigo has created one of the unforgettable figures of French cinema, the mate Père Jules, played with amazing force and genuine strangeness by Michel Simon. The particular poetry of Vigo's work does not preclude a direct look at reality in a way unique in this period of French cinema. The film is not shaped into a neat theatrical pattern and the life of the couple, cooped up on the barge with the mate and the boy (played by Louis Lefebvre, Caussat in *Zéro de conduite*), has the harsh feel of reality. So too has the gap of incomprehension between the barge people and Juliette's parents and the other peasants who follow the couple in procession after the wedding ceremony. Later in the film, when Juliette is alone in the city, we are shown the rarely seen France of the Depression years: the prostitution, the queues of hopeless unemployed, a starving, desperate thief beaten by well-dressed, well-fed bourgeois. Vigo approaches his central couple with the same eye for realistic detail, showing the clumsiness of passion, the inarticulateness of two simple people from very different worlds. But there is no trace of condescension here, indeed *L'Atalante* is shot through with humour, moments of fantasy and imagination (Jean's despairing run down to the sea, after Juliette has left him), and genuinely bizarre characters like Père Jules and the pedlar played by Gilles Margaritis. These are characters which are not the result of observation, but of imaginative insight combined with a willingness to create larger-than-life figures. There is a fascinating conflict between the clumsy but genuinely travelled and devoted Père Jules, and the quick-talking, acrobatic and totally insincere pedlar.

Bored and lonely as Jean gives all his attention to the problems of navigation when she wants to see the sights of Paris and live a little, Juliette is tempted away despite her love for her husband. If Jean's concern with his work is understandable if unromantic (we later see the vicious manager of the company he works for), so too is Juliette's need to escape. Vigo is not afraid to heighten the reality of those situations which draw her away from Jean: first the scene in the exotic, museumlike world of Père Jules's cabin, then the meeting with the pedlar at the *bal populaire*, which emphasises Juliette's physical closeness to the Paris she knows only from the radio. The couple's sensual need for each other when they are separated is conveyed with a directness which no other director attempts in the early 1930s (Renoir, for example, pans away when Madame Lestingois is seduced in *Boudu sauvé des eaux*), so that their eventual reunion thanks to Père Jules comes as a genuine climax to an action which has at times seemed to be digressing from its central concerns into fascinating byways (such as the moments involving Père Jules's old gramophone, or his visit to the clairvoyante). *L'Atalante*, despite the mutilation it received, which has only partially been restored, is a work of unique poetic power. The fact that it is Vigo's sole feature film – and that his entire output lasts less than three and a half hours – does not lessen his status as one of the very greatest of French film makers, and one whose influence on his successors has been uniformly positive.

*

For a time it seemed that Jean Renoir's career would also be impeded. Although his last two silent films had been avowedly commercial efforts, two years passed before he was given a further directorial opportunity. And even then, before he could make the film he planned, he had to undergo a kind of 'test' for the producers, Braunberger and Richebé. This took the form of the cheap, literal and totally conventional filming of a twenty-year-old Georges Feydeau farce, *On purge bébé* (1931). The main interest here – apart from the celebrated sequence in which Renoir recorded the sound of a toilet being flushed – was the renewal of contact with the actor Michel Simon. In this film – scripted in a week, shot in a week, edited in a week (and reputedly in profit by the end of the fourth week) – Simon has little scope for the talents which were to contribute so largely to Renoir's finest work of the early 1930s. However, their next collaboration, *La Chienne* (1931), is one of Renoir's most durable creations and a work in which the complexities of his conception of realism are very apparent. On one level this is a naturalistic slice of low life: a downtrodden clerk, Legrand (Michel Simon), who is also a painter of enormous but unrecognised talent, becomes infatuated with a whore, Lulu (Janie Marèze). After a quarrel over her deception of him, he kills her and allows her pimp Dédé (Georges Flamant) to go to the guillotine. But Renoir prefaces this tale with a tongue-in-cheek puppet-play introduction to the characters and concludes with an epilogue depicting Legrand happy in a new life as a tramp. The plot centres on the incompatibility of the three central characters' dreams – Legrand's for romantic passion, Lulu's for bourgeois respectability and Dédé's for affluence – and the playing, particularly of Michel Simon, constantly stresses the discordant interaction between the various levels of existence and self-presentation. In tone *La Chienne* has the same ambiguity, with the clumsy farce of Legrand's home life balanced by the horror of Dédé's final realisation that he is to die for a crime he did not commit, just as the brutality of the murder itself is set against the everyday bustle of life in the street outside. If it is the complexity of attitude and motivation which interests Renoir, the portrayal of such characters here is accompanied by an awareness that the actors are performing, not living, these roles (critics have pointed to the influence on Renoir at this time of Pabst's version of Brecht's *Die Dreigroschenoper*).

La Nuit du carrefour (1932) is one of Renoir's most mysterious films – the director himself says that the story 'was pretty well incomprehensible, even to its author' and calls the resulting film 'a completely absurd experiment' to which he cannot look back without nostalgia. Although adapted, like Duvivier's *La Tête d'un homme*, from a Simenon novel, *La Nuit du carrefour* places little emphasis on plot or the creation of suspense. The loss of a reel of the film by the assistant editor (and future film historian), Jean Mitry, only partly accounts for the incomprehensibility of certain aspects of the plot. Much of the dialogue is almost inaudible and the camera style concentrates on fog effects and darkness to capture the strange atmosphere of a suburban crossroads on the outskirts of Paris. The director's brother Pierre Renoir gives an excellent performance as

Maigret, but the minor roles are played in a bewildering variety of styles by a largely inexperienced or amateur cast. *Boudu sauvé des eaux* (1932), Renoir's best-known film of the period, is more coherent, although it is a systematic reversal of the values of the play by René Fauchois on which it is based. Whereas in the original the emphasis was on the portrayal of the benevolent bourgeois bookseller, Lestingois (played on stage by Fauchois himself), in the film version the central figure is the anarchistic tramp Boudu (Michel Simon) whom he rescues from drowning in the Seine and who rewards him by seducing first his wife and then his mistress (the maid). Again, as in *La Chienne*, the film opens with a prologue – here a mock ballet, with Lestingois as Bacchus and the maid as Chloe – before settling into a more realistic portrayal of the action. In adapting the play, Renoir has opened out the action so that it takes in the whole of the apartment, shot in deep focus with a constantly moving camera, and the Parisian quayside outside. Within this setting the playing of Michel Simon is the very opposite of his contained portrayal of Legrand. All of Boudu's sentiments are externalised and he is totally uninhibited in all his actions, whether overturning the wine, swinging from the doorframe, polishing his shoes with a bedspread or seducing Madame Lestingois. It is a marvellous performance by Simon to set beside his playing of Père Jules in Vigo's *L'Atalante*. Although there is no deep friendship between Lestingois and Boudu of the kind that leads the two heroes of Clair's *A nous la liberté* to abandon everything and go off together, there is no animosity either. Lestingois fails to civilise Boudu, but he seems to bear his protégé no ill-will, even for the seduction of his wife. The relationship has the characteristic Renoir ambiguity: each has his reasons, his style of coping with life. Thus *Boudu sauvé des eaux*, though parodying and poking fun at bourgeois life, is not a social critique. The mood is one of carefree anarchism which shapes its ending: on the verge of being made respectable by his lottery winnings and marriage to the maid, Boudu overturns a boat and swims away to resume his existence as a tramp.

Neither of Renoir's other two films of the early 1930s matches the exuberance of *Boudu sauvé des eaux*. *Chotard et cie* (1933), one of his least-known works, is a quickly made studio film based on a stage play by Roger Ferdinand. Again the focus is on the disruption of a bourgeois establishment: the son of Chotard the grocer writes poetry. Unlike the previous work, however, *Chotard et cie* ends in a compromise, with honest toil and art reconciled. The most memorable sequence is the fancy dress ball, which is a distant anticipation of that in *La Règle du jeu*. *Madame Bovary* (1934), an adaptation of Flaubert's classic novel made for the publishing house of Gallimard, is a more difficult film to assess, since it was cut by an hour or more before release. The film was not popular with audiences and, although it has its defenders, most critics have tended to see the film's coldly formal style, its unity of tone and its reliance on dialogue as regressive in terms of Renoir's 1930s work. Certainly there is little pleasure to be taken in Valentine Tessier's mannered performance (although Renoir defends it warmly) and the whole film – at least in its shortened form – has the slightly embalmed air of a too solemn and faithful adaptation of a classic novel. Despite this somewhat muted end to 1934, Renoir's work since 1931 had established him as an important film maker and provided the basis of professional experience with sound on which he was to build the series of even greater films, from *Toni* to *La Règle du jeu*.

1934 saw the French film industry on the brink of one of its periodic crises, but there were promising artistic signs of renewal despite the death of Vigo and departure of Clair. Pagnol's return to Marseilles was to herald a masterly series of films made at his studio there – including Renoir's *Toni* (1935) and his own *Angèle* (1934). In 1933 Jacques Feyder had returned from Hollywood and re-established himself as a major director, after years of blocked projects and the shooting of foreign-language 'versions', with *Le Grand jeu* (1934), which is considered together with his subsequent films in the next chapter. If Clair's work for Tobis is particularly indicative of approaches to sound in the early 1930s, it is Feyder's work of the mid-1930s which sets the tone for the series of major productions which brought French film making to the forefront of world cinema in the years immediately before the outbreak of World War II.

*

In retrospect the bitter debate around 1930 about the coming of talking pictures – described by René Clair, for example, as 'a redoubtable monster, an unnatural creation' – seems largely irrelevant. Basically this is because the major polemicists took up positions which subsequently proved quite contrary to their own practice. Jean Renoir, who welcomed the talkies 'with delight, seeing at once all the use that could be made of sound', was unable to work for two years, whereas Clair, who opposed them, was one of the first to use sound with real imagination, achieving still greater international success than with this silent films, despite the barriers which language was supposed to set up. Moreover Clair's masterpiece, *Le Million*, was adapted from a stage work, as was Renoir's *Boudu sauvé des eaux*. Although it was assumed that French cinema would now be taken over by the practitioners of the Parisian stage, the acknowledged king of the boulevard theatre, Sacha Guitry, had only one play adapted in France in the early 1930s – *Le Blanc et le noir* (1931), directed by Marc Allégret – and it was not until 1935 that he began his own directing career with an adaptation of his play, *Pasteur*. Marcel Pagnol, the most vociferous advocate of speech in the cinema and of the adaptation of theatrical works for the screen, had retreated from the world of Joinville and Billancourt by 1933, and his first Provençal film, *Jofroi*, marks the move away from both studio and play adaptation into the sunshine and open air of his native countryside. If the coming of sound was to end the most creative work of some celebrated 1920s figures, such as Gance and L'Herbier, who were by no means hostile to it, other equally celebrated masters of silent cinema, such as Clair and Feyder, continued to do work of the highest level and experienced film makers like Duvivier, Grémillon and Renoir far surpassed their previous endeavours. The reliance on dialogue which it had been feared would make the cinema a prisoner of the perfect enunciation of the Comédie Française, in fact prompted the emergence of a cinema in which dialect could play a real part and a whole new generation of actors – Raimu, Fernandel, Arletty and so on – whose direct approach contrasts most favourably with the theatrical posing of many of the key figures of the supposedly more cinematic 1920s cinema of the image (compare, for example, Séverin-Mars in Gance's *La Roue* with virtually any performance by Raimu). These contradictions occur too on a stylistic level. If the coming of sound led to a new interest in forms of what can be broadly termed 'realism', the range of approaches in the early 1930s is incredibly wide – from Clair's sympathy for characters on the fringes of crime in a Paris rebuilt by Lazare Meerson in *Sous les toits de Paris* or *Quatorze juillet*, Renoir's mixture of naturalism and theatricality in *La Chienne* and Grémillon's treatment of melodrama in *La Petite Lise*, to the new use of location shooting and spontaneity of performance in such very different works as Vigo's *L'Atalante* and Pagnol's *Jofroi*. If a 'poetic realism' can be defined in terms of French late 1930s cinema, its roots in early sound cinema are both diverse and contradictory.

6 The Paradoxes of French Realism
1935–39

Parallèlement à un cinéma traditionnel resté inchangé, il existe indiscutablement aussi un 'cinéma de 36', c'est-à-dire quelques films rompant avec les scénarios et les décors habituels du cinéma français pour témoigner d'un certain changement ou en tout cas d'un espoir sincère, des films portant une attention soudain plus vive aux problèmes sociaux et au monde du travail, des oeuvres avant tout soucieuses de vérité et ne cherchant plus à distraire le spectateur mais le confrontant au contraire de manière critique à ses problèmes quotidiens.

René Predal, 1972

In view of the international reputation acquired by French cinema during the latter part of the 1930s, the actual organisation of production and relation of the film industry to the state are somewhat surprising. These were the years in which directors like Jean Renoir, Julien Duvivier and the young Marcel Carné achieved an impact on film makers and critics throughout the world akin to that made in the 1940s by Roberto Rossellini and the Italian neo-realists or in the late 1950s by the French New Wave. Yet nothing had seemed less likely than this burst of creativity in the early 1930s and the right-wing critics, Maurice Bardèche and Robert Brasillach, conclude the French section of their 1935 *History of the Film* with the observation that 'in 1935 something quite important happened: the French film industry practically disappeared'. In fact production levels remained high – between 110 and 130 features a year during 1934–38 – despite the collapse of the giant combines derived from the old Pathé and Gaumont companies. But the organisation of this production was chaotic, and most of the hundreds of production companies which were founded and vanished within a matter of months existed only to produce a single film and this, in a climate of increasing costs, rising taxation and reduced audience levels, was likely to lose money. The company which Renoir founded specifically to produce *La Marseillaise* was therefore, in accordance with current practice, not an

86

15. Sacha Guitry: Roman d'un tricheur (1936)

16. Jean Renoir: Toni (1935)

17. Jean Renoir: Partie de campagne (1936)
18. Julien Duvivier: Pépé-le-Moko (1937)

19. Marcel Carné: Hôtel du nord (1938)

20. Marcel Pagnol: La Femme du boulanger (1938)

21. Jean Grémillon: Remorques (1939–41)

22. Henri-Georges Clouzot: Le Corbeau (1943)

exception to the rules, and Marcel Pagnol, able regularly to produce two or three films a year in his Marseilles studio, is not a marginalised figure, but one of the half-dozen leading producers of the late 1930s. The same fragmentation was reflected in the organisation of distribution. On average a distribution company would be responsible for no more than a couple of films: in 1936, for example, 46 companies distributed the 91 films actually shot in France (out of a total 'French' production of 116), while the following year 99 films (out of 111) were handled by 54 companies.

Although the major films of the period have an authentically French tone and atmosphere, much of the production finance came from abroad. Most of the major stars of the period worked at some time or other in Berlin, where French versions continued to be made, and links between France and Germany were close, even after the arrival of Hitler. Although Jacques Feyder was later to refuse to work in Paris under the German occupation, his involvement with German finance in the 1930s was considerable. *La Kermesse héroique* was made in two separate language versions – both directed by Feyder – at the Tobis studios in Epinay, where Clair had worked earlier in the decade, and *Les Gens du voyage* was made two years or so later, again in two versions, in Munich. From 1934 the Alliance Cinématographique Européenne (ACE) – a branch of UFA – specialised in producing French films under the supervision of Raoul Ploquin, who was later to play a key role in the organisation of production during the occupation years. From 1936 to 1939 UFA even produced a number of films exclusively in French, among them Marcel L'Herbier's *Adrienne Lecouvreur* (1938). Even as quintessentially French a film as Carné's *Quai des brumes* started off as an UFA project, although it was eventually produced by Gregor Rabinovitch in Paris. In addition to the German involvement, which meant that the major 'French' film-producing companies were foreign firms located outside French boundaries, there was a sizeable but still largely unresearched Anglo-American involvement: Gérard Talon (1975), for instance, claims that over half the 1937 production (some 60 films out of 111) was financed by Lloyd's of London.

The constraints of this foreign-dominated system are very apparent in the career of Jean Grémillon, who was still virtually blacklisted by French producers. After spending the years 1933–35 in Spain, he had to work for three years in Berlin. There he made *La Valse royale* (1935), the French version of a German production, and an original film, *Pattes de mouche* (1936), which showed his unease with comedy and was a commercial failure. *Gueule d'amour* (1937), however, one of the productions made only in French in the Berlin studios, was more successful. Here Grémillon could work from a script written by Charles Spaak and with a cast headed by the two stars who had just made an enormous impact in *Pépé-le-Moko*: Jean Gabin and Mireille Balin. Again the plot is a melodramatic love story which ends in tragedy when Gabin is driven to kill the woman he has loved, but Grémillon avoids both overemphatic dialogue and mere virtuoso scenes. This success was confirmed by *L'Etrange Monsieur Victor* (1938), also shot in Berlin, this time with Raimu as an outwardly respectable man who allows a neighbour to be imprisoned for a murder he himself had committed. Here too Grémillon shows his skill in directing a performer who elsewhere often unbalances a film by the sheer weight of his personality. The adaptation by Charles Spaak, this time supplemented with dialogue by Marcel Achard, allows the director to draw a rich portrait of the confusions and contradictions of his central character, while loosening the stranglehold of the plot sufficiently to enable a wealth of realistic background detail to be offered. Although Grémillon was now at last able to return to France and begin shooting a film on location on the Breton coast, his ill-luck continued. Begun in July 1939, *Remorques*, for which a remarkable cast headed by Gabin, Michèle Morgan and Madeleine Renaud had been assembled, was interrupted by the war and not finished until 1941. The script, on which Spaak, Jacques Prévert and the future director André Cayatte all collaborated, combines a typically Grémillon sense of realism with the fatalistic themes typical of this period of French cinema. As always Gabin's role is a tragic one, and here he plays a rough sailor driven to an adulterous passion with the mysterious woman brought into his life by a storm at the very moment that his wife, unknown to him, is dying. If Grémillon's progress through the 1930s was a painful one, *Remorques* left him poised for his greatest triumphs during the Occupation years.

As in the early 1930s the flow of French talent to the Berlin studios was counterbalanced by the flood of refugees from Nazi Germany and the East. After a brief spell in Hollywood, G. W. Pabst returned to France to direct a couple of spy thrillers, *Mademoiselle Docteur* (1936) and *Le Drame de Shanghai* (1938). In these and the other French productions which preceded Pabst's unexpected return to Germany in 1939 – *L'Esclave blanche* (1938) and *Jeunes filles en détresse* (1939) – the great director's talent was only sporadically apparent. Anatole Litvak's *L'Equipage* (1935) and *Mayerling* (1936) were commercially highly successful and ensured the director's passage to Hollywood, but they made as little lasting contribution to French cinema as the various films directed by Kurt (later Curtis) Bernhardt and Robert Siodmak, or *Ultimatum* (1938), the last film of

Robert Wiene, director of *The Cabinet of Doctor Caligari*. But one German-born director whose work at this period attracted attention is Max Ophuls. Ophuls is very much an international director who also worked in the late 1930s in Italy (*La Signora di tutti*, 1934) and Holland (*Komedie om Geld*, 1936). But from *Divine* (1935), for which the script and dialogue were written by Colette, to *De Mayerling à Sarajévo* (1939–40), a sequel to the Litvak success shot as war loomed, he worked largely in France. His succession of romantic melodramas – including *La Tendre ennemie* (1936), *Yoshiwara* (1937), *Werther* (1938) and *Sans lendemain* (1939–40) – all display the typical Ophuls themes. Whether the setting is the Paris music hall, a Tokyo geisha house or the court at Wetzlar, it will be lovingly reconstructed in the studio and serve as background for a typically unhappy love story. The triteness of the narrative is generally enlivened by Ophuls's sense of decorative poetry and mastery of his fragile atmosphere, but in a sense these films are merely the forerunners of a style which, with growing technical virtuosity and after an interlude in Hollywood, will reach its full flourishing some fifteen years later, once more in France.

Despite the uncertainties of the production and distribution situation, the late 1930s in France were not a time for experiment or, by and large, for new directors with novel ideas. The bulk of the films were the work of well-established and unadventurous craftsmen able and willing to turn out three or four commercially structured films a year. Thus over a quarter of the films of the years 1936 to 1938 (89 out of a total of 346) is the work of just ten prolific directors: Christian-Jaque, Léo Joannon, Pierre Colombier, René Pujol, Jean de Limur, Pierre Chenal, Maurice Cammage, Maurice de Canonge, Pierre Caron and the veteran of silent cinema, Marcel L'Herbier. There is overtly very little connection between this great mass of production – the military farces, stage adaptations and family melodramas produced for the weekly Saturday-night audience – and the qualities which we associate with the films of what is often loosely termed 'French poetic realism'. But this is the true popular cinema of the period, so that even if the films of Duvivier, Carné and Renoir did reach wide audiences, it must be remembered that 1937, for instance, was the year of Colombier's farce *Ignace*, starring Fernandel, as well as Renoir's *La Grande illusion*. Moreover, the films we recall from this period – and there is little dispute as to which are the truly significant and lasting works – have to be seen in this context, since they share many of the formulas of the routine commercial production, such as the importance of script and dialogue writers and the reliance on star performers (albeit Jean Gabin, Louis Jouvet or Raimu).

The connections, which on the surface appear self-evident, between the cinema and the political situation of the period, which saw the establishment and collapse of Léon Blum's Popular Front government, also prove on examination to be less clear-cut than one might imagine from a recollection of the cloth-capped worker played by Gabin in Carné's *Le Jour se lève* or the political involvement which led Renoir to make *La Vie est à nous* for the Communist Party. In fact these few instances which are universally known are virtually the only ones from a period which is typified far more by the fact that union activists of undoubtedly sincere left-wing opinions found themselves in situations which in retrospect seem intolerable: Jean Grémillon, assisted by Louis Daquin, working in fascist Germany, or Marcel L'Herbier making a succession of films in patriotic praise of France's naval might. Where it is not positively reactionary, the bulk of French 1930s production seeks entertainment without social implications, and film makers who sought to give active support to the Popular Front received little encouragement from the politicians, who were clearly unaware of, or indifferent to, the propaganda potential of the cinema. The left-wing coalition raised taxes on the cinema, yet offered no aid to quality production or support for moves aimed at a degree of nationalisation of the industry (the report produced eventually formed the basis of reform under the Vichy administration). Instead, the Popular Front gave assistance to the ruined GFFA, controlled by an opposition parliamentarian, Louis Aubert, confirmed the ban on Vigo's *Zéro de conduite*, and even introduced for the first time into French film production the idea of pre-censorship, in a circular distributed by Edmond Sée in 1937.

These contradictions are to be found in the shaping of the films of the period. If Renoir's *Le Crime de Monsieur Lange* can be seen as looking forward to a new alignment of workers of all kinds – writer and printer, laundress and frontier guard – Duvivier's *La Belle équipe*, made just a year later during the elections, already predicts the failure of working-class unity. The films such as *La Bandéra* or *Pépé-le-Moko* shot partially on location in North Africa show no insight into the realities of life for the Arab population, and in retrospect can be seen to be marked by a latent racism (as in the plot development or the casting of French actresses like Annabella or Line Noro in Arab roles). The respect for the colonist and the legionnaire is absolute and unquestioned, and *La Bandéra* was even dedicated originally to General Franco, who at the time of shooting was commander of the Spanish troops in North Africa. Similarly the Spanish Civil War is passed over in silence (as the Algerian War would be twenty years later), meriting no more than the depiction of the political refugee in *La Belle équipe* and a solitary passing reference in Carné's *Hôtel du nord*. The sole exception is, significantly, a film made by an outsider to the French film industry, the novelist André Malraux (1901–76). Between August 1938 and January 1939, working under extreme difficulties, Malraux shot footage in Spain for a Spanish-language feature film supporting the Republican cause. Originally entitled *Sierra de Teruel* at the time of its first, private, showing in 1939, the film was renamed *L'Espoir* by its distributor prior to its public release in 1945, although in fact it is in no way an adaptation of Malraux's novel of that name. With the material difficulties increased by Malraux's limited command of Spanish and inexperience as a film maker, only a fraction of the planned material could be shot in Spain. But although there were evident problems in matching this footage with the shots taken in the studios in France during April 1939, *L'Espoir* stands out as a committed and eloquent work. Despite its confusing narrative and – because of the date at which it was shot – the fact it could be no more than a tale of heroism in the face of defeat, it sets itself apart from the defeatist French mainstream features of the period. Nothing could be further from the isolated anguish of the characteristic Jean Gabin hero than the respect and solidarity shown by the peasants to the wounded pilots and the bodies of their dead colleagues at the end of *L'Espoir*.

*

In so far as late 1930s French cinema is an affair of individuals, there can be no more striking representatives than two highly successful dramatists whose best work in the cinema dates from this period, Sacha Guitry (1885–1957) and Marcel Pagnol. Guitry's first involvement with the cinema dates from 1915, when a film made up of footage he shot of celebrities from the world of the theatre and the arts, *Ceux de chez nous*, was shown. He also appeared in a single film in 1918, but otherwise he ignored the cinema, even after his play *Le Blanc et le noir* was filmed by Robert Florey in 1931. But by 1935 his interest was engaged by certain possibilities of the new medium, and by 1939 he had completed twelve features, all in the dual role of director and star. Guitry began with a safe subject, an adaptation of his 1919 stage success, *Pasteur* (1935), and six of his subsequent films also fit into the category of filmed theatre, some based on plays that were already ten, fifteen or twenty years old – *Mon père avait raison* (1936), *Faisons un rêve* (1936), *Désiré* (1937) – while others were versions of his 1930s stage successes: *Le Noveau testament* (1936), *Le Mot de Cambronne* (1937), *Quadrille* (1938). The bulk of these are light and witty conversation pieces about adultery or family relations (particularly the father-son relationship which obsessed him, as he continually measured himself against his famous actor father, Lucien Guitry). Although these are all shaped according to the rules of the boulevard theatre, there is nothing impersonal about them, since they are usually expressly written for Guitry himself, his wives, friends and colleagues and parade the particular emotional situation in which he finds himself (upset by the departure of one wife, or excited by marriage to a new one, perhaps twenty years younger than himself). *Pasteur*, however, had a more serious theme, being both a tribute to his father, who originally played the role on stage, and to the great scientist. This interest in the great figures of history is also to be found in two 1930s examples of the star-studded historical conversation pieces for which he was to become famous, *Les Perles de la couronne* (1937) and *Remontons les Champs-Elysées* (1938). Both of these were from original scripts, but Guitry had an enormous facility and flexibility, equally at home with the original scenario, *Bonne chance* (1935), the adaptation of one of his own novels, *Roman d'un tricheur* (1936), or with a film script which could subsequently be turned into a play, *Ils étaient neuf célibataires* (1939).

Guitry was a prolific and unselfconscious dramatist – the kind of playwright who concocts a finished text in a single day: act one before lunch, act two after a nap in the afternoon, and the final act after dinner with a few friends. With the total support from 1936 of his producer, Serge Sandberg, he brought this same nonchalant spontaneity to the cinema, caring little for the technical rules of production and eager always to capture directly the best performance from his actors. On occasion, it seems, he refused to shoot more than one take, convinced that this would contain the freshest rendering of the text. He is therefore at once the extreme example of the 1930s tendency to give predominance to the star and the dialogue, and an exception, in his sovereign disregard for the technical aspects of film making. Guitry's contribution is varied and uneven. Some of his films come strictly into the category of 'canned theatre' – with all its pejorative implications – and others, like *Ils étaient neuf célibataires*, are merely variations on fashionable formulas (in this case the sketch film pioneered by Duvivier with *Un Carnet de bal*). Guitry's historical films are individual if insubstantial, and constitute striking examples of an acting style that owes nothing to the vogue for naturalism, but one film at least stands out as a masterpiece. *Roman d'un tricheur* is totally original within its period and anticipates the kind of interplay between text and image with which Robert Bresson and Jean-Pierre Melville were to experiment in the 1940s and Alain Resnais in the 1950s. It tells the cautionary tale of a young lad who survives the poisoned mushrooms which wipe out his whole family of nine, because he has been sent to bed without any supper for a minor misdemeanour. Learning his lesson, he bases his life on cheating and succeeds in every way, and at no one's expense, until a conversion to honesty ruins him irrevocably. The film's originality lies in Guitry's mode of narration, which develops out of his habit of introducing characters and situations at the beginning of many of his films. Here Guitry tells the whole story while seated in a café, ostensibly writing his memoirs. While the voice narrates, the images unfold in illustration, without dialogue, but often in counterpoint to the words. In none of his subsequent work was Guitry to find quite so perfect a tone or so assured a balance of the elements of his style.

By 1933, at the age of thirty-eight, Marcel Pagnol had achieved sufficient success as a dramatist and as co-producer of *Fanny* to assure his total independence. Withdrawing from the artificial world of the Billancourt studios, he moved back to Marseilles, commissioned a soundtrack from Philips and set about building his own production facilities. Eventually he was to own a three-stage studio in Marseilles, extensive property for location shooting, his own laboratory, production and distribution companies, and a number of theatres including a first-run house in Marseilles. He even had representatives in various French-speaking countries. He was responsible for the production of a number of films in which he was not personally involved – the most notable being Renoir's *Toni* – and scripted a number of films which he did not direct. Later he was to see this business activity as hindering his writing, but in the 1930s his creative energy was boundless. His method of working was unique. Working always from his own scripts and at times placing more emphasis on the dialogue than the visuals, Pagnol would make his films *en famille*. The members of the technical crew seldom varied: photography by Willy and sound by Jean Lecoq, editing by Suzanne de Troye and music by Vincent Scotto. They were on contract and worked, not following some union regulations, but according to the whim of the producer-director-writer. Days spent playing *boules* in the sunshine would be followed by bursts of intense activity. Scenes or even whole films with which Pagnol was dissatisfied would simply be re-shot. Actors, technicians and Pagnol himself would live together on location, dining together at a long table, and outsiders who joined the team would be given plenty of time to find their rhythm. Arthur Honegger, for example, who wrote the music for *Regain*, lived with the crew for two months, during production and even before, while the ruined village that formed the location was built, not as a set, but out of stone like a normal village, by local craftsmen.

The nine feature films directed by Pagnol which were released between 1934 and 1938 fall into two broad categories, those made from his own original scripts or plays and those adapted from the novels and stories of Jean Giono. Paradoxically, in that Pagnol was himself a born story-teller, it is the latter which comprise his finest work as a film maker. He always seems to have been uncertain when working with his own material, which is usually based on his own experiences and has a characteristically satiric flavour. For example, the first versions of both the seventy-minute films which he made from original scripts in 1935 and which were intended to form the complementary halves of a double bill, were scrapped and the films remade the same year. *Merlusse* (1935), the more successful of the two, was re-shot because Pagnol experienced trouble with the sound recording. Shot on location in a school in Marseilles during the holidays, it draws on Pagnol's own experiences as an English teacher in its portrait of a seemingly austere master who shows another side to his character when in charge of the handful of neglected children left in the school when the others go off on vacation. In the first version of the companion piece, *Cigalon* (1935), the title role was again taken, as in *Merlusse*, by Henri Poupon, but Pagnol was unhappy with the interpretation and replaced him with Arnaudy. This story of how the tables are turned on the cook in a village inn who feels himself too good for his clientele, is handled in a more openly farcical way, and though shot on location – in the very inn where the crew took their meals – it seemed contrived to contemporary critics. The double bill was apparently commercially unsuccessful, and Pagnol's next film from his own material had a similar fate. *Topaze* (1936) which starred Arnaudy, was the second version of Pagnol's most celebrated stage work, but it received very little distribution, proving far less successful than the earlier version starring Louis Jouvet which had been directed, without Pagnol's participation, by Louis Gasnier from an adaptation by Léopold Marchand. This version remained in circulation in the 1930s, and Pagnol, clearly dissatisfied, returned to the play to make a third version, this time with Fernandel, in 1951.

By contrast, *César* (1936) remains one of Pagnol's most successful and best-remembered works. This sequel to *Marius* and *Fanny* which forms the final panel of his Marseilles trilogy was written directly for the screen. A fitting farewell to Panisse (Charpin) and a few striking scenes by Raimu in the title role compensate for an occasionally contrived plot centred on the comparatively drab figure of Césariot, the son of Marius and Fanny, who here comes to learn the truth about his parentage. Two years later while simultaneously shooting *Regain*, Pagnol gave in *Le Schpountz* (1938) a further satirical account of his own earlier experiences, reflecting this time on his adventures in the early years of sound in a farcical tale of a simple-minded film fan, Irénée Fabre (played by Fernandel), who is conned into presenting himself at the film studios and who, against all probability, becomes a star. The film – Pagnol's own characteristic homage to the world of the spectacle – bears the marks of its making. Shot on days when rain prevented work on *Regain*, not only was the script improvised day by day, but many of the gags were made up on the set and the concept of the central character shifted as the filming progressed. Even the version first shown to the public was recut by Pagnol, in response to criticisms of anti-semitism in the portrait of the Jewish producer, Meyerboom. *Le Schpountz* has shared the characteristic fate of Pagnol's original screenplays and has been largely ignored by film historians after being coldly received by the critics.

In contrast with the unevenness of such work from his own original material, Pagnol's series of adaptations from stories and novels by Jean Giono have been universally praised. His first film after leaving Paris, *Jofroi* (1934), a fifty-two-minute film adapted from Giono's short tale *Jofroi de la Maussan*, marks a turning away from the precepts of 'canned theatre'. It features a largely amateur cast, with the composer Vincent Scotto in the title role and two non-professionals who subsequently took up acting, Blavette and Henri Poupon. It is also set away from the studio (which was still not completed), beginning in fact in the village where Pagnol was born. In filming his exteriors Pagnol forgets all the rules about studio sound still dominant in Paris and allows his camera to follow the actors. The story itself is slight: an old peasant who has sold his land tries to prevent the new owner from cutting down its unproductive olive trees, even threatening to kill himself if a single tree is touched. But this image of Provence, far removed from the urban world of the Marseilles trilogy, sets the tone of the more substantial works that follow in its preference for nature and human values as against the legal niceties of property ownership.

Angèle (1934) takes only the outline of Giono's novel *Un de Baumugnes*, emphasising such favourite Pagnol themes as the opposition of country virtue and city evil and the clash of generations between an unbending patriarch and his wayward offspring, and featuring, as in the trilogy, Orane Demazis as an unmarried mother redeemed finally by love. The whole film was shot away from the studio and, as in all the Giono adaptations, the landscape plays a key role. The playing here is assured, with a quite remarkable performance by Fernandel in his first dramatic role (after dozens of mindless farces) as Saturnin, who brings Angèle back from Marseilles, where she has

95

been forced into prostitution. As Claude Beylie points out, *Regain* (1937), from the novel of the same name, is in a sense the answering half of a diptych dealing with the redemption of people and the land. Here an almost abandoned mountain village and a desolate landscape are brought to life by an unlikely couple: the giant taciturn peasant Panturle (Gabriel Gabrio) and a girl from the plains, Arsule (again played by Orane Demazis), who has been ill-treated by her companion, the knife-grinder Gedemus (Fernandel), and casually raped by a passing band of migrant farm workers.

After this solemn hymn to the land, shot totally on the almost inaccessible slopes described by Giono, *La Femme du boulanger* (1938) is something of a light relief. The story, taken from an episode in the novel *Jean le bleu*, features Raimu as the village baker, deceived by his wife who runs off with a stranger. Since he now refuses to bake bread, the villagers have to band together to engineer the wayward wife's return and ensure a reconciliation. Ginette Leclerc makes a suitably sultry wife and Raimu, well served by Pagnol's excellent dialogue, gives one of his most memorable performances, though his refusal to perform dialogue scenes in the open air has caused the film to be an odd and rather unsatisfactory mixture of location and studio work. Pagnol had a further film, *La Fille du puisatier*, from an original script, interrupted temporarily by the outbreak of war, but although he continued directing until 1954, nothing he subsequently produced surpasses the artistic and popular success of his 1930s work.

*

The principles on which the artistic renaissance of French cinema in the late 1930s was to be built are to be found in three films by Jacques Feyder, released in 1934–35. Feyder's stay in Hollywood, which had concluded with two mediocre films with Roman Novarro, had not been fruitful. He had therefore to prove himself with *Le Grand jeu* (1934), his first French film for six years. This reunited him with his fellow Belgian, the scriptwriter, Charles Spaak, then at the beginning of a career which was to lead to collaboration with Feyder, Duvivier and Renoir on some of the greatest successes of the period. For this film Feyder also brought together the team of designer Lazare Meerson and cinematographer Harry Stradling, who were to work with him and Spaak on their finest film, *La Kermesse héroique*. In *Le Grand jeu* Feyder took a story which drew specifically on the potentials of the sound film. The hero is involved successively with two women who look identical and may even be the same (the second has lost her memory), but whose voices are quite different. Both roles were played by Marie Bell, but in one she was dubbed with the voice of another actress. For the hero, Feyder and Spaak chose a French legionnaire and as usual the director made full use of the possibilities of his locations, in this case North Africa. The importance of *Le Grand jeu* lies as much in its anticipations as in its achievements, for here we already find a concern with such themes as passion, fate and self-destruction which were to figure so largely in the late 1930s work of Feyder's assistant up till 1935, Marcel Carné. To follow this success Feyder made *Pension Mimosas* (1935) in which a starring role was given to his wife, Françoise Rosay, as the understanding and long-suffering woman who struggles vainly to help her errant stepson. Solidly if, like *Le Grand jeu*, theatrically constructed and painting a vivid portrait of its boarding-house setting, *Pension Mimosas* added further to Feyder's reputation.

His major work – and one of the masterpieces of the period – is *La Kermesse héroique* (1935), in which the tone is lighter and less melodramatic, while the costumes are never less than sumptuous. The film is set in the early seventeenth century in the little Flemish town of Boom. When the inhabitants learn that the Duke of Olivares is to pass through with his Spanish troops, the men are terrified, foreseeing rape, pillage and massacre. But the women, led by the mayor's wife (Françoise Rosay), organise a more fitting reception and during the single night of the Spaniards stay they enjoy company more handsome and gallant than that provided by their dull bourgeois husbands. Although in tone *La Kermesse héroique* is very different from the works of French poetic realism and its visual style breathes the spirit of the great seventeenth-century Dutch and Flemish painters from whom Meerson and Stradling drew their inspiration, it does give a clear indication of the stylistic basis of the best late 1930s French cinema.

Firstly, there is Feyder's total professionalism, the care with which every aspect of the film has been conceived and the precision with which it has been executed. This is typified by the visual style – the carefully controlled camera placing and movement, and the decision to recreate the whole setting within a studio – which is more character-istic of the period than of Feyder's work as a whole. Also crucial to the success of the film is the quality of the scripting, with the overall structure mapped out by Feyder and Spaak and the dialogue written by a specialist, Bernard Zimmer. The importance of writers, especially of dialogue, is very characteristic of this period, and Feyder's work is always the product of weeks spent with his writers at his country retreat in the forest of Rambouillet. The writing is so crucial because cinema at this time is not conceived as a director's visual medium, but as a star vehicle for performers (typified in *La Kermesse héroique* by Louis Jouvet as the wily and worldly priest). It is the players who are the key to success in French 1930s cinema at any level and stylistically everything is shaped so as to foreground the performances: particularly the studio lighting and the design of sets (here in *La Kermesse héroique* prominence is given to the actors by having the houses built slightly smaller than life). Similarly, in terms of narrative structure, the script offers set-piece confrontations and, above all, brilliantly witty or trenchant dialogue. Although the roles are often stereotyped – the fat, pompous mayor, the sexy inn-keeper's wife and so on – the tone is adult, particularly when compared with contemporary work from Hollywood. The interplay of the actors indicates too a further characteristic of this cinema: although the forces shaping the character's destiny may be outside his or her control, the story focuses on social behaviour, with the anarchistic or eccentric escapist mode of the early sound cinema forgotten.

Although Feyder thus set the tone for subsequent developments as early as 1934–5, his own later career is uneven and unsatisfactory, so that *La Kermesse héroique* marks the climax of his work. In 1937 he was tempted to London by Alexander Korda, but *Knight without Armour* was no more than a star vehicle for Marlene Dietrich. *Les Gens du voyage* (1938), made in the German studios in Munich, was a melodramatic tale of a travelling circus which was fairly successful but not as enthusiastically received as the more striking works of Carné and Renoir. *La Loi du nord*, an attempt at renewal starring the recently discovered Michèle Morgan in a script by Alexandre Arnoux, was begun in 1939 and took Feyder on location to the northernmost parts of Sweden. But although shooting was completed before the outbreak of war, the film could not be screened until 1942. By this time Feyder was living in exile in Switzerland, where he completed just one more film, *Une Femme disparaît* in 1942, before his death after a long illness in 1948.

The commercial success which eluded Feyder in the late 1930s was achieved, seemingly effortlessly, by Julien Duvivier, who continued to produce prolifically throughout the period, making eleven films in all from *Golgotha* (1935) to *Untel père et fils* (1939–40). Many of these films are of little lasting value. *Golgotha*, for example, was one of Duvivier's typical religious productions – efficient but totally lacking, it seems, in faith or feeling – while *Le Golem* (1936) and *La Charrette fantôme* (1939) were misguided remakes of foreign silent classics. *L'Homme du jour* (1936) with Maurice Chevalier showed the limits of Duvivier's gift for light comedy, while *Untel père et fils*, made under the shadow of war, was found stilted and contrived when finally shown in Paris in 1945. But even if these films, and Duvivier's Hollywood production, *The Great Waltz* (1938), are left aside, there still remain five films which would figure in any list of key works of the period – three with Jean Gabin (who had earlier appeared in *Maria Chapdelaine* and *Golgotha*) and two with dazzling all-star casts.

La Bandéra (1935), *La Belle équipe* (1936) and *Pépé-le-Moko* (1937) all star Jean Gabin in the role of the defeated hero which was to constitute his trademark at this period. In the first, which has echoes of Feyder's *Le Grand jeu*, he kills a man in Paris, then escapes to join the Spanish foreign legion. Although he loves and marries a Moroccan woman (played by Annabella), he eventually dies fighting heroically. *La Belle équipe* is a potentially affirmative story dealing with a group of unemployed workers who win a lottery and set up a restaurant as a collaborative effort, while *Pépé-le-Moko* returns to North Africa to tell of a gangster tempted out of his retreat in the Algiers casbah by love for a visiting Frenchwoman. Pépé-le-Moko meets his death, watching through the iron barriers as the woman he loves sails away, and in all three stories the mood is one of extreme pessimism, since Duvivier sees his characters as trapped irrevocably by their past or their poverty. Although he shot two contrasting endings for *La Belle équipe* and audiences preferred the happy ending, he himself later substituted the pessimistic end in accordance with his own temperament. In his world there is no hope for collective action, and even if the happy ending had been retained the collective enterprise would still have been shown to be undermined from within by personal failings and jealousies. Duvivier then is the chronicler of the (anticipated) failure of the Popular Front, not its committed celebrant. All that his heroes are allowed is a single glimpse of another world, provoking a longing for escape which can never be fulfilled.

Within this pattern of defeat, Duvivier's narrative sense is superb and many of his individual scenes – such as the death of the informer played by Charpin which triggers off the mechanical piano in *Pépé-le-Moko* – are among the best remembered in French cinema. It is this gift for the striking scene or confrontation which makes his study of a home for retired actors, *La Fin du jour* (1939), so memorable, and underlies the brilliantly successful commercial formula of a film comprising a sequence of separate sketches which he found with *Un Carnet de bal* (1937) and exploited to the full in the Hollywood films he made during the wartime period. Both *Un Carnet de bal*, the story of a newly widowed woman who seeks out the lovers she had danced with twenty years before at her first ball, and *La Fin du jour* are tales of defeat and despair. In each case Duvivier handles his material with a virtuosity which allows him to offer striking roles to his star performers but precludes any depth of feeling. The director collaborated with some of the leading script and dialogue writers of the period: Charles

Spaak on *La Bandéra, La Belle équipe* and *La Fin du jour*, Henri Jeanson on *Pépé-le-Moko*, Bernard Zimmer and a host of others on *Un Carnet de bal*. As a result, these films offer tailor-made roles not only for Gabin, but also for Françoise Rosay, Harry Baur, Raimu and Pierre Blanchar in the various episodes that make up *Un Carnet de bal* and for the remarkable trio of Louis Jouvet, Michel Simon and Victor Francen in *La Fin du jour*. However, the depth of feeling which would allow these films to rank with the masterpieces of Carné and Renoir is missing.

*

At a period when training in film making was acquired through assistantship rather than film schools, no one could be better prepared for a brilliant career than Marcel Carné (b. 1909), who had worked on Clair's *Sous les toits de Paris* and Feyder's three great films of 1934–35. In addition he had already made a short personal documentary, *Nogent, Eldorado du dimanche* (1929), and a number of publicity shorts, but it was only thanks to Feyder, who agreed to supervise the film, and Françoise Rosay, who agreed to star in it, that he was able to make his debut as a feature director at the age of twenty-seven with *Jenny* (1936). More important than the intrinsic qualities of this melodrama is the fact that it allowed Carné to work with the poet Jacques Prévert who was then at the beginning of what was to be a brilliant career as a scriptwriter. The pair together were to make some of the finest French films of the next decade. Carné's second feature, *Drôle de drame* (1937), is a curious work in view of his own preoccupations, but readily understandable in terms of Prévert's taste for comedy which included elaborate gags, surreal fantasy and anti-clerical satire. *Drôle de drame*, which echoes *L'Affaire est dans le sac* and anticipates *Adieu Léonard* in its systematic absurdity and grotesque anti-logic, contains a number of set-piece performances by great actors – Françoise Rosay, Michel Simon, Louis Jouvet (complete with kilt) and offers Jean-Louis Barrault one of his weirdest roles as William Kramps, who kills a butcher 'from time to time' because of his love of sheep. Although the subject is uncharacteristic, Carné has assembled the technical team which will contribute so much to his late 1930s work, adding the talents of designer Alexandre Trauner and composer Maurice Jaubert to those of Prévert.

With *Quai des brumes* (1938) the Carné style is virtually complete. The story brings together a seventeen-year-old orphan, Nelly (Michèle Morgan), and an army deserter, Jean (Jean Gabin), in a dark, misty port which is only nominally Le Havre. They fall in love and, in a hotel room, enjoy the brief moment of happiness which is all Carné allows his characters. Then their idyll is destroyed by the intrusion of the sordid characters around them, as Jean is driven to kill Nelly's hypocritical guardian, Zabel (Michel Simon), and is in turn gunned down by a jealous gangster, Lucien (Pierre Brasseur). These latter characters are the most striking figures in the film – Simon combining a readiness to murder with a taste for religious music and Brasseur alternately strutting and cringing as the half-demented gunman – but Gabin opposes them with a rocklike authority. Although the central couple struggle for their happiness, much of the film is imbued with a sense of defeat, and Carné has recorded that UFA abandoned the production because they found the script too decadent and negative. UFA sold the rights to an émigré Jewish German producer (apparently hoping he would lose money) and he was himself upset when, on the eve of shooting, he finally got round to reading the text. But Carné's pessimism is not as cynical as that of Duvivier, and the themes of an impossible love and the longing for escape are developed in Prévert's script so as to create genuine emotion.

Subsequently the various advocates of either Prévert or Carné have sought to make exclusive claims as to which brought the poetry to the nebulous and ill-defined 'poetic realism' which films like this are said to exemplify. In retrospect, however, the arguments seem over-personalised, since the productions of the writer and director when working alone and after they separated have a remarkable unity in such key areas as the social definition of characters, the role accorded to passion, or the impact of fate on otherwise ordinary, banal lives. The actual split seems related less to conception or artistic approach than to the mode of production. Carné was from the very first in the forefront of a certain tradition of quality film making, the heir of Clair and Feyder, and hence concerned with an industry, a technique, a career. Prévert, by contrast, although a perfect example of the 1930s scriptwriter, able to create striking star roles and write dazzling, memorable dialogue, is not limited to this role and has a whole other identity as surrealist, humorist, poet. In the 1930s the pair seem remarkably well-matched. As *Quai des brumes* shows, Carné's conception of realism is essentially a fantastic one, a studio construct in which fidelity to life is balanced by attention to a certain poetic atmosphere. If Carné's command of technique gives the films their cold formal beauty, this is matched by Prévert's sense of the logic of a tight narrative development. If Prévert's imagination allows him to conceive both the *amour fou* that unites Nelly and Jean, and such picturesque villains as Zabel and Lucien, it is Carné's masterly direction of actors which turns Gabin and Michèle Morgan into the 1930s 'ideal couple' and draws such powerful performances from Michel Simon and Pierre Brasseur.

Hôtel du nord (1938), in which Carné was working from a script by Jean Aurenche adapted and with dialogue by Henri Jeanson, is a less coherent work which allows the contrivance of this French 1930s style to show through as clearly as in any work by Duvivier. Trauner's set, for example, is almost too perfect in its atmospheric studio realism. The characteristic themes of impossible passion, escape and purity are set against sordid existence, crushing poverty and cruelty, but although Jeanson's dialogue is marvellously witty, it lacks Prévert's deeper resonance. The lovers (played by Annabella and Jean-Pierre Aumont) are drab and uninteresting, but the couple part played by Arletty and Louis Jouvet offers sparkling opportunities for star performance. Yet even here Jouvet's multiple identity as Robert/Paolo/Edmond is never remotely convincing and his self-willed death quite unmoving. One is left with a symmetry which, in its very neatness, smacks more of commercial confection than of art or poetry.

No such reservations need to be made about *Le Jour se lève* (1939) which retains its status as a classic of the period. Again the film is built around the performance of Jean Gabin, here bringing his troubled integrity to the role of François, whose life is shattered at the very moment when happiness seemed within his grasp. The pattern which sets François and Françoise (Jacqueline Laurent) against the older, more corrupt couple of Valentin and Clara is more subtly wrought than that of the two contrasting pairs in *Hôtel du nord*. Arletty's earthiness as Clara makes her an admirable foil for Gabin's dogged seriousness, while Jules Berry's performance as Monsieur Valentin, the ageing music-hall star who trains his performing dogs by torturing them, is quite remarkable. This is perhaps the most frightening and pathetic of Prévert's villains, a man who is totally a construct of his words, equally convincing in his portrayal of himself as Françoise's long-lost father or her vile seducer. Berry conveys perfectly the fascination Valentin exercises, making his hold over Françoise and his ability to drive François to murder totally plausible. With his belief in Françoise shattered, François is totally isolated and his rejection of the solidarity of those gathered in the square beneath his window forms a chilling epilogue to a brief period which had opened with the enthusiasms aroused by the Popular Front. *Le Jour se lève*'s rich clash of aspiration and actuality, purity and betrayal, is contained within a structure which admirably reflects Carné's interest in the compression of action and his predilection for the half-light of dawn. The adaptation fashioned by Prévert of an original script by Jacques Viot comprises a masterly flashback pattern, in which a single night leads François to recall the events which have crippled his life and drive him inexorably to suicide. The final image of the tear-gas rising in the room where François already lies dead is one of the most memorable in French cinema.

*

If the late 1930s work of Marcel Carné leads one to seek some unitary definition of a 'poetic realism' of which his work would be the essence, the activities of Jean Renoir over the same period demonstrate the futility of such an undertaking. The terms 'poetry' and 'realism' can be variously applied to all the nine works which stretch in an unbroken line from *Toni* (1935) to *La Règle du jeu* (1939), but there is no single common stylistic paradigm towards which Renoir's work aspires. The only way in which it can be adequately encompassed it to see it as existing in an area of tension between contradictory impulses, and to read each film within its strictly contemporary setting, for Renoir proved himself incredibly sensitive to the shifts within French society and politics in this period leading up to the outbreak of war. Renoir himself has been willing to accept the label of 'poetic realist', attributing the success of French 1930s cinema to 'a certain style. It was called French realism. It was however really a matter of showing – through this realism – a certain kind of poetry'. But for Renoir's own work the terms 'naturalism' and 'theatre' are more useful in defining the range of influence and source of creative tensions.

Within such a scheme, *Toni* (1935), though produced by Marcel Pagnol's company in Marseilles, is furthest from the theatrical pole. Quite unlike Pagnol's own work with Raimu or Fernandel, *Toni* was based on an actual incident, a banal crime that occurred some ten years earlier, and was made on location, without stars or even well-known performers. Perhaps because of its close links to real happenings, the film's plot line is dramatically weak and the characters undergo unmotivated transformations. But to compensate for this there is the great authenticity of the settings, costumes and faces. Far from anticipating the studio realism of French 1930s cinema, *Toni* is often cited as a forerunner of Italian neo-realism. It has close similarities with Luchino Visconti's first film, *Ossessione* (1942): a crime of passion which fails to free the lovers, a strong sense of locality and a considerable degree of implicit social comment. But it differs from post-war neo-realism proper in its lack of both actuality and a true social perspective. In any case it was totally unknown to the Italian directors of the post-war period. Renoir comes much closer to the French tradition with *Le Crime de M Lange* (1936), a project initiated, under the title 'Sur la cour', by Jean Castanier with which Renoir's assistant Jacques Becker hoped to make his debut. Taken over, to Becker's annoyance, by Renoir, the project was developed in ways that made it even more of a collective work. The adaptation and dialogue were written by Jacques Prévert, like Castanier a member of the politically committed theatrical company, the Groupe Octobre, which had toured Russia the previous year. Many of the cast and technical crew (including the writer's brother, Pierre Prévert, who replaced Becker as assistant director) were also members of the group. *Le Crime de M Lange* tells of life in a Parisian courtyard, where the centre of attention is the printing firm run by the dissolute Batala (Jules Berry) who is forced to flee from his creditors. In his absence the printers run the firm as a collective enterprise, achieving enormous success by publishing Lange's *Arizona Jim* stories. When Batala unexpectedly returns, Lange instinctively kills him to protect the collective. This whole story is framed by scenes involving a group of ordinary people at the frontier, who are told Lange's tale and, at the end, allow him to escape across the border. In the complex studio set which forms the location for much of the action, in Prévert's dialogue, in the conception of the villain's role and Berry's masterly performance, Renoir is close to the emerging style of French 1930s dominant cinema. At the same time, however, although depicting suffering, seduction and murder, Renoir is totally free of the pessimism which marks the works of Carné and Duvivier. *Le Crime de M Lange*, made during the months leading up to the formation of the Popular Front government, captures perfectly the confused but sincere aspirations of the left in 1936 and Renoir, without conscious striving or self-analysis, found himself in the forefront of committed film making.

The complexities of Renoir's artistic personality are very apparent in the three films he shot during 1936. *La Vie est à nous* (1936) was an hour-long documentary made with funding from, and in support of, the French Communist Party. Shown in the 1930s only at party gatherings, it received its first public release in 1969, in the aftermath of the events of May '68. Although Renoir was not a party member, his connections with the communists remained close in the late 1930s and he wrote extensively for the communist press. Beginning in a classroom where a teacher sets out to explain the wealth of France to working-class children who have known only poverty, *La Vie est à nous* is an openly didactic work, which mixes well-edited newsreel material, speeches from party leaders and enacted scenes in which many well-known actors of the period appear in tiny roles. In his work of co-ordination, Renoir had the assistance of a team of assistants who included Jasques Becker, Jacques Brunius and Henri Cartier-Bresson. If *La Vie est à nous* was, inevitably, a collective work, *Partie de campagne* (1936–46), adapted from a story by Guy de Maupassant, was one of Renoir's most personal productions. Here in a period piece, set in 1860, the director captured perfectly the atmosphere of his father's paintings. But within the beautiful landscapes, which despite the appalling weather during the shooting convey admirably the feel of a summer picnic, the action is far from idyllic. The bourgeois family on holiday meets up with two young oarsmen and a double seduction ensues. If the flirtations of the mother are grotesquely comic, the daughter's passion, though brief, marks her for life. *Partie de campagne* was abandoned by Renoir, tempted by a new and more commercial proposition, but it was never intended to be more than a fictional short. At its present length of forty minutes, and with a couple of titles to replace the missing interior scenes, it was first shown publicly in 1946 and remains a perfect example of Renoir's art. By contrast, *Les Bas-fonds* (1936), an adaptation of Gorki's play, is an uneven work that hovers uneasily between a French and a Russian setting. With a script by Charles Spaak and a strong cast led by Jean Gabin and Louis Jouvet, *Les Bas-fonds* shows Renoir working once more within the confines of the commercial industry, reflecting the current vogue for studio filming and Russian subjects. The adaptation is by no means a faithful one, and the resulting film has a characteristic Renoir ambiguity, veering between the tragic and the idyllic, the studio-built courtyard and the open air, refusing the fashionable 1930s pessimism but failing too to sustain the optimism that had marked *Le Crime de M Lange*.

La Grande illusion (1937), one of Renoir's most polished, disciplined and successful films, offers little evidence in its final version of the total reworking of the script which was needed when the producer signed Erich von Stroheim, newly arrived in France, to play the prison commandant. Essentially the film, which was again written by Charles Spaak, is the story of three very diverse French officers – an aristocratic career officer, Boeldieu (Pierre Fresnay), a Jew, Rosenthal (Marcel Dalio), and a lower-middle-class conscript, Maréchal (Jean Gabin) – who are thrown together in a German prison camp during World War I. Although Boeldieu's closest affinities are with the German commandant, he gives his life to allow the other two to escape. Throughout the film, class differentiation is shown to be more important than differences of nationality, and national boundaries are viewed as artificial barriers separating people arbitrarily. Just as Boeldieu and Rauffenstein enjoy a mutual respect and sympathy, so too Maréchal, during his escape, enjoys a brief idyll with a German widow. In terms of the film, the great illusion is war and *La Grande illusion* preaches solidarity and internationalism. As always, Renoir extracts remarkable performances from his actors, who have clearly been deeply involved in their roles. There are no heroes and no villains here and though class differences are stressed, they are not felt to be unjust or intolerable. In this way the film, which echoes Renoir's own experiences as a cavalry officer and aviator during World War I, is on one level a nostalgic look back at a now vanished world. Lacking bloodshed (except for the moving and meaningful death of Boeldieu) and without any hint of atrocities, it presents almost too benign a view of war in view of the holocaust which was about to engulf Europe. *La Grande illusion*, perhaps for these very reasons, has proved popular with audiences and its critical reputation has remained high, although it gives only a partial view of Renoir's complex talents.

Continuing this incredible burst of creativity, Renoir had two films released in 1938. *La Marseillaise* accentuates the benevolent contradictions of *La Grande illusion* in its portrait of the 1789 Revolution as an almost bloodless celebration, conducted by ordinary people of the kind one finds in any Renoir film. The contradictions derive in a large part from those of the period in which the film was conceived and shot. Planned as a national epic during the euphoria of the Popular Front, when it was to be financed by public subscription (two francs a head, to be deducted from the price of admission), it was in fact shot as a normal production after the collapse of the Blum government. Its celebration rings therefore somewhat hollow, and characteristically Renoir's sympathy during the shooting moved away from the mass of the people to the court, so that the strongest and most engaging scenes, for him as for the audience, are those involving Louis XVI (played by his brother, Pierre Renoir) and Marie Antoinette (Lise Delamare). There is a sense in *La Marseillaise* that the Revolution is a superior form of theatre, a pageant acted out by a mass of players, all of whom – whatever their loyalties – have their own valid reasons. In sharp contrast, Renoir's second film of the year, *La Bête humaine* (1938) is also his blackest. A commissioned work from a script which Renoir himself drafted in just a fortnight, it transfers the action of Zola's novel to the present day. It also offers Jean Gabin a characteristic role as a likeable, ordinary man who is drawn by chance (when he witnesses a killing) to a career of passion, murder and suicide. The railway setting is beautifully conveyed in a brilliantly edited opening sequence shot on the train, which introduces us to the engine driver Lantier (played by Jean Gabin) and his mate Pecqueux (a brilliant performance by Carette). Quickly the film introduces us to the other key characters, Roubaud (Fernand Ledoux) and his young wife Séverine (Simone Simon) and sets in motion the remorseless logic of the plot. Rouband kills Séverine's lecherous guardian in order to keep his wife, but in doing so inadvertently brings her together with Lantier, whose own homicidal tendencies we have already witnessed in a remarkable love scene where he almost strangles his girl friend. Drawn now to Séverine and fascinated by Roubaud's killing, Lantier is trapped. Although he resists Séverine's urging to kill her husband, his dream of love collapses on the night of the railwaymen's ball. He kills Séverine and next morning, after confessing to Pecqueux, jumps to his death from the train. In *La Bête humaine*, with its stress on hereditary weakness and uncontrollable passions, Renoir comes closest to the pessimism of Carné and Duvivier and this film would have to be included in any list of the principal works of 'poetic realism'.

No such definition can, however, contain *La Règle du jeu* (1939), a film which forms the culmination of a remarkable decade of French film making. If *Toni* reveals most clearly the naturalistic tendency of Renoir's art, *La Règle du jeu* shows his theatrical impulse. Here, at the age of forty-five, after having made fourteen films in the preceding eight years and now working without constraints for his own production company, Renoir was free to express himself fully. Significantly he chose the form of a 'dramatic fantasy' in which the theatrical roots of his style – the debt to Musset, Marivaux and Beaumarchais – are very apparent: in the function of the dialogue, the division of characters into masters and servants, the 'play within a play' structure, the use of both improvisation and very formal placing of characters, and even in the articulation of an action played out in depth and time, allowing genuine performances from the actors. But while *La Règle du jeu* presents itself as a contrivance, a game with emotions, a toying with reality and illusion, it is also a self-portrait of rare depth, not least thanks to Renoir's own appearance in the key role of Octave, the go-between who straddles the worlds of masters and servants and inadvertently triggers off the final tragedy. At the same time the film – like *Le Crime de M Lange* or *La Marseillaise* – is a precise reflection of the time when it was shot, in this case the brief moment between the Munich agreements and outbreak of war. As the director has himself aptly observed, he was absolutely influenced and troubled by the state of mind of French society, but felt that 'one way of interpreting this state of mind to the world at that moment was precisely not to talk of the situation, but instead to tell a frivolous story'.

Although the acting and precise settings of *La Règle du jeu* were largely improvised as the filming was underway and Renoir extended certain roles as he grew more involved with his players, the basic structure remained unchanged. Essentially the film weaves together the lives of eight characters who meet in Paris and move off to the country to enjoy a weekend of hunting and festivity. These eight are arranged in two unevenly balanced groups, with Renoir as Octave constituting the key mediating figure. Around the marquis de la Chesnaye (Marcel Dalio) are grouped his Parisian mistress of whom he has grown tired (Mila Parély), the wife Christine whom he really loves (Nora Gregor) and an aviator with whom the wife is linked in intimate friendship, André Jurieux (Roland Toutain). In the servants' quarters there is a parallel complication as the marquis's gamekeeper (Gaston Modot) tries to keep the poacher-turned-valet Marceau (Julien Carette) away from his wife Lisette (Paulette Dubost), who is Christine's maid. The climax comes when the gamekeeper shoots Jurieux in error, mistaking him for Octave whom he wrongly thinks has seduced his wife. This complicated plot is handled with immense brio and assurance by Renoir, who here indulges to the full his taste for combining opposites. The action moves from bedroom farce to a tragic conclusion, from the ruthlessness of the hunt sequence to the initially good-natured fun of the party entertainments, the beauty of the exteriors and the artificiality of the studio interiors, the quick cutting of the shooting during the hunt and the long takes in depth of the dialogue sequences, and so on. In acting style, the intense professionalism of such performers as Carette or Dalio is set against the clumsy amateurism of Nora Gregor (an Austrian princess in real life) and Renoir himself as the bear-like Octave. Significantly it is this latter pair who cause the complications of the weekend by their inability to take their emotional needs lightly, to live according to the rules of the game, which are here shown to be those of social performance. The key moments of *La Règle du jeu* – and there are many – come when two incongruously linked characters are brought together: La Chesnaye's wife and mistress discussing his faults, Marceau and the gamekeeper musing on life when both think that Lisette has deserted them for Octave, the marquis and his valet discussing women, Octave revealing his true feelings to Christine after years of posing as just her friend. The complexity of the film is enormous and it repays multiple viewings. When first shown, *La Règle du jeu* was a total commercial failure – perhaps the worst in Renoir's career – but since then it has earned universal acclaim and now stands unchallenged as the summation of a decade of French film making which is far richer than any simple notion of poetic realism could define.

7 Four years in a Bottle
1940–44

Le cinéma dit 'de Vichy' au sens idéologique et politique, n'existe pas. Sous le régime de Vichy et sous l'occupation allemande, le cinéma français, en 'liberté surveillée', a été un cinéma de survie industrielle et économique, d'essor artistique toutes les fois que cela lui fut possible, et ce le fut assez souvent grâce à des producteurs, des scénaristes, des réalisateurs, des techniciens qui ne renoncèrent pas à la qualité française.

Jacques Siclier, 1981

The Vichy period may be considered to begin with Marshal Pétain's broadcast speech to the French people on 17 June 1940 and end with the entry of the allied forces into Paris on 24 August 1944. Perhaps the most contradictory and controversial period of French cinema, it has only recently begun to receive the attention it deserves and a really satisfactory account of it still remains to be written. The contradictions begin with the organisation of the film industry. Whereas the German occupying forces might have been expected to seek to eliminate the French film industry and impose their own productions, it was in fact the Paris-based but German-controlled and -financed production and distribution company, Continental Films, which contributed most to the rebirth of the French film industry, producing thirty of the two hundred and twenty features begun in the period 1940–44, as against twenty-two produced by the two major French companies, Pathé Cinéma (fourteen films) and the Société Nouvelle des Etablissements Gaumont (just eight). Moreover, these thirty features were expressly designed as popular commercial films, employing leading directors and stars and, as far as inherent values are concerned, it is impossible to distinguish between films produced by Continental and those of the other French companies of the period.

Although the censorship apparatus was ultimately under German control, the Vichy years also saw a new level of French government involvement in the film industry in response to German initiatives to establish foreign control. Some of the new regulations – such as those requiring professional accreditation for all engaged in the film industry – were clearly not simply designed to assist production, since they formed part of the legislation undertaken by the Vichy government to eliminate Jews from all walks of life. But the setting up of the Comité d'Organisation de l'Industrie Cinématographique in November 1940 – initially under Guy de Carmoy and using a structure he had designed for the Popular Front government of the mid-1930s – allowed the re-establishment of a commercially healthy French film industry. The free circulation of French-made films between the free and occupied zones of France – combined with the closed market resulting from the elimination of all American competition – offered producers the opportunity to recoup their costs and make a reasonable profit from the French market alone. These years of rationing and austerity were the period at which attendance at cinemas, theatres and other permitted forms of entertainment reached its height, and for the first time since before World War I, it is possible to talk of French films dominating their home market.

Many other measures too which were to shape French film making during the post-war period also have their origins at this time. It was the Vichy government which established censorship to protect viewers under the age of sixteen, eliminated the double bill system of exhibition and fostered short and documentary film production, established a Grand Prix du Film d'Art Français, founded the national film school, the Institut des Hautes Etudes Cinématographiques (IDHEC) under Marcel L'Herbier, and granted aid to Henri Langlois's Cinémathèque Française. The propaganda efforts of both the Vichy government and the German authorities were concentrated on the newsreels, which became a compulsory part of all film showings, but were so unpopular that to deter protesters, the lights in the auditorium had to be partially left on. While it is certainly a myth that French audiences boycotted German productions, there was very little French production of an openly propagandistic nature. French film historians have uncovered only two overtly racist fictional films, both of less than feature length, Les Corrupteurs (1942) and Forces occultes (1943), neither of which seems to have had much impact. But this lack of an openly collaborationist cinema should not be taken simply as proof of some underlying spirit of resistance among French film makers: it is at least partly the result of the policy decisions of the German occupying powers who opted for a commercial rather than propagandistic function for French film production.

*

For French audiences of the wartime years the sense of continuity with the 1930s was very strong. True, some of the major figures of the French cinema – directors such as René Clair and Jean Renoir, Julien Duvivier and Jacques Feyder, and stars such as Jean Gabin, Michèle Morgan and Louis Jouvet – chose to go into exile. Also the bulk of the poetic realist films of the 1930s – not only the work of the exiles, Renoir and Gabin, but also Marcel Carné's *Hôtel du nord*, *Quai des brumes* and *Le Jour se lève* – were withdrawn from distribution. But the basic function of popular cinema as a weekly or twice-weekly entertainment medium was unchanged, and many key figures remained. Many of the most popular French films of the 1930s did remain in circulation, and the most prolific directors of the Vichy years are precisely the specialists in melodrama and light comedy who had been most active in the previous decade. Thus Christian-Jaque's six wartime films include the highly successful thriller, *L'Assassinat du Père Noël* (1941), and Henri Decoin, who also made six films in the period, continued in his expert 1930s manner with the delicate comedy of *Premier rendez-vous* (1941), again with his wife, Danielle Darrieux. In retrospect, we can see these early 1940s as a period of renewal, with half-a-dozen important directors either making their first features or gaining control over the choice of subjects for the first time. In fact only nineteen new directors made their appearance in these years (as against sixty-two 1930s figures who remained active) and even this figure includes actors, such as Fernandel and Pierre Blanchar, here making their first directorial efforts.

Among the veterans of the period, Abel Gance made two films, *Vénus aveugle* (1941) – notable for its heady melodrama and dedication to Marshal Pétain – and *Le Capitaine Fracasse* (1943). Sacha Guitry completed three films, including two in his favourite style of historical pageant, while Marcel L'Herbier made no less than six features, including the remarkable *La Nuit fantastique* (1942). This inaugurated a tendency towards the unreal and the illusionary to be found in some of the most striking films of the period. In creating the dream world of *La Nuit fantastique*, which had nothing threatening or troubling, L'Herbier was offering his audience escapism in the purest sense, and the impression of separation from the problems of the moment is enhanced by the style of visual effects used by L'Herbier, which are characteristic of the avant-garde world of the 1920s of which he had been a part.

Another and perhaps more significant example of continuity is furnished by Marcel Pagnol's sole completed film of the period, *La Fille du puisatier* (1940), which was the first film with which French production resumed in 1940 after the hiatus caused by defeat and armistice. The plot uses all the standard melodramatic elements of Pagnol's 1930s films, and as so often in Pagnol's work, the richest opportunities are those offered, not to the lovers, but to such actors as Raimu, here playing the girl's father, and Fernandel, who appears as her loyal if simple-minded friend. This is in essence a timeless world, but Pagnol has situated the film's action so that it coincides precisely with that of the shooting of the film (between February and August 1940) and introduces into it one of the rare notes of actuality to be found in French film making under Vichy, by including a scene in which the characters gather to listen to Marshal Pétain's broadcast to the nation. This scene is very sensitively handled and gives considerable interest to a work which is otherwise a minor effort.

Among the varied paradoxes of French cinema during this period is the fact that though there was undoubtedly a renewal of personnel, and the Vichy years saw the appearance of some of the most forceful and individualistic figures in the history of French cinema, there was no real break between the film makers of the 1930s and their 1940s successors. Certainly such distinctions as can be discerned between generations are less than the rupture one can perceive in the career of a single director – Marcel Carné is the obvious example – and far less than one would have expected from the changed political and economic circumstances.

*

If we consider firstly the tendency towards fantasy – anticipated by L'Herbier in *La Nuit fantastique* – and towards literary or theatrical spectacle, the directors who come immediately to mind are Marcel Carné, one of the great figures of the 1930s, Jean Delannoy, who had made several fairly mediocre films before the fall of France, and Robert Bresson, whose first features date from 1943–44. In all three cases there is a profound ambivalence towards the contemporary scene, which is either depicted in purely allegorical terms or, if the notional 1940s setting is preserved, given symbolic or literary overtones. In purely numerical terms this trend could be described as fairly insignificant, but the handful of films include some of the most prestigious of the period, particularly those of Marcel Carné.

Since the last three 'poetic realist' films which he had made in the 1930s were now all banned by the authorities, it is hardly surprising that Carné, while continuing to work with his habitual scriptwriter, Jacques Prévert, should have found the need to adopt a radically new style. *Les Visiteurs du soir* (1942), co-scripted by Prévert and Pierre Laroche, could hardly be further removed from the dark, contemporary urban world of *Le Jour se lève*. It is a mediaeval fable, bathed in light and set largely in a brilliant white castle. The film tells of an aristocratic world disrupted by the arrival of two strangers, Dominque (Arletty) and Gilles (Alain Cuny), whose apparent amiability masks their identity as emissaries of the devil. But their mission is thwarted when Gilles falls in love with his victim and the devil himself (Jules Berry) has to intervene, giving a welcome lift to a film which adopts perhaps too measured a rhythm in its opening reels. The devil too is eventually foiled: though he turns the lovers to stone, their hearts continue to beat in unison. Although made with limited means, *Les Visiteurs du soir* was conceived as a prestige production to assert the values of French cinema in the face of adversity and austerity, and as such it enjoyed great success. Carné's team – with Alexandre Trauner and Joseph Kosma working clandestinely – matches that of the pre-war years, and though Marie Déa and Alain Cuny as the lovers are somewhat wooden, the cast is a strong one, with Arletty and Jules Berry exuding vitality and commitment. Despite the subject matter, only limited use is made of the camera's potential for trickery in this slow-paced, solemn film which, although occasionally stilted, is unmistakably the work of a major director.

The theatricality of *Les Visiteurs du soir* is enhanced in Marcel Carné's subsequent work, his masterpiece *Les Enfants du paradis* (1943–45). The film has its origins in a story about the nineteenth-century mime Debureau, who struck with his cane at an adolescent who insulted his wife in the street, thereby inadvertently killing him. But oddly enough, although Prévert included the incident – and the subsequent trial and acquittal of Dureau, who had to *speak* to defend himself – in his final script, Carné refused to shoot it, preferring the open ending which the present film has. Running for three and a quarter hours and comprising two parts – 'Le Boulevard du crime' and 'L'Homme blanc' – each of which is of full feature length, *Les Enfants du paradis* is one of the most ambitious films ever undertaken in France. Particularly remarkable is the fact that it was shot – with various delays and interruptions and again with two key collaborators (Trauner and Kosma) working clandestinely – during a period of national turmoil. Originally a Franco-Italian co-production, the film was almost abandoned when the allied invasion of Sicily led the Italian Scalera company to withdraw from the project. Only the intervention of Pathé enabled the film to be completed, and even then some scenes had to be re-shot when Robert Le Vigan, sentenced to death for collaboration by the Resistance, fled from France with his role as a symbolic figure of fate only partially shot.

In addition to Debureau (Jean-Louis Barrault), *Les Enfants du paradis* also includes depictions of other historical characters – the actor Frédéric Lemaître (Pierre Brasseur) and the writer-cum-assassin Lacenaire (Marcel Herrand) weaving them into a totally fictional plot, involving also such invented characters as the beautiful Garance (Arletty) and the comte de Montray (Louis Salou). The latter tries to possess Garance through his wealth alone, but she is loved, in varying ways, by all four men, although she loves only Debureau in return. The title, with its play on the two meanings of 'paradis' – as paradise and also, in theatrical terms, the 'gods' – hints at the nature of the film as a reflection on the spectacle. Here, in their recreation of the Paris of the 1930s (shot largely in the studios at Nice), Prévert and Carné create a world where the action on stage and that in the boulevard du Temple – known too as the boulevard du Crime – merge and fuse, particularly through the riveting character of Lacenaire, the would-be writer whose masterpiece is the (real) assassination of the count. *Les Enfants du paradis* is one of Prévert's richest scripts, studded with memorable aphorisms on art and love, and Carné shows enormous control in his handling both of the crowd scenes and those involving his *monstres sacrés*. The sustained vitality and dynamism of the work as it moves seemingly effortlessly from farce to tragedy, from delicate love scenes to outrageous buffoonery, is exemplary, and it remains the finest filmic achievement of Carné and Prévert, its impact scarcely dimmed by the years.

Jean Delannoy (b.1908) had turned to directing in the mid-1930s after working for five years as film editor and assistant director. His first features went largely unnoticed, although two of them, *La Vénus d'or* (1938) and *Macao, l'enfer du jeu*, starred Mireille Balin, one of the more interesting actresses of the period. *Macao*, an efficiently made exotic melodrama, is recalled today largely for the playing of Erich von Stroheim. The bulk of Delannoy's work during the Occupation years is fairly routine, but he did achieve notoriety with two films, which together point to the difficulty of assessing Vichy cinema. *Pontcarral, colonel d'Empire* (1942), praised by Sadoul and singled out by Courtade as the sole authentic resistance film among the two hundred and twenty features shot in this period, owes its reputation more to Bernard Zimmer's dialogue than to Delannoy's solidly professional direction. Ostensibly just another period drama – it is set under the Restoration of Louis XVIII – the film was able to draw enough parallels with the Vichy situation for its dialogue references to the need for a good man to resist unjust authority to make an oblique point and acquire for the film its later reputation. But if *Pontcarral* can be seen as a work of contemporary significance masquerading as an historical drama, the celebrated *L'Eternel retour* (1943) is a modern-dress version of the myth of Tristan and Isolde. The script is by Jean

Cocteau who in the early 1940s resumed his film activity after a break of some ten years following *Le Sang d'un poète*, and was also responsible for the dialogue for Bresson's *Les Dames du Bois de Boulogne*.

In *L'Eternal retour* – a title borrowed from Nietzsche – Cocteau has transposed the dominant themes of the legend, so as to set his blond-haired lovers – renamed Patrice (Jean Marais) and Nathalie (Madeleine Sologne) – against the forces of evil personified by the dwarf Achille (Piéral). As in his stage adaptations and transpositions of similar legendary source material, Cocteau attempts to re-order and weave together the borrowed elements so that they form a part of his own universe. In this he is only partially successful, and the awkwardness of the transposition, enhanced by the uncertainty of the leading performers, is accentuated by Jean Delannoy's somewhat laboured direction, which creates a sense in the audience of being confronted neither by truly contemporary figures nor by figures of adequate legendary stature. Surrounding himself with some of the most talented technicians in French cinema – Roger Hubert for the photography, Georges Wakhévitch for the decor, Georges Auric for the musical score – Delannoy here inaugurates that particular 'quality' style of film making which is so characteristic of his own later productions and of a whole area of post-war French film making. The Nordic overtones to which so many British critics took exception when it was shown in London in 1945 – Richard Winnington, for example, called it 'a pleasure for the Nazis' – seem not to have troubled French historians, but Delannoy is here far from any hint of the presumed Resistance stance of *Pontcarral*.

Although the two films directed at this period by Robert Bresson (b.1907) may be related to some extent to this literary trend of the Vichy period – particularly in view of the contributions of their dialogue writers – they have certain qualities which set them apart from all other films of the early 1940s. Moreover although thematically they anticipate Bresson's post-war work, they are stylistically very distinct. *Les Anges du péché* (1943) – the title is not of Bresson's choosing – has dialogue by the dramatist Jean Giraudoux. His contribution, however, is subordinated to the intentions of the director who from the start shows great assurance in offering a pared-down and stylised vision of the world. The setting of *Les Anges du péché* is a convent where Dominican nuns go about their task of rehabilitating women criminals, and the film's central spiritual clash is that between a young novice, Anne-Marie (Renée Faure) and a murderess, Thérèse (Jany Holt). The picture of convent life offered by the film has a documentary precision, without a single unnecessary detail. Against this background the few scenes taking place elsewhere have an added impact, particularly the remarkable elliptical scene in which Thérèse kills the man responsible for her unjust imprisonment. Within the white, ordered world of the convent Thérèse sows discord, plotting to destroy Anne-Marie, who has taken upon herself the task of converting her. Playing on the well-bred novice's pride, Thérèse is able to drive a wedge between her and her superiors. Eventually expelled from the order, the once overconfident Anne-Marie is now reduced to anguish and despair. Her health is broken, but at the moment of death she succeeds in her self-appointed mission, when Thérèse pronounces the vows which she herself is now too weak to utter. In the 1950s Bresson was to renounce the use of professional actors, but here he obtains excellent performances from his principal actresses and especially from Sylvie, as the mother superior. Although it does not have quite the quality of Bresson's later work with the veteran cinematographer, Léonce-Henry Burel, the visual style is polished, with only occasional indulgences in mere pictorialism.

If *Les Anges du péché* represents a remarkable debut, Bresson was to surpass it with his second feature, begun the following year, *Les Dames du Bois de Boulogne* (1944–45). Adapted from an incident in Diderot's novel *Jacques le fataliste*, the film is deliberately situated outside time. The brilliant, witty dialogue written by Jean Cocteau bestrides two worlds, recalling the preciosity of the seventeenth century in its politenesses, while never completely leaving the realm of the easily colloquial. Its success is crucial to the impact of the film which is essentially a conversation piece, conducted by articulate characters for whom the forms of expression are as important as the feelings beneath them. The direction emphasises that the contemporary settings is only notional. The decor, through the use of detail and bare rooms, constantly reminds us that this is indeed a studio film, while the style of lighting – again by Philippe Agostini – is controlled and formalised, with only occasional obtrusiveness (as at the end) but with a polished quality throughout. *Les Dames du Bois de Boulogne* is a tale of vengeance which is as pared down as a Racine tragedy. The mechanics of the plot – which depend so largely on the man learning that the seemingly pure girl he has married is in fact a nightclub dancer and prostitute – are excellently handled. The action is beautifully constructed, with every move in the elaborate game shown, so that the film as a whole fits together like a clock mechanism, with every wheel and spindle well-oiled and the rhythm and timing impeccable. But it remains an anachronism, an abstract study of human interaction, even in the upper-class society in which Bresson sets it. The force of Maria Casarès's playing as Hélène, who engineers the whole action to avenge herself on a faithless lover, gives the film a tragic tone which is only partially erased by the ending showing the lovers reunited: for Hélène the outcome can only be a disaster. Casarès has complained of the methods used by Bresson and of his insensitivity to his actors, but her own performance is superb, surpassing even her subsequent role in *Orphée*. She is ably supported by Elina Labourdette as the dancer and by Lucienne Bogaert as the latter's mother. The central flaw of the film is the stilted playing of Paul Bertrand, who was imposed on Bresson by the producers and who never begins to suggest a character capable of provoking the love and jealousy which Hélène lavishes upon him. His insipid presentation – a mere shell of politeness with nothing behind the urbane man-of-the-world façade – unbalances the film and reduces its final impact. One can well understand Bresson's later refusal to use professional actors, but his own move on to a new stylistic approach with the *Journal d'un curé de campagne* in no way lessens the power and effectiveness of this film. *Les Dames du Bois de Boulogne* remains one of the key films of the 1940s.

*

Alongside this literary and escapist tendency we also find in the years 1940–44 a current of cinema, more limited in extent and controversial in impact, which sets out to provoke and disturb. Here one thinks of the collaboration of the Prévert brothers, who in 1932 had made *L'Affaire est dans le sac*, Claude Autant-Lara, whose first feature, *Ciboulette*, also dates back to the early 1930s, and Henri-Georges Clouzot, whose first major film was the most controversial work of the Vichy period. The forms used by these film makers are those familiar at this period in any commercial cinema – the comedy, the period romance, the thriller – but these forms are, in each case, manipulated in such a way as to thwart conventional responses and to reverse the anticipated meaning. We have here a cinema which, beneath its conformist appearance, is profoundly subversive.

Amidst 1940s productions *Adieu Léonard*, which Pierre Prévert directed in 1943 from a script by his brother Jacques, stands out as sharply as did the Jacques Prévert-Marcel Carné comedy, *Drôle de drame*, in the late 1930s. But unfortunately for Pierre Prévert's career, the film instead of simply amusing its audiences, perplexed and frustrated them. One can understand the audience's difficulties, since in *Adieu Léonard* the Prévert brothers amused themselves by poking fun at just about everything. As far as dramatic construction is concerned, they frustratingly delay the appearance of the film's notional star, the singer Charles Trenet, giving us instead the justly celebrated sequence in which Léonard discovers that the elegant woman whose handbag he has been trying to steal is in fact an internationally celebrated thief. They also scorn the Pétain notions of work, family and fatherland; the 'return to the soil' is merely the prelude to a series of bungled murder attempts, and, in place of the customary celebration of honest toil, we have the disconcerting antics of a weird assortment of eccentric craftsmen.

Similar reversals were achieved by Claude Autant-Lara (b.1903) in the world of period romance. Autant-Lara's career prior to 1940 is very revealing of the prevalent attitudes of the French film industry. Son of an actress and an architect, he was involved in the theatre at a very early age and while still in his teens began working as designer for Marcel L'Herbier on some of his 1920s films. A short, *Fait divers* (1923) with Antonin Artaud, was followed in 1925 by a medium-length film, *Construire un feu*, taken from a short story by Jack London and using the wide-screen process and anamorphic lenses developed by Henri Chrétien, which were to form the basis of Cinemascope in the early 1950s. While some of his contemporaries worked on dual-language films in Germany, Autant-Lara spent the years 1930–32 in Hollywood, directing French versions of American films, including some by Buster Keaton. On his return to France he directed *Ciboulette* (1933), based on an operetta by Reynaldo Hahn adapted by Jacques Prévert. But the film was not a success. Autant-Lara was unable to establish himself as a director and so spent the late 1930s credited merely as 'technical advisor' on the films he made for Maurice Lehmann, director of the Châtelet theatre, who claimed sole director credit on *L'Affaire du courrier de Lyon* (1937), *Le Ruisseau* (1938) and *Fric-Frac* (1939). Autant-Lara was therefore both the oldest and the most experienced of the newcomers who made their names during the Vichy years.

The subject matter for Autant-Lara's three films of the period – *Le Mariage de Chiffon* (1941), *Lettres d'amour* (1942) and *Douce* (1943) – could hardly be less promising for a film maker who has always seen his role as that of provoking and disturbing the unquestioned assumptions of his audience. All three are period pieces, set in 1900 or before, and *Le Mariage de Chiffon*, for example, is based on a rose-tinted novel by a countess writing under the pseudonym Gyp. But working with a succession of scripting teams in which Jean Aurenche consistently played a key part, Autant-Lara was able to reverse the expected meaning and turn these films into a sharp and often sardonic querying of bourgeois values. A vital role in making these films acceptable to producers and audiences was played by Odette Joyeux, who became one of the leading stars of the period in this trio of portrayals of beautiful young girls whose impetuosity and honesty –

23. Jean Grémillon: Lumière d'été (1943)

24. Marcel Carné: Les Enfants du paradis (1943–45)

25. Georges Rouquier: Farrebique (1946)

26. Jean Cocteau: La Belle et la bête (1946)

27. Claude Autant-Lara: Le Diable au corps (1947)

28. Jacques Tati: Jour de fête (1949)

29. Jean Cocteau: Orphée (1950)

30. Jacques Becker: Casque d'or (1952)

and resulting tribulations – expose the hypocrisy of the middle-class society in which they live. *Douce*, the finest of the three films and the one in which the upturning of the original meaning of the novel is taken furthest, is the one in which Autant-Lara assembled most of the team which he was to employ in the post-war period: the scriptwriters Jean Aurenche and Pierre Bost, the composer René Cloërec, and the editor Madeleine Gug, who were to be joined in 1947 by the designer Max Douy.

Henri-Georges Clouzot (1907–77) also had an involvement with the cinema dating back to the early 1930s, having directed a short film, *La Terreur des Batignolles*, and begun a career as scriptwriter in 1931. Between 1931 and 1934 he worked on the script, dialogue or lyrics of a dozen or so films, some of them made in Germany. Then illness kept him bedridden for four years in various hospitals and sanitoria. Returning to the cinema in 1938 he worked on a further three scripts – including *Le Duel* (1939) directed by his friend Pierre Fresnay – before the outbreak of war. Engaged by Continental in 1941 Clouzot rapidly became a specialist in thrillers, adapting stories by the Belgian Stanislas-André Steeman for Georges Lacombe's *Le Dernier des six* (1941) and a sequel which he directed himself, *L'Assassin habite au 21* (1942), in both of which Pierre Fresnay as the detective was supported by the young actress and singer Suzy Delair, at this time Clouzot's companion. More substantial was the adaptation of a Simenon novel which Clouzot wrote for Henri Decoin, *Les Inconnus dans la maison* (1942). In this bitter denunciation of respectable provincial society, in which Raimu had one of his best roles, the corrosive tone clearly belongs more to Clouzot than to the director. The film caused some accusations that the German-financed company was indulging in anti-French propaganda. Certainly it did not go unnoticed that the murderer uncovered by Raimu was, in the film as in the novel, a Jew, and that *Les Inconnus dans la maison* was released in a double bill with one of the rare pieces of French anti-semitic propaganda, *Forces occultes*.

The unease provoked by *Les Inconnus dans la maison* grew to a scandal with the release of Clouzot's second film as a director, the masterly *Le Corbeau* (1943). This tale of poison pen-letters in a French provincial town was in fact based on a real incident at Tulle twenty years before and the original script had been registered by Louis Chavance in 1937. Clouzot here paints a masterly portrait of a town in the grip of a frenzy and in which everyone is a suspect. As a flood of letters spreads accusations of adultery, crime and abortion, one particularly vicious example causes a suicide by revealing that a hospital patient has cancer. This bleak and pitiless film was promptly denounced as anti-French in the clandestine press, as if the phenomenon of anonymous letters was unknown in occupied France. As the innuendos spread and it was rumoured that the film had been circulated in Germany under the title *Une Petite ville française*, the reaction began to resemble the action of the film itself. At the Liberation Clouzot was severely censured and deprived of the opportunity to work in the French film industry until 1947, despite the public support of film makers like Carné and Autant-Lara.

*

The third current which can be discerned among the major productions of the Vichy years is what can be broadly termed the 'realistic tendency', the desire to set an action in a clearly defined society whose contradictions and inner conflicts are revealed as the characters begin to interact. Rather than the retreat into the creation of a fantasy world cut off from time or the stance of undermining appearances from within, we find, in the case of these film makers, a concern to assert the dignity of the everyday and a new interest in characters drawn from the working classes. To this broad tendency we can attach the work of Jean Grémillon, a major *cineáste maudit* of the 1930s, Louis Daquin, who was for several years his assistant, and Jacques Becker, one of the most talented and respected figures to emerge in the new 1940s cinema. While a seriousness of approach is common to all three, a certain ambiguity surrounds even some of their best work. This derives from the fact that despite the known political allegiances of the film makers themselves (Daquin, for example, was a key figure in the resistance movement within the film industry and was subsequently to emerge as a militant Communist trade-union organiser), the positive stress which their films lay on the provincial society or village community and on the efforts of ordinary people – whether adults or children – to shape their own lives, is wholly containable within the Vichy ideology of work, family and fatherland.

It is in many ways ironic that for Jean Grémillon the years of material difficulty and hardship constituted by the Vichy period were those in which he was able to express himself most fully in two masterly films which remain his greatest achievements in the cinema. Taking a script by Jacques Prévert and Pierre Laroche, and surrounding himself with a crew of collaborators sympathetic to his ideals, Grémillon shot *Lumière d'été* in 1943. The film, which has a complex plot in which the fates of the individual characters are skilfully interlocked, has many echoes of the cinema of the late 1930s, and can indeed be seen in some senses as a companion work to *La Règle du jeu*. Again we have a society split into two classes, the rich centred on the château and the workers engaged on constructing a dam under the supervision of a young engineer. Here, moreover, this social division reflects the characters' moral worth: the rich are corrupt, and all fresh hope must lie with the workers. The arrival of a pair of outsiders brings these two worlds into collision and at a fancy-dress ball the tensions reach explosion point, leading to death and suicide. *Lumière d'été* is a complex work whose qualities are difficult to pin down. If, with its air of fatalism, its explicitly dialogued confrontations and its final masked ball, it looks back to the 1930s, the use Grémillon makes of landscape and the weight afforded to the world of work is more modern. Grémillon's sense of composition is excellent and the setting, with its hotel perched precariously on a hilltop, takes on an intense life. Although – as always with Prévert – we have been caught up and intrigued by the wicked for most of the film, the final images redress the balance and the villain and his guests, wandering bedraggled in their garish costumes, seem like insubstantial wraiths in a landscape dominated by the workers.

Le Ciel est à vous (1944), dedicated by Grémillon to the real couple whose exploits in 1937 had inspired his film, is undoubtedly his major work. It tells of Thérèse Gauthier, a garage owner's wife (Madeleine Renaud, here making her fourth appearance in a Grémillon film), whose interest is unexpectedly captured by flying. *Le Ciel est à vous* is Grémillon's most eloquent tribute to ordinary people who take their destiny in their own hands and, through their own personal drive and tenacity, create something extraordinary. Working from an adaptation by Charles Spaak of a script originally written by Albert Valentin, Grémillon has put behind him all the defeatist fatalism of French 1930s cinema, looking rather to the future and stressing the value of hard work, devotion and simple courage. *Le Ciel est à vous* is one of the rare French films of the period to put its confidence in the depiction of ordinary lives, capturing the gestures and words of working people, whose life distinguishes itself from the banality around them only through this one act of supreme self-confidence.

The ambiguities of the cinema under Vichy are very apparent, however, in the fact that *Le Ciel est à vous* was widely and warmly praised for its positive values – claimed as those of Pétain's France – by the collaborationist press, led by the infamous François Vinneuil (pseudonym of Lucien Rebatet, author of the anti-semitic *Les Tribus du cinéma et du théâtre* in 1941). At the same time it was seized upon by the underground press as a symbol of French resistance: it seems both sides wished to claim a monopoly of virtue. But Grémillon, a film maker at the height of his powers and able to express openly his love and affection, was far from wishing to laud abstract national values or offer symbols of another reality. His true concern was to create a hymn to the individual, observed with all his faults and petty egotisms, but also in his full potential. A key figure in the movement of resistance in the cinema and a member of the Comité de Libération du Cinéma who was to be responsible in 1945 for the official record of the Normandy invasion, *Le Six juin à l'aube*, Grémillon seemed at this period to be on the verge of a triumphant career. But after the war the production difficulties which had frustrated his career in the 1930s reappeared and the success of *Lumière d'été* and *Le Ciel est à vous* was never to be repeated.

The quality of realism displayed at this period by Jacques Becker (1906–60) also had nothing in it to trouble the authorities. Becker had been Jean Renoir's friend and assistant for most of the films between *La Nuit du carrefour* and *La Marseillaise*. His ambitions to direct were very apparent during this seven-year period but his career got off to a false start at the end of the decade, when *L'Or du Cristobal* (1939), which was to have been his first feature, was abandoned after just three or four weeks' shooting. Becker resumed directing in 1942 with *Le Dernier atout*, a thriller involving American gangsters on the Côte d'Azur and seemingly designed as a substitute for the Hollywood films now banned from France.

Goupi-Mains-Rouges (1943) was a more substantial work, adapted from a novel by Pierre Véry, whose popularity was at its height at this period, when other novels of his were adapted by Christian-Jaque, Jean Delannoy and Louis Daquin. This story of a peasant family, which takes in killing and madness but also the loyalty of the clan which closes its ranks against outsiders and the authorities, is somewhat remote from Becker's central preoccupations. It offers a savagely drawn picture of peasant life which underlines the greed, avarice and selfishness of Véry's characters. But from another point of view it is wholly in line with the ideology of the Pétain era. Its central character, the foppish son supposed to have made good in Paris, is redeemed through his reacquaintance with rural life and the love of his beautiful country cousin. *Falbalas* (1944–45) shows more clearly the mature strengths and limitations of Becker's approach at this period, here applied to a more congenial subject, the world of a Parisian fashion house (where his mother had begun her career). It is significant that Becker's portrait embraces not only the designer but also all those whose humble task it is to realise his creations. The film had only a muted impact, perhaps because the lovingly detailed study of life in occupied Paris which Becker constructed reached its audiences only after the Liberation. The film's strengths, however, lie in its picture of the everyday world with its comradeship but also its tensions. He stresses the minor incongruities of the period and succeeds in presenting the lighter aspects of the sexual sparring between the designer, his best friend and the latter's fiancée (Raymond Rouleau, Jean Chevrier and Micheline Presle). Becker is less at home, however, when the designer's love turns to a hopeless passion and there is a need to motivate the madness which drives this previously frivolous man to the act of suicide which frames the action of the film.

The career of Louis Daquin (1909–80), at one time Grémillon's assistant, echoes his mentor's pattern in its struggles against adversity. After working with Grémillon on several films shot in Germany, Daquin had his first co-directing opportunity with *Le Joueur* (1938), the French-language version of Gerhard Lamprecht's *Der Spieler*. His solo directing career, of which the 1940s form the richest part, begins with *Nous les gosses* (1941), a fresh and lively view of schoolchildren's lives, which captured the mood needed at this period of the Occupation. This optimistic film stressing the self-reliance of the young – to which a tepid love story included at the producer's insistence adds nothing – is situated in a timeless world of childhood (the original script dates from 1936), but its success was enormously encouraging at a low point of French cinema. Even more interesting and significant of the period, however, is Daquin's fourth film, *Premier de cordée* (1944), which has precisely the same ambiguity as Grémillon's *Le Ciel est à vous*. In *Premier de cordée*, a mountaineering film that took him away from the studios, Daquin attempted a tale of human courage struggling against adversity. But, despite the director's political commitment, the final result, far from being an unambiguous expression of the growing sense of French resistance, is in fact, as he himself openly admitted in retrospect, very much impregnated with the political ideology of Pétain, with its themes of return to the land, noble struggle against natural forces, and so on.

The ambiguities to be found in individual works of the 1940–44 period are very evident too in the overall evaluation of French cinema during these years. The roots of the confusion seem to lie less in the films themselves – which reflect the circumstances of their making, both in the conscious efforts of their makers and in the unconscious shaping influences of the times, very much as the films of other periods do – than in the inappropriately simplified social analyses which critics have attempted to bring to bear on them. If the values of Vichy are seen to lie in some such slogan as 'Work, Family and Fatherland', then confusion must clearly arise, since one can hardly imagine the Gaullist resistance attempting to make the population idle, adulterous and unpatriotic. The values appropriated by Vichy are to be found in the work of many film makers of the 1930s, and find their expression too in the post-war world. Marcel Pagnol, for example, had been setting the values of Provence against the corrupt world of Paris and the big city since the early 1930s (even if we limit our analysis to his film work), and he can hardly be accused, in *La Fille du puisatier*, of responding opportunistically to a politician's call for a return to the land and the values of a rural culture. Similarly the documentarist Georges Rouquier responded to the new opportunities for short film makers and, no doubt, to certain ideas 'in the air', by making a number of excellent documentary studies of rural crafts: *Le Tonnelier* (1942) and *Le Charron* (1943). It is in these films, which were in no way calculated to disturb the Vichy censors – quite the opposite – that we find the authentic roots of the approach to peasant life which caused *Farrebique* to be universally hailed as a masterpiece of post-war realism when it appeared in 1946.

It is quite inadequate to base judgments on extrapolated plot synopses or the details from carefully selected moments of a film. To be understood, the films need to be seen in terms of their makers' overall philosophy, as expressed in a wide range of films both before and since. Without such a perspective Delannoy, the patriot, speaking out boldly for the Resistance in *Pontcarral* in 1942, inexplicably becomes Delannoy, the Aryan apologist of *L'Eternel retour* the very next year. But if we consider the director's whole career as a skilled but routine director without a deeply felt range of subject matter, this shift becomes more easily understood, and the superficiality of both approaches can be appreciated. The expression of revolt through isolated symbolic moments in a stylised drama like *Les Visiteurs du soir* does not make Carné a political activist. Nor does the inevitable entanglement with aspects of the Pétain ideological system nullify the attempts of Daquin – who was a militant activist – to express positive values in *Premier de cordée*. Adopting this broader perspective, we do not need Hitler's Aryan philosophy to explain Cocteau's lauding of the blond and blue-eyed in *L'Eternel retour*, and we can understand how a film maker like Clouzot is a disturbing figure for Vichy supporters and Gaullists alike. *Le Corbeau*, the film which, it is well known, led him to be severely censured after the Liberation, had earlier terminated his contract with Continental, who hardly wished for a film maker attacking so bitterly those who denounce their fellows by means of anonymous letters.

8   A Timid Renewal
1945–50

Je me demande même s'il ne faudrait pas, jusqu'en 1950, parler
d'un cinéma postvichyssois. A la surprise amère des militants
clandestins, le Parti Communiste avait, dès la libération de
Paris, repris à son compte les trois mots d'ordre du Maréchal:
travail, famille, patrie. Cette politique pesa sur toute la vie
intellectuelle du pays et la fadeur des films d'après-guerre lui est
largement imputable.

Raymond Borde, 1978

The Committee for the Liberation of the French Cinema, set up early in
1944, made preparations to record on film the allied triumph. Much of
the material shot subsequently appeared in the newly reconstituted
newsreels and in Jean-Paul Le Chanois's compilation, *Au coeur de
l'orage* (1948). After the Liberation the Committee also devoted itself
to the task of restructuring the film industry and carrying out a very
partial and inadequate expulsion from the French cinema of those
elements deemed to have collaborated with the Germans (among
those censured were Arletty, Pierre Fresnay and Sacha Guitry, as well
as Henri-Georges Clouzot). By December 1944 film production was
again under way and the numbers of films produced rose steadily from
about twenty in 1944 to sixty in 1945 and ninety in 1946, to level out
at over a hundred films a year during the 1950s. The achievement of
this level of production was not without its difficulties, however.
While the industry could not hope to maintain the exceptional levels
reached during the Occupation – when some eighty-five per cent of the
films shown were French – producers certainly aimed to achieve the
sixty-five per cent of the local market which they had held in the pre-
war years. A severe threat to this was, however, posed by the
agreement signed in 1946 between Léon Blum and the US representative James F. Byrnes, in which the health of the French film industry
was sacrificed for other political aims. Blum agreed to a quota level of
just sixteen weeks a year for French films – in effect halving the

proportion of screen time local productions had occupied before 1940 – and allowing 'free competition' for the remaining thirty-six weeks. But since the American film industry had a backlog of four years' films – the Hollywood output of 1940–44 banned by the Germans – this competition could never be equal, and the import of American films rose from thirty-eight in the first half of 1946 to three hundred and thirty-eight in the first half of 1947.

The crisis was partially resolved with new government regulations in 1948 which revised the quota arrangement, raising the proportion of time reserved for French films to twenty weeks a year and limiting the number of dubbed films allowed to one hundred and eighty a year, of which one hundred and twenty-one were to be American. The government also began to offer aid to producers and funds for the modernisation of film theatres, thereby restoring confidence. But while production levels rose, there was none of the revolutionary change for which many members of the Committee for the Liberation of the French Cinema had hoped. While René Clément's semi-documentary study of the Resistance, *La Bataille du rail*, was a success, the fictional dramas of Resistance activity – whether given period settings, like Christian-Jaque's *Boule de suif* (1945), or set in the immediate past, like Henri Calef's *Jéricho* (1946) and Raymond Bernard's *Un Ami viendra ce soir* (1946) – were frankly mediocre. There was no resurgence akin to that in Italy with the advent of the neo-realist film makers of the period.

The career of Louis Daquin, who like so many of the new forces in post-war French cinema had made his debut in the Occupation years, is very indicative of the failure of French cinema to achieve a positive renewal and to develop a new link with society after the constraints of Vichy. Daquin, a leading member of the Committee for Liberation and an active trade-union organiser, began his post-war career with a commercial work adapted from a play by Sardou. *Patrie* (1946), although treating in its historical setting themes of occupation and resistance, was essentially conceived as a popular melodrama. Closer to Daquin's central concerns was the adaptation of Jean Prévost's novel, *Les Frères Bouquinquant* (1947), written with the novelist Roger Vaillant, a collaborator on several of Daquin's projects at this period, and offering some location shooting and an examination of certain social issues. Daquin's major achievement is *Le Point du jour* (1949), a study of a mining community from a script by Vladimir Pozner which was set in the North of France where the director was born. Here Daquin's political commitment and his concern with a realist style are both apparent in the shaping of the narrative and in the decision to shoot everything on location, even constructing the interior sets away from Paris and in the area in which the action takes place. *Le Point du jour* marks both the climax of Daquin's career and the end of any French aspiration towards a realist movement akin to that developing in Italy. Two commercial projects in 1949–50 were Daquin's last opportunities to work in the French studios for well over a decade. His only subsequent French-produced feature was *La Foire aux cancres* in 1963 and his career after 1950 has striking echoes of that of Jean Grémillon. Unable to interest French producers in the subjects he developed, Daquin was reduced to merely technical roles and forced to work abroad. His adaptation of Maupassant's *Bel ami* (1954), shot in a dual-language version in Austria, was banned for three years and then allowed to be screened in France only after extensive cuts and the rewriting of key passages of the dialogue. His other films of the 1950s were *Les Chardons du Baragan* (1957), made in Rumania, and *Les Arrivistes* (1959), a version of Balzac's *La Rabouilleuse* shot in East Berlin.

*

The work of the leading directors during the immediate post-war years does not represent a radical break with past traditions. In many ways this is surprising, since many of those who had been active in the 1930s and before – René Clair, Jean Renoir, Marcel Carné, Julien Duvivier, Jacques Feyder and Jean Grémillon – had only limited production opportunities and were no longer the dominant figures. The key role was taken on by half-a-dozen younger directors who had mostly established themselves in the 1940s and were trained as film technicians and craftsmen. Although they had made their first features somewhat earlier, Jean Delannoy and Claude Autant-Lara belong with Henri-Georges Clouzot and Jacques Becker among those who had proved themselves to be important directors with films made between the collapse of France and the Liberation. André Cayatte (b.1909) and Yves Allégret (b.1907) had also made a start with commercial works during the war years. Together with René Clément (b.1913), whose first feature film appeared in 1946, these men were those who set the patterns of French film making up to 1950 and beyond.

The key to the styles and attitudes of the dominant group, who were mostly in their late thirties when the war ended, is to be found in their early careers. Almost all had come to the cinema in a conventional way in the early 1930s and served apprenticeships as assistant directors. This might be a lengthy process and even as gifted a man as Jacques Becker worked for over seven years in this subordinate role before being given a directorial opportunty. In the days before the creation of film schools, assistantship was, in a sense, a form of apprenticeship to the art of film making, and one can sense the deep influence of, say, Renoir on Jacques Becker or Grémillon on Louis Daquin. The majority of these directors had also worked in some other capacity as well: scriptwriters, directors of the French versions of foreign films or short film makers. They were thus highly trained professional film makers who possessed a craftsman's approach to the medium, more technicians and interpreters of the work of others than creative personalities bursting with novel ideas which they needed to express on celluloid. Collectively they made few innovations in film technique and virtually no revolutionary changes in subject matter. Working within a tradition against which they did not rebel, they hardly attempted to get beyond the conventions of the well-constructed film based on an existing work of literature. Their films were meticulously planned and carefully constructed to exploit the wealth of available acting talent, but there was no surge of creative energy.

As much as Clair, Carné or Duvivier, these directors were reliant on the quality of the script for the success or failure of their films and the limitations of the great majority could be ascribed to their reliance on writers. Of the group, only Clouzot wrote his own scripts and even he conceived his films in terms of suspense and dramatic build-up. The other directors leaned heavily on the new scriptwriters whose emergence paralleled their own. Jean Aurenche and Pierre Bost were Autant-Lara's regular scenarists and also contributed to some of Clément's and Delannoy's greatest successes. Other writers made equally important contributions, with Jacques Sigurd scripting Yves Allégret's best films, Jacques Prévert writing Cayatte's first real success, *Les Amants de Vérone*, and Charles Spaak shaping the same director's legal series of the early 1950s. Jacques Becker was perhaps less dependent on his writers, but the contributions of Annette Wademant and Maurice Griffe should not be underestimated. Even when they had ideas to which they were strongly committed, they still continued to use conventional vehicles for their views and to rely on the verbal adroitness of their screenwriters.

Although René Clément ventured outside the studios to make the documentary *La Bataille du rail* and capture the authentic settings of *Au-delà des grilles* and Daquin went to the mining districts of the North for *Le Point du jour*, most of the late 1940s work remains within the French studio tradition. Becker's comedies, for example, take place in a studio world, although the contemporary references are precisely made. Clouzot rebuilds the Paris setting of *Quai des orfèvres*, just as Carné used studio sets for *Les Portes de la nuit* and Duvivier for *Panique*. Clair too returned to a studio world with *Le Silence est d'or*, but whereas his world is deliberately stylised, the concern of the dominant group is the realist reconstruction of their everyday settings. Craftmanship is a constant factor here, but deep involvement with the characters is much rarer. Only Becker fills his films with real human warmth, while the stylistic preoccupations of the others – Clouzot's concern with suspense, Clément's with camera style, Autant-Lara's with the expression of his own idiosyncratic ideas and Allégret's with plot structure – all tend to give their films a certain coldness and remoteness from their characters.

The dangers of such a lack of deep personal involvement with the material are most apparent in the career of Jean Delannoy, who had won a very high reputation for himself with the direction of Jean Cocteau's script for *L'Eternel retour* in 1943. Surrounding himself with skilled and experienced technical collaborators, Delannoy continued after the war to direct ambitious works: scripts derived from Gide (*La Symphonie pastorale*) and Sartre (*Les Jeux sont faits*), for instance, and films treating religious and social problems. Three films scripted by Aurenche and Bost – *La Symphonie pastorale* (1946), *Dieu a besoin des hommes* (1950) and *Chiens perdus sans colliers* (1955) – may be taken as showing Delannoy at his best and representing one aspect of the work of this whole generation. All three films won international awards and are carefully and tastefully directed, but the very smoothness and beauty of the images gives these films a coldness that prevents their characters from coming to life. In retrospect, these works and the dull, over-elaborate period films which followed them epitomise the academicism which haunts many of the more ambitious enterprises of the late 1940s and early 1950s and against which a later generation was rightly to rebel.

French film producers were reluctant in the 1940s to face up to the changed circumstances of post-war France, and film makers sought inspiration instead in the studio-created world of the Gabin films of the 1930s – works like Duvivier's *Pépé-le-Moko*, and the Prévert–Carné films, *Quai des brumes* and *Le Jour se lève*. The result was a naturalistic style of film making – the *film noir* – characterised by the theme of doomed lovers, the setting of urban backstreet squalor and an all-pervading air of fatalism. The first post-war films of Duvivier (*Panique*) and Carné (*Les Portes de la nuit*) are both very much in this tradition. But the qualities and defects of the *film noir* are best seen in the work of Yves Allégret and his scriptwriter Jacques Sigurd who together made *Dedée d'Anvers* (1948), *Une si jolie petite plage* (1949) and *Manèges* (1950). Here Allégret shows clearly his technical mastery and ability to draw performances of high quality from his actors, but these gifts are applied to themes and subjects taken unchanged from the pre-war era. One finds in all three films the same insignificant characters, drab surroundings and extreme, hopeless predicaments. The increasingly static nature of the films' basic situations leads, as with Prévert and Carné, to experiment with narrative structure, particularly flashback technique. It is the lack of connection with the mood of post-war France, rather than any technical or formal weaknesses that makes such films seem artificial. Carné and Prévert had attained a similar degree of blackness in *Le Jour se lève* but were able to strike out afresh and apply their talents to more positive themes in at least two more masterly works. Allégret and Sigurd failed to achieve this renewal and the decline in interest of their work parallels that of the *film noir* tradition into a welter of gangster films and petty little works on prostitution.

*

The most forceful member of the post-war generation was Henri-Georges Clouzot. Because of the scandal surrounding *Le Corbeau*, he had to wait until 1947 before he was able to direct another film, and to re-establish himself, he again turned to a thriller subject. *Quai des orfèvres* (1947), a tale of an unhappily married couple whose problems are increased when they unwittingly become involved in a murder, is remarkable above all for the masterly realism with which the director sketched in the background of police station and shabby music halls. Although the plot is not particularly convincing, Clouzot handles the various threads in an adept fashion, building up considerable suspense and drawing excellent performances from a cast led by Louis Jouvet. The atmosphere of the Quai des Orfèvres is beautifully caught, as in the small incident when the hero has to sign a statement which, translated into police jargon, seems totally false in the absence of all the crucial shades of meaning. The couple's surroundings are thoroughly squalid and Clouzot hints at obsession and corruption. Despite the nominally happy ending, the picture Clouzot draws of this milieu is as depressing as anything in Allégret's work. Moments like the hero's attempted suicide are handled with pitiless realism and the director's approach to the couple is typified by the image he uses to represent their lovemaking: a pan of milk boiling over on the stove. Even bleaker is Clouzot's modernisation of the classic eighteenth-century novel by the abbé Prévost, *Manon Lescaut*. Although the choice of parallels – the Parisian black-market and the illegal emigration of Jews to Palestine – is audacious, *Manon* (1948) loses much in its updating. What is powerfully conveyed, however, is the director's view of passion, summed up by Manon when she comes face to face with her lover in the brothel where she works: 'Nothing is sordid when two people love each other'.

Not surpisingly Clouzot was markedly less successful with his next project, an adaptation of the vaudeville farce, *Miquette et sa mère* (1949), but with *Le Corbeau* and his first two post-war films he succeeded in delineating his own personal filmic world. His personality is stamped on every aspect of this work – on the source material, the studio-built sets, the acting and the plot structure. The characteristics of his approach are an extremely pessimistic view of the world, a ruthlessness and a significant lack of humour. The world of Clouzot's films is one where beauty and tenderness have no place and even love and friendship are rare. It is not at all an unemotional world, but the passions it contains are of the kind which involve dominance and degradation. Whenever he probes his characters he uncovers some unsavoury truth: ambition, lust, hatred or cowardice. The natural outcome is violence and all Clouzot's subsequent fictional works follow the pattern of the 1940s and contain scenes of murder, suicide or at least unnatural death. His natural source material is the thriller and he is at his best in depicting this genre's conventional settings: the schoolroom and the lawcourt, the police station and the provincial boarding house. To all of these he brings a fresh visual imagination and an enormous vigour and vitality, but seldom does he venture any real social comment and, despite the modernising of *Manon*, his world is very much a timeless one of human vices, not the contemporary France emerging from the war.

Like Clouzot, Jacques Becker was already an established director when the war ended, with three feature films to his credit after long years as Renoir's assistant. His first three post-war films form an informal trilogy of Parisian subjects which together add up to a fascinating picture of post-war France. *Antoine et Antoinette* (1946) is ostensibly about a lost lottery ticket but this plot serves as little more than a pretext for a sympathetic portrayal of the everyday life of a working-class couple. The misunderstandings, quarrels and reconciliations of this pair are treated with affectionate insight and without sentimentality. The background of life in a Parisian suburb throbs with life and the various strands of the plot are admirably woven together, including a wedding party observed with a satiric eye worthy of Clair himself. To capture this setting Becker uses the technique of accumulating a mass of tiny detail, but this concentration on the trivial and the everyday, although giving the film a vivid texture, prevents any treatment of the real social issues of post-war France. In *Rendez-vous de juillet* (1949) Becker set out to examine post-war youth but again concentrated on private and personal issues. The film deals with a whole group of young people, their friends, family backgrounds, ambitions and loves. *Rendez-vous de juillet*'s wide focus makes it necessarily diffuse and more loosely constructed than the previous film, but it gives an honest and sympathetic view of youth. It does not put all the blame for their misdeeds on the young, indeed it includes some of Becker's most acid portrayals of smugly successful bourgeois families. The characters are well differentiated and ably acted by a cast of young actors including Daniel Gélin and Maurice Ronet. The tone is essentially lighthearted and it is clear that Becker takes a positive pleasure in the noisy exuberance of his youthful characters. The lightest of the three films is *Edouard et Caroline* (1951) which succeeds totally on its chosen level of comedy, despite an almost total absence of plot. Becker seems indeed to have delighted in the challenge of making a memorable work from the very thin script provided by Annette Wademant. *Edouard et Caroline* combines a study of two young people coping with being married and being in love with the very lightest of portrayals of a pompous and self-satisfied bourgeois world. The handling of the couple's relationship is full of neat, unemphatic touches and precise observation of the little differences which the tension of a big occasion can raise into a full-scale quarrel. But we never doubt that all will eventually be well, and Becker rounds off his film deftly, but as usual without raising any awkward social questions.

Jacques Becker's work provides a necessary answer to Clouzot's bleak world. The centre of interest in any Becker film is humanity, not observed as a collection of isolated individuals but as a society linked by ties of love, friendship, occupation and common interest. His films of the 1940s show his gift of sympathising with people from a wide range of backgrounds and treating their problems with respect. But despite his evident affection for his characters, Becker never sentimentalises. Like Renoir, Becker loved actors and worked sympathetically with them. Thanks to his ability to draw perceptive performances from his actors he is able to create films of lasting value in his Parisian series despite the slightness of the material he handles. Through his actors Becker is able to give a picture of love and affection which, despite the domesticity and the deliberately light comic tone, rings totally true. What he fails to do is move out from his chosen area of the ordinary and commonplace to deal with wider social issues, but within his deliberately limited range Becker's 1940s work shows a total mastery.

Claude Autant-Lara can, on occasion, share Becker's lightness of touch, as his first post-war film, *Sylvie et le fantôme* (1945) shows. Starring Odette Joyeux, it followed the outward pattern of Autant-Lara's previous three films with the same actress, but this time the result is a delicate escapist work – without malice and handled with remarkable elegance. It features Jacques Tati in a tiny role as the ghost with whom the young girl falls in love. Autant-Lara showed the same lightness of touch in *Occupe-toi d'Amélie* (1949), an adaptation of a Feydeau farce starring Danielle Darrieux. Accepting the artificiality of his subject and keeping the plot moving at a cracking pace, Autant-Lara makes the most of the play's ingenuity. Drawing on his own background as a designer, he uses the decor wittily to comment on the intricacies of a play within a play which is itself within a film, and at the same time draws from his leading actress an attractive perform-ance which keeps the film as gay as it is lightheartedly immoral.

Autant-Lara's characteristic style, however, is much more forceful and finds its full expression in *Le Diable au corps* (1947), set during World War I. Like most of the films scripted for the director by Aurenche and Bost, *Le Diable au corps* is an adaptation of a novel, in this case by Raymond Radiguet. It is the tragic love story of an adolescent and a young married woman who defy society even to the extent of longing for the continuation of the war, which alone will keep her husband away and make their continued liaison possible. In characteristic 1940s style the film begins with the funeral of the young woman, who has died giving birth to the hero's child, and as he watches from a distance François relives their now vanished happi-ness. To add to his misery, his loss coincides with the universal rejoicing which accompanies the declaration of the 1918 armistice. The pattern of flashbacks is solidly constructed and the period atmosphere well conveyed through the settings. The script and Autant-Lara's direction offer penetrating insight into the characters of the two lovers and Gérard Philipe in particular captures brilliantly the mental state of a schoolboy, half man half child, who is so confident and demanding of the woman, yet fails her in their moments of crisis.

With *Le Diable au corps* Autant-Lara was able to give a first expression to the themes which dominate all his major work and also consolidate the team of collaborators who were to assist him on most of his films. This establishment of a consistent team – to be joined in 1949 by the cinematographer Jacques Natteau – is characteristic of the director's approach to film making. He eschews formal experiment and returns to this same pattern of narrative construction in later films, including *Journal d'une femme en blanc* in 1965. *Le Diable au corps*, which established Autant-Lara's international reputation after over twenty-five years' involvement with the film industry, has the characteristic Autant-Lara approach to the relationship between characters and society. Although the film has a period setting, its contemporary relevance and unfashionable opposition to war are very apparent. Whereas for Clouzot love is a devouring passion which can only lead to death and for Becker a warm and basically unproblematic relationship between people, for Autant-Lara it is a moment when individual and society inevitably clash. Throughout his subsequent career the director's stance will be emphatically that of *Le Diable au corps*: to vindicate sexual love totally, while not hesitating to reveal its disconcerting truths.

René Clément, the only one of the dominant group who had not made a feature film during the Occupation period, is the most eclectic of them all. His background was in documentary film making and in 1946 he was among the first to confront the recent past in *La Bataille du rail*. Basing his film on actual events (and a script by novelist Colette Audry), using real railway workers supported by just a few professional actors, Clément succeeds admirably in capturing the atmosphere of the Resistance without falling into the trap of false heroics. The material is soberly handled and the various sequences excellently constructed, particularly impressive being the derailment sequence and the scene where engine drivers sound their whistles in protest at the execution of the captured Resistance men. At the time it was the documentary surface of the film which was most striking, particularly in the context of the continuing French studio tradition. It is a work of considerable stature, but in retrospect it is the careful shaping of the film's emotional pattern and the fluid use of camerawork which indicate the direction of Clément's own career.

Clément did not pursue the path which *La Bataille du rail* seemed to open up. After working as technical advisor for Jean Cocteau's *La Belle et la bête* and Noël-Noël's *Le Père tranquille*, Clément turned again to the war period with *Les Maudits* (1947). But this time Clément was firmly within the French tradition of studio film making, for the submarine which forms the film's setting was meticulously rebuilt in the studio. Clément and his director of photography, Henri Alekan, gave much thought to the resolution of technical problems, but the script dealing with the last days of a group of leading Nazis and collaborators under the leadership of a crazed submarine commander is weak and rhetorical *Au-delà des grilles* (1949), the first of several films Clément was to shoot in Italy, is an interesting hybrid work which seems to show a conscious effort to bring together the French tradition and the modern world which the contemporary Italian neo-realists were depicting so forcefully. Based on a story by Cesare Zavattini and Suso Cecchi d'Amico, two of the leading writers of the Italian realist movement, the film gives totally authentic glimpses of the streets of Genoa, so that the tenements, trams and alleyways have absolute authenticity. But at the same time the appearance of Jean Gabin as the hero with only a few days of freedom (before he is hunted down by the police) stresses a link with the 1930s style, which is further emphasised by the solidly constructed adaptation by Aurenche and Bost. The film has a power, however, which is lacking from *Le Château de verre* (1950) in which the script (this time by Clément and Bost) uses a best-selling novel as the basis for a set of games with plot and flashback structure.

As this 1940s work shows, René Clément is both a talented and an eclectic director. Even at this period his films show the power to be derived from creating variations on the French traditional approach to film construction, particularly by the use of location shooting and documentary texture, as in *La Bataille du rail* and *Au delà des grilles*. But equally his failures show the limitations of this tradition: the dangers of substituting meticulous reconstruction (as of the submarine in *Les Maudits*) or technical ingenuity in the camerawork or scripting (as in *Le Château de verre*) for a truly creative treatment of reality which escapes from the confines of the studio and the well-made film. The restlessness evident even in the 1940s will be developed still more during the 1950s and for the whole period up to and beyond the New Wave Clément remains a key film maker whose work reveals the strengths and contradictions of the French approach.

*

Although the work of the most forceful and successful figures of the immediate post-war years is, as we have seen, firmly rooted in pre-war traditions, the veterans of that period all experienced difficulty either in adjusting to the new mood of post-war France or in relating themselves to a French cultural scene from which they had long been separated. Perhaps the most surprising difficulties were those experienced by Marcel Carné and Jean Grémillon, who had been key figures in the 1930s cinema, which still remained a key source of inspiration, and who had both made arguably their best work during the Occupation years. In fact, both were to experience enormous frustrations during the late 1940s.

Marcel Carné was at the height of his fame in 1945. His collaboration with the poet and scriptwriter Jacques Prévert had culminated in two of the greatest films made during the Occupation period – *Les Visiteurs du soir* and *Les Enfants du paradis* – and the director seemed destined to dominate the newcomers who, although lacking his experience, were all of much the same age (he was born in 1909). In 1946 Carné was able to make a film of his own choosing and enjoy the advantages of a large budget. Although given a contemporary setting, *Les Portes de la nuit* had as its source a ballet written by Prévert the previous year and many of its weaknesses stem from this hybrid conception. On the one hand it was ostensibly a realistic film dealing with the black market and the aftermath of the Occupation, on the other it was a poetic work with a melodramatic plot involving a character who personified Fate and introduced the hero to 'the most beautiful woman in the world'. Carné's technical team remained unchanged from the wartime period, but this time the stars for whom the film was written, Jean Gabin and Marlene Dietrich, turned down their roles. Marred by weaknesses of interpretation, the film proved completely out of touch with contemporary taste and Carné's career underwent considerable difficulties.

The abandonment in 1947 of *La Fleur de l'âge* brought to an ignominious end the long and fruitful collaboration with Prévert, who had scripted all Carné's major films up that point. Although Carné collaborated with other distinguished scriptwriters, he never fully recovered his old mastery. When a new film did finally appear in 1950 it was by intention and execution a minor work. *La Marie du port*, adapted from a Simenon novel set in Normandy, was a simple realistic subject lacking the fatalistic overtones of Carné's most characteristic work. Applying his enormous technical skills, Carné captured the authentic Simenon atmosphere and extracted good performances from all his players, particularly Jean Gabin, who here set the pattern for his subsequent post-war career. Clément's *Au-delà des grilles* was the last film in which he appeared in the role which had made him famous in the 1930s: the defeated fugitive from justice. In *La Marie du port* he played for the first time his characteristic 1950s part: a powerful and successful man who, despite a possibly criminal past, remains master of his life and environment.

Jean Grémillon too had achieved popular and critical success with his two striking films during the Occupation years. His first post-war film was the documentary on the Normandy landings, *Le Six juin à l'aube* (1945), which consisted largely of an elegaic meditation on the tragic aftermath of war: the cemeteries and ruins amid which men strive to re-establish themselves. Grémillon's own wonderfully expressive music and the beautifully composed images of his four cameramen make this a very moving if sombre work. Subsequently Grémillon divided his time between administrative roles in the technicians' union and the Cinémathèque française and film making, but was unable to get backing for the ambitious feature films he planned. His two feature films of the immediate post-war years, both from imposed scripts, were full of striking moments but failed to achieve popular success. *Pattes Blanches* (1949), from a script Jean Anouilh had intended to direct himself, is a black tale of obsessive rivalry. The plot is violent and contorted, full of strange scenes and confrontations, but never fully convincing. Grémillon's handling of it, however, was masterly. The Breton backgrounds were lovingly recreated, and the acting of the whole cast of a very high standard. Several sequences were quite outstanding, most notably that of the inn-keeper's wedding, where music, settings and movement combine to splendid effect. *L'Etrange Madame X* (1951), a further tale of impossible love, was less satisfying, although Grémillon again depicted the contrasting social backgrounds with a sure touch. Finding that commercial success in the feature film eluded him, Grémillon turned more and more in the 1950s to the documentary, where much of the most exciting work of the period was to be produced.

Similar difficulties faced the two leading veteran directors who returned from Hollywood during the 1940s. Julien Duvivier chose for his return to the French studios a path similar to that adopted by Carné: a subject from a Simenon novel, set in a Parisian suburb rebuilt at considerable expense at the La Victorine studios in Nice. Duvivier's reaction to the imposed optimism and happy endings of his Hollywood years also served to push him towards a pessimism more suited to the immediate pre-war years in the resulting film, *Panique* (1946), which was scripted by his 1930s collaborator, Charles Spaak. As was to be so often the case in the 1950s, Duvivier's gloom here was all-embracing: the characters are all unsympathetic, the crowd is depicted as a destructive force and no hope or way out is offered to the hapless victim. Despite Michel Simon's masterly performance, the film was in no sense a renewal and Duvivier found it initially very difficult to re-establish for himself the position he had held in earlier years. His unease is clearly shown in the projects he was able to realise in the late 1940s: two British productions, *Anna Karenina* (1948) for Alexander Korda and *Black Jack* (1950), and a fairly routine melodrama set in a girls' boarding school, *Au royaume des cieux* (1949), co-scripted with Henri Jeanson, which offered little that was fresh to its hackneyed subject.

René Clair's return to France to make his first film there for thirteen years was more immediately successful. *Le Silence est d'or* (1947), although described by Clair himself as a comedy, reflected the new and changed mood which was to dominate all the director's post-war work. The youthful exuberance of the 1930s had been replaced by a more serious attitude to life, and although humour was never absent, greater depth was given to the characters who were never the simple marionettes of *Le Million*. For *Le Silence est d'or* Clair drew inspiration from Molière's *L'Ecole des femmes* treating the predicament of a middle-aged film producer who gives lessons on life and love to his timid assistant, only to watch the latter profit by his teaching to the extent of winning the young girl with whom the producer himself has fallen in love. The film exploits to the full the ironies of this situation and is built around a series of repetitions: the café where Monsieur Emile and his assistant each in turn take Madeleine and where they meet again after their quarrel; the sentimental tune played there which serves as the film's leitmotif; and, most strikingly of all, the helpful advice given by M. Emile which helps his assistant win the girl and subsequently rebounds on M. Emile. As so often in Clair's work, the men are more sharply characterised than the women, and Maurice Chevalier, who brings all his debonair charm to the role of the producer, is outstanding. The film is set in the Paris of 1906 and is an explicit homage to the directors of those days whose pupil Clair acknowledges himself to be. The period background is lovingly recreated in Léon Barsacq's sets and Clair includes a number of the tiny film dramas of the kind made in those years. There are also many of those characteristic touches one remembers from Clair's films: the imperturbable card players who continue their game whatever may be happening around them, and two scenes in which reality and theatricality coincide: the second meeting of Madeleine and the young assistant who, all unsuspecting, come face to face as princess and explorer in one of M. Emile's oriental tales, and the final scene where M. Emile gives the young couple his blessing under the pretext of directing them in a further scene.

Despite the success of Le Silence est d'or Clair did not work again in France for five years. His sole work of the intervening period, La Beauté du diable (1949), written in collaboration with the playwright Armand Salacrou, was shot in Italy. In this Clair broke new ground by tackling the Faust legend, being particularly attracted by the question of how Mephisto manages to trick a man as intelligent as Faust into selling his soul for worldly power. The solution devised in this very free version of the legend is characteristic of Clair's interest in dream and reality: Mephisto gives Faust youth and love, power and success without asking anything in return, and then reduces Faust to insignificant poverty again, so that he begs for the return of what he has lost. This idea is ingenious but it is also irrelevant to the legend's central concerns with good and evil. The latter in particular is a notion from which Clair shies away, and he gives his film a happy ending which negates the logic of what had gone before. Despite the playing of Michel Simon and Gérard Philipe the film is never wholly satisfying and it remains, despite its ambitions, one of the director's minor works.

*

The strength of the dominant style in France during the immediate post-war years can be measured by the difficulties faced by those directors who stood aside from its preoccupations. Robert Bresson and Jacques Tati (1908–82) belong to the same generation as the traditionalist group, but were unable to establish themselves in the 1940s. Subsequently, however, both were able slowly to build up a body of independent work, and the innovations for which they have been responsible are among the principal achievements of French cinema.

Jacques Tati, who had begun his career in the music hall and appeared in several short films from the early 1930s onwards, began his feature career with *Jour de fête*, which was finally completed, after considerable financial difficulties, in 1949, although not in colour as Tati had planned it. The film is set in a French village on the day of its annual fair, with its action framed by the arrival and departure of the lorry carrying the wooden horses for the roundabout. The action concerns the village postman (played by Tati himself) who is incited to imitate the delivery methods of the US postal service and briefly outdoes even such a rival in the speed and frenzy of his deliveries. But by the time the fair leaves all has returned to normal and François is back in his old way of life. *Jour de fête* mixes comedy of all kinds – gentle rustic humour, pure slapstick and satire on the modern craze for speed. Tati was a mime before becoming a film maker and this first film recalls silent comedy in its reliance on visual humour. He shows a predilection for long shots in which the whole action can be enclosed in a single frame and close-ups are rare. His gangling postman acts with his whole body, and the humour comes less from his facial expressions than from his antics with the ancient bicycle to which he is almost inseparably attached. François, like the villagers of Sainte-Sévère-sur-Inde (where the film was shot on location), is sympatheti-cally drawn but his predicament never gives rise to pathos. The lack of technical polish is very apparent, but music and soundtrack are used inventively and Tati's music-hall training has allowed him to master the essential of all screen comedy: the art of timing his gags. *Jour de fête* is an isolated work in the French cinema of the 1940s. It heralded no new school of comedy and four years passed before another film of Tati's appeared, but even alone it was sufficient to mark out its director and star as a wholly original talent.

Equally isolated is Robert Bresson's sole film of the period. Although he had directed two striking films during the Occupation years, it was not until 1950 that he was able to resume his career with *Journal d'un curé de campagne*, adapted by the director himself from the Georges Bernanos novel. In this adaptation Bresson was concerned to seek out the central core of the book – the spiritual development of the young priest – and prune all side issues not directly relevant to this, thereby intensifying the story and giving it the purity of a Racinian tragedy. The film traces the solitary battles fought against illness, despair and death by the young priest, played with total conviction by the hitherto inexperienced Claude Laydu. Although the film is concerned essentially with an inner conflict, contact with the outside world of the village is maintained, particularly through a subtle use of sound effects. Bresson makes every aspect of the film his own. His script rejects the conventions of the well-made 1940s film and the various episodes are held together by shots of the curé writing his diary and by his voice recounting calmly the sequence of events. In a similar way to this refusal to dramatise the conflict in some invented, external scenes, Bresson reserves the music for the emotional climaxes. The quality of the photography of the veteran Léonce-Henry Burel (a collaborator of Gance in the World War I period and in the 1920s) is superb. It never obtrudes to disturb the balance of the film, but makes skilful use of the possibilities of patterning light and shade.

The director's personality is to be felt too in the film's tone: all the emotions are muted and there is a total lack of violence or outwardly expressed passion. Bresson chose non-professionals for the minor parts and all the playing – particularly that of Laydu – is restrained and stylised, reflecting Bresson's conception of the various roles, not the actors' own interpretations. This continual understating of the emotions, together with the hero's own essentially passive submission to God's will, gives the film its particular rhythm and makes the curé's death a real climax. In his handling of this moment, Bresson's approach is revealed most clearly: a letter recounting the curé's death is read by his only real friend and gradually the image of this man is replaced by that of the Cross, which fills the screen as the voice records the curé's last words: 'Tout est grâce – All is Grace'. *Journal d'un curé de campagne* confirmed Bresson as one of the truly great directors. The very difficulty of giving the apparently unfilmic subject matter of a man's spiritual development a filmic expression seems to have prompted him to create a work in which he not only developed a highly original and personal style, but also attained a degree of depth and truth rarely equalled in the cinema. But despite the artistic success of his film Bresson had to wait five years before he was able to direct a further feature.

Other striking isolated works were made by directors previously active in documentary film making. Roger Leenhardt (b.1903) was already an influential film critic and experienced director of short films when he made *Les Dernières vacances* (1947). This film, which has become something of a minor classic, has all the personal style and scope of an autobiographical novel. It studies with sensitivity and intelligence the first awakenings of adult emotion in two young people who have grown up together, setting their problems against those of their elders who have assembled to debate the necessity of selling the family estate. The background of holiday life in a country house during the 1920s is beautifully evoked, and although the amorous intrigues of the adults are perhaps given excessive weight, the truth with which the adolescents are observed more than compensates for Leenhardt's occasional awkwardness in handling his material. It was fifteen years before Leenhardt was given a similar opportunity to make a feature and he devoted the intervening years to short film production.

Georges Rouquier (b.1909), whose first contact with the cinema had been the silent documentary, *Vendages*, shot in 1929, had returned to the film world during the Occupation to make a number of films on rural crafts. His masterpiece, however, is the feature-length documentary, *Farrebique* (1946), which took a year to shoot and traces life on a farm in the Massif Central from autumn to autumn. Inevitably it is a fragmentary work, but its very unevenness adds to its air of absolute authenticity. *Farrebique* has a double focus: the farm itself and the pattern of the seasons. The manner in which the everyday life of the family is observed – the bread-making, ploughing and harvesting, evening prayers and trips to church and bistro – recalls Rouquier's earlier shorts. The major events that take place within the family in the course of the year – the grandfather's account of the family history, his death and the birth of a baby, the younger son's injury and engagement – are all underplayed, and the slight clumsiness with which they are handled is in perfect keeping with the film's tone. Parallel to the life within the farm is the pageant of the seasons, and here Rouquier constantly stresses the dynamic aspects, particularly in the long lyrical passage celebrating the coming of spring. Rouquier once described *Farrebique* as a diary of childhood memories and this admirably defines its special quality. He does not attempt to relate rural life to wider social issues (as Luchino Visconti was to do with the life of the fishermen in *La Terra trema* two years later), and in *Farrebique* virtually the only contact with the outside world is the installation of electricity and even this is treated as a minor incident. The simple life led by those on the farm is seen as satisfying and is observed with a warm and good-natured attitude utterly lacking in condescension. Rouquier's view is always optimistic and affirmative and significantly he breaks with chronology at the end of the film so as to close not with the grandfather's death, but with the son's engagement and the promise of spring.

Unable to follow *Farrebique* with the further studies of French life which he planned, Rouquier turned back to the short film. He collaborated with Jean Painlevé on *L'Oeuvre scientifique de Pasteur* (1947), resumed his studies of craftsmanship with *Le Chaudronnier* (1949), and produced a remarkable epic of land reclamation in the Camargue, *Le Sel de la terre* (1950), in which his personality found as rich an expression as in *Farrebique*. The 1940s were a rich period of production in the area of the documentary. One of Jean Epstein's last works was a poetic documentary about the Breton coast, *Le Tempestaire* (1947). The doyen of French scientific film makers, Jean Painlevé, contributed a number of films from which his sense of humour and his inventiveness were never absent, among them *Le Vampire* (1945) and *Assassins d'eau douce* (1947). Younger film makers were also beginning to make their mark. Alain Resnais, who had worked as editor on Nicole Védrès's widely seen *Paris 1900* (1948), produced a series of masterly studies of painters and paintings: *Van Gogh* (1948), *Gauguin* (1950) and *Guernica* (1950). 1949 also saw the appearance of Georges Franju's riveting study of the Paris abbatoirs, *Le Sang des bêtes*, followed in 1950 by *En passant par la Lorraine*. Other striking documentaries of the 1945–50 period include Eli Lotar's *Aubervilliers* (1945), Roger Leenhardt's *La Naissance du cinéma* (1946), Yannick Bellon's *Goëmans* (1948), and *Les Charmes de l'existence* (1949), co-directed by Grémillon and Pierre Kast.

Aside from this documentary stream, Jean-Pierre Melville (1917–73) began his career without union membership (or indeed the rights to the novel) with an adaptation of Vercors's *Le Silence de la mer* (1947). Melville followed the original closely, powerfully conveying the Occupation atmosphere and obtaining excellent performances from his actors. *Le Silence de la mer* has some of the stiffness one might expect from a first film made on a very low budget, but its originality is striking. In its combination of a spoken commentary and illustrative non-synchronous images it anticipates a whole area of French 1950s production and the photographic style of Henri Decaë is quite remarkable. As in his later work Melville draws on his knowledge of classic Hollywood cinema to build up atmosphere. Two years later Melville worked in close collaboration with Jean Cocteau on a low-budget adaptation of the latter's novel *Les Enfants terribles*. The film lovingly reconstitutes the characteristic elements of the Cocteau universe: the fatal snowball fight (with which the film opens, echoing *Le Sang d'un poète*), the incestuous relationships, the notions of order and disorder and the underlying obsession with death. The collaboration of two such contrasting personalities as Melville and Cocteau was not entirely successful and the latter's insistence on the same actress playing the parts of both Dargelos and Agathe is at least a partial failure. But the success in capturing so much of the tone of a difficult book may be attributed partly to Cocteau's own spoken commentary and Melville's idea of using classical music (Bach and Vivaldi) to accompany the action.

Jean Cocteau himself was the only one of these independents to work consistently on projects of his choice in the cinema of the 1940s. He had resumed work in the cinema with several scripts directed by others during the Occupation. Then, in 1945, he himself directed an adaptation of the fairy-tale, *Le Belle et la bête*. Cocteau's version is very much a personal·one and his approach is far from the childlike innocence which he asks of his audience in a spoken prologue. Visually the film is most sophisticated: costumes and photographic style are decorative rather than functional and have their roots in the Dutch paintings of Vermeer. The handling of the supernatural elements exemplifies Cocteau's search for a 'realism of the unreal' and he has solved the problems of characterisation by adopting parody and humour in his treatment of the minor figures. With the two central characters he emphasises the ambiguity of the situation: in Belle's attitude towards the Beast (whose animal qualities are emphasised in Jean Marais's make-up and gestures) and in the double use of Marais as dissolute lover and Prince Charming. After this appropriation of a fairy-tale to his own personal mythology, Cocteau turned to the adaptation of his own works. In addition to his work on *Les Enfants terribles*, he also directed versions of two plays: a stilted version of *L'Aigle à deux têtes* (1947) and a far more interesting version of *Les Parents terribles* (1948), in which the intense theatricality of the original is emphasised by the florid acting style, unusual cutting and refusal to broaden out the play and take the action outside its key interior sets.

Orphée (1950) is undoubtedly Cocteau's major achievement in the cinema. It depicts the love of the poet Orphée (Jean Marais) for the Princess (Maria Casarès) who is 'one of the innumerable functionaries of Death' and whose constant journeying between this world and the next have made her susceptible to human emotions. *Orphée* makes full use of the trappings of the real world: black-clad motorcyclists, machine guns, Rolls-Royces and mysterious messages which echo wartime Resistance codes. At the same time the solidity of the world is disturbed by Cocteau's delight in the conjuring possibilities of the medium, which he uses more extensively than in *La Belle et la bête*:

trick shots using mercury tubs, plain glass substituted for mirror, duplicate rooms, doubles, and on occasion rear projection. The film embodies perfectly Cocteau's personal mythology and conception of the poet as an exceptional being who has a unique and intimate relation with death. Cocteau regarded the myth of Orpheus as *his* myth, for he felt himself to be a man with one foot in life and the other in death. For him the conflict of life and death was not a contrast of light and darkness, but a matter of degrees of greyness and twilight merging into each other. For a work dealing so largely with death, *Orphée* is remarkably idyllic in tone. There is no sense of terror here, for death is a beautiful woman. There is no sense of physical decline or decay and death is totally lacking in irrevocability or awesomeness. *Orphée* is a remarkable personal work, realised in the conventional production structures of French cinema and its existence – like the isolated works of Bresson and Tati – throws into perspective the traditional, backward-looking quality of the bulk of French production of the period.

*

The limitations of the renewal of French cinema after 1945 are very apparent in retrospect. The effect of making their debuts amid the ambiguities of the Occupation period seems to have remained with the 1940s generation of film makers, and Raymond Borde even goes so far as to speculate that the period up to 1950 should perhaps be described as 'post-Vichy'. The enthusiasm generated by the Liberation was soon dissipated, and the new freedom they enjoyed was not accompanied by any spontaneous rediscovery of reality. Seen today, *La Bataille du rail* is more remarkable for its careful shaping than any sense of an immediately lived past. True there were limitations of formal censorship, but it seems fair too to talk of self-censorship, as directors and writers avoided confronting the realities of post-war France and shaped even material relating to the values they held most strongly into carefully constructed commercial packages. The persuasive tone of much of this late 1940s work was a self-defeating irony – which united works otherwise as different as Autant-Lara's *Le Diable au corps*, Allégret's *Une si jolie petite plage* and Clair's *Le Silence est d'or*. This tone found its perfect expression in the calculated effects of the meticulously shaped flashback structure which characterised the dominant output of the period. This was a time of predominantly studio filming, with strongly hierarchical crews of specialist technicians whose skills were the result of long training and the acceptance of given rules of performance and procedure. The lack of an authentically personal approach was in part a function of the conception of the director's role as the person who realises a given script, in the writing of which construction and dialogue are seen as essentially distinct (and often the work of different specialists). Even those, like Clair, who were the complete authors of their work, attributed less importance to the moment of directing than to the composition of the script. It was the avoidance of these constraints which made the spontaneity of some of Becker's lighter work so refreshing and which characterised such master works as *Jour de fête, Journal d'un curé de campagne* or *Orphée*. The restrictions of the dominant style, by contrast, became more and more apparent in the 1950s as the academicism which characterised Delannoy's work from the very start engulfed most of the others of his generation.

9   The Tradition of Quality
1951–57

Si le cinéma français existe par une centaine de films chaque année, il est bien entendu que dix ou douze seulement méritent de retenir l'attention des critiques et des cinéphiles . . .
Les dix ou douze films constituent ce que l'on a joliment appelé la *Tradition de la Qualité*, ils forcent par leur ambition l'admiration de la presse étrangère, défendent deux fois l'an les couleurs de la France à Cannes où à Venise ou, depuis 1946, ils râflent assez regulièrement médailles, lions d'or et grands prix.

François Truffaut, 1954

The interventions of the state in the organisation of the cinema during the 1950s took on a paradoxical role. On the one hand, the legislation concerning state aid was renewed in 1953, accompanied by an important new criterion: to gain state support, a film had not simply to be seen as a potentially viable commercial proposition (as was the case in the United Kingdom) but also to have a certain aesthetic quality. This notion of quality had a very positive long-term impact, particularly as the 1953 legislation was concerned with offering support to a high level of production of first-rate short films. On the other hand, the early 1950s saw a great deal of state interference in terms of censorship – the banning of such anti-colonial short films as René Vautier's *Afrique 1950* or Alain Resnais and Chris Marker's *Les Statues meurent aussi* and demands for radical changes in certain projects proposed by feature directors like André Cayatte and Louis Daquin.

But neither the state involvement nor the censorship rulings is an adequate explanation of the extent to which the French cinema of the early and mid-1950s became so largely a period of stagnation. The dominance of the traditionally minded 1940s group led by Clouzot, Clément, Becker and Autant-Lara remained unchallenged, despite the return of two further distinguished veterans, Max Ophuls and Jean Renoir, for there was no breakthrough by a new and younger generation. In this mainstream of French cinema there was no real sense of innovation and it was as if these directors, having established themselves in the late 1940s after long years of assistantships and routine technical assignments, were principally concerned with building themselves careers which would last through the 1950s and beyond. In itself this was no bad thing, but for this particular group it implied an inward-looking cinema which turned its back not only on the profound changes undergone by society in metropolitan France but also on events in the French overseas empire. For these were years which saw the end of the French war in Indo-China with the fall of Dien-Bien-Phu and the beginnings of the Algerian revolution – events which the film making of the period totally ignored.

Faced with such momentous events, this generation, which had lived through the Occupation during its formative years, retreated into a studio world of film making and used scripts which were expertly made, but tailored to a formula which reduced Raymond Radiguet and Stendhal, Marcel Aymé and Zola to identical patterns of style and narrative construction. The notion of 'quality' film making began to take on a pejorative meaning and in his critical article on 'A Certain Tendency of the French Cinema', François Truffaut, then a critic on the *Cahiers du cinéma*, attacked the leading scriptwriting team, Jean Aurenche and Pierre Bost:

> To their way of thinking, every story includes characters A, B, C, and D. In the interior of that equation, everything is organised in function of criteria known to them alone. The sun rises and sets like clockwork, characters disappear, others are invented, the script deviates little by little from the original and becomes a whole, formless but brilliant; a new film, step by step, makes its solemn entrance into the 'Tradition of Quality'.

The 1950s saw many remarkable works of sound craftsmanship, but the focus was always away from actuality, from the present itself, and on to a past which could perhaps be better controlled. These directors were not seeking to create their own personal worlds; they remained dependent on pre-existing literary works, on their very professional scriptwriters, on star performers who frequently had a background in theatre, and on a host of highly talented specialist technical collaborators. It was the meticulous, at times almost maniacal, reconstruction of the surface detail of their period settings which concerned these directors, not the relevance of their stories to the contemporary world in which they, and their audiences, lived. Only Autant-Lara, himself a designer by training, experimented with the symbolic use of a deliberately unreal decor – in *Marguerite de la nuit* – but this film was in fact more of a nostalgic look back at the film maker's debut in the

1920s than a genuine release into a fresh world of the imagination. The sense of distance is increased by the directors' own detachment from their characters. Already apparent in the late 1940s, this tendency grew during the 1950s, overtaking even Jacques Becker in many of his later, more routine, works.

During these years of the 1950s, the qualities lacking are those of innovation and risk. Significantly those of this generation who did at times seek to escape from the styles which, by the middle of the decade, had become rigid formulas, dreamed of films they were never to make. Thus, during the last five years of his life, Becker longed to be given a little money, a cameraman and some Eastmancolor film, so as to be able to emulate Robert Flaherty and shoot what he called 'his little Moroccan Nanook'. What he in fact made in North Africa was a version of *Ali-Baba* with Fernandel. Likewise Clouzot turned down various offers in 1950 and set out to make 'Le Voyage au Brésil', which was to be an account of his discovery of the homeland of his new wife, Véra, but this project too ran into production difficulties. What Clouzot shot was one of the great suspense thrillers of the decade, *Le Salaire de la peur*, set in a Latin America reconstructed on the outskirts of Nîmes. René Clément ventured outside the confines of the studio and used his camera in quite a new and fluent way while on location in England for *Monsieur Ripois/Knave of Hearts* in 1954. But back in France, he once more turned to the studio reconstruction of a period setting with *Gervaise*.

In some ways the directors of this generation became the victims of their own critical and commercial success. Throughout the 1950s they moved slowly but seemingly inevitably towards bigger production budgets, colour and wide-screen. Soon they had to face the whole machinery of the expensive international co-production, designed for an anonymous multinational audience and with pretensions which were commercial rather than artistic. Significant works in this respect are the film on which Clément worked during 1957 (and which was released in May 1958), *Barrage contre le Pacifique/La digua sul Pacifico*, Becker's trivial later films such as *Ali-Baba et les quarante voleurs* or *Les Aventures d'Arsène Lupin*, and Jean Delannoy's empty period spectacles like *Notre-Dame de Paris* and *La Princesse de Clèves*. With the true independents of this generation still marginalised – Tati and Bresson again each made only one film in the five-year period – much of the best work of the time was accomplished outside the mainstream: in little-seen, low-budget works like the early films of Astruc and Varda and, above all, in the documentary school which reached new heights at this time.

*

One of the few film makers of the 1940s generation to confront the realities of contemporary French society was the ex-lawyer and novelist, André Cayatte, whose first work of value was his tenth film, *Les Amants de Vérone* (1948) which was made, significantly enough, from one of Jacques Prévert's last scripts. The films on which Cayatte's reputation rests are films of a rather different kind, in which he revived, briefly at least, the interest of the *film noir*. In four films – *Justice est faite* (1950), *Nous sommes tous des assassins* (1952), *Avant le déluge* (1953) and *Le Dossier noir* (1955) – Cayatte and his scriptwriter Charles Spaak tackled a variety of social and legal problems, such as euthanasia, the death penalty and juvenile delinquency, in a mood of black accusation. Carefully realistic settings, unknown young players and solid character actors, together with sober if unexciting camerawork are used to focus the audience's attention on the film's argument, which is expounded with all the explicitness of a legal testimony. The films themselves are sincere, forceful and courageous, but they suffer from the sacrificing of all to polemics. In addition, Cayatte is unable to evolve a visual style adequate to encompass his savage insights into the working of society. Cayatte continued directing prolifically into the late 1970s, but none of his later films – which include such popular successes as *Le Passage du Rhin* (1960) – has the same interest as this early 1950s work. With Cayatte's decline into routine commercial work and the parallel loss of vigour in the work of Yves Allégret (despite occasional interesting works such as *Les Orgueilleux* (1953) and a version of *Germinal* (1962)), the interest of the *film noir* as the characteristic product of the first post-war generation of film makers comes to an end.

For Henri-Georges Clouzot, the early 1950s were marked by the production, after numerous difficulties, of one of his finest and most successful films, *Le Salaire de la peur* (1953). The construction is such that the film may be divided into two parts. The first sets the scene in the hot, squalid little town of Las Piedras and revolves around a group of European layabouts trapped there. Their situation seems as hopeless as that facing Jean Gabin in the pre-war *Pépé-le-Moko* or *Le Jour se lève*, until suddenly a means of escape is offered. The American oil company which virtually owns the town needs four men to drive two lorries loaded with nitro-glycerine three hundred miles to a burning oil well. Under the strain of the nightmare drive, which occupies the whole second half of the film, the characters of the four men are laid bare. The horror and tension are skilfully maintained throughout, up to a final ironic crash on the hillside, when the sole survivor meets his death. The stress on the comradeship of men facing death together makes this Clouzot's most optimistic statement about human nature, although in the end nothing, it seems, can avert disaster. There is even a touch of sentimentality here to lighten the gloom, as the two Frenchmen in the group exchange memories of Paris. If the opening sequences of *Le Salaire de la peur* show Clouzot's ability in fixing his characters in their settings, the latter scenes show his unrivalled mastery in the creation of suspense. By using the very simplest means with the utmost skill and concentration, he plays on the audience's nerves. Most of the time the camera is focused on the faces of the four characters as they tackle a succession of hazards – a rutted stretch of roadway, a rotting bridge, a huge rock that has to be dynamited and, for the Frenchmen, the oil-filled pool left by the explosion of the preceding lorry. In terms of sheer construction and narrative skill, the film is a masterpiece; its tension, relieved only by a few necessary touches of humour, is utterly unrelenting.

Clouzot's subsequent two thrillers, *Les Diaboliques* (1955) and *Les Espions* (1957) are more difficult to evaluate since in each case the director first painstakingly establishes a solidly realistic setting in the manner of *Quai des orfèvres* and *Le Salaire de la peur*, then – seemingly gratuitously – moves away from it in the latter part of the film. In *Les Diaboliques* the setting of a shabby, provincial private school is thoroughly and methodically built up, the tensions between the three principal characters revealed and a first murder shown in brutal and convincing detail. Then inexplicable things start to happen and the suspense that has been built up is dissipated in a virtuoso display of plot-twisting, which leaves the audience reeling, but destroys the credibility of all that has gone before. *Les Espions* too shows the intrusion of the unreal into a French provincial setting – in this case a psychiatric clinic – which has been carefully documented. In this case the characters are shown from the first to be caricatures and the dividing line between the insane and the spies hiding in their midst is never clear. The film's mixture of real violence and torture with moments of pure farce is unsatisfying, and the whole lacks both logic and tension. Both films are clear signs of an attempt to move beyond the psychological realism which characterises the bulk of the work of this generation of film makers, but for Clouzot such an escape can only – it seems – be towards the over-elaboration of plot and a parodistic pseudo-logic that in no way relates to our experience.

With *Le Mystère Picasso* (1956), an hour-long documentary depicting the great painter at work, Clouzot broke away from the constraints of the thriller genre, but characteristically it is Picasso's ability to create an image out of nothing, to modify, magnify or invert it, which attracts the director's camera. This draws attention to the continued paradox of Clouzot's situation, torn between realism and the unreal but never quite attaining the Kafkaesque illogicality to which he aspires. Everything in a Clouzot film is pre-planned, every movement of the camera is plotted and the actors are ruthlessly drilled to produce the effects which the director has anticipated. But then he seems to revolt against the ordered, too easily comprehensible world he has created and seeks to prove his own dominance by turning it – and the spectator's assumptions – upside down. The result is an enormously powerful, but in some fundamental ways unsatisfying, form of cinema.

Jacques Becker's progress through the 1950s begins brilliantly, but subsequently tails off into near insignificance (although he was to show the full scope of his powers in a last film made shortly before his death in 1960). *Casque d'or* (1952), a tragic love story set in Paris at the turn of the century and based on law reports of the period, is undoubtedly Becker's masterpiece. Here the director appears as a genuine creator, for the whole conception of the film, as well as most of the script and dialogue, is his. In its final form the film is beautifully constructed, moving from the untroubled life of the craftsman, Manda, through his meeting and love for the beautiful Casque d'or, to the murders he is driven to commit and on to the final horror of condemnation and execution. Becker shows all the hurried ugliness and squalor that surrounds the guillotine, so that we feel this execution to be an affront to humanity. The scenes within the film unfold with a fine sense of rhythm and the action moves easily from the studio-built interiors to the open air and back again. No attempt is made to romanticise the pimps, prostitutes and criminals who form the centre of the film's action, and the playing of Charles Dauphin, as Leca, their leader, reveals a character as complex as he is unlikeable – one of the few such in Becker's work. The playing of the two lovers is exceptional. Serge Reggiani brings to the part of Manda an inner strength, only partially concealed behind a frail exterior, that drives him twice to murder: once to obtain Casque d'or and again to avenge the treachery of Leca. Simone Signoret as Marie, nicknamed Casque d'or because of her flowing blond hair, reveals a ripe beauty and moves convincingly from carefree enjoyment of her own power over men to tragic helplessness as she watches Manda's death. The idyllic love scenes between these two have a truth and sensuous quality rare in cinema. In *Casque d'or* all Becker's key qualities are present: a concern with love and friendship, an exactitude in the handling of background detail and an ability to sustain transitions of mood and atmosphere. But here too, in *Casque d'or*, there is the added dimension of death, for in this film the love is of a kind that drives a man to murder and the friendship of a degree that demands self-sacrifice.

Nothing Becker directed in the following five years measures up to *Casque d'or. Rue de l'Estrapade* (1953) echoes, without developing or adding to, the late 1940s Parisian trilogy. *Touchez pas au grisbi* (1954) initiates – along with Jules Dassin's *Du rififi chez les hommes* (another Albert Simonin adaptation made the following year) – a vogue for thriller subjects, but it is a minor work, where the mark of the director is to be found less in the narrative development than in the *temps morts. Ali-Baba et les quarante voleurs* (1954) and *Les Aventures d'Arsène Lupin* (1956) are merely commercial works and the director is never truly engaged even in the more immediately fascinating story of Modigliani's later years, *Montparnasse 19* (1957), a project on which Ophuls had been working at the time of his death.

While Becker treated contemporary France only in the form of a light comedy and a thriller, Autant-Lara made exclusively films with historical settings in the first post-war decade. *L'Auberge rouge* (1951) was a period comedy which used the elements of farce for a remarkably outspoken attack on Catholicism. Although Aurenche and Bost's script is at times a little over-explicit, the film contains a wonderful collection of priestly and bourgeois foibles, at the centre of which is Fernandel's portrait of a monk who combines cowardice with cupidity. Throughout the film appearances are deceptive: the welcoming inn is a veritable slaughterhouse, the respectable travellers a collection of mean and callous gluttons, the friendly-looking snowman a dead man's resting place. Much of the humour is coarsely anticlerical and the makers exploit with relish the scenes of Fernandel carrying out his priestly functions. After a minor work (made without Aurenche and Bost), *Le Bon dieu sans confession* (1953), Autant-Lara adapted Colette's novel, *Le Blé en herbe* (1954), in which he and his writers capture perfectly both the embarrassments and uncertainties of adolescence and the plight of a woman who retreats from an affair with a much younger man when she finds the situation impossible to handle. The playing is uniformly good, especially the beautifully judged performance of Edwige Feuillère, and the whole film is handled with great delicacy and insight, so that the theme, though disturbing, is never offensive.

In *Le Rouge et le noir* (1954) Aurenche and Bost made an honourable attempt at transposing the complexities of Stendhal's novel, but even three hours of screen time was insufficient to capture its full richness. The most successful scenes are those at the beginning of the film depicting Gérard Philipe and Danielle Darrieux as lovers separated, as so often in Autant-Lara's work, by both age and social position. The later parts of the film showing the hero's hesitations between the scarlet of the military uniform and the black of priesthood are less satisfying. Despite an attempt to order the material into a pattern of flashbacks and the employment of a first-person narration, the film fails to encompass adequately Stendhal's combination of analytic style and melodramatic plot development. After this over-ambitious film, *Marguerite de la nuit* (1955), a version of the Faust legend set in the 1920s, was an experiment using deliberately stylised and unreal settings, with changes of colour to indicate mood and atmosphere. The film is a reminder that the director began his career in the 1920s as designer on Marcel L'Herbier's films, but its final effect is cold and stilted. *La Traversée de Paris* (1956), which was another partial success, is set during the Occupation and tells of two men who carry four suitcases full of pork across Paris for a black-market butcher. The details of the journey are fascinating and often very funny and the contrast of the two men (played by Jean Gabin and Bourvil) is vividly drawn. Satire and irony abound and Autant-Lara is not afraid to question cherished beliefs about the period, although some of the transitions from farce to tragedy are awkwardly handled.

While Autant-Lara's attempts to widen the scope of his work to take in Stendhal or the Faust legend cannot be deemed wholly successful, he does show a consistency in the way in which he expounds his idiosyncratic views through a wide range of subjects. The themes of opposition to war and vindication of adolescent sexuality are con-tinued and developed in this 1950s work, and *L'Auberge rouge*, which has claims on being considered one of the most anti-clerical films ever made in France, reveals most distinctly the opposition to the Church, which – along with opposition to the army and the bourgeoisie – gives his work its characteristic tone. Autant-Lara's ability to express himself forthrightly within the context of the commercially successful feature film is refreshing, even though the formal structures of his work are unoriginal.

The youngest member of this leading group of directors, René Clément, produced the most satisfying group of films in the early 1950s. *Jeux interdits* (1952), a return to the theme of war made from a script by Aurenche and Bost, dealt with the subject obliquely, seeing it through the eyes of two children. After a strikingly edited opening sequence showing the machine-gunning of a column of refugees, the film concentrates on a little Parisian girl whose parents are killed in the attack and on the young peasant boy who befriends her. The film draws us into their secret world, where, away from adult eyes but influenced by the carnage around them, they build a cemetery for dead animals. The adult world is caricatured, but the children are observed with real sympathy and understanding. Clément has drawn from his young players performances of great naturalness and his recreation of their private world and growing obsession with death is conveyed in masterly fashion through the images and Narcisco Yepes's sensitive guitar accompaniment. Undeterred by his own inability to speak English, Clément went to London to make the dual-language film *Monsieur Ripois/Knave of Hearts* (1954), in which Gérard Philipe was supported by a largely English cast. The film is a sophisticated comedy telling of the adventures of a young Frenchman who fills the emptiness of his life in London with a succession of amorous conquests. The film's flashback technique, whereby the hero gives an account of his four principal loves in an attempt to convince a fifth young woman of his sincerity, is effective and gives the film the ironic tone so necessary for this style of comedy. But the film's greatest merit is its photographic style (under the direction of Oswald Morris) which captures the unfashionable face of London with great fluency and total authenticity. *Gervaise* (1956), Clément's return to French studio film making, was an adaptation by Aurenche and Bost of Zola's *L'Assommoir*. As the title indicates, the emphasis has been shifted from the problems of alcoholism to the specific fate of the individual characters, the young Gervaise and her drunken husband. Clément's method of approach to his period setting was to demand absolute fidelity of detail, but this does not prevent the film from coming alive in a whole succession of superbly vivid scenes. Nor does Clément show squeamishness in his portrayal of the story's horror: all the degradation is here, from women wrestling to the husband lying in his own vomit.

While Clément already showed in the 1940s and 1950s the taste for international film production which was to become dominant from the 1960s onwards, his finest work of this period is deeply rooted in French life and history: the world of the Resistance in *La Bataille du rail*, that of the contemporary peasant in *Jeux interdits* and that of nineteenth-century Paris in *Gervaise*. Each of these worlds is treated with complete realism, so that every word and gesture is convincing. Clément's approach is obsessively meticulous: to prepare François Périer for his role of the alcoholic husband in *Gervaise* Clément took him to mental asylums and made him take notes of his observations. Overshadowing the characters in Clément's best work is the reality of death: the execution which awaits the Resistance workers in *La Bataille du rail*; the slaughter that grows to obsess the children of *Jeux interdits*; the madness and delirium preceding the death of an alcoholic in *Gervaise*. In this way the experience mirrored in these films is heightened to near-tragedy, while their dramatic force is created by the contrast of the vitality with which the characters confront their fate.

*

Max Ophuls returned to France, which had been his home from 1933 till 1940, in 1949. *La Ronde* (1950), adapted from a play by Arthur Schnitzler and set in a fairy-tale Vienna of 1900, was one of the director's greatest successes and with it he formed the team of collaborators he was to work with until his death in 1957. The film is full of cynicism and worldly wit, and Ophuls takes an apparent delight in the manipulation of his characters. He exploits to the full the irony of their situation: the fact that while the characters change their partners, their gestures remain the same, so that they are in turn deceivers and deceived, involuntarily echoing each other's words and sentiments. To link the various episodes, Ophuls used a waltz by Oskar Straus, the recurring image of a roundabout and the *meneur de jeu* played by Anton Walbrook. The latter is in a sense a personification of the director himself, manipulating the characters and making them dance to the tune of the waltz. The freedom of the *meneur de jeu* contrasts with the captivity of the other characters. The fact that the circle is never broken gives a sense of fatality to the coupling of the characters and the dialogue is littered with epigrams about the incompatibility of love and happiness. Next Ophuls chose three stories by Guy de Maupassant to make up *Le Plaisir* (1952). Despite the unifying theme – pleasure has nothing to do with happiness – this is the most disjointed of Ophuls's films. He strove to give it unity and shape by balancing the longer and humorous central story – *La Maison Tellier*, about a brothel closed for the first communion of the madam's niece – with two shorter ones. In the first story, *Le Masque*, we see a woman who sacrifices herself to the man she loves, while in the third, *Le Modèle*, the roles are reversed and it is the man who makes the sacrifices. As in all his films, Ophuls indulges his passion for tracking and crane shots. Typical in this respect is his treatment of the Maison Tellier: although the interior was built in the greatest detail, the camera never enters it, contenting itself with circling the exterior, climbing the walls and peering in through the windows at the activity within.

For *Madame de . . .* (1953) Ophuls adapted a story by Louise de Vilmorin, which attracted him because the action turned, like a roundabout, around a scarcely visible axis: a pair of earrings. Husband, wife and lover all own them at some time or other, until they complete the circle to give the husband proof of his wife's infidelity. Decor and costumes play a vital part in the film and the camera tracks and whirls amid the curtains, mirrors and chandeliers, catching all the glitter of the ball, pursuing the characters as they move between theatre, dance and reception. The freedom with which Ophuls handles his marionettes and subordinates them to his aesthetic design is perhaps best shown in the dance sequence which condenses a whole series of meetings between Madame de . . . and her lover into a single waltz. *Lola Monte's* (1955), Ophuls's last film, was a fitting culmination to his life's work, in which he was given the sort of resources normally available to the tried commercial director (such as the star, Martine Carol's husband, Christian-Jaque): a large budget, a thirty-three-week shooting schedule, colour, cinemascope and a cast of international stars. When completed, the film turned out to contain the very essence of the director's art and to be, at the same time, an enormous commercial failure. The subject of the film was of little concern to Ophuls: all the interest lay in the treatment. The film begins and ends in the circus, where Lola (once the mistress of Liszt and of the King of Bavaria) is reduced to selling kisses, and her story is told in flashbacks, provoked by the ringmaster's narration. Ophuls's camera, in this his only colour film, is never still: it pivots and circles restlessly through the extravagant decor crammed with grills and stairways, performs arabesques within the ever-changing decor of the circus ring, sweeps after the characters, and peeps through windows, curtains and doorways.

For Ophuls the essence of the cinema lay in the play of light, the juggling with surfaces. His camera tracks, turns and zigzags in virtuoso fashion so as to catch every facet of the intricate settings through which – simply to multiply the difficulties – the characters move incessantly. The themes of the transitoriness of pleasure and the precariousness of happiness recur again and again, their reappearance emphasised by the continual recourse to a dream-world turn-of-the-century setting. The same images crop up continually in films made over a period of twenty-five years (the lovers' meeting in the snow, the duel . . .) to give Ophuls's work its striking stylistic unity. The stories Ophuls chooses are slight, tending to the episodic, and great care is expended on the shaping of the pattern of events, but never does Ophuls' camera pause to analyse or probe his ever-recurring subject: the tribulations of a beautiful woman in love.

For Jean Renoir, who had left France after completing *La Règle du jeu* in 1939, the years of exile in Hollywood had brought mixed fortunes. Although a new period of his career opens with the making of *The River* in India in 1950, it was not until four years later that he explored his new approach in France. In between he made *The Golden Coach/Le Carrosse d'or* (1952), an international production shot in three languages in Italy. Like this film, *French Cancan* (1954), which marked Renoir's return to the French studios after an absence of fourteen years, was a homage to the theatre. Set in the Paris of the 1880s *French Cancan* was an evocation of the world of the director's father, with street scenes carefully designed to recall the paintings of the Impressionists and a particularly subtle use of colour. The film's visual qualities were perhaps Renoir's prime concern, for the plot, dealing with the founding of the Moulin Rouge, is no more significant than that of the average backstage musical and the characters hardly count. But the whole film, building up to a twenty-minute cancan climax, leaves an impression of intense vitality. The same qualities are to be found in *Elena et les hommes* (1956) which Renoir described as a musical fantasy and which dealt in a lighthearted way with General Boulanger's bid for dictatorial power in Paris during the 1880s. All the characteristic elements of the late Renoir films are here: colour and movement, good humour spilling over into awkward farce and a wildly satirical look at the rich and ambitious.

Renoir's films of the 1950s are strongly marked by nostalgia. *The River* is set in a dream India of happy understanding between colonists and Hindus where sorrow and tragedy are swallowed up in gay, colourful native festivals. *The Golden Coach* takes us to an eighteenth-century colony where the underprivileged are notably lacking, while both *French Cancan* and *Elena et les hommes* give a very romanticised view of Paris in the 1880s. Jean Renoir always had a hierarchic view of society and much of the impact and comedy of his best work comes from the interaction of two worlds, masters and servants. This vision carries over into the later films, so that we find colonists and natives in *The River*, actors and courtiers in *The Golden Coach*, the rich and their servants in *Elena et les hommes*. The fusion of these two worlds, where it does occur, happens through the medium of love. But if love knows no boundaries, it remains a transient emotion and these relationships are just part of the eternal changing of partners that characterises Renoir's universe. The real impact of Renoir's later work comes from the director's handling of the elements of spectacle. Only two of his films after 1950 were shot in black and white and the others all rely for their effect on the interweaving of colour, movement and music. All were made in conscious opposition to the naturalistic and pessimistic conception of life which was so prevalent in post-war French cinema. Two of these works, *French Cancan* and *The Golden Coach*, exalt the theatre as the antithesis to life, more real it seems than dull reality itself. In others, such as *The River*, nature is contrasted with human society. The affectionate humour, zest for life and warm humanity of these 1950s films would rank Renoir high among film makers, even if he had not made an even greater succession of films twenty or so years before.

René Clair also turned his back on the contemporary world in his 1950s films. *Les Belles-de-nuit* (1952) marked his return to pure comedy. The initial idea was to create a comic version of *Intolerance* in which – through the use of dreams – interwoven stories would build up to a simultaneous climax. The film is neatly constructed and the balance between dream and reality always held. All the dreams of the music-teacher hero (Gérard Philipe) grow out of his everyday life and all the women in them are romanticised versions of people he meets every day. The various epochs in which these dreams are set – Paris in 1900, the Algeria of 1830, the French Revolution and the age of the Three Musketeers – are linked by the recurring figure of an old man whose continual reminders of the superiority of the 'good old days' serve to trigger a new jump back in time. The sounds which plague the music teacher are balanced by the lighthearted rhythms of the music by Georges Van Parys (who worked on *Le Million*) and the carefree tone is preserved throughout.

With *Les Grandes manoeuvres* (1955) and *Porte des lilas* (1957) Clair adopted a more serious dramatic tone. The first is a love story with near-tragic overtones set in a provincial garrison town in the summer of 1914. The setting of this classic tale of a nonchalant seducer who falls in love but is unable to convince his beloved of his sincerity allows Clair to draw yet another portrait of bourgeois society and show its underlying hypocrisies and deceits. The numerous scenes of background detail and the large number of subplots are not gratuitous, for society plays a crucial role in determining the romance of the central couple, most of whose meetings take place under the keen eyes of those around them and give scope for malicious tongues. Yet it is the figures of the two lovers – beautifully played in their very different styles by Gérard Philipe and Michèle Morgan – that stand out as Clair's most fully rounded characters. *Porte des lilas* is perhaps Clair's major treatment of the theme of friendship, just as *Les Grandes manoeuvres* was his most revealing analysis of love. The tone of the film is generally sombre – Clair himself described it as a dramatic comedy – and comic highlights are rare. The Parisian setting which forms the background to the film and gives it its title has been lovingly recreated by Clair and his designer Léon Barsacq, and the best scenes are those that grow directly out of it and share its air of slight stylisation: the muted scenes between the hero and the girl he ineffectually loves and those among the regulars in the bistro owned by the girl's father.

The sense of continuity in style and vision in Clair's work is very strong but the later films of the 1950s have their distinctive tone and mood. The most successful of the post-1945 films are the dramatic comedies. *Les Belles-de-nuit*, though charming, is an insubstantial work and the happy ending of *La Beauté du diable* negates what has gone before. The tendency towards the tragic at times threatens to destroy the delicate balance of Clair's world, which is not really robust enough to encompass death. The logic of *Le Silence est d'or* points to an unhappy ending, which is avoided only by M. Emile's sense of humour (his last words are: 'Do you like happy endings, Mademoiselle? So do I'). Clair apparently shot a suicide scene for *Les Grandes manoeuvres*, although he rejected it at the editing stage, and it is the violent ending of *Porte des lilas* which prevents the film from being more than a partial success. This new seriousness derives from the greater weight given to the emotions of the leading characters. Clair has always been a complete author, writing his own scripts and dialogue as well as directing. His work increasingly reflects both his own nostalgia and his literary interests. When, in *Les Belles-de-nuit*, he satirises those who believe in the superiority of the 'good old days' he is dealing with a tendency in himself. The commentaries he wrote to accompany his published scripts show that he has consciously written his own versions of *L'Ecole des femmes* and the legends of Faust and Don Juan. His comments too tend to play down the directing role, yet the scenes one remembers from a Clair film are precisely those where his sense of *mise-en-scène*, his humour and his irony fuse completely: the scene where M. Emile and his young assistant, both in love with the same girl, carry on their private dialogues, on opposite sides of the angle of the studio wall; the lovers' stroll in *Les Grandes manoeuvres* which is commented on and dialogued by a succession of interested onlookers; or the small boys in *Porte des lilas*, seen through a window, who mime the gangster's actions as they are read out from a newspaper.

The work of two other veterans of the 1930s, Marcel Carné and Julien Duvivier, does not hold the same interest. *Juliette ou la clef des songes* (1951) was a project which Carné had first developed as early as 1939. It contains the same themes of fatalism and impossible love as his best work of that period, but lacks the sense of poetry possessed by Carné's work with Jacques Prévert. As a result, despite an interesting opening, the impression left by the film is one of coldness and, ultimately, banality. *Thérèse Raquin* (1953) was a modernisation of Zola's novel, scripted by Charles Spaak and set in present-day Lyons. Carné deliberately sacrificed the social pressure of nineteenth-century provincial bourgeois life which Zola had seen as decisive in shaping the heroine's life, attempting instead to invest the story with the aura of fatality which is to be found in all his most characteristic work. The weaknesses of *Thérèse Raquin* derive almost entirely from this deterministic conception of life, which fails to motivate adequately the conduct of the characters, particularly when the modernisation of the work entails a number of disturbing inconsistencies. But there is much to admire in the film: the acting, the studio-built exteriors and Carné's handling of composition and editing. *Thérèse Raquin* is perhaps Carné's most accomplished post-war work, far superior to the two rather routine films that followed it: *L'Air de Paris* (1954) and *Le Pays d'où je viens* (1956).

Duvivier is easily the most prolific of the veteran directors during the 1950s with nine films in the period from *Sous le ciel de Paris* (1951) to *Pot-Bouille* (1957). Of these the most interesting is *La Fête à Henriette* (1952), which satirises the old notions of black fatalism to which Carné still kept, and the most successful commercially was *Le Petit monde de Don Camillo* (1952), made in Italy with Fernandel in the leading role. The rest of Duvivier's work of the period has no more than commercial pretensions.

*

In the early 1950s, as in the late 1940s, two of the most talented of French directors, Jacques Tati and Robert Bresson, were able to make only one film each, although both works are films of outstanding interest. In *Les Vacances de Monsieur Hulot* (1953) Tati appeared as a new comic character, Hulot, who is less farcical than his predecessor, the postman François, but equally an outsider and disrupter of everyday life. In repose, Hulot is a normal enough type, solid and pipe-smoking, with a battered old car that is his counterpart to François's bicycle, but his gait marks him out as an oddity and sets him apart from those around him. As in *Jour de fête*, the construction is simple, with the action enclosed between shots of the arrival of Hulot and the other guests at their hotel and their departure a week or so later. The principal gags constitute a succession of classic comic sequences, in which Hulot leaves havoc behind him when carrying out the simplest of acts: painting a canoe, rowing, repairing a flat tyre or even entering the hotel with wet plimsolls. Beaten at tennis he learns a pulverising service (which recalls the sporting mimes with which Tati first made his name). As a climax to his holiday and to the film, he contrives to set fire to a hut full of fireworks. In none of these situations does Hulot actually take the initiative and invent his gags and Tati has used this fact to define a difference between his own work and that of Chaplin. *Les Vacances de Monsieur Hulot* also lacks totally the sentimentality which colours so much of Chaplin's later work. As in *Jour de fête* virtually all the humour is visual. Words play only a minor part (the early scene at the railway station with the loud-speakers blaring out incomprehensible instructions sets the pattern) and the music, a catchy tune by Alain Romans, serves chiefly to help capture the holiday mood.

In his first two features, Tati created two outstanding and unforgettable comic characters. François, the postman in *Jour de fête*, is the
more obviously funny of the two. He is, at one and the same time,
unthinkable outside this particular village community, and at a
distance from the other characters, a brilliant mime's comic act amid a
carefully observed and realistic setting. Tati put much more of himself
into his second comic persona. Hulot is a realistic character and fits
more closely into the life around him. In appearance he is quite ordinary and Tati takes care that he never becomes exaggerated. We smile
at his actions, rather than laugh outright, but his ordinariness means
that he can participate more in the life around him, belong to a family,
even become, eventually, a real if marvellously entertaining uncle.

Robert Bresson's sole film of the mid-1950s, *Un Condamné à mort
s'est échappé*, is the story of a prison escape, based on the true account
of a wartime escape from the Nazi prison of Fort Montluc. At first
sight this subject may seem far removed from *Journal d'un curé de
campagne*, but its subtitle, 'The Wind Bloweth Where it Listeth',
reveals both the significance for Bresson of the events related and the
link with the previous work: the escape is seen as the working out of
the divine will. In this respect the music employed in the film is
significant. Mozart's C Minor Mass is used to accompany scenes of the
prisoners going about their everyday tasks and serves to underline the
hidden meaning behind their actions and the supreme order behind
even the carrying out of menial tasks. Again Bresson concentrates on
his single theme, the prison escape planned and executed by the hero
(here known as Lieutenant Fontaine), and all that is irrelevant to this is
omitted. For this reason we learn nothing of the prisoner's antecedents
or even the reasons why he is in prison; we can see what sort of a man
he is from his actions and this suffices. Similarly the camera rarely
leaves the prison. Only the muffled sounds reaching Fontaine's cell
remind us of the life going on outside. Probing close-ups of Fontaine's
face are used to give us insight into his personality, and again, as in
Journal d'un curé de campagne, the hero's voice is heard linking the
scenes, commenting on the action and revealing his own thoughts. In
this film the physical details of Fontaine's escape are of very great
importance and so the camera dwells on his hands as well as on his
face, and on the objects in his cell which he utilises for his escape.
Calmly and patiently Fontaine prepares to cheat his executioners,
benefiting from another prisoner's unsuccessful attempt to escape. All
seems ready, when unexpectedly a young lad, Jost, is put into his cell.
Fontaine, torn by doubts, finally reveals his plan to the newcomer and
persuades him of the effectiveness of his plan. Together they make the
escape.

Bresson builds up tension and suspense during the escape but never by the obvious and more melodramatic methods of Clouzot. Equally significantly Bresson is totally free of the irony which pervades the characteristic works of this first post-war decade of French cinema. The ultimate outcome is never in doubt, but the method of escape is always totally absorbing. The photography, again by Léonce-Henry Burel, is outstanding: greys and blacks are used to convey the claustrophobic prison atmosphere, so that one is made to feel the prisoners' need to escape. The players are all unknowns, none of them professional actors (although François Leterrier, who plays Fontaine, later became a director), and even more than in *Journal d'un curé de campagne* the director's presence can be felt in the acting and even in the manner of talking. Throughout the film there is a sense of control, and an incident like Fontaine's hysterical laughter on being returned to his own cell after his death sentence has been confirmed is muffled and passes almost unnoticed. The whole film has an evenness of tone that marks it as the product of one man's personality. Fontaine has remarkable similarities with the curé d'Ambricourt: he is intelligent, withdrawn, in control of himself even in moments of crisis and endowed with considerable force of character which allows him to impose his will on his fellow men and on his physical surroundings. Confidently he awaits the success of his plan, and this calm passivity gives the film its rhythm and atmosphere.

*

Among the other 'outsiders' of the period, Roger Leenhardt was completely excluded from feature-film production and turned his attention to a series of documentary portraits of great men: *Victor Hugo* (1951), *François Mauriac* (1954), *Jean-Jacques* (1958) on Rousseau, *Paul Valéry* (1960) and *L'Homme à la pipe* (1962) on the painter Gustave Courbet. Neither Jean Grémillon with his fictional feature *L'Amour d'une femme* (1954) nor Georges Rouquier with *Sang et lumières* (1953) and *S.O.S. Noronha* (1957) made any appreciable impression, and both also returned to documentary film making. Rouquier's *Malgovert* (1952) celebrated the building of a hydro-electric power station in the mountains of Savoie. As in *Le Sel de la terre* the director's sympathy with the workers and ability to capture and record the gestures of everyday life are very apparent, and through the combination of music and editing he makes the building of the tunnel into an enthralling crescendo. In a very different mood, *Arthur Honegger* (1955) traced the composer's career by means of a filmed interview and excerpts from his work. Probably Rouquier's finest work after *Farrebique* was *Lourdes et ses miracles* (1954), a three-part examination of the Lourdes phenomenon from an admirably detached viewpoint which posed the question as to whether faith is strengthened by the miraculous (or at least inexplicable) cure of the few, or whether one is horrified by the disappointed hopes of the commercially exploited majority. Grémillon's major documentaries of the period were art films which rank with Resnais's work of 1948–50. *Au coeur de l'Ile de France* (1954) traces the architecture and painting of the Ile de France from Gothic to Impressionism, *La Maison aux images* (1956) looks at the etchers and engravers of Montmartre, and *Haute Lisse* (1957) deals with the weaving of tapestries at the Manufacture des Gobelins, leaving a lasting impression with its images of craftsmen at work. Grémillon's finest achievement in the documentary, completed in the year before his death, is *André Masson et les quatre éléments* (1958), which took a year to complete and was shot in and around the home and studio of the tachiste painter in Aix-en-Provence. It traces with penetrating insight the intimate connections between Masson's abstract paintings and collages and the Provençal landscape. The film is both a meditation on the mysteries of artistic creation and also itself a fully realised work of art in which vision (landscapes, paintings and the gestures of Masson) and sound (Grémillon's voice and music) fuse perfectly.

Equally distinguished work was produced during the period by a whole range of documentarists, among them Georges Franju, Alain Resnais and Chris Marker. Franju's early documentaries, all powerful and lovingly shaped works, are haunted by death. *Le Sang des bêtes* moves alternately between the beautifully composed landscapes photographed by Marcel Fradetal and its central slaughterhouse horrors, and *En passant par la Lorraine* emphasises less the achievement of the workers (which Rouquier captures so well) than the physical dangers they undergo, for example, when working with white-hot metal. Likewise *Hôtel des invalides* (1951) uses its apparently banal tourist images to make an impassioned attack on the myths and glorifications of war. Many of Franju's works contain moments of surrealistic horror and beauty: the worker in *Le Sang des bêtes*, for example, who sings Charles Trenet's 'La mer' as he swills down the blood-soaked floor, or, in *Hôtel des invalides*, the mutilated veterans gathered for mass beneath a banner inscribed 'Paradise lies in the shadow of the sabre'. By contrast, Franju's two documentaries of 1952–53, the affectionate portraits of *Le Grand Méliès* and *Monsieur et Madame Curie*, show the more sentimental side of his character. These five films alone would give Franju a very high place in French documentary film making, but unable to make features, he continued in the short film area for a further five years.

Alain Resnais followed his art films of 1948–50 with a wide variety of subjects. *Les Statues meurent aussi* (1953), which he made in collaboration with Chris Marker, dealt with the destructive impact of western civilisation on African art and was banned for ten years. *Nuit et brouillard* (1955), his most powerful documentary, was a sombre meditation on the concentration camps with an impressive commentary by the novelist Jean Cayrol (later to script *Muriel*) and music by Hanns Eisler. The film's calm, thoughtful rhythm derives from the alternation of the tracking shots, in colour, of the camps today with the harsh black-and-white realities caught by old photographs and by the newsreel shots taken when the camps were first opened up. Resnais has had the audacity to make a film which is beautiful while not shrinking from the atrocities which it depicts, and *Nuit et brouillard* points to the dominant trends of his 1960s feature-film work: the use of a tracking, probing camera and the themes of memory and forgetfulness. *Toute la mémoire du monde* (1956) is a lighter film, full of personal references, but the impact of the concentration camps on Resnais's sensibilities is very apparent in the way the Bibliothèque Nationale, the film's subject, emerges as a kind of prison for books. *Le Chant du styrène* (1958), Resnais's final short, is a carefree work with a commentary by Raymond Queneau celebrating the manufacture of polystyrene.

Chris Marker, Resnais's collaborator on *Les Statues meurent aussi*, was a poet and essayist before turning to the cinema. *Dimanche à Pékin* (1955), his first solo effort, shows the basis of his style in its witty commentary full of private allusions, a humorous delight in contradictions and oddities and a vision of China coloured by memories of Jules Verne and of Humphrey Bogart in the opium dens of Chinatown. *Lettre de Sibérie* (1957), the product of a trip to Russia, is one of his freest and most original films. Marker's own sincere commitment to his subject in no way precludes humour and irreverence. Mocking the clichés and conventions of the documentary genre, he includes parodies and pastiches along with his reportage, and at one point repeats the same images of the town of Iakoutsk three times on each occasion with a different commentary.

Despite this vitality in the documentary, there were few signs of innovation by young directors in the feature film, with not a single newcomer of any importance emerging in the seven years that followed the debuts of Tati and Jean-Pierre Melville in 1947. Melville himself, after an uninteresting and unambitious commercial work, *Quand tu liras cette lettre* (1953), made in the late 1950s two interesting and personal films, *Bob le flambeur* (1956) and *Deux hommes dans Manhattan* (1959). The more fascinating of the two,

Bob le flambeur, is a very individual study of an ageing gangster, superficially in the genre established by Becker in *Touchez pas au grisbi* and Dassin in *Du rififi chez les hommes*. On a deeper level the film is a nostalgic study of the now vanished Montmartre of Melville's youth and the plot little more than a pretext leading deliberately to an anti-climax (Bob wins a fortune, legally, in the casino he planned to rob). In his films up to 1959 Melville worked as an independent in a unique way: he owned his own little studio in the rue Jenner and worked on occasion as his own producer, scriptwriter, director of photography, set designer, editor and leading actor. His example was one of those followed by the directors of the New Wave in the late 1950s.

Two young directors who succeeded in making a feature in 1955 were the critic Alexandre Astruc (b.1923) and the still photographer Agnès Varda (b.1928). Astruc had already completed a remarkable forty-five-minute stylistic exercise, *Le Rideau cramoisi* (1953), based on a mystery story by the nineteenth-century novelist, Barbey d'Aurevilly. Shot without synchronous sound in a style which drew on silent cinema, it used a voice-over narration to tell its story of an impossible love. The more ambitious feature *Les Mauvaises rencontres* (1955), co-scripted with Roland Laudenbach (a collaborator of Delannoy and Autant-Lara), is less successful. Its contemporary setting and thriller plot do not justify Astruc's over-elaborate camera style which makes great use of the play of light and shadow, the pattern to be derived from mirrors and pillars and the selection of expressive and unusual camera angles. Agnès Varda's *La Pointe Courte* (1955) is a direct precursor of the feature work of Alain Resnais, who edited the film. Deliberately literary in tone (with inspiration drawn from William Faulkner's *The Wild Palms*), the film set the emotional problems of a nameless, unpersonalised couple against the lives of the inhabitants of the fishing port of La Pointe Courte. While the couple are treated in a stylised, theatrical manner – their conversation has a distinctly literary ring – the background is observed in documentary style and the film's impact derives from the delicately held balance between the two. Unable to make a further feature for seven years, Varda turned to the documentary, making two stylistic exercises for the tourist board, *O saisons, ô châteaux* (1957) and *Du côté de la côte* (1958), and a remarkable subjective study of the Mouffetard district as seen through the eyes of a pregnant woman (Varda was herself expecting a baby at the time), *Opéra Mouffe* (1958).

At this time too a number of the critics working on *Cahiers du cinéma* began to experiment with short fictional subjects. After two films shot in Geneva, where he lived at that time, the documentary *Opération béton* (1954) and the ten-minute fictional piece, *Une*

Femme coquette (1955), Jean-Luc Godard made three further shorts in which the themes and styles of his first features are already apparent in embryo. *Tous les garçons s'appellent Patrick* (1957) and *Charlotte et son Jules* (1958) are lighthearted pieces which introduce some of the characters and actors (Jean-Claude Brialy and Jean-Paul Belmondo) of the New Wave features of the 1958–62 period. *Une histoire d'eau* (1958) is also interesting in that it combines images shot by François Truffaut with a characteristic Godard commentary crammed full of literary and filmic allusions. Truffaut himself completed a charming story about a gang of schoolboys who torment the beautiful Bernadette and her gym instructor boyfriend, *Les Mistons* (1957), and introduced two further key New Wave players, Bernadette Lafont and Gérard Blain. At this time too Jacques Rivette made an elegant if unsubstantial study of the sexual manoeuvring of a handful of characters, *Le Coup du berger* (1956), and Eric Rohmer, who scripted Godard's two films of 1957–8, made a whole series of little narratives, of which the best known is *Véronique et son cancre* (1958).

All these little films were, of course, marginal to French commercial production, although in retrospect they have a considerable interest as the first works of directors who were to dominate the French cinema of the 1960s and 1970s. In the mainstream of production itself there were also a few seemingly promising signs in the years 1956–57. Two new directors tackled themes related to the war in Indo-China: Marcel Camus (1912–82), after ten years' work as assistant, made *Mort en fraude* (1957), the first film in an output marked chiefly by exoticism and purely commercial ambition; and Claude Bernard-Aubert (b.1930), who was to become a prolific director of pornographic films in the 1970s (under the name Burd Tranbaree), made *Patrouille de choc* (1957). Roger Vadim (b.1928) made an enormous commercial impact with *Et dieu créa la femme* (1956), starring his young wife Brigitte Bardot. This film and the two which followed it – *Sait-on jamais* (1957), with Françoise Arnoul, and *Les Bijoutiers du clair de lune* (1957), with Bardot once more – had a genuinely youthful quality in a French production which was otherwise clearly ageing and offered the (unfulfilled) promise of a director with something new to say. More substantial was the debut of Louis Malle (b.1932), who had worked as Bresson's assistant and co-directed the underwater documentary, *Le Monde du silence*, with Jacques-Yves Cousteau. *L'Ascenseur pour l'échafaud* (1957) was a thriller with a complicated plot, enlivened by a lively jazz score by Miles Davis, some striking camerawork by Henri Decaë and, above all, by a remarkable performance from Jeanne Moreau.

*

In retrospect it is the limitations of the mainstream film production of the period up to 1958 which strikes one most forcibly. Local film audiences continued to grow throughout the period (reaching a peak in 1957) and the well-made, solidly constructed films in what François Truffaut so aptly named the 'tradition of quality' – those of Clément, Clouzot, Autant-Lara and Delannoy – maintained a major share of this public. Early 1950s cinema was indeed an inward-looking cinema, produced specifically for a local audience (which would be steadily lost with the advent of television) and largely unconcerned with foreign markets except those covered by the international co-production agreements which had been concluded with Italy in 1949, West Germany in 1952 and Spain in 1953. But the steady rise of such co-productions from about a dozen in 1951 to over ninety ten years later led to cumbersome, often ill-cast commercial vehicles which were no longer rooted in French culture.

French cinema has always been at its richest when it has direct contact with the world of the arts in general, but the major currents of thought and literature hardly find their reflection in the cinema of the 1950s, whose concerns remain, essentially, professionalism, attention to detail in setting and acting, and commercial viability. In this sense it was a cinema without risks which could hardly attract the young aspirants who were nurtured by the growth of the ciné-club movement in France after 1945, by the activities of the Cinémathèque française which maintained a lively and eclectic approach under Henri Langlois, and by the new generation of film critics. When *Cahiers du cinéma* was founded by André Bazin and Jacques Doniol-Valcroze in 1951, it could draw nothing from the mainstream French production. Bazin and the young critics like Eric Rohmer, François Truffaut and Jean-Luc Godard whom he gathered around him took a wider view of cinema, being particularly concerned to give new importance to Hollywood. The French film makers singled out for praise in the early numbers of *Cahiers du cinéma* included Renoir, Ophuls and Cocteau, but also the two great independents of the 1940s generation, Bresson and Tati. Whereas the mainstream directors had almost all produced their major work by the mid-1950s, Bresson and Tati who were each able to produce only two films in the first post-war decade continued to develop creatively through the 1960s and 1970s.

Cahiers du cinéma also drew attention to the wealth of short film production in France at this time. In addition to such major figures as Franju and Resnais, there was a whole new generation of short film makers emerging in this first post-war decade. The new documentarists were ten to fifteen years younger than the mainstream feature directors (being in their early twenties when the war ended) and, unlike their elders, they showed an amazing vitality and an incredibly wide variety of styles and personal approaches. Good films of every conceivable kind were made: from the passionately committed shorts of the Marxist Robert Ménegoz (b.1925) to the poetic fantasies of Albert Lamorisse (b.1922); from the parodies of Hollywood devised by Paul Paviot (b.1925) to the meditations on art of Carlos Vilardebo (b.1926) and the skilful reportage of François Reichenbach (b.1928). Around 1959, when conditions were most favourable for a young director to make his first feature, many of these short film makers seized their opportunity. Although results were very mixed, comparatively few succeeded in imposing themselves on the feature film industry, but their work over the preceding ten years gave French cinema a much-needed life and vigour.

La Nouvelle Vague? Elle est très vague et fort peu nouvelle.
Bernard Chardère, 1962

1958 was a year of political upheaval and change in France with the constitution of the Fifth Republic by Charles de Gaulle under the impact of the stresses caused by the continuing conflict in Algeria. It was also the year in which the first undeniable signs of a renewal in French cinema occur. The two are, however, not closely linked and if changes are made in society as a whole, the institutions of cinema undergo no substantive modification, merely a change of personnel. The New Wave – however we define it – captures the surface texture of French life in a fresh way, if only because the low budgets with which most young directors work initially necessitate a certain contemporary flavour lacking in the 1951–57 period, when the characteristic works were (as we have seen) period reconstructions. The newcomers had no money to build elaborate sets, pay for costumes or employ star names: they shot on location, with reduced crews and fresh young performers. But this contemporary flavour was not accompanied by any real social or political concern on the part of the new film makers. The newcomers who have left-wing political views (Alain Resnais or Chris Marker, for instance) are more than balanced by those whose claims to be apolitical (François Truffaut, Claude Chabrol, the Jean-Luc Godard of 1958–62) mask a complicity with the values and forms of bourgeois society. If the 'tradition of quality' of the early 1950s could be characterised and attacked by Truffaut as 'an anti-bourgeois cinema made by the bourgeois for the bourgeois', the New Wave, it must be said, offers in the period 1958–62 no more than a bourgeois cinema made by the bourgeois for the bourgeois. Key contemporary themes – the war in Algeria, the need for social change in metropolitan France – are as absent from French cinema after 1958 as they were before. Even the kind of socially analytic film making which was favoured by British Free Cinema or which existed in French documentary production in the 1950s, is lacking from the post-1958 feature-film industry, which remains essentially a Parisian cinema, dealing with middle-class problems in middle-class terms, and above all concerned with the 'eternal' issues of human emotions and relationships.

1958–62 is a confused period of intense activity in which some of the older directors – Becker, Bresson and Tati among them – made some of their best work, but in which the key factor demanded of a film director was youth. Or at least the semblance of it, for it must be remembered that many of the new directors were young only in comparison with the established generation of the 1940s. If we go back further in French film history we find that at thirty – the age at which Jean-Luc Godard made his first feature – René Clair had made all his silent films, Marcel Carné had completed five features culminating in *Le Jour se lève*, and Jean Vigo, of course, died at the age of twenty-nine. Nonetheless this was a period of renewal, with some ninety-seven first features completed and commercially released in the period of four years from 1958 to 1962, in addition to a number of films, like Jean-Daniel Pollet's *La Ligne de mire* or Paul Gégauff's *Le Reflux*, which were made but not released.

In retrospect it is clear that there was not just one renewal in 1958 but several concurring. On the one hand the late 1950s saw the death or retirement of a dozen or so of the most prolific commercial directors of the first post-war decade, among them André Berthomieu, Maurice de Canonge, Léonide Moguy and Henri Diamant-Berger. These were replaced by a whole succession of newcomers who had no pretensions of revolutionising the art of cinema but who had spent up to ten years as assistant directors. Among those who had served this kind of traditional apprenticeship and emerged simultaneously with the New Wave we find: Edouard Molinaro and Michel Deville in 1958, Georges Lautner in 1959, Philippe De Broca, Jacques Deray, Michel Drach and Claude Sautet in 1960, Pierre Granier-Deferre and Alain Cavalier in 1962. In addition a number of actors graduated from theatre to film directing at the same time, Yves Robert, Jean-Pierre Mocky and Gérard Oury among them. Most of these directors would no doubt have emerged in any case, although perhaps the enthusiasm of producers for new talent around 1959–60 may have hastened a few debuts: Claude Sautet, for example, had to wait five years before he could direct a second feature and Michel Deville waited three. The more dependable commercial talents among this group had an enormous output – Lautner with twenty-six films and Molinaro with twenty-four over a twenty-year period – but this work had as little to do with the art of the cinema as that of such predecessors as Gilles Grangier or Henri Verneuil. Others produced work which would merit consideration here if space allowed. Michel Deville and Michel Drach, for example, both produced a number of delightful and sensitive works, and Jean-Pierre Mocky, with an output of a film a year for twenty years, remains an unclassifiable and slightly disturbing film maker.

While this progression from assistantship to direction was generally fruitful, the cross-fertilisation between cinema and television, which also occurred in this period, was far less so. The major television directors usually made just one or two feature films for cinema release before returning to their previous role, and such works as *Cette nuit-là* (Maurice Cazeneuve, 1958), *Climats* (Stellio Lorenzi, 1961) or *Le Monte-charge* and *Carambolages* (Marcel Bluwal, 1961 and 1962 respectively) brought little that was new. Perhaps the most successful work by a director trained in television was Jacques Rozier's *Adieu Philippine*, made in 1961 and released only two years later. Made, it seems, in a fairly chaotic fashion, *Adieu Philippine* is one of the best monuments to French producers' brief enthusiasm for fresh and untried talent. Its chief qualities are its youthful vitality and the improvised, *cinéma-vérité*-style authenticity of its language, characters and settings. The film's weaknesses are largely those of construction: it is a disjointed and often somewhat incoherent telling of what is essentially a simple story of a television technician who takes out two girls alternately in Paris and then spends a holiday with them both in Corsica, before being called off to his national service in Algeria. Rozier's passion for irrelevant detail (for example, the extensive footage devoted to satirising television commercials) and the abundance of material deriving from his television style of shooting (often with three cameras simultaneously) make the film harder to follow than it need have been, but it remains an enormously engaging minor work. Rozier's subsequent features, made some ten or more years later, did not have the same impact.

In addition to these two groups of film makers, whose impact alone would not have justified talk of a New Wave of cinema by journalists seeking in their articles symbols of the rejuvenation and renewal of France under the Fifth Republic, we may separate out three other groups of young film makers: those whose beginnings pre-date 1958; the group who graduated to film direction from *Cahiers du cinéma* (and were the most successful in publicising the idea of a new cinema coming into existence); and a very heterogeneous group of former documentary film makers, led by Georges Franju and Alain Resnais.

Curiously enough the strongest lead did not come from those who had made their debuts before 1958. Jean-Pierre Melville, for example, remained as unclassifiable as ever. *Bob le flambeur* gave the tone and visual style to much of the work produced after 1957 (Malle, Chabrol and Truffaut all used Melville's photographer, Henri Decaë, on their first films) and Melville's independent mode of production inspired many young film makers to take the risk of making films instead of just dreaming about them. But after *Deux hommes dans Manhattan*, shot partly in New York in 1958, Melville gave up this personal style of film making, resolving henceforth to make solidly commercial films for a wide audience, using larger budgets, star performers and saleable subjects. This new approach is very apparent in *Léon Morin, prêtre* (1961), adapted from a largely autobiographical novel by Béatrix Beck, and featuring two of the biggest stars of the early 1960s, Jean-Paul Belmondo and Emmanuelle Riva. The spiritual conflict between the unhappy young woman and the handsome youthful priest who tries to comfort and convert her is superficially handled and their exchanges lack intellectual depth. The inner turmoil of the woman is excellently captured by Riva's performance, but the character and motives of the priest remain shadowy. A comparison with Bresson's work shows the extent to which Melville, an avowed non-believer, is concerned to do little more than create a smoothly running narrative which will interest audiences but not disturb them in any way. Although he can capture the atmosphere of occupied France with a few sharply drawn characters and deftly chosen details, Melville hedges when he comes to the central spiritual issues which his film raises. What is particularly interesting about *Léon Morin, prêtre* is the extent to which it anticipates the conformity which was to follow the breakthrough of the New Wave for so many of its key figures in the mid- and late 1960s.

Roger Vadim, who had seemed to offer a new tone with his first films, produced little of note after 1958. *Les Liaisons dangereuses* (1959), a modernisation of Laclos's novel fashionably set in a ski resort, is notable more for the scandal it provoked (with protests from defenders of the book) than for any intrinsic merits, while *Et mourir de plaisir* (1960) was a lush but tedious adaptation of a Sheridan le Fanu tale. *La Bride sur le cou* was no more than a commercial job, taken over at short notice when the production ran into trouble, but *Le Repos du guerrier* (1962), again with Brigitte Bardot, was intended to be a more personal work. Unfortunately it is impossible to lend credence to this story of a love affair between a prim young girl and an anarchist student who, after dominating her physically, is brought to his knees by love. The colour views of Florence and the obligatory nude shots of Bardot are pleasing, but none of the characters come to life and the trite and unconvincing script plunges into bathos in the climactic final meeting in a ruined chapel. This is conformist cinema at its worst.

1958–62 was Alexandre Astruc's most prolific period, but the three films produced are of very varying interest. *Une Vie* (1958) was an expensive co-production filmed in colour and starring Maria Schell, then at the height of her international reputation. The source of the film was a novel by Guy de Maupassant and again, as in *Le Rideau cramoisi*, Astruc retained the period setting. *Une Vie* is a film of great visual beauty, from the opening scene of two girls running down to the sea up to the final sight of two bodies amid the wreckage, and the director has taken enormous care with the colours, costumes and photography (by Claude Renoir). Astruc shows here the same dislike of the sordid as Vadim: there is no dirt or disorder and the costumes are always spotless and unworn. Beneath this often ravishing surface the characters fail to come alive and *Une Vie* increased Astruc's reputation as a 'cold' director. The low-budget black-and-white feature, *La Proie pour l'ombre* (1961), is in many ways Astruc's most personal film, shot from an original script and lacking the elaborate visual style of the earlier features. As a record of a woman's struggle to maintain her identity within her marriage, the film shows considerable insight and for once the characters are people with whom we can involve ourselves. But Astruc appears troubled by the slightness of the work and at several points in the film – particularly at the end – he attempts to put more weight on the story than it can stand. *L'Education sentimentale* (1962), a modernisation of Flaubert's novel, is a hybrid work, exploring Astruc's characteristic themes of the difficulties of human communication but without engaging us deeply in the actions and motivations of the characters. Astruc is a paradoxical figure, a novelist most of whose work comprises adaptations, a film critic whose work is weighed down – not liberated – by his attention to camera style. In his theorisation of the 'caméra-stylo' he looks forward to the freedom and fluidity of the best work of the late 1950s, but his own output is ponderous and fits all too easily into the conformist patterns of the 'tradition of quality'.

Of the other newcomers who had made their debuts in 1957, Pierre Kast made three films – *Le Bel âge* (1960), *Merci Natercia*, which was never released, and *La Morte saison des amours* (1961) – which in conception and execution represent the New Wave sensibility at its most fragile and superficial. By contrast, Louis Malle used the years 1958 to 1962 to consolidate the basis of what was to be a very considerable career. *Les Amants* (1958), made from a script written in collaboration with Louise de Vilmorin, confirmed the promise contained in *Ascenseur pour l'échafaud*. *Les Amants* begins as a study of high society and shows the love affair of a bored older woman and a young student which is born and consummated in a single night in the gardens of her husband's villa and in her bedroom. While one may find the ending, in which the woman and her lover drive off to begin a new life together, a trifle naive, the romantic love scenes combine a delicate lyricism with (for the period) a great frankness and truth. Among other successes of the film are Henri Decaë's photography and the satirical portrait it draws of polite society (which Malle knows well from his own wealthy background). In *Zazie dans le métro* (1960) Malle tried his hand at filming the unfilmable. The basic idea of Raymond Queneau's novel is of a very young girl with a startling vocabulary of vulgar words who is more mature and balanced than all the adults around her and who spreads havoc wherever she goes. But this plot is little more than a pretext for a series of subtle and often very funny variations on language and orthography. Seeking visual equivalents for Queneau's puns and word-play Malle created a film which is beautiful in its imagery, technically exciting and set in a constantly shifting decor. He uses a welter of trick shots, unexpected cutting and superimpositions, varies the projection speed and includes a mass of parodies and filmic references. But this very abundance of detail tends to weigh the film down and Malle does not quite possess the sense of comic timing necessary to sustain his slapstick ending. In *Vie privée* (1962), starring Brigitte Bardot and to some extent built around the star's own life, Malle continued his experiments with narrative method. His unexpected cutting and freezing of images, particularly in the early scenes, parallel Resnais's experiments at this period and his use of colour and camera movement is always exciting. Yet for a number of reasons *Vie privée* remains one of Malle's least satisfying films. The characters lack substance and the film's documentary aspects – the recording of Bardot's own personal mannerisms and facial expressions – do not compensate for this. Similarly the idealisation of the heroine leads not to insight into the phenomenon of the star but to an absurd and miscalculated lyrical ending. The years 1958–62 were a period of experimentation for Malle: while the films produced were uneven, the gain in technical mastery was to be crucial for Malle's later career.

Among others whose work anticipated the 1958 breakthrough was Agnès Varda, whose second feature, *Cléo de cinq à sept*, was not made until 1962. Varda's husband, Jacques Demy (b.1931), worked as assistant and made a number of documentaries before making *Lola* (1961), his first feature. In a totally different vein, Pierre Etaix (b.1928), who had appeared in Bresson's *Pickpocket* and assisted Tati on *Mon oncle*, made two inventive and very funny shorts, *Rupture* and *Heureux anniversaire* (both 1961), and Claude Lelouch (b.1937) made two features in the years 1960–62, *Le Propre de l'homme* (1960) and *L'Amour avec des si*, but the latter was not released until 1966. Lelouch's career, like those of Varda, Demy and Etaix, is considered in the following chapter.

*

It will have been apparent from the preceding pages that the appearance of the majority of the newcomers who emerged in the late 1950s would have caused little stir. Among the dozen or so names already mentioned only Malle, Varda and perhaps Astruc had been able to create more than a single really original film. For the appearance of new directors to become a social phenomenon – that is the New Wave – a different kind of energy, originality and publicity sense was required, and this was provided by a group of highly articulate young writers from *Cahiers du cinéma*. The very divergent careers of these men in the 1960s and 1970s and their enormous differences of temperament mean that their similarities should not be overemphasised and certainly the present grouping is intended as no more than a way of mapping the field. Three of the group – Claude Chabrol, François Truffaut and Jean-Luc Godard – established international reputations with thirteen feature films between them in the period 1958–62. Three others – Jacques Doniol-Valcroze, Eric Rohmer and Jacques Rivette – also made first films, although with markedly less critical and popular success. But if Doniol-Valcroze's career as a film maker was to peter out inconclusively, both Rohmer and Rivette went on to establish themselves as major directors ten or twelve years later.

One thing which all this group had in common was a view of criticism as essentially a step towards directing, so that for all of them there was a sense of continuity when they moved from *Cahiers du cinéma* into the film industry. Their film making, like their writing, shows their awareness of being heirs to a long film-making tradition. While they contemptuously rejected the work of their immediate predecessors, their early films are full of allusions to the directors they consider truly great. Thus we find, for example, direct quotations from Lang's *Metropolis* in Rivette's *Paris nous appartient* and from Dreyer's *La Passion de Jeanne d'Arc* in Godard's *Vivre sa vie*, while Godard uses Jean-Pierre Melville as an actor in *A bout de souffle*, just as he will subsequently use Lang, Leenhardt and Sam Fuller. More important than these references to past films and film makers is the fact that their background gave the *Cahiers* group their own particular view of the relationship of cinema and life. Crime is not a social problem, it is a film genre; a new film is not an attempt to capture reality but an attempt 'to film an Antonioni subject in the manner of Hawks or Hitchcock' (Godard on *Le Mépris*); the whole texture of a film is made up of shots and sequences remembered from favourite Hollywood movies. The group was subject to continual shifts over a period of twenty years. If Godard and Truffaut dominated the period from 1960 to 1967, Chabrol produced key works in the period 1968–71, Rohmer made his most significant work between 1967 and 1972, and Rivette's most creative period did not begin until 1969. In 1958 the key figure was the first of the group to break into feature-film making, Claude Chabrol.

Chabrol's first film, *Le Beau Serge* (1958) has a considerable historic interest. Shot entirely on location, with unknown players and financed with money inherited by the director's wife, it depicts the return of a young man to his native village and his attempts to rehabilitate his childhood friend, now the village drunkard. Henri Decaë's photography captures beautifully the bleakness of autumn and winter in the Sardent area and the documentary aspects – the village and the countryside, the dance and indeed all the background elements – are sharply and successfully drawn. The contrast in acting styles of the two leading players (Jean-Claude Brialy and Gerard Blain) is neat and the courage and independence of Chabrol's approach are never in doubt. But a gap remains between the characters and the background in which they are set and the elements of melodrama, incest and rape mar the unity of the film. The artificiality of the plot's resolution is increasingly apparent and the ending with its Christian overtones is an incredibly glib oversimplification of complex issues. Chabrol was aware of these latter defects and the religious themes and imagery (perhaps a misguided homage to Alfred Hitchcock about whom Chabrol wrote a book with Eric Rohmer) are absent from his later films.

Les Cousins (1959), begun immediately after *Le Beau Serge*, is in many ways its companion work. Again the film is built around the contrast and rivalry of two young men, this time both students: the polished, bullying carefree Paul and the honest, clumsy and provincial Charles. Chabrol is fully at home in this overglamourised undergraduate world, his handling of the material is assured and the photography (again by Decaë) is dazzling and exciting. The film's principal strength is again the acting of Brialy and Blain as the two contrasting cousins, but the other roles are either underdeveloped (Juliette Mayniel as the girl they both love) or caricatured (Claude Cerval as Paul's hanger-on Clovis). The film is virtually plotless, comprising a succession of set-pieces, of which the party scenes are the most successful, since they reveal clearly Chabrol's taste for the theatrical and flamboyant. The contrived ending of unwitting murder – inspired no doubt by the theme of the exchange of guilt which Chabrol and Rohmer analysed in Hitchcock – bears little obvious connection with what has gone before.

Keeping up his breathless flood of films, Chabrol turned, with *A double tour* (1959) to the world of colour, big budgets and international co-production. The intentions of Chabrol and his scriptwriter Paul Gégauff (who had also written the dialogue for *Les Cousins*) do not seem to rise beyond the production of an entertaining thriller, built around the impact of two outsiders on a bourgeois family. The construction is original in its use of overlapping fragments of action, so that we live through the same time with various characters successively, but this method merely dissipates suspense and draws attention to the wooden quality of the dialogue. Chabrol's lack of feeling for his characters and love of overacting become evident in his handling of the minor characters, and the love scenes which should be moving are simply cinematic clichés. Continuing his collaboration with Gégauff, Chabrol next made *Les Bonnes femmes* (1960), about the dreams and ambitions of four shopgirls. The note of condescension in the title remains apparent throughout the film; none of the characters is presented sympathetically and the most sympathetic of the four is, predictably, the one who is murdered. The masterly way in which this scene is set, photographed and handled shows Chabrol's sheer professional ability. Henri Decaë's photography is fluid and assured throughout, with a harsh reality in its grey tones, and on a superficial level the film is highly successful, despite the denigratory tone Chabrol adopts. Chabrol's work from 1958 to 1960 played a key role in the establishment of the new generation of film makers. But with *Les Godelureaux* (1961), which marked the temporary end to his collaboration with Gégauff, it was clear that Chabrol's career was losing its momentum. His inability to take the subjects of his films seriously is very apparent in his interview comments of this time and his own lack of profound involvement with his work coincided with a loss of box-office success for both *L'Oeil du malin* (1962), an intended psychological thriller, and *Ophélia*, a mediocre and unconvincing modernisation of the Hamlet theme.

In contrast to Chabrol, François Truffaut was able to make three successful but highly differing films during the period. *Les Quatre cents coups* (1959) recaptures all the qualities of the preceding short, *Les Mistons*, together with a portrait in depth of its adolescent hero. It traces with sympathy and insight the career of the thirteen-year-old

Antoine Doinel from schoolboy pranks to reformatory and the performance of the young Jean-Pierre Léaud makes this Truffaut's finest character study. The boy's school and home background are totally authentic and the whole world around him is observed with remarkable freshness and insight. The script, by Truffaut and Marcel Moussy, captures very well the sense of transition in Antoine's life. He is half-adult, half-child, and this is revealed particularly clearly in the scene where he talks to the prison psychiatrist about his sexual experiences. The tone of *Les Quatre cents coups* is remarkably even, and the director's attitude is strictly neutral: he observes without comment and there is no sense of protest in the handling of Antoine's fate. The technical qualities of the film are very high and, as in the first films of Malle and Chabrol, Henri Decaë's camerawork is fluent and assured. Indeed only the music, which is lush and over-orchestrated, strikes a discordant note. *Les Quatre cents coups* is the cinematic equivalent of an autobiographical first novel and the figure of Antoine Doinel is one to which Truffaut was to return four times in the next twenty years. As a critic, Truffaut had made virulent attacks on the conformism of the older generation of film makers – the stalwarts of the 'tradition of quality', but there is little that is revolutionary in *Les Quatre cents coups*. For all the undeniable qualities of intelligence and sensitivity that Truffaut displays, his film cannot be said to represent a stylistic revolution akin to the first films of Godard and Resnais.

Tirez sur le pianiste (1960) was a far freer work, derived from an American *série noire* thriller by David Goodis, and dealing with the double life of a pub pianist (Charles Aznavour) who had once been a successful concert pianist. While the scenes of his earlier life, told in flashback, are pure melodrama, the scenes of the hero's subsequent life are handled in a loose, humorous and affectionate manner, full of irrelevancies and parody and with some striking camerawork by Raoul Coutard. As is inevitable in a work of this nature, it is the comic elements that come across the best: the two wildly improbable, pipe-smoking gangsters with whom the hero becomes involved, the opening sequence of a meeting between two strangers, and the crazy song of Bob Lapointe concluding 'Avanie et framboises sont les mamelles du destin'. The film as a whole is disjointed, constantly changing its moods and continually surprising the audience with a new turn of the plot or a fresh idea. This makes the film lively and entertaining, but lessens the impact of the more serious passages. The final transition to solemnity, with the death in the snow of the woman the hero loves, is flatly handled and leaves the spectator unmoved.

Truffaut's third film, *Jules et Jim* (1962), was also an adaptation, this time from a novel by the septuagenarian Henri-Pierre Roché, which confronted him with the problem of how to handle the tangled relations of two friends, one German and one French, and the woman they both love. The period atmosphere is deftly handled through reconstructed pre-1914 settings and photographic tones and textures recalling the films of the period. The passing of time (depicted through the use of newsreel inserts and successive stages of Picasso's painting style used for posters) is less important than the shifting patterns of the trio's twenty-year *ménage à trois*, from its inception until the moment when it can be no longer sustained as the woman, Catherine, drives herself and Jim to their deaths. As so often in Truffaut's work, the most memorable scenes are those with only the most tenuous of connections with the ostensible plot: the discussion of the Swedish play, Jeanne Moreau as Catherine singing 'le Tourbillon', the story of the soldier who wooed and won by post a girl he had met only once, the career of Thérèse, whom they meet on several occasions, and so on. The mood is marvellously sustained and in the taste and delicacy with which the emotions of Jules, Jim and Catherine are handled, Truffaut's creative personality is fully apparent. Having given the new French cinema three of its most successful and universally acclaimed works, Truffaut turned again to the character of Antoine Doinel in the episode he contributed to the collective film, *L'Amour à vingt ans* (1972). *Antoine et Colette* is a rueful little tale about how Antoine wins the girl's parents but loses Colette herself, told with all Truffaut's usual insight into the quirks of human behaviour and the hesitancies and uncertainties of young love. The flow of events is smoothly controlled and all the irony of the situation is fully exploited.

Jean-Luc Godard did not complete his first feature until 1960, but *A bout de souffle* (1960) proved to be one of the most startlingly innovative films of the period, which was to have an enormous impact on film makers both in France and abroad. On the surface the plot is that of a not very original thriller, but Godard made it completely his own in conception and execution. *A bout de souffle* examines the last hours of Michel Poiccard (Jean-Paul Belmondo), his relationship with Patricia (Jean Seberg) and his attempt to escape the police net tightening around him. Godard's debt to American 'B' picture mythology is obvious (and acknowledged when Michel – and the film – observes a minute of silence in memory of Humphrey Bogart). The interest comes from the way Godard handles his material. All the rules of conventional film making are scorned: Raoul Coutard's camerawork is rough and unrefined and the script and editing are jumbled, rambling, repetitive and inconclusive, full of irrelevances and abruptly changing moods. The style is set in the opening sequence of Michel driving inconsequentially towards murder while directing at his audience a welter of comment and selected insult. At the centre of the film is the portrait of Michel and Patricia, sleeping together without really knowing each other, sparring and probing, lying and concealing, until finally it is she who denounces him to the police. *Le Petit soldat* (1960–63) was banned for two years by the government. In the hero, Bruno (Michel Subor), Godard expands the autobiographical aspects of Michel Poiccard into a full-length portrait. The wordiness of *A bout de souffle* here becomes a running commentary by Bruno on the images as they unfold, an outpouring of private likes and dislikes, with mention of Klee, Velasquez, Gauguin and Van Gogh; Bach, Beethoven, Haydn and Mozart; Camus, Cocteau and Malraux; T. E. Lawrence, Drieu la Rochelle and Aragon. Nominally the hero of *Le Petit soldat* belongs to a fascist terrorist organisation confronting the FLN in Switzerland, but the film's political analysis goes no further than to assert that there is nothing to choose between the two sides and illustrates this by giving them identical dialogue. This is itself a very right-wing political stance, but on another level *Le Petit soldat* is a new variant on the gangster film, with all the usual violent trimmings and rules of gang loyalties. Raoul Coutard's camera is constantly on the move, marvellously catching the atmosphere of Geneva by day and night, giving an almost documentary realism to some scenes, and in others isolating characters in significant close-up, often against a blank background. The shots of Bruno's girlfriend, Véronique, are a poem in praise of Anna Karina's beauty, but despite the strongly autobiographical aspects of the work, Godard remains strangely aloof and detached from the action and unusually reticent in the love scenes.

If Godard's first two features had been in the nature of partial self-portraits, the next two were both studies of this wife, Anna Karina, who is at the centre of both films. In *Une Femme est une femme* (1961) the plot turns on the need of a young woman to have a baby. When Emile, the man she loves and lives with, refuses, Angela turns to their friend Alfred. Shot in the studios, in colour and cinemascope, *Une Femme est une femme* is a comedy of changing moods, veering from farce to seriousness, full of the usual Godard quirks and references to his favourite directors and concealing a profound analysis of contemporary France beneath its inconsequential surface. Despite the agreeable playing of Karina, Brialy and Belmondo, the film disconcerted its first audiences and had little commercial success. Godard gave an even fuller portrait of Anna Karina in *Vivre sa vie* (1962). Indeed the sole *raison d'être* of this film was to place Karina in as wide a range of emotional situations as possible, and it had as little to do with the social problem of prostitution as *Le Petit soldat* had with the realities of fascist politics. Godard has ordered the material by dividing it into twelve tableaux preceded by explanatory titles, a device which recalls both Brecht and silent cinema. *Vivre sa vie* was shot quickly in Godard's usual manner, on location and without a clear-cut script. Some scenes, such as the heroine Nana's dance around a young man in a deserted billiard room, succeed beautifully, but other's, like Nana's meeting with the (real) philosopher Brice Parain fail to come fully alive. The technique is bold but sometimes obtrusive, as in the opening scene shot from behind the heads of Nana and her husband. Often the patterns which the camera makes in its incessant tracking to and fro have a beauty and impact that owe nothing to dramatic necessity. The film is a stylistic exercise, detached and impersonal about its theme of prostitution, but passionately involved with its heroine. All kinds of fragments are brought together to make up the portrait of Karina: shots from Dreyer's *La Passion de Jeanne d'Arc*, statistics on prostitution, a child's essay, a philosopher, a dance, a pop song and a story by Poe. This portrait, which is the core of the film, remains essentially romanticised, for Nana is a descendant of 'la dame aux camélias', selling her body, but keeping her soul.

The first feature films of Eric Rohmer and Jacques Rivette received only a muted appreciation and it is fair to say that their significance emerged only much later, in the light of subsequent and much more successful works. Rohmer had been one of the first of the *Cahiers* group to make short fiction films in the 1950s, but his first feature, *Le Signe du lion* (1959), made with the aid of Claude Chabrol, had to wait three years for even a partial release. Set in Paris in the summer when most of the residents have gone away on holiday and the streets are full of tourists, *Le Signe du lion* traces the gradual degeneration of a bohemian musician who finds himself penniless and alone in a hostile city. The film's chief virtues are its authentic view of Paris and its lack of compromise. With the failure of this film, Rohmer had to return to 16 mm production and it was in this format that he began the series of six 'moral tales' which were to occupy him until 1972.

Jacques Rivette's *Paris nous appartient*, shot between 1957 and 1959 and released in 1961, is in total contrast with his first short, *Le Coup du berger*, being quite loaded down with portentous significance and deep meaning. It mixes its story of a group of conspirators bent on world destruction with the account of a group of actors attempting to mount a production of Shakespeare's *Pericles*. *Paris nous appartient* is quite uncompromising in its avoidance of any sort of flamboyance, wit or humour. The tone never varies, the dialogue is flat and the photography, although competent, is never striking. The film's major defect is its failure to create any sort of dramatic tension. The problems of mounting the stage production and the Paris of intellectual dinner parties and drab bedsitting-room life, are skilfully evoked. But when Rivette attempts to lift his film above the realistic plane, so that, like *Pericles*, its parts come together on another level, he fails. The underlying menace of imminent annihilation is neither convincingly evoked nor maintained and the constant talk of conspiracy and nameless horror is altogether out of proportion to the actual happenings of the film – an inadequacy for which the inclusion of a few minutes of Fritz Lang's *Metropolis* cannot compensate.

*

Among the many who made the move from documentary to feature production at this time, the emergence of Georges Franju is of particular importance. For his debut Franju chose a subject closely related to his earlier documentary work. *La Tête contre les murs* (1958) dealt with a young man committed to an asylum by his father who escapes in order to prove his sanity, only to be recaptured and dragged back to confinement. The film was shot on location and the picture of life inside the asylum is utterly convincing. The pair of doctors representing new and old approaches to the treatment of the mentally ill are excellently played (by Paul Meurisse and Pierre Brasseur) if a trifle over-schematised. The major problem with the film is the unresolved ambiguity concerning the sanity of the hero (played by the film's scriptwriter, Jean-Pierre Mocky). But Franju's formal preoccupations – his concern with plastic values, visual patterns and symbols – are admirably supported by the photography of the veteran German Eugen Schüfftan and the musical score of Maurice Jarre. *Les Yeux sans visage* (1959) lacks the 'problem picture' overtones which Mocky had brought to *La Tête contre les murs* and is essentially a stylistic exercise, using the elements of plot (the mad surgeon who kills young girls in order to attempt to transplant their faces onto his own disfigured daughter) much as Clouzot used them in *Les Espions*. The strengths of the film lie less in its narrative command or creation of suspense than in its moments of pure visual effect (most obvious in the handling of Edith Scob as the heroine, as when she vanishes, white-clad and accompanied by doves, after setting loose the hounds which will tear her father to pieces).

Pleins feux sur l'assassin (1961), Franju's least demanding feature, has the plot of a conventional thriller (concerning the mysterious disappearance of a wealthy count) but contains some of the most remarkable sequences Franju has directed, particularly a 'son et

31. René Clément: Jeux interdits (1952)

32. Jean Renoir: Le Carrosse d'or (1952)

33. Alexandre Astruc: Le Rideau cramoisi (1952)

34. Henri-Georges Clouzot: Le Salaire de la peur (1953)

35. Jacques Tati: Les Vacances de M Hulot (1953)

36. Robert Bresson: Un Condamné à mort s'est échappé (1956)

37. Max Ophuls: Lola Montès (1955)

lumière' spectacle, when the soundtrack and Maurice Jarre's music combine with Marcel Fradetal's photography to create an eerie tension out of (literally) nothing, and a speeded-up funeral when the joyous heirs finally bury the count's body to the accompaniment of a cheerful little song by Georges Brassens: 'Où sont les funérailles d'antan?'. *Thérèse Desqueyroux* (1962), in which Franju returned to the more humane and realistic vein of *La Tête contre les murs*, marks his maturity as a feature director. It was derived from a novel by the Catholic novelist François Mauriac, who adapted it for Franju in collaboration with his son Claude. The action is transferred to the present day but otherwise the adaptation largely respects the pattern of the original. Shooting on location in the very settings that had inspired Mauriac, Franju gave a very convincing portrayal of the power exercised by the forests over the minds of the inhabitants and of the suffocating nature of French upper-middle-class life. *Thérèse Desqueyroux* is a film of shades and nuances, and Franju captures admirably the novel's claustrophobic atmosphere and sense of deep regret at Thérèse's inability to find the happiness which is always so near and so inaccessible. The director was again greatly helped by Maurice Jarre's music with its theme for solo piano, an instrument which, for Franju, symbolises provincial life. Georges Franju occupies a unique place in French cinema. His first connection with the cinema was as co-founder of the Cinémathèque française in 1937 and his work shows a particular love of the pioneer film makers. In particular he sees the key element of a film not as the narrative development but as the interplay of images and music. With his particular conception of realism and atmosphere Franju provides an invaluable link between the cinema of the 1930s and that of the 1950s. But in essence the tradition to which his work attaches itself is less that of Carné than of Vigo, and his genuinely anarchistic approach provides a touchstone against which the supposed non-conformity of the younger film makers can be measured.

Alain Resnais waited an equally long time before making his first feature but then chose an original script by Marguerite Duras for *Hiroshima mon amour* (1959), a film that proved to be as masterly and revolutionary as Orson Welles's *Citizen Kane* eighteen years earlier. *Hiroshima mon amour* tells of a French actress whose brief affair with a Japanese architect prompts memories of an earlier unhappy love, for a German soldier during wartime in provincial France. In the film Resnais and Duras explore the workings of the woman's memory. Initially it is simply the movement of her Japanese lover's hand that recalls the past. Then the horrors of Hiroshima, when she comes to feel them deeply, lead her to remember her own personal loss, humiliation and madness at Nevers. As past and present become one, the Japanese and the German lovers fuse into one being. To relate this narrative the authors devised a quite novel flashback pattern. The images of Nevers rise up unheralded and unexpected, and the past is revealed not in any logical order but only as it imposes itself on the woman. As the memories grow in intensity, so the flashbacks reach greater length and the music of Giovanni Fusco serves to unify the film by a repetition of its principal themes. Visually the film is always exciting: the first enigmatic shots of embracing bodies; the tracking shots – familiar from Resnais's documentaries – through the museum in Hiroshima; the neon-lit harshness of the modern riverside café; the softer light of Nevers and the scenes of young love. *Hiroshima mon amour* is a remarkably ambitious film. It comprises a documentary on Hiroshima past and present, and an indictment of our forgetfulness of the atomic horror. It deals with human situations of rare complexity and, discarding conventional notions of plot and story development, it invents a new narrative technique of balancing image and text, uniting the various elements by a highly original use of music and recitative.

L'Année dernière à Marienbad (1961), from a script by the novelist Alain Robbe-Grillet, is an even more complex and ambiguous work. Even the makers in their numerous and contradictory discussions of the film were not prepared to do more than say what seems to happen. Namely, that a man, X, attempts to seduce a woman, A, away from M, who is perhaps her husband. Eventually, despite a succession of defeats every time he encounters M, he succeeds and the couple leave together. Various explanations to account for this story spring to mind: that it is a version of the Orpheus-Euridice myth, for example, or that it depicts in visual terms the relationship between patient and psychoanalyst, but the authors, although drawing on a rich set of fictional archetypes, have ensured that no single explanation is wholly satisfactory. The whole film is built up in a fragmentary and confusing manner, with the time sequence deliberately destroyed and short scenes following each other without apparent logic. Some images evidently depict the thoughts or fears of the characters, but real and imaginary are never distinguished. The possibility that the whole film happens in the woman's mind is left open, just as events of this year and last year are shown as part of a single, disjointed flow which it is impossible to analyse chronologically. On the surface, *L'Année dernière à Marienbad* is a cold film with a technical perfection that leaves little room for emotion. The setting has few points of contact with our everday world (a remoteness emphasised by the film's organ accompaniment) and the acting is totally stylised and closer to opera than film naturalism. Yet the underlying structure devised by Robbe-Grillet has a very precise pattern, dependent on symmetry and reversal, and if the film is experienced in terms of a musical flow of feeling, rather than confronted as an intellectual puzzle to be resolved, it is a deeply satisfying and emotional work.

Resnais's concern with time and the mind, the interaction of past and present leads him to a fresh approach to film structure in which the role of editing is crucial. Rejecting the all-too-logical patterning of the previous generation, he builds his films in more adventurous ways. In the documentaries, this meant reconstructing in time the various elements that Picasso had integrated in space in his great painting *Guernica* or deriving the impact and rhythm of *Nuit et brouillard* from the balance of colour images of the camps today with black-and-white newsreel footage. In *Hiroshima mon amour* the Nevers story is integrated into the Hiroshima relationship by means of the steadily growing flow of flashbacks and in a similar way the reality of any given image in *L'Année dernière à Marienbad* can be assessed solely from its position, length and lighting. Even more original is the way in which the patterns of counterpoint between these images and the music and commentary track worked out in the documentaries is taken over to become the basis of a totally original narrative construction in the first features. In this way Resnais gives his films all the interest and fluency of the contemporary novel.

Resnais's impact on all the writers with whom he was to work in this period was considerable. In the years up to 1962 there were also several films influenced by, or developing parallel to, his work. Henri Colpi, his editor on *Hiroshima* and *Marienbad*, directed a further Marguerite Duras script dealing with the themes of identity and memory, *Une Aussi longue absence* (1960), with great precision and polish. The success of this film makes one regret that Colpi, who made three further and very varied features in the 1960s, was never able to establish himself fully as a director. Another isolated work was *La Jetée* (shot in 1962, but not released until 1964), the sole fiction film directed by Chris Marker. This thirty-minute short, shot almost entirely in still photographs and edited in masterly fashion, is a strikingly original experiment which treats material closely related to the feature work of Resnais and Agnès Varda: a love story of nameless individuals existing outside time, set against a background of war and concentration-camp horror, concerned with the problems of time and memory and the interaction of past and future. Marker's other works of the period were studies of two emergent societies: Israel in *Description d'un combat* (1960) and Cuba in *Cuba si!* (1961). In both documentaries the characteristic Marker humour is present, but they also reveal the director's keenness on asking questions about the problematic future of the countries concerned.

*

The bulk of Jean Rouch's work, which extends into the 1980s, comprises ethnographic films relating directly to his work in Africa which have received only limited European showings. A compilation of his early films, *Les Fils de l'eau*, was made in 1952 but was not shown publicly until six years later and the first of his films to receive wide attention was *Les Maîtres fous* (1955) which dealt with a small African religious sect drawing its members from the illiterate sections of the population and reflecting in its rites both the struggle of the blacks against white supremacy and the disorientation caused by contact with an alien culture. But it was with the films shown or made in the period 1958–62 that Rouch came to exercise a real influence on French cinema and emerged as the leader in France of the movement variously known as *cinéma-vérité* or direct cinema. These years coincided with the development of lightweight 16 mm Arriflex and Nagra synchronous sound film system and Rouch was both one of the prime instigators in the development of this equipment and also one of the keenest advocates of its use in both documentary and fictional film making. The aesthetic of *cinéma-vérité* is in many ways at odds with that of the classic narrative film in that both an interesting visual style and strikingly beautiful effects are rejected as a hindrance to truth and there is a constant attempt to blur the distinction between reality as it exists in the world and the image of reality as captured with a camera and tape recorder. Another key influence is television for which the new balance of word and image and the lower visual quality of 16 mm production could be acceptable. The key meeting of *cinéma-vérité* film makers from all over the world, which took place in Lyons in 1963, was sponsored under the auspices of Radio Télévision Française.

Rouch's work reflects all the confusions, enthusiasms and ambiguities of the movement in its initial stages and moves steadily from a concern with documentary recording to an attempt to create new forms of fiction. For *Moi un noir* (1958), his first feature film, Rouch began by filming an objective account of the life of a stevedore in the slum district of Treichville in Abidjan, then, by persuading him to record the commentary, was able to convey in the film the man's dreams and ambitions, reflected in the name he has chosen for himself, Edward G. Robinson. The stevedore, Oumarou Ganda, later returned to his native Niger and became one of the pioneer film directors of black Africa. In *La Pyramide humaine* (1961) Rouch used a fictional story to provoke and record interaction between black and white pupils at the Abidjan grammar school. Shot in a spontaneous, improvised manner with a silent camera, the film showed Rouch's increasing interest in fiction as a means of understanding questions of cultural interaction. *Chronique d'un été* (1961), made with the sociologist Edgar Morin, applied the approach of Rouch's African films to the very different milieu of Paris. Working for the first time with lightweight synchronous sound equipment, Rouch and Morin used interview techniques to probe the fears and anxieties of a wide range of people and as in his earlier work Rouch showed his interest in filming the discussions and interactions of the people he brought together. Freed from the problem of post-synchronisation, Rouch here had to cope with the complexities of editing the twenty-one hours of material shot by his two cameramen, the Canadian *cinéma-vérité* film maker, Michel Brault, and Godard's cameraman Raoul Coutard. Despite the interest aroused by *Chronique d'un été* it was not a commercial success, but Rouch was able to proceed with his idea of trying to shoot a feature-length fiction film in a single weekend. *La Punition*, shown on television in 1962, applied the methods of the previous film to fiction, but despite its technical innovation, the film was widely criticised, since the players were ill-rehearsed, the dialogue inadequate and the relation of the shooting style to the action and to the needs of editing never resolved. In retrospect it seems clear that Rouch's work in the crucial period of 1958–62 is notable more for the questions it raises about film and reality than for the specific answers it gives.

Two film makers who in the 1960s followed in the paths opened up by Rouch are Mario Ruspoli and Chris Marker. Ruspoli, a former painter and journalist, had made his first film, *Les Hommes de la baleine* (1956), in classic documentary style. In 1962 he used the new lightweight synchronous sound equipment for two remarkable studies, *Les Inconnus de la terre* and *Regard sur la folie*. Where Rouch shows his interest in situations and subjects created at the actual moment of shooting, Ruspoli eschews fiction and is concerned with filming only what exists in as true and spontaneous a fashion as possible. The versatile Chris Marker's *Le Joli mai* (first shown in 1963, but shot in May 1962) falls into two parts, the first exploring the private lives of a range of people, and the second dealing with the wider issues of the time: the trial of General Salan, the railway strike, the problems of Algerians living in France. Lacking the characteristic Marker commentary, the film is almost as formless and uneven as Rouch's work, but contains a number of brilliant moments and some invaluable insights into the state of French public opinion.

*

During the period 1958–62 it was the young film makers who received most attention – regardless of the intrinsic value of their work – and several of the older directors seem to have felt the need to come to terms with the new generation. Henri-Georges Clouzot, for example, chose Brigitte Bardot as the star of his only work of the period, *La Vérité* (1960), a return to the theme of amoral youth which he had earlier treated in *Manon*. The film's contemporary theme is, however, packaged in an essentially 1940s narrative structure built around flashbacks and, while the characteristic Clouzot themes of the destructiveness of passion and the humiliations of love are very apparent, the picture offered of contemporary youth is unconvincing. In *Les Tricheurs* (1958) and again in the less successful *Terrain vague* (1960) Marcel Carné turned to a similar subject matter. But despite a number of superficially modern touches, *Les Tricheurs* is also basically a conventional piece, with no originality in construction to match the new subject matter. It is the set-pieces that succeed best and little insight is shown by either Carné or his writer, Jacques Sigurd, into the motives and feelings of their rebellious young characters. René Clément was much more successful in capturing a new tone with *Plein soleil* (1959) on which he worked with Chabrol's scriptwriter Paul Gégauff and the director of photography Henri Decaë. An ingenious if not altogether convincing thriller adapted from a Patricia Highsmith novel, the film starred Alain Delon and Maurice Ronet and allowed Clément to continue the experiments in fluidly moving camerawork which he had begun in *Monsieur Ripois*. Clément's visual sense never deserts him, but his international co-productions of the period show the first signs of the decline in his work which was to occur in the 1960s and especially the 1970s. If *Quelle joie de vivre* (1961), a tragicomic burlesque set in Italy at the time of Mussolini's march on Rome, is handled with a verve and technical skill that compensate for Clément's lack of an instinctive flair for comedy, *Barrage contre le Pacifique/La digya sul Pacifico* (1958) is a sprawling epic which never unites its themes or gets below the surface in tracing its characters' actions.

The decline apparent in Clément's work is also to be found in that of other veterans of the period. When Jean Renoir returned to the cinema in 1959 after three years largely devoted to the theatre it was to make two very uneven works in a semi-improvised style based on television methods of shooting. *Le Testament du Docteur Cordelier*, released in 1961, two years after its completion, was a modernised version of the Dr Jekyll and Mr Hyde theme starring Jean-Louis Barrault. Originally intended as a live television production, the film retains its air of spontaneity but its visual quality is poor, the plot schematised and unconvincing and the performance of Barrault undisciplined, provoking laughter rather than horror. *Le Déjeuner sur l'herbe* (1959), shot in the same semi-improvised manner, mixes its genres – farce and poetry, satire and hymn to nature – in characteristic fashion. There are some striking images of the Provençal landscape and Renoir's family home, Les Collettes, but although Renoir's theme of the necessity of submission to nature comes across strongly, the action is schematised and never convincing. With *Le Caporal épinglé* (1962) Renoir returned to some of the themes of *La Grande illusion* but now the tone and range are quite different, and the new film, for all its lightness and humour, is perilously near to standard army farce.

Renoir's later work found plenty of warm support from the members of the younger generation who idolised him (particularly Truffaut, who was later to edit the drafts of André Bazin's unfinished book on the director). But there is little that can be said to the credit of René Clair's *Tout l'or du monde* (1961), an exaggerated and unconvincing farce peopled by stereotyped peasants which lacks even Clair's customary tight construction. Claude Autant-Lara's extensive output – eight films between *En cas de malheur* (1958) to *Le Comte de Monte-Cristo* (1961) – is also largely without interest, apart from the realisation – in Yugoslavia in 1960 – of the director's long-projected anti-war film, *Tu ne tueras point* (released only in 1963). But even here, despite his evident sincerity and passion, Autant-Lara has not succeeded in making his film more than a somewhat ponderous if well-intentioned tract.

The years 1959–62 did, however, see worthy farewells to the cinema from three distinguished directors. Roger Leenhardt's *Le Rendez-vous de minuit* (1962) was less deeply felt than his other feature, *Les Dernières vacances*, but its complex working out of its film-within-a-film theme sustained intellectual interest. Jacques Becker's last film before his death, *Le Trou* (1960), was a masterly success after eight years of failures and half-achieved projects. The subject of a prison escape is treated so as to offer the detailed observation of people in which Becker delighted. From the beginning the humiliations of prison life are made clear and we can understand the men's need for freedom. Nothing is allowed to distract us from the action: the camera style is marvellously assured but unobtrusive, and there is no music, only natural sound used to create atmosphere. The tension and suspense are maintained throughout, up to the final agonising scene of betrayal. The five main characters themselves, all played by nonprofessionals, are not romanticised, nor are the moments of violence that flare up glossed over. But the co-operation and common need for freedom shared by these men bring out other qualities in them:

persistence, ingenuity, courage and, above all, loyalty. By concentrating on these Becker was able to give *Le Trou* a sense of affirmation which makes it a fitting conclusion to his work.

In 1959, nine years after completing his major work, *Orphée*, Jean Cocteau returned to make *Le Testament d'Orphée* which is, in many ways, a summing up to his career, full of allusions to his earlier work. Taking on the leading role himself, Cocteau meets on his travels the Sphinx and Jean Marais in the role of Oedipus, as well as the Princess of Death and her attendant Heurtebise from *Orphée*. He travels on the same boat as Isolde and the smoke that comes from his mouth as he lies 'dead' before Minerva recalls that issuing from the statuary in *La Belle et la bête*. Cocteau also passes in front of his own mural of Judith and visits the Eglise St Pierre which he decorated. His adopted son Edouard Dermit reappears as Cégeste and others of his acquaintances, ranging from Picasso to Yul Brynner and the bull-fighter Luis Dominguin, put in brief appearances. Cocteau also reveals here to the greatest extent his delight in the conjuring possibilities of cinema, the ability to move freely through time and space, or to perform (by means of reverse projection) such impossible feats as making a picture appear by rubbing it out, reassembling a shattered flower or creating a photograph from the flames. While the personal mythology of the film is often obscure, there is no mistaking the poet's serenity and good humour, here emphasised by his own slightly awkward performance. Cocteau's reputation as a film maker rests largely on his three original filmic creations: *Le Sang d'un poète* (1930), *Orphée* (1950) and *Le Testament d' Orphée* (1959). In these films Cocteau reveals his status as a film maker entirely free from the limitations of a conventional approach, able to express his personal views, quirks and obsessions while using a whole variety of stylistic devices.

Major work outside the mainstream was again produced by the French cinema's two great independent innovators of the post-war period, Jacques Tati and Robert Bresson. Tati's *Mon oncle* (1958) again featured Hulot, but tackled wider issues than either *Jour de fête* or *Les Vacances de Monsieur Hulot* and is indicative of the director's increasingly serious attitude to comedy. The film attacks the soullessness of modern life in the manner of Clair's classic *A nous la liberté*, resting on a contrast between the worlds of Hulot and his brother-in-law Arpel. The latter lives in an ultra-modern house with a bare, functional, open-plan interior and a completely symmetrical garden so tidy and geometrical that even a single leaf on the path is a cause for surprise. Hulot by contrast lives in the dilapidated old quarter of the town where life is more leisurely and humane. The contrast of Hulot and Arpel is expressed in other ways too: Jean Bourgoin's colour photography brings out the essential difference in its tonal qualities and, on the sound track, there is a huge gulf between the mechanical rattling and whirring of the innumerable gadgets in the Arpel house and the laughter and talk in the square overlooked by Hulot's apartment. The gags in *Mon oncle* have been meticulously worked out. The tone of the film is leisurely and Tati aims to provoke smiles rather than guffaws. To hold the film together he employs a number of running jokes and as usual the construction is neat, simple and well thought out. As in previous films the music serves to give unity and to maintain the mood, while the dialogue is unimportant. Occasionally too here are touches of almost surrealist humour, as in the scene where the two Arpels appear at their windows so that the house appears to be rolling its eyes, and sometimes the film raises the ordinary rhythm of life into an almost formal ballet. Despite these moments there is an increasing preoccupation with realism in *Mon oncle* which has caused some critics to evoke comparisons with Italian neo-realism. But Tati is resolutely non-political: he views the old quarter inhabited by Hulot with nostalgic affection and his attack on modernity in the person of Arpel is much in line with the attitudes of René Clair. Tati's realism lacks an essentially critical edge.

With the two films made between 1958 and 1962 Robert Bresson completed his series on the achievement of sainthood or, at least, a state of grace. The original scenario for *Pickpocket* (1959) was clearly inspired by Dostoievsky's *Crime and Punishment* and tells of a young man who tries to prove his superiority to the world by a life of crime but achieves salvation through the love of a young girl. Michel, the pickpocket of the title and narrator of the film, has the face we associate with a Bresson hero – sensitive, alert and unemotional – and his commentary recounts, but never justifies or excuses, his conduct. *Pickpocket* takes us more into the everyday world than before, but this is a world where God plays no part and Michel's life here has no spiritual meaning. Although the core of the film is formed by Michel's inner struggle, Bresson shows no interest in individual psychology and Michel remains expressionless throughout. The secondary climaxes of his life, such as the death of his mother, are played down so that attention is concentrated squarely on the conflict within him. In this way his final arrest, which is the climax of this conflict and hence of the whole film, is made to stand out. Jeanne, whose love for Michel is the means of his salvation, introduces a new note into Bresson's work and anticipates the submissive victims of the late 1960s films. Every aspect of *Pickpocket* bears the stamp of its maker. The actors are drilled to present the characters precisely as he sees them, the rhythm is slow and measured and it is typical of the control exercised that the final embrace of Michel and Jeanne is through the bars of his cell. The film's camera focuses throughout with mesmeric intensity, whether on the ballet-like play of the pickpockets' hands or on the faces of Michel and Jeanne.

Procès de Jeanne d'Arc (1962) concentrates on the imprisonment and trial of Joan and culminates in her condemnation and execution. Where in his earlier films Bresson had distilled a single thread of action from the diversity of life, here he attempted to breathe life into the historical record of Joan's trial. In his quest for absolute authenticity, these records were Bresson's only conceivable source and he allows himself to invent nothing, though in his *mise-en-scène* he does include a few anachronisms in order to avoid any of the picturesque atmosphere of the conventional historical film. Words are as important as ever in *Procès de Jeanne d'Arc* but they serve a different function from that exercised in the earlier films. Here they record not an inner struggle but an outer clash – Joan's verbal duel with Bishop Cauchon – and this is perhaps the key to the peculiar coldness of the film. Stylistically too the film shows Bresson at his most austere. Only at the beginning and end of the film are the full resources of the cinema used, while the long central interrogation is filmed almost entirely in medium shots relentlessly cross-cutting between Joan and her interrogators. This method allows Bresson to create a sense of the monotony of prolonged imprisonment and trial and gives the film a weight out of proportion to its length (a mere sixty-five minutes). But it does not allow the director to penetrate deeply into the character of Joan. As depicted here, she has virtually no doubts or regrets at leaving this world. She is content, such is the strength of her faith, to submit herself totally to God's will. The resolute march of a saint to martyrdom may fill us with awe, but we do not feel any personal involvement with her.

*

The period 1958–62 saw the French cinema in the forefront of what was to be a worldwide reshaping of the whole notion of how a fictional feature film should be constructed. Perhaps the fact that French mid-1950s cinema was so moribund helped the new generation there to make the initial breakthrough so decisively, but one should not underestimate the drive and resourcefulness of the *Cahiers du cinéma* group in achieving the ambitions they had first nurtured in the darkness of Henri Langlois's Cinémathèque française in the early 1950s. The example they set was to be followed by dozens of groups calling themselves 'new cinemas' or 'young cinemas' throughout the world in the 1960s.

The New Wave aimed at change on virtually every level of film style. First, as far as the film maker himself is concerned, his work could be as directly personal as a first novel (Truffaut's *Les Quatre cents coups* was a key example) and could reflect a direct and immediate response to a particular time and place, filmed on location, not reconstructed in a studio (in the way that Rohmer's *Le Signe du lion* captured the tourist Paris of the dead summer months). All the rules of conventional 1950s narrative continuity editing, with its careful establishing shots and patterned use of close-ups, its separation of dialogue from structure and total rejection of any trace of spontaneity or improvisation, could be questioned. Here the change has been most radical and, twenty years after its first release, it is now virtually impossible to see Godard's *A bout de souffle* as the revolutionary work it looked in 1960, so universally accepted have its structural advances become. Abandoning the sacrosanct text, the film maker could also forgo the services of stars who had developed their own theatrical mannerisms and indeed reject the conventions of a cinema built on typecasting and the careful gradation of roles. All the time-consuming paraphernalia and massive crewing of studio work could be abandoned and a new use made of lightweight cameras, location sound-recording equipment, portable lighting and fast film stocks. Then, having given up so much of the conventional artifice which aligned it to the patterns of nineteenth-century narrative, the cinema could forge new links with modern literature – here Resnais was to play a key part – and use flashbacks and dislocations of time with all the freedom of a contemporary novelist.

The great achievement of the young (and not so young) French film makers of this period was to accomplish this within the mainstream of production, so that their low-budget features were not marginalised but competed in the same cinemas and on the same terms as the major productions of Clément, Cayatte or Delannoy. New sources of finance were also discovered by producers who found that there was an international market for a new Godard or Truffaut film. The latters' breakthrough not only opened the way forward for themselves, it also allowed such innovative older directors as Tati and Bresson to work with the assurance of an audience and with new possibilities of raising funding for ambitious and unorthodox works (Truffaut's assistance in the financing of Cocteau's *Le Testament d'Orphée* symbolises the new links between generations). The transformation achieved in four years was enormous: it only remained for these new foundations to be built upon, and in particular for the new stylistic freedom to be applied creatively to the changing face of France.

11 Ebb Tide
1963–68

C'est une autre tradition de tout un cinéma français. Pour ne pas se compromettre avec une réalité trop souvent conflictuelle, on conjugue le temps dans une dimension que les grammairiens n'ont pas prévue: le contemporain vague. Il s'agit, tout en travaillant apparemment au présent, d'en évacuer toutes les asperités, tous les signes qui exigéraient une prise de position, un choix politique.

Jean-Pierre Jeancolas, 1979

After the surge of excitement occasioned by the advent of a hundred or so new directors during the years immediately following 1958, the eight years from 1963 to May 1968 seem comparatively dull and timid. It becomes increasingly clear that the advent of a new generation of directors has not led to a new relationship between French cinema and French society. Some of those who seemed destined to be key names in the 1960s lose their touch and plunge into mediocrity, while others rise to prominence. But in the period up to 1968 one has the sense of a game of musical chairs, rather than a real building on the renewal which the New Wave, for all its ambiguities, constituted. The institutional structure of the cinema remained unchanged, the vogue for the young and untried gradually subsided as luckless producers found themselves with a dozen or two films which were, quite literally, unshowable. Some of the major established talents rose to new heights, but there were more careers coming to an end, it seemed, than were being launched. The standard cycles of the period in the commercial film are sadly predictable – thrillers and period dramas, low-budget spy films and vehicles for such established stars as Jean Gabin and Louis de Funès. Nowhere is there a willingness to come fully to terms with the contradictions of the present or to probe the evasions of the past: even the major talents of the period seem to be turning their backs increasingly on reality as the 1960s advance.

The change of fortunes and retreat from actuality are nowhere more clearly shown than in the case of those who had anticipated the breakthrough in 1958 and had at one time seemed destined to be among the major forces of the subsequent decade. Roger Vadim had the advantages of gifted technical collaborators, large budgets and star performers (including Catherine Deneuve and Jane Fonda), but the succession of films he produced from *Le Vice et la vertu* (1963) to *Barbarella* (1968) is of very little lasting interest. Alexandre Astruc's two war films, *La Longue marche* (1966) and *Flammes sur l'Adriatique* (1968), the last fiction films for which he was to be responsible, are seriously intended attempts at demystification (of the Resistance in the first instance) which, although quite unexceptional by international standards, did have a local interest in raising issues too often ignored in France.

In contrast to these muted efforts, the work of Jean-Pierre Melville reached new heights during this period. If *L'Aîné des Ferchaux* (1963), an adaptation of a Simenon novel, offered a subject remote from his central concerns, Melville's other films of the period form the very core of his achievement in cinema. In this trio of masterly gangster films – *Le Doulos* (1963) with Jean-Paul Belmondo, *Le Deuxième souffle* (1966) with Lino Ventura, and *Le Samourai* (1967) with Alain Delon – the director's concern with film as narrative spectacle is totally vindicated. Drawing on his own 1930s viewing and his adolescent reading of American thrillers (Dashiell Hammett was naturally a favourite), Melville manipulated the whole mythology of the gangster film. His criminals are idealised figures, their appearance stylised (with raincoat, hat and gun predominant) and their behaviour oddly blending violence and ritualised politeness. The director has no interest in the realistic portrayal of life as it is and disregards both psychological depth and accuracy of location and costume. He uses his stars to portray timeless, tragic figures caught up in ambiguous conflicts and patterns of deceit, relying on the actor's personality and certainty of gesture to fill the intentional void. *Le Samourai* in particular is a perfect distillation of the cinematic myth of the gangster. Melville's mid-1960s works, together with Jacques Becker's earlier *Touchez pas au grisbi* and *Le Trou*, stand head and shoulders over all opposition.

The mid-1960s were also a period in which Louis Malle's work took on a new force and authority. *Le Feu follet* (1963), adapted by the director from a novel by Drieu La Rochelle, was Malle's finest film to date. Gone were the hesitancies and uncertainties of the previous work. The characters continually hold the interest, the fluent camerawork never obtrudes and the awareness of impending death gives the film a dimension new in Malle's work. *Le Feu follet* recounts the last forty-eight hours in the life of Alain Leroy (Maurice Ronet), whose past is gradually revealed to us from casual remarks by his friends, while the utter emptiness of his present becomes clear from his lack of vital contact with any of them. The rhythm of Alain's progression towards death is slow and measured. Malle is not afraid of *longueurs*, the tone is consistent throughout, with only occasional touches of humour, and the mood is greatly fortified by the use of a piano piece by Erik Satie. The colourful *Viva Maria* (1965), shot in Mexico as a lighthearted diversion after the seriousness of *Le Feu follet*, was designed to exploit the combined impact of two of the most distinctive French stars of the 1960s, Jeanne Moreau and Brigitte Bardot, here making their first appearance together. On the lightest level of undemanding entertainment, *Viva Maria* functions excellently, full of witty gags, catchy tunes by Georges Delerue and beautiful colour images by Henri Decaë. On another level the film can perhaps be seen as a reflection on the interplay of life and the theatre in the tradition of Renoir's *The Golden Coach*, with Jeanne Moreau using Shakespeare to rouse the masses and Brigitte Bardot a machine-gun to lead a music-hall version of revolution. As if to prove his versatility, Malle remained with a period setting but returned to a more serious tone with *Le Voleur* (1967). Again, as in *Le Feu follet*, he adapted a novel but treated material very close to his own personal concerns. The story is that of a young man from a wealthy background who has turned to crime because of his hatred of society and whose whole life is exposed in a single night: the recurring presence of death, the increasing solitude, and the implacable drive to theft.

Agnès Varda's progress through the mid-1960s, though on a less commercially successful level, has a similar artistic consistency. Varda's second feature film, *Cléo de cinq à sept* (1962), traces two hours in the life of a successful pop singer awaiting a hospital report. Cléo (Corinne Marchand) finds her secluded little world of maid, lover and composers constricting – the white airiness of her flat emphasises the unreality of her life – and goes out into the Parisian streets. But the world outside is indifferent, even on occasion menacing, until a chance encounter brings a promise of love. *Cléo de cinq à sept* is an attempt to probe into the life and motivations of a beautiful woman who seems at first sight merely frivolous but who grows increasingly sympathetic as the film progresses. The film is not without its flaws (a cliché carnival sequence and a very unfunny silent-film insert), but as a whole is scrupulously planned, full of convincing detail and, as one would expect from a professional photographer, visually most exciting. Subsequently Varda went, like Chris Marker, to Cuba and on her return produced a short documentary homage to Cuba, *Salut les cubains* (1963), from the four thousand still photographs she had shot there.

Varda's feature work in the 1960s does not, however, reflect her political views directly. *Le Bonheur* (1965) is disturbing precisely because it leaves aside social issues, as well as all considerations of psychology and morality. We are left with a structure that is more of a symmetrical pattern – the substitution of one loved woman for another – than a plot in the conventional sense. Although the intrusion of a new woman into the artisan hero's life drives his wife to suicide, the tone of *Le Bonheur* is uniformly idyllic, reinforced by the music of Mozart, and nothing could be further from social realism than the make-believe world it constructs. *Le Bonheur* is Varda's most decoratively resplendent work, showing perhaps the influence of her husband, Jacques Demy, and echoing Renoir's use of landscape in *Le Déjeuner sur l'herbe* (a clip of which is included). Throughout nature is of crucial importance: the film begins with a summer picnic which is the perfect picture of happiness and ends with an autumnal one in which the replacement of wife by mistress is the only alteration. Throughout colour is used symbolically and *Le Bonheur* remains in the memory as a film of flowers and sunlight. With *Les Créatures* (1966) Varda examined the interrelationship of reality and fiction, taking as her subject a writer whose fantasies become so real in his own mind that eventually he finds himself playing chess with one of his characters to decide the fate of the others. The degree of reality of any particular scene is often left in doubt and order is only fully restored at the end when the writer's wife gives birth to a child. The beautifully photographed *Les Créatures* represents the extreme example of Varda's manipulation of characters who are denied any human depth or psychological complexity but, lacking *Le Bonheur*'s simplicity of form, its rhythm is less compelling.

*

Among the group constituted by the former critics of *Cahiers du cinéma* fortunes were mixed during the mid-1960s. For Claude Chabrol, after a succession of box-office failures, the period up to 1967 comprised purely commercial assignments through which he strove to re-establish the confidence of producers and recover control over his work. *Landru* (1962), a study of the mass murderer scripted by Françoise Sagan, was a first step in this direction. The subject afforded Chabrol great scope for an attack on bourgeois values, but with the tone veering unevenly and inconsistently from farce to serious drama, the main impact was made less by the narrative than by the lush sets and vivid colour photography (by Jean Rabier, Chabrol's customary director of photography throughout the 1960s). Subsequently all pretension to the production of anything but undemanding entertainment films vanished as he made in quick succession a series of comedy thrillers whose titles speak for themselves: *Le Tigre aime la chair fraîche* (1964), *Marie Chantal contre le Docteur Kah* (1965), *Le Tigre se parfume à la dynamite* (1965). Gradually, however, Chabrol succeeded in restoring himself to something like his old position of eminence. *La Ligne de démarcation* (1966) was a Resistance melodrama with certain similarities to Astruc's *La Longue marche*, released the same year. *Le Scandale* (1967), an ingenious detective mystery recalling Chabrol's admiration for Hitchcock, and *La Route de Corinthe* (1967), a further spy-film parody, marked further stages in the slow recovery which was to be confirmed with the appearance of *Les Biches* in 1968. This film is considered, together with the masterly series of studies of bourgeois manners which it initiated, in the next chapter.

After the muted reception of *Paris nous appartient*, Jacques Rivette had to wait several years before he could realise a second feature project. Having directed a version of Jacques Diderot's novel on stage in 1962, Rivette decided to transpose it onto the screen as *Suzanne Simonin, la religieuse de Diderot*, with Anna Karina maintaining the leading role. Unexpectedly three successive scripts were rejected by the censors and religious organisations were mobilised to prevent the film being shown even before it was completed. The final film, passed by the board of censors, was promptly banned by the Minister of Information, although it was simultaneously selected as one of the official French entries at the 1966 Cannes film festival. The cause of this censorship was Diderot's subject – the misuse of convent life in eighteenth-century France – but its effect was to give the film enormous audiences when it was eventually shown in Paris after a year or so's delay. This success is paradoxical, since *La Religieuse* is one of Rivette's most austere works, a totally sober and unsensational narrative tracing the fate of a young girl forced into a nunnery against her will and then finding, when she breaks her vows, that there is no place for her in society. In the context of Rivette's later work, this film is quite conventional and unexperimental – the nearest of his films to the classic cinema of Hollywood for which the director has such affection.

Eric Rohmer was similarly unable to impose himself fully until the end of the 1960s after the commercial failure of *Le Signe du lion*. Undeterred, he worked for educational television and turned back to 16 mm production of short films, continuing to work in the way he had begun his career in the early 1950s. Among the films to which he contributed was *Paris vu par . . .* (1965), a collective work which also included sketches by Claude Chabrol, Jean-Luc Godard, Jean Rouch,

Jean-Daniel Pollet and Jean Douchet. In 1962 Rohmer also began work on the project to film six 'moral tales' which was to occupy him for ten years. The first two episodes, *La Boulangère de Monceau* (1962) and *La Carrière de Suzanne* (1963), were both short films shot in black and white and in 16 mm, but in 1967 Rohmer was able to return to 35 mm feature-film production with *La Collectionneuse*, the fourth in the series of six, but the third to be filmed. We shall return to this series of tales in the next chapter.

In contrast, François Truffaut was able to extend his range of film-making styles during the mid-1960s with four varied but personally chosen films without losing the favour of the public. None of the films realised at this period has, however, quite the impact of *Les Quatre cents coups* or *Jules et Jim*. *La Peau douce* (1964), for example, his fourth feature, is a serious study of the dissolution of a marriage, examining the adultery of a middle-aged literary critic with an air hostess he meets on a plane taking him to Portugal. This situation is a stock ingredient of much conventional commercial film production and it is only by his choice of detail and clear, compelling characterisation that Truffaut asserts his originality. The film's crucial weakness is the ending, when the wife, having discovered some incriminating photographs of the now terminated affair, carries a shot-gun into the restaurant where the husband is contentedly eating and shoots him dead. Truffaut derived this ending from a newspaper report and incorporated it into his film in a fairly arbitrary way so that it contrives to damage in retrospect much that has gone before. *Fahrenheit 451* (1966) was again something of a new departure, being an adaptation of a Ray Bradbury science-fiction novel, made in London with Julie Christie in a double role. The title refers to the temperature at which paper catches fire, and the story is set in an age when the role of firemen is not to prevent fires but to burn books. Despite the subject matter, Truffaut shows little interest either in the sociological aspects or with the future itself. He uses contemporary settings but without defining at all the time or place of the action, and totally excludes all Bradbury's futuristic gadgetry (like the mechanical hound). The film has quite a number of echoes of the director's earlier work, but in essence remains a limited, slightly impersonal work showing some signs of Truffaut's unease with the English language.

1967 saw the publication of Truffaut's book of interviews with Alfred Hitchcock and the latter's influence is clearly visible in his next film, *La Mariée était en noir* (1967). There are echoes of specific Hitchcock films (such as *Marnie*), the music is by Bernard Herrmann, and the script itself derived from a novel by William Irish, the author of *Rear Window* and countless other thrillers. *La Mariée était en noir* deals with a woman (Jeanne Moreau) whose relentless quest for vengeance leads her to murder the five men involved in the accidental shooting of her husband on the steps of the church on her wedding day. As Truffaut himself pointed out, the film contains American themes treated in a European spirit rather than mere imitation, and the heritage of Jean Renoir is apparent in the handling of actors and in the inability to create convincing villains. Pursuing what seems to have been a conscious policy of following each completed project with a new one which is in some ways the opposite (the pattern also chosen by Louis Malle), Truffaut next returned to a more personal tone and recounted a further series of adventures of Antoine Doinel, his alter ego played by Jean-Pierre Léaud. *Baisers volés* (1968) takes up the story after Antoine's dishonourable discharge from the army, which he has joined after a quarrel with his girl, Christine. While attempting to regain her love, Antoine makes his living as, successively, a hotel night porter, a private detective (in which role he is magically seduced by Delphine Seyrig) and as a television repair man. It is in the latter job that he is reunited with Christine who agrees to marry him. *Baisers volés* is a slight and affectionate little film with nothing revolutionary to offer in its form or content, but with a splendid performance from Léaud (capturing just the right note of adolescent blundering tentativeness and insouciance) and a whole mass of brilliant humorous and affectionate detail, such as the slow track up to the *wrong* bedroom when Antoine and Christine (Claude Jade) are making love, or the tender scene of Antoine's proposal.

The most startling creative achievement of the 1960s was that of Jean-Luc Godard who followed his four features of 1960–62 with a further twelve completed by mid-1968, becoming in the process the most influential figure in world cinema of the decade. Godard films follow each other in a rich but confusing flow, each film both constituting a revaluation of progress to date and looking forward to new, still untried paths for cinema. *Les Carabiniers* (1963) makes a good starting point, since this film, on which Roberto Rossellini worked as one of the original script collaborators, sets out to re-invent the cinema. Shot very quickly and in a style intended as a homage to Louis Lumière, it makes interesting use of silent-film gestures and conventions and of the photographic texture of primitive film. Telling the story of two brothers, Ulysses and Michelangelo, who are persuaded to become soldiers of the king, and indulge in a riot of rape and killing, only to find that a revolution has taken place when they go to claim their reward, *Les Carabiniers* opens inventively and contains several very funny sequences, such as the remakes of such Lumière classics as *Arriveé d'un train à la Ciotat* and *Le Repas de bébé*. But the inclusion of newsreel footage of war atrocities is more questionable, as the film's tone hovers uncertainly between the farcical, the horrific and the merely facetious. Certainly the most memorable aspects of the film have little to do with the central theme: a few of Godard's most outrageous puns, the scene in the cinema when Michelangelo tries to join in the projected action of a film and the cataloguing of the brothers' collection of postcards.

Le Mépris, also made in 1963, was based remotely on Alberto Moravia's novel, *A Ghost at Noon*, and shot in colour and cinemascope on location in Rome and Capri. It depicts the break-up of the marriage of a young woman (Brigitte Bardot) and her writer husband (Michel Piccoli) when he is engaged to rewrite the script of a version of the Odyssey being shot by Fritz Lang. *Le Mépris* is in many ways a summary of Godard's work to date: there is the usual wide range of quotations and references; Fritz Lang appears in the role of the father figure who dispenses wisdom (recalling Brice Parain in *Vivre sa vie* and anticipating Roger Leenhardt in *Une Femme mariée*); there is a virtual documentary on Brigitte Bardot (who makes the obligatory nude appearances); and Godard offers his own reflections on the film world. The structure of the dialogue is a perfect symbol of non-communication, as none of the principals can speak the others' languages and need constant recourse to an interpreter. A key to the understanding of the film is the long scene (reminiscent of *A bout de souffle*) in which the incompatibility of the couple becomes apparent as Raoul Coutard's camera fluently, and with a bold use of bright splashes of colour, achieves some labyrinthine movements from room to room in their shared apartment.

The first of the two films released in 1964, *Bande à part*, is a fresh handling of *série noire* material about a trio of inefficient crooks (two men and a girl) who conspire to rob the rich woman with whom the girl (Anna Karina) lives. The plot is no more than a pretext for Godard to display all his mannerisms with an air of absolute certainty which leaves one in no doubt about his mastery of the film medium. The personal element is strong, since the story is accompanied by a commentary spoken by Godard in which he resumes the plot so far for the benefit of late-comers, gives his views on the Place de Clichy, compares the Seine to a Corot painting or tells us what the characters are thinking. Despite a drab setting of suburban Paris, *Bande à part* is a gay and tender little film, full of jokes, puns, parodied death scenes and all sorts of quirks. *Une Femme mariée* (1964) is a fresh and more serious departure, a study of woman's role in society, featuring Macha Méril. The film's subtitle is 'Fragments of a Film Shot in 1964' and it contains an incredible mixture of styles and approaches. Apart from the love scenes (as cold as they are outspoken and accompanied by passages from Beethoven's string quartets), there are interviews, long passages of quotation (Céline and Racine), a dialogue between husband and wife in which they describe their flat in estate-agents' jargon, a long sequence printed in negative, a virtual documentary on women's underwear advertisements and frequent references to the concentration camps (including a clip from Resnais's *Nuit et brouillard*). The views of the heroine and the people around her form the core of the film and are given in labelled, mock *cinéma-vérité* interviews (on memory, the present, intelligence etc.).

Alphaville (1965) is one of Godard's most satisfying films. An interesting mixture of science fiction and *série noire* it stars Eddie Constantine as Lemmy Caution, a secret agent who enters Alphaville to destroy its master, Professor von Braun, and escapes with the professor's daughter (Anna Karina). Godard has kept to many of the conventions of the Eddie Constantine-type melodrama (including the gunfights at beginning and end) and made excellent use of contemporary Parisian settings to evoke the futuristic world of Alpha 60. Raoul Coutard's camera makes full use of the dramatic contrasts of total blackness and dazzling neon and Paul Misraki's music contributes much to the meaning by serving as a reminder of the world of feeling outside the computer-run city of machines. Containing few of the usual jokes and digressions, *Alphaville* is by far the director's most disciplined work of the period. Elusive and unclassifiable as ever, Godard proceeded to make *Pierrot le fou* (1965), which is equally satisfying but completely undisciplined. Here he again goes back to a standard pulp-fiction plot concerning a hitherto respectable (if disorientated) young man (Jean-Paul Belmondo) who meets an enigmatic girl (Anna Karina) and becomes involved through her in murder. Forced to flee from Paris, they live for a while in idyllic harmony, but eventually incompatibility and betrayal lead to a climax of ugly violence. The early Parisian scenes are highly organised, including some fascinating experiment with fragmented narrative, a few stylised night driving scenes, a large number of references to paintings (especially Renoir), and a number of notable asides, such as the appearance at a party of Sam Fuller defining cinema as 'Like a battleground. Love. Hate. Action. Violence. Death. In a word, emotions'. A clue to Godard's intentions in the film is the reference to Velasquez who in his old age was concerned to paint 'not so much clearly defined objects as what lies between them'. The ending comes when Belmondo, in a memorable sequence, paints his face blue, ties dynamite around his head, lights the fuse and then (too late) changes his mind.

In contrast, *Masculin féminin* (1966) returned to the inquiry film framework of *Une Femme mariée* to consider, in 'fifteen precise facts', the problems of the younger generation, whom Godard characterises as the children of Marx and Coca-Cola. The basic story line, about an affair between a muddled young man (Jean-Pierre Léaud) and a young pop singer which ends with her pregnant and him dead, is far less important than the incidental confessions and comments scattered throughout the film, in which young people talk about their lives, their beliefs, politics, contraception and so on. All the affection and tenderness that characterised *Bande à part* are missing here. Paris is depicted as a sordid, depressing place, full of squalid sex and meaningless violence, and viewed by Godard and his hero with a total indifference and blank unrelieved pessimism.

Godard's work reached a new intensity in 1967, when four new feature films were released. *Made in USA* (1967), like *Deux ou trois choses que je sais d'elle* which was made simultaneously with it, allows other concerns – in this case politics – to take precedence over narrative, thereby showing the direction of Godard's work in the late 1960s. Godard has recorded that his initial idea was to do a kind of remake of *The Big Sleep*, but with a woman (Anna Karina) in the Humphrey Bogart role. There are many incidental touches that point to the same kind of Hollywood source: a dedication to Sam (Fuller) and Nick (Ray), the naming of the characters – David Goodis (author of the book on which *Tirez sur le pianiste* was based), Donald Siegel, Richard Widmark and Inspector Aldrich. There is also a Japanese girl called Doris Mizoguchi, a personal appearance by Marianne Faithfull and a pair of assassins called Nixon and McNamara. Despite this somewhat whimsical level of allusion, *Made in USA* was also intended to contain serious comment on current political issues: the Ben Barka affair, and the role of the left. But the film's closing message – 'The right and the left are both the same, they'll never change. The right because it's as stupid as it's vicious. The left because it's sentimental' – marks no advance on *Le Petit soldat*. Indeed the world of screen make-believe continually engulfs the depiction of real political violence, and the tone of *Made in USA* is well summed up when the commentary refers to it as 'a film by Walt Disney, but played by Humphrey Bogart and therefore a political film'.

Deux ou trois choses que je sais d'elle (1967) shows an analogous concern with social issues, being inspired by a newspaper report about women living in the expensive new blocks of flats on the outskirts of Paris who have to resort to casual prostitution to acquire the luxuries which are so necessary a part of modern life. The element of personal degradation is hardly touched upon in Godard's typically uninvolved handling of this theme, and prostitution is used as a general metaphor for human existence and as a peg on which to hang reflections on a whole range of issues. Godard even parodies his own seemingly random use of quotation through two figures, called in the script Bouvard and Pécuchet, who read a selection of disconnected sentences chosen haphazardly from a pile of books. The disjoined aspect of the film is always apparent and Godard aptly described it as 'not a film, but an attempt at a film... It is not a story, it is intended as a document'. On yet another level the film is one of Godard's crucial reflections on the problems of communication, the choices facing a film maker and the nature of language.

La Chinoise (1967) is about a group of young students who set up a Maois cell during their summer holidays. For much of the time the film hardly moves from the borrowed apartment in which they live and which they decorate with slogans, aphorisms, blackboards and a mass of Mao's little red books. The five students argue, discuss, and lecture each other, trying to evolve a common programme of action, but eventually each goes his or her own way. La Chinoise is a striking anticipation of the events of May 1968, but in other ways it is one of Godard's least satisfactory works. Though colour is used with great simplicity and effect – with the red of Mao's book a dominant feature – the characters are no more than semi-coherent puppets cut off from social reality, and the whole work is drowned in a mass of talk, allusion, and quotation. Far more striking is Weekend (1967), which is by far Godard's most virulent attack on the values of western civilisation. A deceitful married couple set out for a weekened drive to visit her mother, deciding en route to kill her for her money. On the way they undergo a series of bloody mishaps and pass through a landscape of rural France littered with blazing cars, dead and mutilated bodies, and all the violence that can be unleashed by the automobile. Their trip becomes a journey through a dream landscape as they encounter figures like Saint-Just, Emily Brontë and finally a band of cannibalistic hippies (the Seine-et-Oise Liberation Front). As usual Godard expresses the view that there is nothing to choose between the two sides in a situation of revolutionary confrontation. And the analysis of both sex and violence contains all the usual Godardian paradoxes – a cold involvement in sexual perversion and a parody revulsion against violence. But here in Weekend there is a new tone of bitterness and a new edge to the humour. The variations in mood remain, however, as abrupt as ever: bursts of savagery alternating with long-held shots in which nothing at all happens (the slow 360 degree panning shots of a pianist playing Mozart in a farmyard), and monologues on Vietnam or the role of the left set against scenes of cannibalism or pure whimsical fantasy. What makes Weekend so startling is the lack of any sense of the creation of formal culture or preservation of any degree of love or tenderness.

Although Godard's pre-1968 work lacks real or adequate political orientation, it does show a progressive movement away from notions of narrative and conventional cinematic representation. The film he began early in 1968 took him to the very brink of the style he was to adopt after May 1968. *One plus One* (1968), shot in England and starring Godard's second wife, Anne Wiazemsky, was originally to have shown its heroine's involvement with two men, a neo-fascist and a black militant. In the final film, however, all trace of narrative has disappeared. The film is largely shot in long takes, with those featuring the Rolling Stones rehearsing a new number used to form a kind of linking framework. Intercut with these rehearsal scenes are sequences involving a group of black militants who talk about revolution and execute two white women in white nightdresses, a fascist reading *Mein Kampf* in a Soho pornographic bookshop, and an interview with Anne Wiazemsky as 'Eve Democracy'. The whole film is held together by a commentary comprising extracts from a pornographic political novel. With *One plus One* Godard turns his back on most of the conventional attributes of the commercially produced feature film: a story, acting, cutting etc. His ideas are no longer dramatised, but presented bluntly in the form of slogans or tirades, so that the film is a collage of surface reflections. When he turns to political film making after May 1968 Godard has little to discard from the style towards which his work has evolved. The crucial addition will be a defined stance from which to attempt a coherent analysis of society. But the series of features which he completed between 1960 and 1968, which avoids or toys with most of the conventions of narrative cinema, forms a uniquely personal analysis of cinema and view of the moods and tensions of France in the 1960s.

*

While Jean-Luc Godard's prodigious output dominated the mid-1960s other film makers offered work of high quality. But even those who had first made their reputations in the documentary tended to shy away from the contemporary realities of French society. Typical in this respect were the two films produced by Georges Franju in the mid-1960s. *Judex* (1963) is an explicit homage to the filmic past in the form of a re-make of Louis Feuillade's serial of 1916. Predictably Franju would have preferred to retell the story of Fantômas, the master criminal, and his *Judex* is explicitly dedicated to the Feuillade of 1914. The figures of the masked avenger, the evil banker and the innocent victim are never more than cardboard cut-outs, and the plot is deliberately improbable, so that the film's impact is almost purely visual. Franju and Marcel Fradetal succeeded in recapturing the vivid contrasts of black and white that are to be found in the primitive silent cinema, above all in the pale figure of the innocent Jacqueline (Edith Scob) and the masterful silhouette of the black-cloaked avenger (Channing Pollock). In condensing Feuillade's seven-hour original the authors concocted a number of unforgettable scenes: a murder staged at a fancy dress ball, the villainess abducting the heroine while disguised as a nun, an aged man discovering, in his would-be assassin, his own long-lost son, and a rooftop battle to the death between two women.

Franju's subsequent film, *Thomas l'imposteur* (1965) was a film he had wanted to make while still a documentarist, but although Cocteau had collaborated on the adaptation of his own novel, many years passed before a producer could be found. Like the heroes of *Les Enfants terribles*, Thomas is an adolescent whose life is an inextricable mixture of fiction and reality. Under an assumed identity he participates in what his patroness calls 'the glorious theatrical spectacle of war' and his somnambulistic progress is halted only when he is shot: '"A bullet", he said to himself. "I'm lost if I don't pretend to be dead." But fiction and reality, in him, were one. Guillaume Thomas was dead'. Franju is a pacifist, but the fascination which World War I holds for him was already apparent in *Hôtel des invalides*. In *Thomas l'imposteur* this intense involvement finds an outlet and, with a minimum of props and a few bizarre images (a horse with its mane aflame, a totally unexpected death from a stray bullet), he creates a powerful vision of the destructiveness of war.

Alain Resnais's *Muriel* (1963), by contrast, marks its director's return to the contemporary everyday world, but the stylistic pattern chosen by Resnais and his scriptwriter, Jean Cayrol (who had previously written the commentary of *Nuit et brouillard*), means that an air of mystery and strangeness persists. Although the film is set in Boulogne in 1962 and, in the script, each scene is given a precise time and date, none of this is apparent in the completed film, where the technique of observing absolute chronology while simultaneously following a number of characters and treating even casual passers-by in the same manner as the main characters gives rise to a hallucinatory realism. In every aspect of the film disruption and uncertainty are emphasised. Early scenes abruptly alternate daytime and night-time, and when filming two separate conversations in a café, Resnais cross-cuts indiscriminately between the four people involved. Twin stories utilising themes of time and memory are interwoven in *Muriel*. The heroine (Delphine Seyrig) tries vainly to revive a past love, while her son is driven to murder by his inability to cope with his own past, as a participant in torture in Algeria. A set of contemporary references rare in 1960s cinema is present in *Muriel*, but the film's structure and its theatrical tone and non-naturalistic acting style serve to distance its impact.

La Guerre est finie (1966), made from a script by the Spanish novelist Jorge Semprun, marks a departure in that it is resolutely realistic in style: scenes are dated and located precisely; the surface detail is wholly contemporary and the acting (particularly that of Yves Montand as the political activist Diego) lacks the theatrical overtones present in the performance of Emmanuelle Riva in *Hiroshima mon amour* and Delphine Seyrig in both *L'Année dernière à Marienbad* and *Muriel*. The earlier explorations of time and consciousness are present only as isolated moments in *La Guerre est finie* and no longer have a dominant role in the shaping of our response, although Diego himself is a man with so many aliases that he admits to being startled if anyone calls him by his correct name. What is of interest in *La Guerre est finie* is that despite this ever-present surface realism, the true subject of the film – the struggle in Spain – is absent, just as it is absent from Diego's life as a long-term exile. The fact that these two mid-1960s films did not mark a desire on Resnais's part to move into a new relationship with reality is borne out by his next project, *Je t'aime, je t'aime* (1968), which is a deliberately distanced work, a conscious play with science-fiction themes of time and logic. Chronology has been totally lost here and the interweaving of reality and dream seems totally random, although the events eventually lead, as if inevitably, to the hero's death. *Je t'aime, je t'aime*, like its predecessors, shows Resnais's enormous technical command and his continual concern to explore new and untried paths. But it also demonstrates clearly how individual his approach is, and how impossible it is to fit him into any neat categorisation of post-1958 French cinema.

Chris Marker showed himself, both before and after 1968, to be much closer to the mood of contemporary France. It was Marker who, in 1967, served as organiser of one of the most striking collaborative efforts in the history of French cinema, *Loin du Vietnam*, an exposé of the problems of the war in Vietnam as seen from Europe, which contains a wealth of fascinating material and episodes, some documentary, some meditative and one (that made by Resnais) fictional. Among the other contributors were Joris Ivens filming in Hanoi, Claude Lelouch in Saigon, the journalist Michele Ray in the battle zone and William Klein in the United States. Marker's own personal works of the mid-1960s are more muted and introspective. *Le Mystère Koumiko* (1965), shot on the occasion of the Japanese

Olympics, was a fairly inconclusive portrait of its heroine, although it contains the usual wide range of material: a strip cartoon opening, some irreverent comments on de Gaulle, allusions to *L'Année dernière à Marienbad* and a parody of Demy's *Les Parapluies de Cherbourg*. *Si j'avais quatre dromadaires* (1966) was also very much a personal work, using still photographs taken by Marker in twenty-six countries over a period of ten years, concentrating particularly on the USSR. The structure, admirably supported by Marker's customary eloquent commentary, is akin to that of a photographic exhibition with the images grouped in clusters to illustrate Marker's particular interests and enthusiasms.

The close connection between film and literature to which Alain Resnais's films bear witness led an increasing number of writers to turn to the cinema in order to direct as well as to compose scenarios. Certainly Resnais's seriousness of approach seems to have had a very positive effect on those with whom he has worked. Marguerite Duras, for example, co-directed her first film, *La Musica*, in 1967 and, as we shall see, the cinema became a prime creative outlet for her after 1968. Jean Cayrol too became very involved with the cinema in the early 1960s, publishing a volume of essays examining the possibilities offered by the medium, *Le Droit de regard*, and directing, with Claude Durand, a number of fascinating shorts from *On vous parle* (1960), to *La Deésse* (1967). His major work, *Le Coup de grâce* (1964) is a feature film dealing with the interaction of past and present and reflecting his own experience of having been betrayed to the Nazis while working with the Resistance in wartime France. In *Le Coup de grâce* Cayrol adopts the same stylistic techniques as in *Muriel* and, although he lacks Resnais's supreme technical skill, he shows the same concern with painting a portrait of provincial life, with tracing the tensions among a group of related characters and with showing the shadows cast on the present by the events of a generation before.

During the period 1963–68 the most important work produced by a novelist was that of Alain Robbe-Grillet, the writer of *L'Année dernière à Marienbad*. Robbe-Grillet shot his first feature, *L'Immortelle* (1963) in Turkey without any prior technical experience and from a script to which he adhered rigidly. The subject of *L'Immortelle* has close analogies with *L'Année dernière à Marienbad* and plots the relationship of a trio of semi-anonymous characters, designated in the script by the initials N (the narrator-hero), L (the enigmatic heroine Leila) and M (the husband – 'le mari' in French – who comes between them). The film's handling of narrative is most striking and revolutionary. In the opening shots the basic elements of the film are stated: a car crash, a room, a dog barking, a motor boat, a woman, views from a window. These are then arranged in some provisional order, full of contradictions but building up a fairly consistent relationship between the hero and the woman. Then, with Leila's death, the images of the narrator's world become corrupted. The relationship is relived in distorted fashion and the progression of the narrative leads only to the narrator's death in circumstances identical with Leila's. Robbe-Grillet, although shooting entirely on location, is particularly successful in creating an autonomous world of narrative and although the events related do not conform to any external logic they do build up the tension of a well-resolved narrative.

Trans-Europ-Express (1966) shows the same preoccupation with reality and imagination and is, in effect, a reflection on the process of composition of a narrative. The title gives the setting of much of the action, the train which takes two sets of characters – the 'authors' and their imagined figures – from Paris to Antwerp. The whole film is full of mirror images, disguises, duplications, distortions of reality and impossible happenings, which are nowhere more apparent than in the handling of the characters. Robbe-Grillet appears in the film as a director called Jean, whose secretary is played by Robbe-Grillet's wife Catherine and who is planning a film to be called 'Trans-Europ-Express'. Jean boards the same train as that taken by his invented hero whom he names Elias (Alias?) but who refers to himself as Jean. Elias is played by Jean-Louis Trintignant who, to complicate things further, makes at least one appearance in the film as himself and at the end figures in a shot parodying Lelouch's *Un Homme et une femme* in which he had also played the lead. The two sets of Robbe-Grillet's fictional characters, who should be on different levels of reality, in fact keep coming impossibly face to face. Moreover, although Elias is allegedly the creation of Jean, he has a whole personal sex life with a prostitute whom he eventually strangles which forms no part of Jean's narration. A new and important dimension of the film is the use of humour as a distancing device and as a means of complicating the narrative, its value being particularly apparent in the erotic sequences. Again no pretence at a conventional story line is attempted: the plot invents itself as it proceeds, creating and ignoring problems, inconsistencies and downright impossibilities.

L'Homme qui ment (1968), Robbe-Grillet's major work as a film maker, carries through the formal experiments of the earlier films to their logical conclusion. It is the story of a man who invents his own character, his past and his emotions as he goes along. Made on location in Czechoslovakia and set in an old château amid the forests, the film again stars Jean-Louis Trintignant, whose lightness of touch is as crucial here as in *Trans-Europ-Express*. Boris, who is both hero and traitor (according to his own conflicting accounts), weaves stories around the missing Resistance leader Jean and, with his words, seduces in turn the man's maid, his sister and his wife. But as Jean is created by his words, he becomes more and more powerful, and on his eventual return to the château turns the tables on Boris, who is expelled, nameless and without identity now, to the forest from which he emerged. *L'Homme qui ment* allows Robbe-Grillet's narrative methods to be seen with clarity. None of his films has a coherent plot in a conventional sense but each is able to offer many of the same satisfactions as a normal story because of its extreme patterning in terms of symmetry, reversal and inversion. The pattern is indeed very much akin to a musical structure. Rather than simply creating and then breaking story-within-a-story patterns, Robbe-Grillet is concerned with setting the elements – the narrator and the woman he remembers/imagines in *L'Immortelle*, the 'authors' and Elias in *Trans-Europ-Express*, and Boris and Jean in *L'Homme qui ment* – in shifting, fluid opposition to each other. By fastening on two basic but very simple aspects of the film image: its uniquely present-tense quality (you cannot photograph yesterday's happenings today) and the inextricable mixture of reality and falsehood in any fictional film (real actors playing imagined characters etc.), Robbe-Grillet fashions films which are both approachable and immensely innovative in the context of French 1960s cinema.

*

The films of such literary figures as Duras, Cayrol and Robbe-Grillet were fairly marginal to the mainstream of French cinema in the 1960s, but two other newcomers of the decade did capture the public attention with films which painted a very rose-tinted picture of the world. Jacques Demy had already found an audience with his first feature, *Lola*, in 1961. This lighthearted work which is a sort of musical without songs and dances owes much to Raoul Coutard's flowing camerawork. Demy, like so many of his contemporaries, includes a whole mass of filmic references ranging from Bresson's *Les Dames du Bois de Boulogne* to Gary Cooper, with the title itself explicitly recalling the heroines of such totally divergent films as Ophuls's *Lola Montès* and Sternberg's *The Blue Angel*. *Lola*'s setting is Nantes, where Demy grew up, and all its characters are fragments or reflections of the relationship of the central couple: the patient Lola (Anouk Aimée) and her lover Michel, who returns to reclaim her after seven years' absence. Demy here maintains the dance of his puppets adroitly and succeeds in creating a make-believe world all of his own, where love rules, and evil, envy and jealousy are absent. His second film, *La Baie des anges* (1963) is set in Nice and on the Riviera and stars Jeanne Moreau as a blonde gambler who arouses the love of a holidaying bank clerk, played by Claude Mann. This work shows the same preoccupations with chance and fortune as *Lola*, and lightly skirts the real social problems to which compulsive gambling gives rise. Its general mood is as light as that of *Lola* and at the end it is implied that love triumphs and that Moreau will abandon the gambling tables.

Finally Demy was able to make the musical films he had long planned with Michel Legrand, who had composed the music for his first two features. *Les Parapluies de Cherbourg* (1964) achieved almost universal acclaim. In it the director recaptures the mood of *Lola*, treating the same themes and in part the same characters with music and colour, and finding in Catherine Deneuve a worthy successor to Anouk Aimée. All the dialogue of *Les Parapluies de Cherbourg*, even the most banal conversation, was set to music by Legrand, and Demy worked by welding the actions of the cast onto a prerecorded score. Again, as in *Lola*, the basic situations are those of seduction and abandonment which have always been the stock ingredients of film melodrama (witness the success of Marcel Pagnol's *Marius* trilogy) and the rather pretentious three-part structure – Departure, Absence, Return – is redolent of the atmosphere of the prewar Carné–Prévert films. Here, however, all these elements, which could have been treated with heavy solemnity, are seen as the basis for songs, set against the vivid decor designed by Bernard Evein and photographed in glowing colours by the sweeping uninhibited camera of Jean Rabier. Demy and Legrand worked on *Les Parapluies de Cherbourg* for a whole year and the film is both a totally original work and a labour of love. *Les Demoiselles de Rochefort* (1967) was made with equal dedication by the same team of Demy, Legrand, and Evein with Ghislain Cloquet this time in charge of the camera. The film attempts to repeat the popular success of *Les Parapluies de Cherbourg* and again the setting is a seaside town in which a group of characters meet, love and dream. The inclusion of Gene Kelly in the cast alongside Catherine Deneuve and Françoise Dorléac points clearly to Demy's desire to emulate the Americal musical, but the film lacks the requisite narrative drive and the underlying melodramatic seriousness that had characterised Demy's previous work. With its emphasis on prettified settings and dazzling costumes, *Les Demoiselles de Rochefort* never becomes more than an agreeable if totally undemanding spectacle.

A director who shared Demy's desire of reaching the widest possible audience and likewise reaching a peak of public success in the otherwise fairly bleak years of the mid-1960s was Claude Lelouch. But whereas Demy had received critical acclaim from the very beginning of his feature-film-making career with *Lola*, Lelouch's early work met with virtually no critical or commercial success. *Le Propre de l'homme* (1960) was a failure that left him deeply in debt; *L'Amour avec des si* (made in 1962) did not achieve a commercial release until four years later; and *La Femme spectacle* (1964) received no showing at all. If *Une Fille et des fusils* (1965) did at last achieve the showing and box-office success Lelouch was seeking, it hardly seemed to point in the direction of a major film-making career. Lelouch was still unable to establish himself with any kind of certainty and his next feature, *Les Grands moments* (1965) went completely unnoticed.

Total success came with *Un Homme et une femme* (1966) which tells a basically simple love story of two people, both of whom have been battered by life, who meet by chance and fall in love. Like Demy's first success, *Lola*, the film stars Anouk Aimée, here partnered by Jean-Louis Trintignant, and the playing of the two principals is the least controversial aspect of the film. For the rest, Lelouch turns his story into the feature-length equivalent of a television commercial, set on the picturesque beaches of Deauville in winter. The two leading characters are both given spectacularly melodramatic pasts, glamorous jobs (she works in films; he is a racing driver) and unbelievably sweet and photogenic children. Like so much mid-1960s French film making, *Un Homme et une femme* refuses all but the most superficial connection with French society. The handling of music (by Francis Lai), colour and cutting reveals an impulse to paint no more than a glossy surface and Lelouch, who was his own cameraman as well as co-editor and co-scriptwriter, never misses the opportunity for a gratuitously elaborate camera movement. As a result *Un Homme et une femme* has an air of total contrivance and self-conscious charm. With *Vivre pour vivre* (1967) Lelouch repeated his commercial success, telling the story of an affair between a television reporter and a beautiful young model (Yves Montand and Candice Bergen). The now familiar arsenal of gimmicks, beautiful locations and heavy mood music from the same team as that used for *Un Homme et une femme* assured the film of popular acclaim, but would not conceal the essential superficiality of both plot and treatment. *Vivre pour vivre* touches on more serious issues when Montand's duties take him to the Congo and Vietnam, but the limitations of Lelouch's political awareness are all too apparent in the material he shot for *Loin du Vietnam*, in which his approach contrived to make the US bombers setting out to raid Hanoi look simply decorative.

None of the other newcomers of the mid-1960s had popular successes as great as those of Demy and Lelouch, but a number of interesting debuts were made. Alain Jessua (b.1932), for example, began with *La Vie à l'envers* (1963), a study of the progressive alienation of a young man who gradually retreats from the cluttered world of reality to the bare whiteness of what is, though he is not fully aware of it, a mental asylum. The film is extremely persuasive in the way that it insidiously makes one share the hero's view, see the world and people as slightly ridiculous and rejoice at the superiority of the contemplative mind. *Jeu de massacre* (1967) was an equally interesting if ultimately less successful work. It too probes the interaction of fantasy and reality, dealing with a wealthy young man who becomes obsessed with the heroes of his favourite comic strip. Jessua plays his realistic images of the main action against the vivid comic-strip images drawn by Guy Peellaert and, as in *La Vie à l'envers*, maintains a balance between humour and involvement, so that *Jeu de massacre*, like its hero, remains poised between real life and imagination. The promise of these two first films was not fully maintained, for when Jessua returned to directing in 1972 after a break of five years it was as the maker of solid, big-budget commercial films.

Equally striking was the debut of René Allio (b.1924), a painter and theatre designer, who began with two remarkable studies of characters who deliberately change their identity to the consternation of those closest to them. *La Vieille dame indigne* (1965) was adapted from a Brecht story – relocated in Allio's native Marseilles – and offered the veteran actress Sylvie one of her best roles as the old woman on the verge of death who suddenly decides to spend the little money she has on herself rather than leave it to her heirs. *L'Une et l'autre* (1967), although having an explicitly theatrical setting, shows the same mastery in the capturing of everyday detail and the tiny gestures by which people relate. Here the heroine is an actress who, realising that her life has become meaningless, takes on the identity of her sister as a prelude to being able to express openly to the man she lives with the fact that she needs a new and independent life for herself.

In the realm of alternative production, feature-length innovation was limited in France in the mid-1960s. In the short film, however, the Polish-born Walerian Borowczyk (b.1923), whose first French production had been *Les Astronautes* (1959), an animated short made in collaboration with Chris Marker, continued as an animator with first a short and then, in 1967, a feature showing the ferocious couple, Monsieur and Madame Kabal. He also experimented with the formal parameters of filmic expression in a series of masterly, totally individual and quite unclassifiable short films: *Renaissance* (1963),

Rosalie (1966), *Gavotte* (1967) and *Diptyque* (1967). These served as a prelude to his feature debut with *Goto, l'île d'amour* (1968), which will be considered in the next chapter.

For Marcel Hanoun the early 1960s were difficult years, for *Le Huitième jour* (1959) was the first and last of his films to gain a proper commercial release. He resumed production, however, with total independence but minuscule budgets, beginning in 1964; with *Octobre à Madrid*, which contains a recollection of his earlier work, reflections on the production context and a meditation on how a film is prevented from being made. Subsequently he set out to explore in a totally individual tone the nature of fascism and the concentration camps in the austere and distanced *L'Authentique procès de Carl Emmanuel Jung* (1966). These were also the years in which the French-born Jean-Marie Straub and his inseparable companion Danièle Huillet began their film-making career, in exile in Germany, with the shorts *Machorka-Muff* (1963) and *Der Bräutigam, die Komödiantin und der Zuhalter* (1968), the fifty-minute *Nicht versöhnt* (1965) and the feature-length *Chronik der Anna Magdalena Bach* (1968).

*

With rare but significant exceptions, the years 1963–68 were barren ones for the older generation of film makers who had dominated the early post-war years. Marcel Carné produced three routine works: a comedy thriller, *Du mouron chez les petits oiseaux* (1963); a Simenon adaptation, *Trois chambres à Manhattan* (1965); and a further unsuccessful attempt to come to terms with the younger generation, *Les Jeunes loups* (1968). Of Autant-Lara's five films of the period only *Journal d'une femme en blanc* (1965), which tackled questions of abortion and contraception, showed anything of the old ambition. René Clément's output comprised only big-budget works compromised by international co-production requirements and bilingual production difficulties: the Resistance story, *Le Jour et l'heure* (1963); the stylish thriller, *Les Félins* (1964); and the ponderous and overloaded epic, *Paris brûle-t-il?* (1966).

Two great names of French cinema made their last films. If René Clair's *Les Fêtes galantes* (1965), a period piece of tragi-comedy shot in Roumania, is without question one of his lesser works, marked by the same laboriousness and hollow joviality as *Tout l'or du monde*, Henri-Georges Clouzot's farewell to film making was more substantial. *La Prisonnière* (1968) is the characteristic story of a young woman, neglected by her kinetic artist husband, who becomes totally fascinated by a perverted gallery owner and comes to share his vices,

38. Albert Lamorisse: Le Ballon rouge (1956)

39. Roger Vadim: Et dieu créa la femme (1956)

40. François Truffaut: Les Quatre cent coups (1959)

41. Jean-Luc Godard: A bout de souffle (1960)

42. Jacques Rivette: Paris nous appartient (1961)

43. Alain Resnais: L'Année dernière à Marienbad (1962)

44. Georges Franju: Judex (1963)

45. Jean-Luc Godard: Bande à part (1964)

enjoying against her will the total submission he imposes on her. The film shows the persistence of a key theme in Clouzot's work: a study of evil where, as in *Manon* twenty years before, nothing is too sordid if two people love each other. There are close personal references: Clouzot himself had dabbled in kinetic art and published a volume of nude studies, and his treatment of actors had earned him a reputation for sadism on the set. Yet the film is far from a modern piece of self-expressive cinema: despite a seven-minute sequence of 'pure cinema' (picturing the heroine's nightmare on the verge of death) and a few Lelouch-style episodes of glamour and radiant love, the structure of psychological interplay based on explicit dialogue and big confrontation scenes is one that Clouzot could have used unchanged at any time in the previous twenty-five years.

Offsetting this decline is the totally unexpected return to French studios of Luis Buñuel who, although having made three Franco-Mexican co-productions in the late 1950s – *Cela s'appelle l'aurore* (1955); *La Mort en ce jardin* (1956); and *La Fièvre monte à El Pao* (1959) – had not worked in France itself for over thirty years when he returned to direct Jeanne Moreau in a solid if fairly traditional version of *Le Journal d'une femme de chambre* (1963). More astounding was *Belle de jour* (1966), the first masterpiece in the last and incredibly productive period of Buñuel's creative life. This seemingly simple study of the obsessions of a young woman, Séverine (played by Catherine Deneuve), is a masterly fusion of surrealism and narrative, mixing without distinction reality and dreams or imaginings and throwing doubt onto every seeming certainty that the narrative proposes. While celebrating the purity of his heroine's sexual needs, Buñuel maintains a total ambiguity about the film's action and about the reality or otherwise of the brothel scenes in which Séverine submits willingly to passion, sadism and nameless perversion.

Equally creative was the work of both Jacques Tati and Robert Bresson who both produced major films in the period. Tati spent three years and a reputed million pounds to shoot *Play Time* (1967) using the full resources of colour, 70 mm film stock and stereophonic sound. The resulting work originally ran for some two and a half hours but rests on the slenderest pattern of plot. This concerns a group of tourists on a lightning tour of Paris who see nothing of the traditional city, only the modernistic steel and glass structures familiar in any modern capital. But in the evening their newly opened hotel disintegrates into a more human chaos under the benevolent eye of Monsieur Hulot as the forces of order and efficiency are totally routed. With *Play Time* Tati achieved his long-held ideal of democratising comedy by making a film in which Hulot is reduced to an episodic character on the same level as all the others, not presented as a privileged figure inventing a multitude of gags. In this film the gags belong to everyone and emerge from the intensity with which everyday life is observed, not from any contrived sequence of farcical actions. The costly sets of *Play Time* were constructed not to stylise or distort, but to allow Tati total control over the creation of his effects. Here he brings to its highest point the conception of comedy, already hinted at in *Les Vacances de Monsieur Hulot*, as a window opening out onto the world and permitting the spectators to see and laugh at their own and others' foibles and follies. Significantly *Play Time* – a film to which seeing is crucial – contains an extraordinary number of marvellously realised gags using glass and windows. *Play Time* is uncompromising in the demands it makes on its audience. In conventional comedy spectators are constantly provoked by a welter of incidents and heavily emphasised effects. Here they are required to remain alert and observant at all times, as crucial events may be happening in a remote corner of the huge sets or on the edge of the 70 mm frame. *Play Time*'s calm, reflective rhythm, which allows deliberate *longueurs* and an affectionate repetition of little scenes or incidents, marks Tati's maturity as a film maker. As few directors before or since have managed to do, Tati has taken the technical resources of the big-budget spectacular film and used them to create a tender, delicate and totally personal statement about life as he sees it.

Tati's position in French cinema also looked – briefly at least – less isolated with the appearance in the 1960s of the first features of Pierre Etaix. The latter, who had worked in a circus and as assistant on *Mon oncle*, was principal actor, director and co-scriptwriter for his first feature, *Le Soupirant*, made in 1962. The film's thread of plot is very simple, dealing with a man who gives up his studies of astronomy to devote himself wholeheartedly to the problem of getting married and approaching successively (and vainly) a number of possible – and impossible – young women. *Le Soupirant* avoids the glib dialogue humour of standard French comedy but, although containing a wealth of good gags, it is an uneven work. The basic problem which Etaix and his habitual co-scriptwriter Jean-Claude Carrière have not resolved is that of how to sustain a ninety-minute narrative. The film comprises a succession of more or less comic scenes, some of which are beautifully timed and executed and would have made perfect short films on their own, while others are obviously planted or padded out to unnecessary length. These problems are largely resolved in Etaix's major work, *Yoyo* (1965), set in the circus which has been the decisive influence on his work, much as mime was for Tati. The plot is more complicated, dealing with a father and son who both successively abandon a life of empty luxury to join the circus. The early scenes, set in the 1920s, are perhaps the most successful, being entirely free of dialogue though making inventive use of sound and being filmed in a parodied silent film comedy manner. Although there is a wealth of good gags throughout, the narrative is satisfyingly shaped, and *Yoyo*, while abounding in humour, leaves behind it at the same time a feeling of melancholy. *Yoyo* proved to be the most satisfying and best-rounded of Etaix's films and nothing he made subsequently has the same unity of tone and impact. In *Tant qu'on a la santé* (1966), for example, the comments on the stresses and strains of modern life do not add up to a coherent feature-length narrative. *Le Grand amour* (1969) and *Pays de Cocagne* (1971), his last features before he abandoned the cinema, added nothing to his reputation. Throughout his work after *Yoyo*, Etaix maintains the calm mask of the true film comedian, but too many of his situations are contrived and there is a basic lack of commitment to any coherent attitude or view.

With *Procès de Jeanne d'Arc* in 1966 Bresson appeared to have reached the *ne plus ultra* of his stylistic development and it was difficult to foresee ways in which he would proceed. In fact, however, his mid-1960s work marked quite a new level of mastery. *Au hasard, Balthazar* (1966) not only forged a fresh stylistic approach, it also covered a new range of material with an inclusiveness that the earlier works had lacked. It takes in jazz and teenage dancing, violence and nudity, cruelty and leather-clad motorcyclists, while still preserving a Bressonian atmosphere. The director contrives to distance this material by means of a film structure that achieves an effect of de-dramatisation by breaking the action into a succession of tiny elliptical scenes connected in ways that are not immediately apparent. The film has the richness of a Dostoievskian story and an added element of strangeness in that its eponymous hero is a donkey. Balthazar begins life as a children's pet. He is cosseted and formally christened, a witness to the innocence of childhood, and virtually worshipped like a pagan idol by the young Marie, who adorns him with flowers. Then brutally the world of work intrudes: he is broken in, beaten and tormented, accompanies a half-crazed murderer on his wanderings in the mountains and works in a circus. Bought by a miser, he is worked almost to death grinding corn; rescued, he walks in a church procession and is hailed as a saint, only to be stolen by smugglers and, shot by customs men, left to die on the mountainside amid a flock of sheep. Balthazar's story is itself impregnated with Christian overtones (the seven deadly sins) and is linked to that of the film's other victim, the girl Marie. Balthazar is present at most of the crises of her life, when her submission brings only humiliation from the man she loves abjectly, Gérard. If Marie is the embodiment of submission, Gérard is an incarnation of evil: thief, seducer, bully and hooligan. The film's distinctive blend of obscure meaning (the donkey) and quite blatant symbolism (Gérard's leather jacket and motorbike) is held together by Bresson's extraordinary stylistic control. Characteristic Bressonian touches, such as the discreet use of Schubert's music and the uniform style of gesture and enunciation, are combined with moments of quite unique unreality: the donkey in a deserted house or amid traffic, with the sheep on the hillside or confronted by the animals in the zoo. The vision which emerges is that of a world where evil flourishes and secret vices eat at the hearts of men, where simple love and laughter vanish with childhood, but where grace is never wholly absent.

Mouchette (1967), adapted from a novel by Georges Bernanos, who had also furnished the subject of *Journal d'un curé de campagne*, is similarly a story of humiliation and defeat. It is set too in a world made to seem unreal by the juxtaposition of traditional life and modernity: the heroine wears clogs and a smock but also rides in a dodgem-car at the fair to the sound of jazzy modern music. Bresson's quest for authenticity has never made him shun anachronism and here, in adapting Bernanos's novel, he has only half-modernised it. *Mouchette* traces the experience of a whole lifetime, but obliquely, in a succession of fragmentary shots and scenes fused in an almost musical rhythm. The fourteen-year-old heroine does not need to seek humiliation; it comes her way spontaneously at home and at school. When she befriends the epileptic poacher Arsène and nurses him after a fit, he rewards her by raping her brutally; when she runs off home, it is to arrive just in time to witness her mother's death. The failure of love and all her tentative attempts at human contact drive her to a pitiful revolt that can only be negative and self-destructive. Her suicide – like the film's opening – is accompanied by portions of Monteverdi's *Magnificat*, although elsewhere the director relies entirely on natural sound and fragmentary snatches of dialogue. *Au hasard, Balthazar* and *Mouchette* show Bresson's art at its finest: the ability to remain faithful to a literary source and yet produce a work that is wholly his own; to shoot with non-professional actors on location and yet give his film an air of the supernatural; to insist on total realism at every stage and yet achieve a result that is a marvel of stylisation.

*

Despite such isolated successes, it is difficult not to see the period from 1963 until May 1968 as a time of retreat comparable to the early and mid-1950s, with the decline emphasised by the sharp fall of almost a third in film audiences as the number of television sets, which was below a million in 1959, rose from 3.4m in 1963 to 8.3m in 1968. 1960s film production levels were maintained, however, and there was even a small but significant rise in features with full French financing, but the creative excitement which the emergence of a new generation in 1958–62 had promised was lacking. Apart from the unique and astonishing achievements of Jean-Luc Godard in the 1960s, the picture echoed that of a decade earlier. Chabrol, Truffaut and Malle followed the example of Jean-Pierre Melville and resolutely set out to build themselves the basis of a prolific career. As in the early 1950s some of the most distinctive talents of the generation (Rivette, Rohmer) were marginalised, and some of the most innovative work of the period, such as Alain Robbe-Grillet's *L'Homme qui ment* and Jacques Tati's *Play Time*, failed to get the attention it deserved. *Cinéma-vérité* failed to achieve the total modification of feature-film making which it had once seemed to promise – Chris Marker's *Le Joli mai* is its swansong – and even documentary production lacked its old impact. In the feature-film scene, the characteristic pull was away from reality – in Varda as much as Demy, in Franju as in Lelouch – and the issues at stake in French society and politics continued to find no echo on the screen. In France the stylistic revolution of the New Wave remained limited to a formal restructuring, not accompanied by any new content. Major issues were ignored to such an extent that even the oblique handling of some of the consequences of the Algerian war in Resnais's *Muriel* seemed daring. The events of May 1968 therefore burst upon this cinema with as great an impact as the New Wave's appearance in 1958: now, at last, French cinema would have, it seemed, to face up to reality.

A l'image des cinémas italiens ou américains, le cinéma français
se fait miroir de l'époque. Pas un très bon miroir. Un miroir qui
souvent réfléchit drôlement, déforme, enjolive, ou, pour
employer un mot qui fit fortune à l'époque, récupère.

Jean-Pierre Jeancolas, 1969

The participation of film makers and technicians in the strikes and
debates provoked by May '68 seemed to herald, if not a total shift in
the relation between cinema and society, at least a more socially
engaged form of film making than actually emerged. The film world
had already been mobilised earlier in 1968 by the scandal surrounding
the dismissal of the revered Henri Langlois as head of the nominally
independent Cinémathèque française. The efforts which resulted in his
reinstatement – though at some considerable cost to the
Cinémathèque – formed perhaps the organisational basis for the
creation, in May 1968, of the Estates General of the French Cinema by
several thousand film makers, critics and technicians. The intention
was to revolutionise French cinema, but the Estates General showed
all the contradictions of May '68 itself and, ironically, one of the few
really revolutionary proposals was put forward by a group in which
Claude Chabrol played a key part (although he later claimed that May
'68 had no influence on his life or career). The Estates General did get a
number of immediate documentary projects under way, but it was
never able to agree a coherent policy and perhaps the greatest impact
was made in the area of film theory, with the radicalisation of *Cahiers
du cinéma* and the founding of *Cinéthique*.

The involvement of many film makers – including Jean-Luc Godard
– alongside the students at the barricades in May is reflected in the
group of tiny 'slogan' films – the anonymous *Ciné-tracts* – produced
with the immediacy and inventiveness of the wall posters and graffiti
which were such a feature of the times. Records were also made of the

impact of May '68 on the workers whose involvement rapidly became as intense as that of the students (although often directed towards rather different political ends). Among such immediate records initiated by the Estates General are *Le Cheminot, Travailleurs émigrés* and *Comité d'action*, whose titles reflect their direct involvement. *Oser lutter, oser vaincre* (also 1968), made by Jean-Pierre Thon, was a forceful statement of the view that the workers' struggle at the Flins Renault factory had been betrayed by the unions. The material was subsequently remade by a group of film makers with a rather different political viewpoint, the Cinéastes révolutionnaires prolétariens, as *Flins 68–69*, while the unions themselves replied to criticism with compilations such as *La CGT en mai* (Paul Séban, 1968). Indeed material shot at the period has been constantly used and re-used in different contexts by film makers of varying political persuasions.

A feature of 1968 was the development of film-making collectives in which the makers' identities were shrouded in anonymity. In addition to the Maoist Cinéastes révolutionnaires prolétariens and the more orthodox Communist Dynadia, the most notable were the Dziga Vertov collective and SLON (later Groupe Medvedkine), both of which contained major film makers. SLON had been formed in 1967 and grew out of the collective work which Chris Marker organised for *Loin du Vietnam*. Marker and Mario Marret together made *A bientôt, j'espère* (1968), about militant workers at Besançon and were later instrumental, after May '68, in allowing the workers themselves access to film-making equipment. When SLON decided to distribute Alexander Medvedkine's 1934 Soviet film, *Happiness*, Marker shot an introductory film, *Le Train en marche* (1971), containing film clips, documents and an interview with the seventy-one-year-old director. Other films for SLON on which Marker collaborated were the shorts, *La Sixième face du pentagon* (with François Reichenbach, 1968) and *Jour de tournage* (on the shooting of Costa-Gavras's *L'Aveu*, 1970) and the medium-length *La Bataille des dix millions* (1970) on the sugar harvest in Cuba. It was not until 1974 that Marker re-emerged as a personal film maker with a further striking documentary, *La Solitude du chanteur de fond*, which traces the appearance of Yves Montand with a one-man show at Olympia in aid of Chilean refugees. As in his earlier work, Marker shows his mastery of reportage, his ability to present a situation or a personality directly, without either lauding or patronising, and to produce images which, even without his habitual precise and witty commentary, convey the essence of his subject.

After *One plus One* Jean-Luc Godard had the unique distinction of producing works commissioned by major television companies in

France, the United Kingdom, Italy and West Germany, all of whom subsequently refused to transmit the films in question. This period up to 1972, during which Godard attempted to re-create the cinema from zero in the light of Marxist-Leninist analysis, was therefore one in which his work – previously a key feature of art cinema distribution throughout Europe and the USA – became invisible. *Le Gai savoir*, made before and after May '68 for ORTF, sets the pattern. A conversation piece, located in a void, between two symbolically named characters (Emile Rousseau and Patricia Lumumba) intercut with newspaper and magazine clippings and slogans, it shows a characteristic predominance of sound over image and a questioning of the nature of communication. *Le Gai savoir* ends with Godard's comment that this is 'not the film that has to be made'. *Un Film comme les autres*, a feature-length discussion between workers and students interspersed with May '68 footage, was shot in August 1968 but received virtually no distribution, even in militant circles. After failing to complete a documentary with Leacock and Pennebaker in the USA and conceiving and abandoning projects in Canada and Cuba, Godard went to London to shoot *British Sounds* in February 1969 for London Weekend Television. The film contains a variety of material – shots in a BMC factory, a mock television news report, discussions with workers and students – but shows little real insight into the nature of the class struggle in Britain. However, the explicit statement of its aim to smash the system of representation whereby 'the bourgeoisie recreates the world in its own image' led to its transmission being refused.

Paradoxically, while working anonymously with Jean-Pierre Gorin in the Dziga Vertov collective in 1969–70, Godard used his name and past reputation to obtain funding for works which radically questioned everything he had achieved before 1968. Four films were completed: *Pravda*, shot in Czechoslovakia with finance from the Grove Press of New York; *Vent d'est*, produced by a left-wing Italian producer; and *Luttes en Italie* and *Vladimir und Rosa*, commissioned – and rejected – by RAI and Munich Tele-Pool respectively. The most substantial of these is the colour 16 mm feature, *Vent d'est*, which combines deliberately banal, home-movie-style images of figures in period costume with a soundtrack that questions the nature of political action and offers reflections on the problems of revolutionary cinema. Throughout this period of films which remained virtually unseen in France, Godard's stated aim was not to make political cinema but to make cinema politically. However, the extent to which he became marginalised in political as well as film-making circles is a measure of his failure to achieve this aim. After one further 'invisible' film – the forty-five-minute analysis of a still photograph of Jane Fonda in Vietnam, *Lettre à Jane* – Godard and Gorin re-emerged from semi-clandestinity with a commercially financed feature, *Tout va bien* (1972), with Yves Montand and Jane Fonda. Here the contradictions of Godard's position, even after long years of analysis and experiment, were very apparent and the film had only a muted impact. All the narrative logic which Godard questioned in his pre-1968 features is reinstated, and the subject – the reactions of the boss, the workers and media intellectuals to a factory strike and occupation – is treated without fervour or intellectual rigour. The attempted distanciation, through the use of caricature and stereotype, blurs rather than clarifies the impact, and the film is not helped by the impotent, self-pitying monologues about the difficulties of communication in which both the principal characters indulge. After the break-up of the Dziga–Vertov collective Godard retired to Grenoble and for many years devoted himself to video production.

*

Moves towards a more realistic approach after May '68 occurred on a variety of levels. Louis Malle, who had worked with Cousteau on his documentary *Le Monde du silence* in 1956 but subsequently concerned himself exclusively with fictional subjects, visited India and returned with a feature-length documentary study, *Calcutta* (1969), and a seven-part television series. Malle's view of India is never an official one: he offers few interviews and little commentary, allowing the images to convey a reality which is often hard to comprehend. A few years later, working with the same team, he applied a similar documentary detachment to everyday French subjects in two short features, a study of a square – *Place de la République* (1974) – and a depiction of working-class factory life – *Humain trop humain* (also 1974). These same years were also marked by several compilation films which looked at aspects of recent French history in a new and questioning way. The most important of these, *Le Chagrin et la pitié* (1971), was the work of three men who had worked together regularly for ORTF's current affairs programmes in 1967: the director Marcel Ophuls (son of Max) and the producers André Harris and Alain de Sedouy. Although the new work was made independently (after their series was discontinued in the aftermath of May '68), it was shot on 16 mm and designed for television showing. ORTF did not need to exercise censorship and reject the film: they simply refused to view it even after it had received widespread praise. Running over four hours, *Le Chagrin et la pitié* takes as its subject the town of Clermont-Ferrand under the German occupation, investigating it by means of interview material interspersed with contemporary news footage. Statesmen like Eden and Mendès-France set the general pattern and the local detail is provided by men like the local German commander (who knows nothing of any persecution) and the peasant Resistance man who still lives in the same village as the man who betrayed him to the Germans. The result, skilfully pieced together by Ophuls from sixty hours of interviews, is totally fascinating in its presentation of the facts beneath the legend, the sorrow and the pity of the Occupation. While Ophuls returned to television work, Harris and de Sedouy continued in the same vein with *Français, si vous saviez*, a three-part look at the effects of France's military ventures from World War I to the Algerian Revolution, again mixing contemporary footage and present-day interviews to explode some of the prevalent myths.

In the fiction film a fresh tone was given by two or three directors who, in very different ways, confronted aspects of reality hitherto absent from the French screen. Costa-Gavras had already completed two fairly conventional films, the well-received thriller *Compartiment teurs* (1965) and a Resistance drama, *Un Homme de trop* (1966), when he directed *Z* (1969). This bold film managed to combine impeccable left-wing sentiments with a sure sense for commercially successful structuring. The opening of the film, featuring such actors as Yves Montand, Jean Bouise and Bernard Fresson and constructed so as to allow the flow of the narrative to be interrupted by thought flashes, has distinct echoes of Resnais's *La Guerre est finie*. *Z* was in fact co-scripted and had dialogue written by Resnais's scenarist, Jorge Semprun, but unlike the earlier film it analyses the repercussions of a political assassination, not the mind of a political activist. Securely based on a real-life Greek incident of 1963 (the Lambrakis affair) and constructed so as to unfold with the intricacy of a good detective story, the film is a vigorous and entertaining piece of work. It is not without its flaws – it has moments of facility and melodrama and the use of well-known actors for all the major parts is questionable – but in political terms it is irrefutable and its stance represents something new in French cinema. Being himself of Greek origin, Costa-Gavras was able to handle the labyrinthine political manoeuvrings with a sure touch and yet give his film a note of wider accusation.

The choice of Raoul Coutard as cameraman for *Z* is indicative of Costa-Gavras's extrovert style which found him a wide audience both in France and elsewhere. However, the dangers as well as the virtues of this approach to political subjects using all-star casts and big budgets are shown by the director's subsequent works. *L'Aveu* (1970), made by the same team the following year, is also a study of political oppression, this time that of Stalinism in Czechoslovakia in the 1950s.

Again the basic events are real (the film is based on Artur London's autobiography) but the political analysis offered is counterbalanced by the thriller aspects of a plot designed to extract the maximum of drama from the situations it confronts. Costa-Gavras's third political study and perhaps the best of his work at this period, *Etat de siège* (1972), was scripted by Franco Solinas who had earlier written the script of Gillo Pontecorvo's internationally successful *Battle of Algiers* (1966). Dealing with the role of an American 'advisor' tried and executed by Tupamaros guerrillas in Uruguay, *Etat de siège* generates the same forceful emotional impact as Costa-Gavras's earlier work, although it too has moments at which political events are manipulated so as to achieve an overemphatic dramatic effect.

To set against the occasional excesses of Costa-Gavras is the restrained and understated work of Maurice Pialat (b.1925). Much of Pialat's work had been done for television – most notably a serial *La Maison des bois* shown in 1971 which acquired wide acclaim. He was in his mid-forties when the first of his mere handful of features for the cinema was released and all his works are among the most austerely independent films of the period, applying a realistic approach uncompromised by fashion or ostentation. Almost all his films deal with social issues of a kind ignored elsewhere in French cinema: the problems of an unwanted child in *L'Enfance nue* (1969); the end of a love affair in *Nous ne viellirons pas ensemble* (1972); the difficulties faced by a woman suffering – and dying – of cancer in *La Gueule ouverte* (1974). Pialat shows equal skill in handling non-professional players and such forceful personalities as Jean Yanne (in *Nous ne viellirons pas ensemble*), and his sensitivity to the nuances of human behaviour is unsurpassed. Pialat's difficulty in establishing himself are paralleled by those of a number of younger film makers who emerged in the aftermath of the New Wave, among them Paul Vecchiali (b.1930), Jean Eustache (1938–81) and Claude Feraldo (b.1936).

*

If the films of Costa-Gavras and Pialat in their very different ways opened new areas of interaction between film and politics or society, the dominant trends of the post-1968 realism were of a far more conventional and familiar kind. For a number of directors who had made their first appearance in the midst of the enthusiasm generated by the New Wave, these years were ones devoted to film making of a more measured and sober kind. In their very different styles, Chabrol and Rohmer, Truffaut and Malle all offered striking portraits of French bourgeois society from within its own perspectives. Here the youthful impetuosity of their earlier work was replaced by a cool professionalism, and in many ways it is possible to argue that these were years in which the New Wave moved back towards that very 'tradition of quality' so derided in the 1950s and from which all traces of social or political engagement were strenuously excluded.

For Claude Chabrol 1968 was the year in which he once more acquired full control over his work and he exploited this new freedom to the full by making *Les Biches* (1968), arguably his finest film to date. Returning to his original scriptwriter Paul Gégauff and to his favourite theme of the interaction of a trio of characters, Chabrol told the story of two women united in love (beautifully played by Stéphane Audran and Jacqueline Sassard) and the man who enters their lives with disastrous consequences. All the characteristic Chabrol elements are there: opulent settings and overplayed farcical minor parts, twisted relationships and a cold detached tone, quite free from all moralising comment. What is new is the discipline and sheer technical polish with which these elements are welded together and the total control of the medium within his chosen range which Chabrol here displays. Capitalising on this success, Chabrol went on to explore analogous themes in five more films made in quick succession between 1969 and 1971. The extent to which these are all variations on a theme is emphasised by the recurrence of characters' names, players and structures. The basic pattern is that of a conflict between a bourgeois husband Charles and an outsider or intruder called Paul, both rivals in some way for Charles's elegant wife Hélène (played, except in *Que la bête meure*, by Stéphane Audran). If there is a child, he is invariably called Michel. Audran's excellent performances are more than matched by those of Michel Bouquet, the image of bourgeois propriety as Charles in *La Femme infidèle* and *Juste avant la nuit*, and of Jean Yanne as the intruder (Paul or Popaul) in *Que la bête meure* and *Le Boucher*. The sense of continuity is enhanced further by the fact that all six films were produced for the same company and with the same technical crew, in which the cinematographer Jean Rabier played a key role.

In *La Femme infidèle* (1969) the impeccable surface of a bourgeois marriage is troubled when the husband discovers his wife's infidelity. Trying to react with his customary suave self-control, Charles is nevertheless driven to murder his rival, an action and its aftermath described by Chabrol with a clinical precision worthy of Hitchcock. *Que la bête meure* (1969), co-scripted once more with Gégauff, is a beautifully shaped thriller with a genuinely enigmatic ending. While never relaxing the tension after an opening sequence depicting the death of a child and never weakening his picture of the complexity of human motivation, Chabrol is able to include all his obsessional quirks. Here his fascination with the limitlessness of stupidity, with the brutal rapacity of the bourgeois mind and with the pretensions of the half-educated is used to lighten and counterbalance the story of a relentless vengeance carried out by a writer on those responsible for his son's death. In *Le Boucher* (1970) the figure of the husband/father is absent and the film portrays the love which unites the gentle school-teacher Hélène and the village butcher Popaul. Although she discovers that the latter is in fact a sadistic killer of young girls, her love persists and they share a first chaste kiss before he dies of self-inflicted wounds. *La Rupture* (1971) is perhaps the bleakest of this whole series of films as the life of a wholly innocent woman struggling to protect her son is subjected to a succession of inexplicable disasters and cruel manipulations which leave her on the brink of insanity. For once the tranquil surface of bourgeois life cannot be restored. But this occurs in *Juste avant la nuit* (1971) which effectively closes the series and provides a perfect counterbalance to *La Femme infidèle*. Whereas the complicity of the couple in that film was founded on a shared silence, here the husband (again Michel Bouquet) seeks absolution, after killing his mistress, by confession. But neither his wife nor the husband of the dead mistress (and his own best friend) offer anything but love and understanding. Unable to erase his sense of guilt, he is on the brink of confessing to the police when his wife intervenes to prevent him and to maintain the immaculate surface appearance of their shared life. Chabrol continued producing prolifically but, despite marvellous sequences, none of his subsequent four films of the period had the same force and unity.

A series of bourgeois portraits of a very different kind is provided by the six 'moral tales' directed by Eric Rohmer, the most secretive and elusive of the New Wave directors, between 1962 and 1972. These tales constitute a virtually unique group of films. All treat what is essentially the same story: a man, married or engaged to one woman, is tempted by another. After a momentary hesitation he returns to his first love, usually having enjoyed no more than a token 'victory' over the temptress. As if to balance the appearance of two women in each story, the hero, through whose eyes each tale is told, is given a male friend who usually plays a key role in the unfolding of the story. All of Rohmer's tales were initially written in literary form before being adapted by their author for the screen, although they were not published in book form until 1974. Their style remains distinctly literary, with a great importance attached to the hero-narrator's commentary, and their tone of psychological questioning is highly reminiscent in some ways of eighteenth-century French fiction. Yet at the same time the images retain their independent interest and the action is firmly placed in a specifically contemporary time and space. The hero reflects this ambiguity: though tempted briefly away from the path which he has chosen for his life, his final choice is always taken in conformity with the demands of conventional morality. Like Chabrol's very different films of the same period, Rohmer's tales dissect bourgeois life from within its norms and conventions.

Rohmer conceived his set of six films at the lowest ebb of his career – after the commercial failure of *Le Signe du lion* – and he was compelled to begin the series with two short black-and-white 16 mm films using unknown players or non-professionals, *La Boulangère de Monceau* (1962) and *La Carrière de Suzanne* (1963). These received virtually no showing at the time they were made in the early 1960s, so that the moral tales, like their author, emerge only slowly from obscurity. *La Collectionneuse* (1967) was the first of Rohmer's tales to achieve a commercial success, allowing the series to be completed in 35 mm and (except for *Ma nuit chez Maud*) in colour. It also marked the beginning of Rohmer's collaboration with the photographer Nestor Almendros, who gives this tale of shifting Saint-Tropez holiday romances a visual clarity and sensuality new to Rohmer's work. With *Ma nuit chez Maud* (1969) Rohmer's moral tales achieve a new level of complexity. In part this stems from the fact that the characters are this time mature adults able to talk eloquently about their experiences and ambitions. Although the provincial setting of Clermont-Ferrand in winter is given considerable weight, *Ma nuit chez Maud* is above all a conversation piece – witty, literate, amusing – with its dialogue expertly delivered by a cast led by Françoise Fabian and Jean-Louis Trintignant. The talk skips lightly around the themes of Pascal and chance, love and marriage. Rohmer brilliantly sustains the central situation of his hero spending the night in the bedroom of the glamorous Maud, shamefacedly defending his belief in Catholicism and morality and declining (but only just) a fairly open invitation to share the lady's bed. *Ma nuit chez Maud* marked the climax of Rohmer's work in that its hero and heroine are so well matched. In *Le Genou de Claire* (1970) the balance is no longer there between the mature Jérôme, holidaying at Annecy on the eve of his marriage, and the beautiful seventeen-year-old Claire, whose knee he decides to caress as a test of his power over women. But the emptiness of the gesture once accomplished (it is received by Claire not as a sexual advance but as a gesture of consolation in her tearfulness) denies the film any weight or ultimate seriousness. Yet its tone is better sustained than that of *L'Amour l'après-midi* (1972), the last of the series, which is also perhaps the most frustrating, in that Frédéric, having dreamed throughout the film of an adultery which will enliven a life burdened with wife and children, flees abjectly when confronted with the naked and willing Chloé. Again, as in *Ma nuit chez Maud*, there is ambiguity, but Rohmer seems ultimately to accept as valid and eternal a marriage without either conviction or honesty. The most agreeable and delightful sequence in *L'Amour l'après-midi* is the lighthearted episode in which Frédéric imagines the seduction of a succession of women encountered in the street, all of whom are played by actresses from earlier tales in the series. Rohmer's basically realistic stance in the six moral tales (with this one highly successful exception) combines effortlessly with the shaping impact of his classicism, which lays great stress on the traditional unities, particularly the unity of the action. All is pre-planned and pre-scripted, with no space left for chance or improvisation, yet in the best sequences – the central passages of *Ma nuit chez Maud*, for example – he achieves a rare impact.

The early 1970s also saw the appearance of two striking films directed by Louis Malle, both of which offer striking portrayals of adolescents while refusing to take any stance outside the consciousness of the central figure. *Le Souffle au coeur* (1971) is a paradoxical film in that though it is traditional, even conventional, in form, its climax is furnished by a scene of incest between mother and son. All Malle's best work grows out of genuine personal feeling – the suicidal despair of *Le Feu follet* or the anarchistic revolt of *Le Voleur* – but previously the emotion has always been distanced by the methods of literary adaptation and professional production. Here, by contrast, he has discovered in his ninth film the kind of directness which a film maker like Truffaut could achieve in his first work. For all its very real sense of involvement, the film is not directly autobiographical. The setting is 1954 – the year of Dien-Bien-Phu and the end of France's dreams of empire – while Malle's own adolescence was during the 1940s. The period is captured with loving detail – Charlie Parker, Camus, the advent of television, the political argument – but, like *Les Quatre cents coups*, *Le Souffle au coeur* is a film which adopts totally the viewpoint of its adolescent hero. Seen through his eyes, the drinking, whoring and stealing of his brothers and his own passion for his mother cease to be scandalous and become instead the natural expression of his own intense sense of revolt. If, ultimately, the couching of the film in comedy terms seems to take away some of the necessary virulence, the film nonetheless marks an important new stage in Malle's career.

This is emphasised by *Lacombe Lucien* (1974), a striking portrait of a seventeen-year-old collaborator during the Occupation. The film shows the strength of the classic narrative tradition. It offers no flashbacks or visually emphatic sequences, contenting itself simply with showing, without explanation or apology. In this it recalls Malle's early work as assistant to Cousteau and Bresson and his mid-1970s' concern with documentary approaches. He offers a striking re-creation of 1944 French society and shapes his film around the powerful clash of the over-civilised Jew Horn and the suspicious peasant Lucien, triggered off by the latter's involvement with Horn's daughter. This is a cinema of physical action, of gesture not psychology, and Lucien's drift into fascist activities is depicted rather as Cousteau might picture an exotic fish in his 'world of silence'. Honest portrayals of the usually glossed-over ambiguities of life in occupied France are rare and *Lacombe Lucien* confronts its subject forcefully. But, as in so much early 1970s French cinema, there is no point from which the social and political issues raised can be judged. We follow the actions of a young man for whom killing people is no more important than killing chickens and the film accepts his perspective, implying ultimately that there is no difference between collaboration or resistance (Lucien could happily have joined either side).

The most striking example of the void in which French realist cinema of the early 1970s operated is undoubtedly François Truffaut's *L'Enfant sauvage* (1970), the first film in which he appears as an actor. Truffaut plays Dr Itard, the eighteenth-century doctor who attempts to educate Victor, a wild child found in the wood near Aveyron where he had grown to the age of twelve without human contact (the film is based on the doctor's account of this real-life situation). Truffaut's fascination with language and with the teaching methods employed by Itard is clearly apparent, and he brings all his insight and more than a touch of autobiographical concern to the central relationship of adolescent and adoptive father (echoes of Truffaut and Bazin?). The portrayal is lovingly exact and holds the attention completely, but on the key issues raised by the film concerning the relation of nature and society, the status of 'civilisation' and the aims (rather than the methodology) of education, he has nothing to say. The ending is deliberately open, like that of *Les Quatre cents coups*, but here it seems doubly ambiguous in that the director seems both to accept without question Itard's eighteenth-century notions of civilisation (table manners, wearing a top hat) and to ignore the terror of the wild boy's final situation, suspended for life between savagery and civilisation.

In his other works of this period Truffaut is content to echo in a minor vein themes and stories already explored earlier in his career. The sense of continuity is remarkable, but the individual works tend to lack exciting new resonances. *La Sirène du Mississippi* (1969) and *Une Belle fille comme moi* (1972) are explorations in Truffaut's familiar pseudo-Hitchcockian style of material drawn from American thrillers and offer portrayals of two highly contrasting but equally dominating women: the enigmatic Marion (Catherine Deneuve) and the nymphomaniac Camille (Bernadette Lafont). *Domicile conjugal* (1970) is a further instalment of the Antoine Doinel saga, taking him through marriage, parenthood and initial adultery (with an enigmatic Japanese) with an agreeable lightness of tone but a striking absence of depth. Despite the opportunities offered by its opening style in *Les Quatre cents coups* and the frequency with which Truffaut returned to it, the Antoine Doinel story is in no way a social (let alone political) history of its period: all issues outside those concerning personal relations are resolutely ignored. Similarly *Les Deux anglaises et le continent* (1971) adapts a second novel by Henri-Pierre Roché, the author of *Jules et Jim*, without equalling the memorable charm and power of the earlier film. Truffaut's most striking film of the period is *La Nuit américaine* (1974), a vigorously drawn portrayal of action on and off the screen on a film set, with Truffaut himself giving an authoritative performance as the director around whom the tragic and farcical events revolve. The film is inevitably loaded with allusions to other films and the emotional tangles are handled with Truffaut's customary delicacy. *La Nuit américaine* is a complex work which deals affectionately with film making without ever attempting a serious questioning of the relationship between cinematic fiction and reality.

In addition to these former members of the New Wave, two other film makers became, as it were, the official chroniclers of the bourgeoisie of the 1970s. Claude Sautet (b.1924) had made his debut with a thriller, *Classe tous risques*, in 1960, completed a second feature, *L'Arme à gauche*, in 1965 and worked on a large number of scripts during the decade. But his career did not really get under way until he completed *Les Choses de la vie* (1969). This film set the pattern to be followed in the years up to 1974 and beyond: *Max et les ferrailleurs* (1970), *César et Rosalie* (1972) and *Vincent, François, Paul. . . et les autres* (1974). The core of any Sautet film is a fairly banal emotional problem – a man caught between two women in *Les Choses de la vie* or a married woman confronted with a former lover in *César et Rosalie* – handled in ways that do not ultimately give offence to conventional morality. Around this central situation Sautet and his customary scriptwriter Jean-Loup Dabadie weave a rich pattern of bourgeois life: concerns with home and family, with money and possessions; and it is this sense of group interaction that gives his films that particular tone. Problems and motivations are always explicitly spelt out, for this is a style of psychological realism in which the individual not the social forms the focus of attention. Sautet's style is a sober classical one built on the model of the traditions of Hollywood narrative: action, movement, vitality. Although his style can encompass elaborate set-pieces, the director is most concerned with the unfolding of a strong and involving narrative line. A key feature of all his work is the confrontation scene, and his films offer excellent opportunities for such solid and talented actors as Romy Schneider and Michel Piccoli (three films each), Yves Montand, François Périer, Serge Reggiani. Sautet's work is impressive, but always marked by more complicity than criticism in its portrayal of bourgeois life.

At the opposite pole stylistically to Sautet's cool classicism, but ideologically fairly close in its portrayal of bourgeois life, is the frenetic and often over-emphatic work of Claude Lelouch who, throughout the 1970s, built on the reputation acquired with *Un Homme et une femme*. It is generally the glossier side of life that attracts Lelouch. Thus after a seriously intended look at capital punishment, *La Vie, l'amour et la mort* (1969), he returned to romantic love with *Un Homme qui me plaît* (1970), which contained star performances, glamorous American settings and a story moving easily from chance meeting to passionate love and sad final parting. Lelouch, though working within a consistent system of values, is an erratic and uneven director, mixing moments of genuinely captured humour and drama with grossly pretentious sequences and scenes. Three very varied films – the parody thriller *Le Voyou* (1970), the inexpensive and improvised *Smic, smac, smoc* (1971) and the big-budget satire on world politics *L'Aventure c'est l'aventure* (1972) – all deal with the role of money in society, but their critical impact is very muted. With *La Bonne année* (1973), a sumptuously told story of a gangster who fails his biggest coup but finds true love, and *Toute une vie* (1974), a family chronicle extending over several generations, Lelouch moved into the territory in which his most characteristic 1970s work is located: the complaisant portrayal of a society from which politics is excluded and where love and comradeship will always triumph.

*

Many of the major figures of French cinema were virtually excluded from production in the early 1970s. Alain Resnais's *Stavisky* (1974) was his first feature for six years and marks the resumption of his collaboration with the writer Jorge Semprun. Resnais treated this tale of a 1930s swindler (played by Jean-Paul Belmondo) with a cold and dazzling style. It is a formidable work – clearly that of a major director – but unengaging in its brilliance. Despite Semprun's device of setting the public drama of Stavisky's scandals against the more private story of Trotsky's arrival in exile, the film remains an entertainment, not a historical study. As an entertainment, it is most notable for its discreet reflections on the nature of spectacle, showing the world of business and politics as no more than an extension of the theatre which forms so large a part of Stavisky's life.

Agnès Varda too made only one film during this period, *Lions Love* (1969) and this was shot independently in Hollywood. The film is a remarkable collage of real and imagined events set against clips of Capra's *Lost Horizons* and television footage of the assassination of Robert Kennedy, in which the cast, led by Warhol's star Viva, act even when they are being real and indulge in grotesque parody when called upon to act. Varda's husband Jacques Demy had earlier gone to Hollywood to make *The Model Shop* (1968), a muted attempt to take his personal mythology – along with one of his favourite stars, Anouk Aimée – to the United States. The essay is not without interest, although the gap remains unbridged between the director's dream America and the actual Los Angeles locations used for the filming. On his return to France Demy entered the bleakest period of his career. Successively he made two fairy-tales – the pretentious and over-elaborate *Peau d'âne* (1970) and the British-made *The Pied Piper* (1972) – and a disastrously miscalculated comedy, *L'Evénément le plus important depuis que l'homme a marché sur la lune* (1973), which was followed by long years of silence.

Other newcomers of the 1960s were more fortunate. René Allio, for example, was able to continue his career with three very diverse films characterised by his particular blend of realism and theatricality (he began his career as a stage designer) and his intense sympathy for ordinary people, captured with all their banality and also all their dreams. The life of Pierre, the hero of *Pierre et Paul* (1969), is so ordered and well-regulated that he does not realise the extent to which it depends on credit until his father's death plunges him deeply into debt, and drives him to violence. In contrast, *Les Camisards* (1972) is a historical study without stars or even star roles which traces the failed revolt of the protestant people of the Cervennes who rose against the oppression of Louis XIV at the beginning of the eighteenth century. *Rude journée pour la reine* (1973), another quite fresh departure, is both a personal work and a stylistic exercise, capturing with precision and an involving rhythm the interaction of dream and reality in the head of an ordinary housewife, played with characteristic forcefulness by Simone Signoret. All of Allio's films are engagingly original and exact in execution and his intelligence as a film maker is never in doubt.

Equally personal is the film work of Walerian Borowczyk, the graphic designer and film animator, whose first feature, *Goto, l'île d'amour* (1968) was followed by a second, *Blanche*, in 1971. Both are haunting tales of love born and destroyed and star Borowczyk's wife, Ligia Branice. The setting of *Goto l'île d'amour* is an imaginary island which serves as a distorting mirror for the fascist dictatorships of our own time, a world of Kafkaesque ritual, cruelty and hate. Within this dreary world Glossia's brief but passionate love for an officer takes on an enormous sensuality but, like Glossia herself, it is inexorably doomed. Borowczyk's formal control and visual sense are remarkable and the drab greyness of the images is broken not merely by glimpses of Glossia's naked beauty but also by snatches of Handel and occasional totally enigmatic brief bursts of colour. *Blanche* offers a similar tale of doomed love, this time in a historical setting, recounting the love of an aged thirteenth-century lord's young wife for her handsome stepson. Again the love must be affirmed against a background of hate and lust, but none of the lovers' sincere but despairing efforts can stave off the inevitable disaster which comes with the death of all the principal characters except the cruel and conniving king who is left to rule over a desolate world.

The formal qualities of Borowczyk's work are still apparent in the four tales which go to make up the *Contes immoraux* (1974). The stories range widely in content and setting, and Borowczyk's aim is clearly to provoke, but the impact of his eroticism is distinctly muted, hampered rather than enhanced by his decorative sense. These hymns to the sensuality of human flesh are memorable less for their stories or structure than for moments of figures set in a landscape or objects isolated with all their curious inherent power.

Alain Robbe-Grillet's colour films of the 1970s are as innovative in terms of structure as his earlier black-and-white films, but far less successful in terms of communication with an audience. The problem of these films is precisely that of Borowczyk's *Contes immoraux* – the concern with blatant eroticism that undermines the interest of the formal experiment. Instead of presenting themselves as works of intellectual and artistic complexity, they invite a reading in terms of their content alone and in this respect seem, at first sight, no more than unusually disjointed examples of the soft-core pornography which swamped French screens from the mid-1970s onwards. The added difficulty of Robbe-Grillet's work is that even when the formal patterning is uncovered through analysis, it is still incredibly difficult to experience the films in these terms. *L'Eden et après* (1970), for example, is on one level a disjointed adventure story involving a group of students, the search for a stolen painting, games, drugs, escape to a dream orient and so on, and enlivened by a particularly uninhibited performance by Catherine Jourdan. Beneath its apparently incoherent surface, however, is a complex attempt to structure a film narrative on the lines of serial music, with twelve themes varied in ten series. But even Robbe-Grillet has been forced to admit in interviews that he himself finds it impossible to experience this formal pattern while viewing the film. *Glissements progressifs du plaisir* (1974) and *Le Jeu avec le feu* (1975) continue and develop Robbe-Grillet's formal concerns, exploring circular patterns of film structure akin to those used in his 1970s novels. But increasingly it is the director's obsession with women's flesh that strikes the spectator. Robbe-Grillet talks of using merely the familiar stereotypes of eroticism and containing these within the formal play of the work, but the distance he aims for is never achieved.

Equally demanding and formally innovative – but totally lacking any trace of eroticism – are the contemporary works of Jacques Rivette, for whom this was and remains the richest creative period. *L'Amour fou* (1969) deals with Rivette's favourite subject – a group of actors rehearsing a play – and is a major work of the decade. Running for four hours and twelve minutes, it brings together and interweaves a number of threads: a group rehearsing Racine's *Andromaque* and a television documentary being made about them, the professional work of the director (Jean-Pierre Kalfon) and the disintegration of his relationship with his wife (Bulle Ogier). The texture of the image (with the 16 mm documentary footage intercut with 35 mm material) is crucial to the understanding of the work and despite the apparent looseness of the structure there is nothing arbitrary about the film. Aside from the remarkable sequence in which the couple destroy the contents of their flat in a frenzy of obsessive violence, there is little drama in a conventional sense. Instead Rivette uses his huge time span to create a closeness to and awareness of the central figures that seem to deny the conventional barriers set up by the concept of the fictional character. Yet despite the stress throughout on reality – we feel the players are living their parts, not acting, and the production of the play is an authentic one devised and rehearsed by Kalfon – the film remains a fiction, filled with all the magic and sense of mystery which characterises Rivette's finest work.

Out one (1971) is one of the legendary works of French cinema, running for twelve hours forty minutes (Rivette had hoped to sell it as a television serial) and shown only once, in the form of a work print, in Le Havre in October 1971. From the material Rivette constructed what he insists is a radically different work (not a condensation) which was released commercially as *Out one spectre* (1974). Here Rivette takes even further than in *L'Amour fou* the techniques of improvisation and involvement of the actors in the creation of their roles. Balzac's *Histoire des treize* is used to give a vaguely unifying basis to the film and the character played by Jean-Pierre Léaud serves as a link, bringing together a whole set of quite diverse characters, as he attempts to solve a mystery that continues to elude him and the other characters. Here Rivette pursues his questioning of the most fundamental aspects of film: the nature of narrative; the relation of acting and being; the spectator's response to duration (the film lasts four hours twenty minutes); and the necessity of editing. Once more there is an interplay of textures (colour film images and black-and-white stills) and the reduction of the action to a series of conversations recorded at length with a camera that never draws attention to itself. Since each actor or actress was responsible for the construction of his or her role in isolation from the rest, the fictional world of *Out one spectre* has a unique quality, as we watch the group try out their roles, invent relations among themselves and seek connections and explanations which continually evade them and us.

In comparison to the preceding works, *Céline et Julie vont en bateau* (1974) is both short (a mere three hours twelve minutes) and light-hearted. Just as *L'Amour fou* could have been extended by a further two hours by the inclusion of the whole of the play which we see being rehearsed, so too *Céline et Julie vont en bateau* with its circular structure could recommence at the end and run for a further three hours. The tone is much as before, with Juliet Berto and Dominique Labourier contributing much to their roles as well as to their performances, but here Rivette's attention is directed far more at questions of shaping and editing material. The interplay of heterogeneous levels is taken to its extreme point: there is absolutely no connection in style, form or cutting between the free and spontaneous acting of the two young women and the claustrophobic world of repetitious melodrama that they enter by taking magic potions and sucking mysterious sweets. For once the mystery is fully resolved: the action of the inset play, which is quite incomprehensible when we first see it, is shown to be about to culminate in the killing of a child whom Céline and Julie rescue. In addition to its cyclical overall structure, *Céline et Julie vont en bateau* is full of repetitions and parallels, with Céline and Julie continually mirroring each other's thoughts and actions and even exchanging identities completely on occasion. This is a world of playful fantasy, where the delight comes from our awareness and acceptance of the contrivance of a plot which, if more rigorously planned than before, is still full of loose ends and non-sequiturs.

The post-1968 period was one rich in filmic experiment. In addition to the films of such experimenters as Robbe-Grillet and Rivette, there was also fascinatingly original work from such innovators as Marguerite Duras, Marcel Hanoun and, in exile, Jean-Marie Straub. Although the latter's version of the Corneille play, *Othon* (1969), had a French text it was made with an Italian crew and largely non-professional actors in Italy, where Straub and Danielle Huillet lived from 1969. Thus, like Straub's other remarkable features of the period – the Brecht adaptation *Leçons d'histoire* (1972) and the film version of Schoenberg's opera *Moïse et Aaron* (1974) – *Othon* falls outside the scope of this volume.

Marcel Hanoun too continued a career begun in the late 1950s with a remarkable series of films which have never received the attention they deserve. *L'Eté* (1968) mixes visual references to the events of May '68 and other contemporary political issues with quotations from a range of literary sources and a stream-of-consciousness narration. *L'Hiver* (1969) is set in Bourges and offers a meditation on the problems of organising a film on location there as well as a personal story. *Le Printemps* (1970) brings together two sets of images – a man pursued and a child who is perhaps his daughter – without allowing one to separate reality from imagination, to know, for example, whether the man is real or simply imagined by the child. *L'Automne* (1972), which was followed by a version of the story of Christ, *La Verité sur l'imaginaire passion d'un inconnu* (1974), is perhaps the most fascinating of the series in the reflections it offers on the nature of cinema. For most of the film we see only two people, a man and a woman, engaged on editing a film which we do not see, since the camera is placed at the very point at which they are looking – the screen of the editing bench. Yet the sounds heard and the images described and commented on present us with an imaginary film which unfolds alongside the developing relation between the two film makers in the claustrophobic setting of the editing room adorned with stills from earlier Hanoun films. For Marguerite Duras too the post-1968 period was one of renewed involvement with the cinema. *Détruire dit-elle* (1969), *Jaune le soleil* (1971), *Nathalie Granger* (1973) and *La Femme du Gange* (1974) are a series of meditative studies poised between literary texts and filmic narratives in which all sense of dramatisation is lost and the interplay of voices take precedence over the flow of images. The themes of Duras's work – love, loss, death – are those of traditional story-telling but in her films they remain abstract, rarified, unable to accede to the weight and solidity of a story. Allegories of the imagination, these films prepare the way for the still more radical series which Duras was to realise during the late 1970s.

*

Luton Sixth Form College Library

The period up to the mid-1970s saw the end of a number of directing careers. Most of Jean Renoir's later years were devoted to writing: his book on his father, *Renoir* (1962), and a number of novels beginning with *Les Cahiers du Capitaine Georges* (1966). *Le Petit théâtre de Jean Renoir* (1969), a group of four short pieces made for television and presented by the director himself, forms an agreeable if insubstantial ending to his long career. Marcel Carné also published his memoirs in the 1970s, but his own last films were less satisfactory. While the loose, improvisatory style of Renoir could be seen as relating to modern tastes, neither the Cayette-style cinema of social protest exemplified by Carné's *Les Assassins de l'ordre* (1970) nor the would-be poetic fantasy of his *La Merveilleuse visite* (1973) corresponded to contemporary conceptions of cinema. Equally unsatisfactory was the work made during this period by René Clément, who ended his career with a series of thrillers, made as expensive co-productions with international stars, in which the director's technical command in no way compensates for the lack of conviction and narrative drive: *Le Passager de la pluie* (1970) with Charles Bronson, *La Maison sous les arbres* (1971) with Faye Dunaway, *La Course du lièvre à travers les champs* (1972) with Robert Ryan and Aldo Ray, *La Baby-sitter* (1975) with Maria Schneider.

Two other key directors of the 1950s and 1960s also concluded their careers at this time. Jean-Pierre Melville followed his masterly trio of gangster films with *L'Armée des ombres* (1969), one of the French cinema's few adequate depictions of the Resistance. Adapted from a novel by Joseph Kessel, it traces the activities of one Resistance group over a period of some five months during 1942–43. Melville constructs his narrative with great economy and draws his characters with deft precision. The wartime period, to which he returns here for the third time, is an ideal one for the director. In *L'Armée des ombres* he can combine his nostalgia for the past (a different Paris and a different style of film making) with his interest in comradeship and heroism, loyalty and betrayal (the mainsprings of his gangster films). Melville's use of Lino Ventura, Paul Meurisse and Simone Signoret in this film is a reminder of the extent to which the cinema of the late 1960s was once more becoming an actor's medium, as it had been in the heyday of Raimu or Gabin. *Le Cercle rouge* (1970) is a return by Melville to the pure thriller atmosphere of *Le Samourai*. Once more the star is Alain Delon (seconded this time by Gian Maria Volonté) and again there is a touch of the oriental, in that the film's title comes from the allegedly Buddhist notion of a 'red circle' in which men, predestined by fate, will be re-united, however much they may struggle against this. The whole action takes place not in present-day reality, but in the mythical world of the fictional gangster. This is a dark and claustrophobic world (no light enters the shuttered apartment where the detective, Bourvil, lives alone with his three cats) and in it the characters continually deceive and double-cross each other. Melville avoids all social criticism but the parallels drawn in the film between the world of the detectives and that of the crooks have a precision worthy of Fritz Lang.

Un Flic (1972), the last film completed by Melville before his death in 1973, was less successful, though still recognisably the work of a master craftsman. The plot elements are much as before, with the policeman (Alain Delon) evenly matched against the gang-leader (Richard Crenna) with whose mistress he is having an affair. Critics were generally troubled by the model work in a train-robbery sequence and, above all, by the increasing austerity of Melville's style. With *Un Flic* the passage towards abstraction begun in the earlier gangster films is virtually complete, and we are left with a derisory world lacking even the human warmth of loyalty and friendship which the director had once celebrated. The mood of this last film is in fact summed up by Delon when he explains that 'ambiguity and derision are the only feelings which man has ever been able to inspire in a policeman'.

Georges Franju's last two films reflect yet again the two contrasting poles of his feature-film making: the literary adaptation and the pure stylistic exercise. *La Faute de l'abbé Mouret* (1970), Franju's first film for the cinema after a break of five years and a project first conceived seventeen years earlier, is very much a part of his customary world – violently anti-religious and unwavering in its advocacy of *amour fou*. The film, adapted from a Zola novel, is built on patterns of contrasts, with the liberating purity of young love set against a Catholic Church which is both an oppressive tool of the rich and a fountain of crippling superstition. Much of Franju's best work in the cinema – *Hôtel des Invalides* or *Thérèse Desqueyroux*, for example – makes its point subversively. Here in *La Faute de l'abbé Mouret* the director is able to make almost too direct a statement of his basic beliefs and much of the customary tension of his work is missing.

Nuits rouges (1974), made after a further gap of four years, is a return to the world of the primitive film serial which had been a constant source of inspiration for Franju. Working once more with Jacques Champreux (co-scriptwriter of *Judex*), the director lovingly created a totally fantastic and claustrophobic world of underground passages and labyrinths, in which a struggle for power is fought out between the Man Without a Face (played by Champreux) and the Knights Templar who guard their treasure ruthlessly. Franju has described his film, which is made with a complete unconcern for any form of realism or even credibility, as 'a purely fictional adventure story, a chimeric action spectacle, a dramatic *divertissement*'. He was never to make the planned sequel and his work in the feature film seems to have been cut off, perhaps even before the ultimate masterpiece which his first documentaries seemed to promise. But for all its unevenness, Franju's feature-film career assures him of a place apart in French cinema, as both innovator and one of the most faithful preservers of its greatest traditions.

While Melville and Franju offer lessons in film making which look back to earlier styles (their own included), film makers of an even earlier generation undertook in these years works which attempted a radical redefinition of the film narrative. While retaining a basically realistic conception of the film camera as a means of capturing reality, Robert Bresson, Jacques Tati and Luis Buñuel resist in their varying ways the claims of linear narrative. All three directors base their films on quite other principles, seeking new relationships between the characters and the action, between the audience and the film.

For Robert Bresson, *Une Femme douce* (1969), adapted from a story by Dostoevsky, proved that the necessity of working in colour in no way lessened his ability to create a totally personal vision. The film is the story of the wretched marriage of two ill-assorted young people, told in flashback after the wife's suicide, as the husband looks at her body stretched out on the bed. The progress of the couple's relationship is beautifully captured without recourse to psychological 'explanations' and the whole tone of the acting, shooting and cutting bears the imprint of Bresson's personality. His strength as a director lies in his ability to select and juxtapose elements drawn from reality. His handling of the suicide at the beginning of *Une Femme douce* exemplifies this; a shot of a table slowly tipping over in front of an open window, a white scarf drifting slowly to the ground, over which is laid the sound of screeching brakes. All the elements selected are 'real', but the whole incident acquires a new poetry and mystery. At the same time the effect of such an extreme selection is to isolate the incidents from the flow of everyday life: the world becomes a prison.

Quatre nuits d'un rêveur (1972) was a further adaptation of Dostoevsky, this time the story, *White Nights*, which Luchino Visconti had filmed fifteen years earlier. It tells of a young girl waiting for her student lover who promised to marry her a year before and of the young man who keeps her company for four nights and falls in love with her. The combination of a nineteenth-century story and a modern hippie setting around the Pont Neuf in Paris sets up the double time-scale which characterises Bresson's literary adaptations. The heroine is played by Isabelle Weingarten who, like Dominique Sanda, the star of *Une Femme douce*, trained as a model and maintains an impassivity throughout. The new erotic tone which entered Bresson's work with *Au hasard, Balthazar* finds expression here, especially in the brief but effective images of the naked lovers embracing. Both the obsessed heroine, who falls totally in love with a man she has never actually seen, and the shy hero, who with his tape-recorder turns every woman he meets into a figure of fantasy, reject reality in the name of a dream. *Quatre nuits d'un rêveur* is less tragic than its predecessors, in that the heroine is saved from suicide and in the end has her deepest wishes granted. But the very banality of the appearance of her bespectacled student lover, arriving four nights late to claim her, empties the dream of its romance.

Likewise *Lancelot du lac* (1974) empties its subject – the Arthurian legend – of its conventional overtones, presenting only anonymous, helmeted figures whose passage is marked by the sound of horses' hooves, by killing, looting and burning. All the mystery and romanticism is peeled away: the director begins with the failure of the quest for the grail and charts the parallel failure of Lancelot and Guinevere to conquer the human weaknesses of passion, pride and treachery. Love of man and love of God are seen as incompatible. Guinevere is unable to sublimate her love for her chosen knight Lancelot so as to remain true to her marriage vows. But equally, when Lancelot has carried her off, she is drawn back to Arthur. Lancelot attempts to achieve sainthood by an effort of will, and even succeeds briefly, at least in the eyes of his closest friend, Gauwain. But ultimately he fails both the king and Guinevere, wins only the enmity of Modred and even kills his companion, Gauwain. For lovers such as Lancelot and Guinevere the only outcome can be death – brutal, anonymous, and futile. There is no more glory in their end than in the search for the grail with which the film opens: only crude, violent acts of sword and hand, the needless spilling of blood in an indifferent landscape. Bresson removes all the traditional depth from his narrative, but his construction obeys a tighter logic: the remorseless working out of the tragic failure to achieve divine grace.

For Jacques Tati too the early 1970s were years of high achievement. *Trafic* (1970), his meditation on the motorcar, is at the very opposite pole to Godard's *Weekend*. Its car-crash sequence is not a scene of carnage, but an automobile ballet which provokes exaggerated politeness and *joie de vivre* on the part of everyone concerned and culminates in the unforgettable image of a cleric tinkering with his engine employing all the gestures of a priest celebrating mass. Tati's attitude to such notions as progress, mass production and public relations is one of gentle irony. As always in his films an alternative to modern life is discovered by Hulot – here it is a country garage alongside a Dutch canal, with the waterways offering a glimpse of a more leisurely – and more human – rhythm. As in *Play Time* the plot as such is virtually non-existent, comprising simply the efforts of the company for which Hulot works to get their latest camping car to an international exhibition in Amsterdam. Inevitably, with Hulot in charge, they arrive only after the exhibition has closed. But although Hulot is back in the centre of the action, after his virtual disappearance from *Play Time*, the film continues to use the long shot as the basis of its style, the mood being set in the brilliant opening sequence of planners hastening to and fro, stepping awkwardly over the invisible trip-wires marking out the exhibition spaces in the vast hall. *Trafic* completely disregards the possibilities of verbal humour and Tati has no interest in building up chain reactions by steadily increasing the exaggeration and absurdity of a situation. Instead he prefers a sequence made up of a dozen or more equal and tiny fragments or the isolated confrontation (as when a fluffy dog watches with enigmatic interest as a car salesman uses an equally fluffy cloth to clean a car). No film maker at work in commercial cinema demands a closer attention to detail from his audience than Tati. *Trafic*, like *Play Time*, is a film that demands to be seen and reseen.

On the surface Tati's *Parade* (1974) is no more than an evening's unassuming entertainment, a visit to the circus, built round the performances of the players including Tati himself. There is no trickery or elaborate stylisation involved in the presentation of any particular act, and the film's basic unit is an almost documentary-style record of performance, the film's richness coming from the interweaving and interaction of these performances over time. Here Tati at last records on film the sporting mimes with which he made his initial reputation in the 1930s. His use of the circus metaphor is personal and distinctive: for him there is no pathos or nostalgia for a past tradition. The clowns and the elephants are missing; instead we find youth, agility and simple – if polished – talents. Tati offers a democratisation of the spectacle. Performers and audience within the film (and hopefully the film's spectators too) are linked in a common celebration. Tati appears as the *meneur de jeu*, performing his mimes but never assuming the airs of a star. Around him forms the world familiar to us from his earlier films – one where pomposity is deflated, the tiny human detail takes precedence over the grand performance and the eternal cycle of creation and destruction takes its course. After the supreme achievement of *Play Time* and the occasionally strained effect of *Trafic*, *Parade* is a more relaxed work, characterised by its informality, good humour and fundamental respect for human skill and oddity.

For Luis Buñuel, *Belle de jour*, made at the age of sixty-six, heralded an unbroken series of masterly films whose originality and modernity is astounding. Throughout a key element in the director's approach is humour, for the films of Buñuel's maturity are both totally approachable comedies and subtle games with narrative and realistic expectations. *La Voie lactée* (1969) is a somewhat esoteric and episodic film, built loosely around the adventures and visions of two rather shabby pilgrims. In a sequence of episodes set at varying times and in diverse locations, Buñuel reviews the range of heresies that arise from the six major dogmas of the Catholic Church. Despite the almost pedantic exactness of Buñuel's chronicling of heresy, the film is light, at times even farcical, though its full impact depends (ironically since Buñuel is a self-proclaimed atheist) on a knowledge of and involvement with Church dogma which is no longer universal. Buñuel's subsequent films of the 1970s have more widely accessible targets, particularly those confronting the ideology of the bourgeoisie. This is particularly apparent in the film Buñuel made after a brief return to Spain (where he made the masterly *Tristana*, 1970), *Le Charme discret de la bourgeoisie* (1972). Like *La Voie lactée*, this is an episodic work, but here the structure is stronger, being built around a group of half-a-dozen bourgeois characters and their endless, never-satisfied pursuit of dinner. While their incidental behaviour and conversation gives Buñuel scope for a searching portrait of their greed and sexual appetite, the drama of the film is that of the constant frustration of their desire to eat. At first the obstacles are predictable, 'realistic' ones: arriving on the wrong day, visiting a restaurant where the *patron* has just died and so on. But as the film proceeds, the distinction between reality and dream is lost. The hindrances become more and more bizarre: army manoeuvres, finding oneself in a stage scene of a dinner party, being arrested by the police or gunned down by gangsters. But the frustration remains and the final images show the characters – despite being shot – eternally, optimistically *en route* for the missing meal.

The advance which *Le Charme discret de la bourgeoisie* represents – in terms of structure – in relation to *La Voie lactée*, is echoed in *Le Fantôme de la liberté* (1974). Here Buñuel rediscovers the freedom of *Un Chien andalou* (1929), basing the whole one-hundred-minute structure on a systematic non-sense and non-sequentiality of events. The film begins with the execution of Spanish patriots who shout 'Down with Liberty!' as they are executed by Napoleonic forces in 1808 and ends with the same cry superimposed over shots of animals in the Vincennes zoo. Between these two moments, at which the significance of the title is most explicit, the film concentrates on a range of characters drawn largely from contemporary French bourgeois life. The links between the episodes are deliberately disconcerting, as Buñuel plays with our narrative expectations and frustrates our desire to know the ending of the various stories he begins. Every story is cut off before the climax is reached. We discover, for example, that it is merely a tale being told by someone else, or follow a minor, hitherto uninteresting character into a new episode – which likewise remains unresolved. Stylistically we have a denial of narrative logic and continuity, of the hierarchy between major and secondary characters, and of the need to differentiate between different levels of reality. This startling formal structure is a perfect frame for the world which Buñuel depicts. Gone is the logic of cause and effect, the reality of death, our moral certainties and customary practices: instead we are offered a derisory world of upturned values.

*

The half-dozen years following May '68 – those of Georges Pompidou's presidency – form a contradictory period, whose difficulty of interpretation comes only partially from its closeness to us. There is a real attempt at politicisation of the cinema to be found in the non-commercial documentary production of the late 1960s and early 1970s. Marker and Godard take up positions of a kind seldom, if ever, occupied by earlier film makers. There is an admittedly confused attempt to rethink the fundamentals of film production and to create a new relationship with the audience, and this fresh approach finds expression not only in the documentary movement but also in the feature film, with the political concerns of Costa-Gavras and social films of Pialat. Yet, within a few years, the overtly committed approach begins to lose its appeal, while the work of such talented directors as Robbe-Grillet and Borowczyk shows the beginnings of a shift towards a quite unpoliticised eroticism. The characteristic social cinema of the mid-1970s – from Chabrol, Rohmer and Melville to Truffaut, Malle and Sautet – questions bourgeois society, but only from very bourgeois standpoints. Moreover many of the major achievements of the period lie outside this area of social engagement altogether, as in the deliberately esoteric work of film makers like Jacques Rivette and Marguerite Duras or in the rethinking of realist narrative cinema undertaken by such veterans as Bresson, Tati and Buñuel.

13   The Liberalisation of Cinema
1975–81

Pour le cinéma français, les années 70 auront été la décennie *post* par excellence: post-Nouvelle Vague, post-68, post-moderne. Pas de lame de fond, de mouvement, d'école: presque un désert esthétique. On ne sait pas en quoi cette décennie regarde déjà vers les années 80. On saura plus tard ce qu'elle y aura préfigurée. En attendant, il faut hasarder une description: ni à froid, ni à chaud: à tiède.

Serge Daney, 1980

One of the more unexpected results of Giscard d'Estaing's presidency was the rise of the pornographic film to prominence in France during the mid-1970s. The abolition of censorship came at a time when the vogue for eroticism in the cinema was at its height. The key film in this respect is the phenomenally successful *Emmanuelle* (1974) which had been seen by a reputed eight million spectators in France when the same director's version of the *Histoire d'O* opened the following year. Just Jaeckin, the director, is a former fashion photographer whose compositional sense and decorative talents are more developed than his awareness of narrative. The plot action – the sexual initiation of an innocent young French wife in the brothels of Bangkok in *Emmanuelle* and the total sexual humiliation of the tormented masochistic heroine in *Histoire d'O* – is dully handled. But both films are given an amazingly glossy finish with a photographic style akin to that used in the most chic and expensive Parisian magazines (*Vogue, Lui*) in which Jaeckin's photographs had earlier appeared. The softening of the contours of the photographed world (rose-tinted views of the Bangkok brothels and the château de Roissy) is accompanied by a dilution of any provocative element which the original novels – particularly the *Histoire d'O* – might contain. Just Jaeckin's eroticism is a soft-focus vision of beautiful young models locked in tender embrace with others of their kind, or submitting, dewy-eyed, to nameless (and generally unseen) humiliations at the hands of ravaged-looking male survivors of a very different kind of cinema (first Alain Cuny, then Anthony Steele).

This style of film making is anaemic and totally conformist, offering only muted satisfaction despite the evident charms of Sylvia Kristel as Emmanuelle and Corinne Cléry as O. Its continuation in the various sequels to *Emmanuelle*, in Jaeckin's own *L'Amant de Lady Chatterley* (a 1981 travesty of D. H. Lawrence) and in the work of yet another photographer specialising in the photographing of adolescent girls in tasteful yet provocative poses, David Hamiliton (*Bilitis*, 1976; *Laura, les ombres de l'été*, 1979), is of little consequence. What is troubling is that this unappealing form of cinema has become an area of concern for certain major film makers of the 1970s. Simulating intercourse for an audience of voyeurs securely hidden in the darkness, the softcore semi-pornographic film offers an ersatz confection of sex reduced to mere nudity and heavy breathing. Its economic basis – the exploitation of the frustrations of its audience – is equally unsavoury. Its shoddiness from an artistic perspective is usually only too clear in the mere decorativeness of its visual style, and its ideology in the basic (and well-founded) assumption that it is cheaper to persuade pretty girls to take off their clothes as a way of getting into the movies than to use actresses who can hold the attention fully clad. The hazards of the genre are self-evident, yet the fundamentally joyless and dispiriting exercise of offering naked flesh to an audience has attracted a number of film makers of undoubted intellectual and artistic pretensions, foremost among them some of those European film makers born in 1922–23 to whom we owe many of the major cinematic advances of the 1960s.

As examples from outside France one might cite some of the later work of Miklos Jancsó (*Private Vices and Public Virtues*) and Pier Paolo Pasolini (the 'trilogy of life'), in which the potential provocative power of the naked body as an expressive symbol of the untouched force of the people is sadly dissipated. The problems raised by this form of cinema have already been touched upon in our consideration of Alain Robbe-Grillet's 1970s films. *Le Jeu avec le feu* (1975) was the last Robbe-Grillet film for eight years, but Walerian Borowczyk continued working prolifically throughout the late 1970s and his work raises similar problems. The titles of Borowczyk's films give a clear picture of his preoccupations: *La Bête* (1975), the Polish-made *The Story of Sin* (*Dzieje Grzechu*, 1975), *La Marge* (1976) from a story by André Pieyre de Mandiargues, *Intérieur d'un couvent* (1978), *Les Héroines du mal* (1979), *Lulu* (1980) and *Docteur Jekyll et les femmes* (1981). For both Robbe-Grillet and Borowczyk the confrontation with the censors is less a matter of politics than of breaking sexual taboos – a stance which can allow an otherwise esoteric author the chance to gain a wider audience for his work. At first sight the female nude has enormous potential as material for use in stylistic exercises involving either the plasticity of the image (Borowczyk) or new and mobile narrative structures (Robbe-Grillet). The latter's novels of the 1970s show the scope which the translation of the visual imagery of advertising and pornography into verbal terms offers an artist. But current film practice shows equally convincingly that if it is simply reproduced in film terms, such imagery remains exploitative and invites a degrading complicity between author and audience. The very language of film – as well as the production structure – needs to be transformed if the spectator is not to be forced into a purely voyeuristic role. The ambiguities of Borowczyk's work are illustrated by *La Bête*, a feature film whose starting point was an episode discarded from the earlier *Contes immoraux*. The previously shot tale of an eighteenth-century beauty and a marauding beast is used as a dream sequence in an otherwise contemporary story. The latter is structured as a rather uneasy and overlong farce, set in a house of erotic secrets inhabited by a collection of perverted and obsessed characters: the curé with his choirboys, the duke with his hair fetish, the daughter with the negro servant and the son with his animals. Many shots of isolated objects and the shock images of mating horses are extremely powerful, but the antiquated and anti-clerical plot fails to maintain interest. The transitions from reality to dream summoned up by the masturbatory activities of the charming young heiress are striking and the pursuit of the bewigged shepherdess through the forest becomes a sophisticated striptease to the music of Scarlatti which is a *tour de force* of directorial organisation. Yet the beast himself, with his rubber penis oozing gallons of artificial semen, lacks the necessary Cocteauesque poetry, and the climax of the framing story is ludicrous in quite the wrong way. At the same time, the film's final image – the shepherdess suddenly aware of her own nakedness, like Eve, in the forest – is extremely beautiful and effective.

There is no such ambiguity with regard to the hardcore pornographic film which made its first appearance in the elegant cinemas of the Champs-Elysées with Jean-François Davy's *Exhibition* in 1975. Although the production of pornographic films – a genre in no way to be confused with the decorative provocation of Jaeckin or Borowczyk – reached such a level as to constitute almost half the number of French films made in 1978 (157 out of 326 films completed) and though pseudonyms are common among the directors employed, no major figures have become involved in this area. With its tiny budgets and plots limited to a rigid set of actions, the pornographic film constitutes a definition of film as a basic commodity in an unambiguous commercial sense unknown since the days of Charles Pathé. The first unexpectedly blatant flourishing in the immediate aftermath of the lifting of censorship made the re-imposition of regulations of some kind inevitable. Rather than re-introduce censorship, the government brought into force a classification system and set of tax disincentives for productions given the 'X' label at the beginning of 1976. In this way, though production has continued to flourish, the consumption has been pushed back into the ghetto of the sleazier big-city cinemas and so removed from too obvious public view.

Exhibition constitutes an excellent example of the basic hypocrisy of the hardcore pornographic film. While on the surface offering an investigation into the mechanics of the pornographic film, both in terms of the atmosphere of shooting (the difficulties of performing sexual acts on cue in public) and the background of the leading actress (her past as a prostitute, her current boyfriend, her attitudes to her work and the money she is paid), *Exhibition* gives us no insight into anything that might be uncomfortable to the director or crew. The reasons for their involvement, together with the financial operation of marketing the end-product, are omitted from this account of pornographic production. While ostensibly sympathising with the leading performer (Claudine Beccarie) as a human being, the director exploits her mercilessly to obtain the effective footage he needs. The somewhat battered, wordly-wise actress gives a spirited performance, and she clearly thinks herself free in indulging in such activity at a rate of a thousand francs a day, but her inability to see how her evident honesty is exploited by Davy in this contemptible film is pathetic in the extreme.

*

The late 1970s were a contradictory period of French cinema. While production remained at a comparatively high level despite the continuing decline in the number of spectators (even when the mass of pornographic films produced is discounted), many of the established directors found their careers faltering. A huge number of young film makers – perhaps as many as three hundred in the 1970s – were able to make a first feature, but some of these debuts were outside the confines of professional film production (with its implication of full union crewing and a 35 mm format) and most were very low-budget, personal films which received at best only very limited commercial showings. As a result, many young directors were unable to proceed to a second or a third film, and few have been able to establish a real oeuvre. Although in terms of sheer numbers the renewal of the mid-1970s can be compared to the New Wave of 1958–62, the international impact of the new film makers has been muted. Few, if any, have found audiences abroad for their work in the way that Truffaut or Chabrol did, and for these reasons any definitive assessment at this stage is impossible. The following pages therefore attempt to pick out for detailed discussion a few key figures whose work seems to hold particular interest in the period up to 1981. But this is no more than a very provisional listing of newcomers to French 1970s cinema.

Many young directors adopted the tactic of taking a seemingly scandalous subject but filming it in a way which ultimately denuded it of its potential provocation, in the manner of, say, Louis Malle's treatment of incest in *Le Souffle au coeur* or Just Jaeckin's of sado-masochism in *Histoire d'O*. Thus Jean-Claude Tachella (b.1939) gave a lyrical picture of innocent and blatant adultery amid bourgeois hypocrisy in his second feature, *Cousin Cousine* (1975), achieving a level of success unequalled in his subsequent films. In similar fashion Michel Lang (b.1939) exploited the theme of adolescent lust – together with a fair measure of anglophobia – in *A nous les petites anglaises* (1975), then resurrected similar themes, this time in a French setting but with no greater subtlety, in *L'Hôtel de la plage* (1978). The specialist in questionable subjects would seem, however, to be Bertrand Blier (b.1939), who belongs to this generation despite the 'false start' of two films in the 1960s, *Hitler connais pas* (1963) and *Si j'étais un espion* (1967). Getting his career under way again in the mid-1970s, Blier offered carefully calculated treatment – often in comedy form – to such subjects as youthful sexual (and criminal) delinquency in *Les Valseuses* (1974), the superseding of two adult men by a thirteen-year-old boy as lover of the frustrated heroine of *Préparez vos mouchoirs* (1976), and incest between father and under-age step-daughter in *Beau-père* (1981). Blier's undeniable talent is shown with greater clarity in the equally pessimistic but more ambiguously surreal *Buffet froid* (1979).

One of the most talented of the new generation, Alain Corneau (b.1943), who spent several years as assistant director, has been deeply influenced by Hollywood cinema, particularly the thriller genre. Since the lack of real box-office success for the ambitious social and political stance of his first film, *France société anonyme* (1974), he has produced a series of thrillers which promise to rank him with Jean-Pierre Melville among the masters of the genre. The titles – *Police Python 357* (1976), *La Menace* (1977), *Série noire* (1979), *Le Choix des armes* (1981) – give a clear indication of the line which he has followed. These films are thrillers in the true sense of the word, designed for a mass audience and employing stars and impressive budgets, but in them Corneau is able to express his own particular concerns. His handling of actors is masterly and at the centre of each of his films is a study in disintegration or madness which offers remarkable opportunities to such powerful actors as Yves Montand, Patrick Dewaere and Gérard Depardieu. Working persistently with the cinematographer Pierre-William Glenn, Corneau has set these stories of torment haunted by the inevitable approach of death in precisely observed contexts – Orleans in *Police Python 357*, Montreal in *La Menace*, the Parisian suburban landscape in *Série noire* – which, through tight control of light and colour, become the abstract universal settings of human tragedy. Corneau's work is exemplary in its use of conventional forms to express a personal vision. Many of those who have attempted to follow less commercial paths have encountered difficulties. The Argentinian-born Hugo Santiago (b.1939), for example, has so far been unable to follow up his over-ambitious intellectual parody of the thriller genre – using Catherine Deneuve as an unlikely Marlowe substitute – *Ecoute voir* (1977). René Feret (b.1945) was able to follow his first 16 mm black-and-white feature *Histoire de Paul* (1975) with the very well-received and better-financed *La Communion solennelle* (1977), but *Fernand* (1980) added nothing to his reputation. Similarly Benoît Jacquot (b.1947) earned wide praise for his second film, *Les Enfants du placard* (1977), but his subsequent feature, *Les Ailes de la colombe* (1981), was a facile and unconvincing up-dating of a complex Henry James novel.

Among those critics who successfully made the transition to feature-film making, the most prolific is Bertrand Tavernier (b.1941), whose debut dates from *L'Horloger de Saint Paul* (1974), an adaptation of a Simenon novel. Like Alain Corneau, Tavernier has been deeply influenced by Hollywood cinema, but the stress in his films is less on action than on introspection. The pattern in this sense is set by *L'Horloger de Saint Paul* where the tranquillity of the watchmaker's life is unexpectedly shattered when his son commits a murder and has to flee from the police. This moment of change in a life of hitherto calm acceptance forms the core too of Tavernier's 1981 film, *Coup de torchon*, which is set in Senegal in the late 1930s and shows an indolent police chief suddenly reaching the decision to eliminate all the riff-raff of the little town who up till now have shown him open contempt. The difference in tone and setting between these two films – the meditative portrait of Tavernier's hometown of Lyons set against the strident reconstruction of European expatriate society in *Coup de torchon* – is very indicative of Tavernier's range, which is apparent in the five films he made between 1975 and 1980. *Que la fête commence* (1975) was an unexpected topic – a period piece set at the court of Philippe d'Orleans – but *Le Juge et l'assassin* (1976), though again a historical study, set this time in the 1890s, brings the director back to his central preoccupations in its study of the clash between magistrate and killer. Both *Des Enfants gâtés* (1977) and *Une Semaine de vacances* (1980) take a moment of respite – a film director seeking peace and quiet so as to be able to finish a script or a French schoolmistress taking a week's holiday – and use this as the basis to probe lives which have hitherto been unexamined. Tavernier's other 1980s film, *La Mort en direct/Death Watch*, was made in English and is a more striking study of a society in which death has replaced sex as the new pornography. Of all the new French directors of the 1970s, Tavernier seems most assured of creating an output to set against that of, say, Truffaut.

The career of another former critic – and editor of *Cahiers du cinéma* – André Téchiné (b.1943) has been more difficult and contradictory. His first film, *Paulina s'en va*, was completed in 1969 but not given a commercial showing until 1975. A study of madness, it draws on both Rivette's stress on improvisation (as in *L'Amour fou*) and the 'conversation in a void' style perfected by Godard in *Le Gai savoir*. It is filmed totally from the perspective of the girl, Paulina, and offers a key to the dominant situation of all Téchiné's characters – caught in a world they can neither change nor overcome. *Souvenirs d'en France* (1975) – a film which captures extremely well the pun (en France/enfance) contained in its title – is made in a very real sense *against* the earlier work. Where *Paulina s'en va* is a deliberately difficult, hermetic work, this second feature is open, full of incident and rooted in the popular genre of family history. It traces in chronicle form, without interest in suspense or overt tension, the progress of a bourgeois family over several decades. The dating of the action is difficult – if not impossible – because although the events are clearly located (via film posters) as occurring between 1937 and 1973, the characters themselves do not age. Téchiné shows us bourgeois life on its own terms, with all elements falling outside it – such as working-class movements during and after the Popular Front – merely caricatured. In this sense Téchiné's first two films are consistent: nowhere does the director show a concern for surface realism or psychological depth, and there is no way in which plot developments can carry the characters outside of the situations in which they are fixed.

Barocco (1976) is a film that has its profound sources in classic Hollywood style. It was easily Téchiné's most expensive production, a sumptuous recreation of Amsterdam as a mythical city of depravity and death, splendidly photographed by Bruno Nuytten. The director takes a plot that could easily have come from Hitchcock (seen in the light of French theories about the 'transfer of guilt') but though packed with references to Téchiné's favourite directors (Lang, Ray, Hitchcock), *Barocco* has, however, none of the Hollywood cinema's exemplary unity of style. As usual with the director, the wider social implications of the underworld plot (the framing sequences of the electoral campaign, for example) are neglected in favour of the contradictory actions and impulses of the characters. In *Les Soeurs Brontë* (1978) all options are closed from the outset. Indeed the whole film can be read as an uneven conflict between the static, shadow-ridden landscape – again photographed by Nuytten – and the vitality of the young Brontës as they struggle to act and express themselves. The landscape, which exists as a setting, a decor for the action rather than as an evocation of place, is the inevitable winner, particularly as Téchiné, despite the presence of a trio of talented and distinctive actresses, never probes the sources of the sisters' marvellous creativity but concentrates instead on the doomed figure of Branwell, frustrated and self-defeating in love as in art.

In *Hôtel des Amériques* (1981) the ostensible subject is once more passion, and for once the elements of the setting (the hotel in mid-transformation, the mansion that symbolises the heroine's lost love) are less oppressive. Yet the action – as so often with Téchiné – moves around the characters rather than animating them or propelling them towards each other. As almost always, the outcome is no more than a failure to achieve release from the cage of existence whose bars are here formed by the differing past experiences of two protagonists linked only by chance. Caught in a shifting moment between past and future, they have no solidity and their failure to build on their initial passion has a total logic. André Téchiné's work is most interesting for its contradictions within the overall richness of a highly personal style. The director tries to combine his own radical transformation of the elements of traditional nineteenth-century narrative into self-defeating stories which are viewed peripherally with all the paraphernalia of the big-budget commercial feature film. As a result, the expectations set by his use of stars, expensive location shooting and romantic musical themes are undermined by the films' refusal to offer coherent characters and well-engineered plots. Or, to put it another way, the depth of his theoretical insight into the demands of modernist narration is negated by the very skill of his lushly traditional *mise-en-scène*. As so often in French cinema, the contradiction and ultimate limitation come from an attempt at a purely formal rethinking of film structure, which leaves the social content unchanged and unexamined.

Another young director who seems well established at the beginning of the 1980s is Claude Miller (b.1942), a former assistant of Truffaut and Godard, whose work combines a profound interest in the abnormalities of human response and interaction with a growing concern to produce the smooth flow of a well-shaped narrative. Again the influence of the American *film noir* of the 1940s is apparent. Miller's first and lightest film, *La Meilleur façon de marcher* (1975), is a story of adolescent problems of sex and identity, set in a 1960s summer camp. Although it toys with themes of homosexuality and transvestism, the film really sets the pattern for Miller's later work by being a study of the ambiguities and transformations in the relationship of two boys over a period of years, tracing successive humiliations and successes. The precision of observation is partially concealed beneath a seemingly casual surface, but the plot is subtly shaped to lead convincingly to the emergence of the seemingly weaker of the boys as the stronger of the pair. *Dites-lui que je l'aime* (1977) is a more ambitious film, adapted from a Patricia Highsmith novel and dealing with material central to Miller's preoccupations. It traces the baffled obsession of a psychologically unhinged young man who is twice rejected by the woman he loves passionately, each time in favour of a seemingly loveless marriage with an insignificant man whom the hero despises. The film is fleshed out with filmic references – especially to Hitchcock's *Rebecca* – and great care has clearly gone into the shaping of the plot with its calculated patterns of duplications and misrecognitions. But here the over-elaboration works against itself: far from working on multiple levels of reality, *Dites-lui que je l'aime* exists solely as a narrative line and the unfolding of this unfortunately lacks the remorseless and merciless logic of the Highsmith original. Typical in this respect is the ending, after the hero has killed both himself and his beloved by falling with her from a balcony into a swimming pool: in his moment of death he sees again a moment of imagined bliss and the film magically whisks him back onto the balcony with the woman in his arms.

Garde à vue (1981) shows Miller's skills at their finest. Sacrificing the apparent advantages of cinematic time and space, the director has chosen the classical unities, using little more than a single set and virtually real time, to tell of a duel between police interrogator and possible child murderer. The shifts in balance and movement of control between the two are acutely observed. As the questioning shifts to and fro between them, Lino Ventura and Michel Serrault are so perfectly cast for their outward roles that we never doubt that we are watching a painful but remorseless progression towards the truth, till the film's ending shatteringly destroys all our certainties. *Garde à vue* is a pure, hundred-minute spectacle, a story that holds the attention unerringly but which in its unfolding destroys its own painfully built logic. In the end, we know that the policeman has manufactured his solution and imposed it on his victim, who in turn has accepted it not because it is true, but because so much of the rest of his life seems to need absolution. But of what lies behind this confession, the film gives no more than tantalising hints and unanswered questions.

*

The more realistic approach to society which began to emerge after May 1968 tended to lose its impetus in the late 1970s. Chris Marker, who participated in the collective study of Allende's Chile, *La Spirale* (1976), summed up the feelings of the era from a very personal standpoint in his massive four-hour compilation, *Le Fond de l'air est rouge* (1977). The film, which opens with scenes from *The Battleship Potemkin* intercut with contemporary actuality footage and set to the music of Berio, falls into two parts, 'Les Mains fragiles', which starts with Vietnam and its lessons, and 'Les Mains coupées', which moves from Prague to a consideration of the interaction of politics and the Olympic games. Although many areas of conflict are inevitably ignored, Marker stresses the world perspective of struggle, particularly in the response of left-wing parties and representatives. Most of the material – a mixture of new footage, stills and interviews – is fresh and all of it is assembled in a typically original and eclectic fashion. *Le Fond de l'air est rouge* is a major document on the state of left-wing politics in France in the mid-1970s. Attempts to combine political views and insights with fictional subjects were less positive. Costa-Gavras's *Section spéciale* (1975) about the operation of justice in Vichy France seemed somewhat contrived, a tired variant on a style which had seemed so fresh and welcome in *Z*. Costa-Gavras himself seems to have felt the dissatisfaction and sought renewal, first by turning to a non-political subject – the story of a tormented couple in *Clair de femme* (1979) – and then by working in English with Jack Lemmon and Sissy Spacek on the widely praised, Hollywood-produced *Missing* (1981), which considers CIA involvement in the torture and murder which occurred in Chile after the fall of Allende.

For François Truffaut the late 1970s were years of considerable achievement. He completed seven films between 1975 and 1981, works which reveal a talent turning in on itself and a new awareness of loss, madness and death. The tone is set by *L'Histoire d'Adèle H* (1975), which, like several other films of the 1970s, is based on authentic documents, in this case the diaries of Victor Hugo's daughter Adèle. The film tells in strict chronological fashion of the obsessive love of Adèle for a handsome French lieutenant she has met in Guernsey. Her passion makes her follow him first to Halifax, Nova

Scotia, and then on to Barbados, pester him and send him presents, then humiliate herself totally until a point of madness is reached. This is a tale of *amour fou* fluently told in a succession of beautifully expressive images and accompanied by music written by Maurice Jaubert (who died in 1940 after writing music for Clair, Vigo and Carné). *L'Histoire d'Adèle H* is a celebration of love – with no external perspective on the passion which animates Adèle – yet the key moments of connection and humiliation are omitted, so that the effect is both frighteningly claustrophobic and tastefully muted. *L'Argent de poche* (1976) is, by contrast, a minor film. Apparently derived from a project first conceived at the time of *Les Quatre cents coups*, this tale of children's joys and sorrows unfortunately shows the distance which now separates Truffaut from direct involvement with children and displays to an excessive extent the charm which always lurks just below the surface in the director's later work.

L'Homme qui aimait les femmes (1978), although largely couched in light comedy tones, begins with the hero's funeral, attended exclusively by women. Bertrand (Charles Denner) is a man whose sole interest in life has been women, yet his story as told by Truffaut is less one of active passion than of a despairing quest which, although resulting in a book, bears all the marks of renunciation, absence and loss. The lack of dynamism is emphasised by a complicated flashback structure which denies any sense of progression. Inevitably the scenes we see are not those of requited love but failed attempts which leave us as unsatisfied as the hero. Perhaps the extreme point of Truffaut's obsession with loss and death is furnished by *La Chambre verte* (1979), the fourth successive film of Truffaut's to use the music of Maurice Jaubert. Again, as in *L'Enfant sauvage* and *La Nuit americaine*, Truffaut himself plays the leading role with an engaging non-professional awkwardness. A kind of anti-Bertrand, Julien Davenne rejects the people and reality around him in order to devote himself to the preservation of the past, the memory of his wife and his other dead, to whom he dedicates this shrine, the green room of the title. Julien's purely negative stance (he makes his living by writing obituaries for the local paper) can only lead to his own death. But on the way Truffaut offers us a meditation not only on loss itself but on the cinema conceived in the terms in which many of its originators saw it: as an object of sentimental devotion and a way of preserving the image of the dear departed.

Although it had seemed that the Antoine Doinel saga was complete with the making of *Domicile conjugal* in 1970 and the publication, that year, of the four scripts as *Les Aventures d'Antoine Doinel*, Truffaut returned to this key autobiographical figure with *L'Amour en fuite* in 1979. Like the fictional Antoine, Jean-Pierre Léaud had reached the age of thirty without losing his essential boyishness, and in keeping with the general mood of Truffaut's work at this period, the film is retrospective, looking back on the hero's childhood, his first romance with Colette and his failed marriage to Christine. These seem as real to Antoine as his present affair with Sabine, whom he pursues with his customary combination of engaging romanticism and off-handed absent-mindedness. The plot itself is inconsequential, full of coincidences and chance meetings and its best moment – characteristic of the film's strangely compulsive blend of autobiography and fiction – is the revelation that the story Antoine recounts as the plot of his new novel is in fact the true story of how he met Sabine. What gives *L'Amour en fuite* its particular interest for filmgoers is the fact that Truffaut not only employs the actresses Marie-France Pisier (Colette) and Claude Jade (Christine) from the earlier films, but also includes, as flashbacks, some eighteen minutes of footage from these earlier films. These have a unique quality, both in the differing image textures they bring to *L'Amour en fuite* and in the view they give of the players in the same roles some ten or even fifteen years before. In particular we have a virtual documentary on Jean-Pierre Léaud seen here at key moments of a twenty-year career. The effect too is to enhance the 'reality' of Antoine. Always a curiously solid fictional character because of the extent to which he was an autobiographical extension of both director and actor, here he seems an authentic representative of twenty years of French cinema in his own right.

If *L'Amour en fuite* is one of Truffaut's more engaging films of the 1970s, *Le Dernier métro* (1980) was his most successful in commercial terms. This is partially explicable in terms of the reassuring picture which it offers us of one of the most troubled periods of recent French history, the German Occupation (the title refers to the last train which actors and spectators had to catch before the curfew came into force). The setting of *Le Dernier métro* is a theatre, and although some of the detail gives us an insight into the pressures of the period, the film's emphasis is very much on the interplay of acting and reality in a small group of players linked in and through the theatre in moods and manners which recall a Renoir film. Truffaut's warm romanticism has never been more apparent than in this sympathetic portrait of the emotional turmoil of an outwardly cool and self-possessed woman. In its calm acceptance of the vagaries of human emotion and attraction *Le Dernier métro* is a counterpart to *La Nuit americaine* which similarly mixed life and cinema. In comparison with the richly wrought *Le Dernier métro*, *La Femme d'à côté* (1981) is a lightweight film, though it purports to tell a tale of passion leading to death.

Somehow the contrivances (the hero's former mistress, now happily married, coming unwittingly to live next door) and the coincidences (the narrator had a similarly destructive affair twenty years before) fail to cohere, and one has the sense of a demonstration of the outward forms of passion rather than an involvement in its essence. Despite the muted impact of *La Femme d'à côté*, Truffaut's career throughout the 1970s is exemplary in its tenacity and impressively rich in the expression of its chosen themes. The director retains the personal touch for which he has always been famous, even though the mood is now more melancholy and introspective. If Truffaut's work offers limited insight into the workings of contemporary French society, it nonetheless ranks him as the finest storyteller to emerge from the New Wave.

Claude Chabrol's late 1970s career has no such pleasing unity: having won universal praise at the beginning of the decade for a series of masterly studies in bourgeois behaviour in which every touch and word of dialogue was calculated for maximum effect, he proceeded to lose critics and audience with films in which everything is reduced to the same derisory level. *Une Partie de plaisir* (1975) was something of a new departure: an autobiographical film written by his customary script collaborator Paul Gégauff about the break-up of his own marriage and acted by Gégauff himself, his ex-wife and their small daughter. The result is a disturbing experience, but Gégauff's personal world emerges as disconcertingly close to that of the mediocre middle-class intellectuals whom he and Chabrol had derided for so long. In contrast, *Les Innocents aux mains sales* (1975) showed a return to the familiar thriller format. What was new here was that the plot itself, once so crucial a mechanism in Chabrol's work, was now just another of the elements held up for derision, as the film charts a most improbable sequence of deaths and resurrections. In a sense, Chabrol was here using a trick plot rather in the manner of Clouzot in *Les Diaboliques*, but far from being a temporary aberration, this whole attitude to aspects of his work which had once been vital to him persisted through the 1970s. Although Chabrol succeeded in assembling large budgets and international casts, he lost contact with his audience in a series of extravagantly derisory films. His most interesting film of the late 1970s is *Violette Nozière*, based like *Les Noces rouges* on an actual occurrence. Chabrol uses this 1930s story of a young girl whose quest for freedom and love leads her to poison her parents as the basis for a characteristically savage onslaught on the bourgeois family. But whereas the early 1970s films had lucidly explored the ambiguities of human behaviour, here the ambiguity has enveloped everything – the angle of vision, the motivation of the central character and even details of the action. After a break during which he devoted himself to television production, Chabrol returned to the cinema with *Le Cheval d'orgueil* (1980), an ambitious but only partially successful attempt to tackle a quite new area of subject matter: the life of a French rural community in the years leading up to World War I.

In sharp contrast to the hesitancies and contradictions of Chabrol's work are the careers of the two directors who had emerged in the 1970s as the ideal chroniclers of the bourgeoisie on its own unquestioned terms. Claude Sautet made only three films in this six-year period – *Mado* (1976), *Une Histoire simple* (1978) and *Un Mauvais fils* (1980) – but each is characterised by a total assurance and mastery of the medium. This mastery, however, is exercised within very precise limits, not in terms of the subject matter which continues to widen to take in the problems of affluence, women's independence, and delinquency but in the manner in which such issues of the moment are approached. Sautet's work has all the classicism of form of Hollywood cinema and is clearly able to communicate with its audience in much the same fashion, but it lacks the social resonance of the best American cinema. Seeking to move his audience rather than to enlighten it, Sautet uses powerful actors cast to type in carefully constructed roles, but any probing of essential contradictions is avoided by a *mise-en-scène* which keeps rigidly to the surface of life, the given patterns of bourgeois social activity. His approach is condemned to a certain schematism, particularly in the handling of dialogue scenes, but his work gets its sense of vitality from the vigour with which the group scenes – the meals and excursions – and the locations of café or railway station are handled. Sautet offers a facsimile of life, a reflection of current problems and issues, but contained within a form calculated not to trouble the spectator after he has left the cinema. The uneven, at times chaotic output of Claude Lelouch is at the opposite pole to the calculated effects of Sautet, except in the ideological picture of contemporary French life which it offers. Producing features at a rate of more than one a year between *Mariage* (1975) and *Les Uns et les autres* (1981), Lelouch offered his faithful audience reassurance through plots which skirt the issues they apparently raise in order to reach the obligatory happy ending. Music lushly underlines the emotional certainties and Lelouch's visual style always aspires to the pictorial effects of the glossier magazines.

*

For the established directors working outside the confines of a conventional realism of surface detail, the late 1970s tended to be difficult years. If Claude Autant-Lara's last film, the melodramatic *Gloria* (1977), was little more than an anachronism, the farewell film of Luis Buñuel was more relevant and substantial. *Cet obscur objet du désir* (1977) is a complex and ironic deconstruction of film narrative in the manner of the earlier 1970s films, marked by the audacious device of having the central role played alternately by two separate and very different actresses. This deconstruction of the conventional certainties of cinema is accompanied by a similar play with audience expectation: the ignoring (until the very end) of the succession of terrorist bombs which litter the storyline and the constant frustration of the hero (and the spectator) in his quest for the object of his dreams and desires. The stress on an irrational *amour fou* – which the bourgeois hero, to his credit, lives through to the full – recalls Buñuel's earlier surrealist masterpiece *L'Age d'or*, as does the constant stress on the venality of the police, the rapacity of mothers and the dubiousness of virginity. This final assault on bourgeois order and propriety is a dazzling display of Buñuel's essential modernity. Equally impressive, but in a very different mode, is Robert Bresson's *Le Diable probablement* (1977). It too frustrates the spectator – by fragmenting the narrative and holding back information which, in conventional cinema, would be essential. Here we have not a celebration of love but its negation. *Le Diable probablement* is perhaps the bleakest of Bresson's films, a final point in the descent into a hell on earth which began with *Au hasard Balthazar* in 1966. The setting is resolutely contemporary – a group of young people living disordered lives and concerned with questions of belief, with issues like pollution and with their personal relations. From the faces of his young protagonists and images of Paris, particularly the Seine at night, Bresson builds up an image of a world without grace but still imbued with mystery and the power to enthral.

Alain Resnais completed two films of very differing ambition in the late 1970s. *Providence* (1977), an English-language film starring John Gielgud and Dirk Bogarde and made from a script by David Mercer, reflects the writer's obsession with the weaknesses of the flesh in its story of a dying novelist struggling to cope – in imagination and in reality – with his family on the occasion of his sixty-eighth birthday. To this subject Resnais brings a mass of personal allusions, a homage to Hollywood in the use of Miklos Rozsa's musical score and a structure which links this film closely to his earlier work. The opening of *Providence* is deliberately enigmatic and we only slowly realise, as the scenes unfold, that the images we see of inconsistent characters moving through a shifting decor are in fact a first draft of a novel on which the hero is working. But finally the film moves towards an idyllic resolution which finds its perfect expression in Rozsa's music and a three-hundred-and-sixty-degree pan around the glories of the novelist's garden. Ultimately *Providence* emerges as Resnais's most optimistic film and – despite passages of ambiguity and moments of horror – as proof of the importance to him of the traditional virtues of order, harmony and coherence. *Mon oncle d'Amérique* (1980) – scripted by Jean Gruault who had worked extensively with Truffaut – is one of Resnais's most structurally audacious works and at the same time his biggest (and most surprising) box-office success. The film combines explanatory accounts of biological experiments and theories of motivation and behaviour made, direct to camera, by Professor Henri Laborit with a fictional story concerning three very diverse characters whose lives cross and interact over a period of years. A further level of complexity is added by the inclusion of black-and-white film clips featuring the stars with whom the three characters identify themselves in their fantasies (Danielle Darrieux, Jean Marais and Jean Gabin). The interrelation of these three levels of imagery is always subtly controlled and the fictional episodes never degenerate into mere illustrations of the theories advanced by Laborit. Indeed the accessibility and charm of the film stems largely from the way in which the characters are engagingly suspended between the experimental rats of the Professor's laboratory and the larger-than-life world of their screen heroes. As in his earlier documentary work, Resnais shows a refusal of neat pedagogic solutions and, as in *Providence*, allows himself to include enigmatic moments of surreal imagery.

For Louis Malle the late 1970s were a period of increasing inter-nationalisation of his work, so that by the beginning of the 1980s it is difficult to see him as a contributor to French cinema. His feature films of the 1970s, whatever their production context, have in common the fact that they are all disconcerting visions of some kind of innocence. *Black Moon* (1975) is a journey into a total fantasy world. The young heroine passes, as it were, through the looking glass into a dream world where humans converse by touch and animals by words, and which is ruled over by a strange old woman at home in both spheres. The elements of this fantasy existing on the fringes of a bitter futuristic war are startling: animals appearing from nowhere, a talking unicorn, naked children endlessly cavorting with a fat pink pig, chickens pecking the breast of a dead soldier. But the mysterious inhabitants (played in startlingly heterogeneous styles by Brechtian veteran Thérèse Giehse, Warhol's Joe Dallesandro and film actress Alexandra Stewart) never engage us fully. The film is beautifully shot by Bergman's habitual cameraman Sven Nykvist, but the elements somehow never coalesce, as the dream world fails to generate its own inner coherence and anti-logic. As a result, the would-be Wagnerian climax seems both contrived and banal and the final shift back to the girl about to breast-feed the unicorn, as war threatens to engulf the house, seems merely odd and stilted. While several notable French directors, Chabrol and Resnais among them, made English-language films during this period, Malle is the only one to establish himself fully as an American director. His subsequent films – a further study of childhood innocence, *Pretty Baby* (1978), with Brooke Shields as a twelve-year-old girl brought up in a New Orleans brothel who falls in love with the photographer E. J. Bellocq, *Atlantic City* (1980), starring Burt Lancaster, and the unexpectedly successful conversation piece *My Dinner with André* (1981) – all fall outside the scope of this study.

For Eric Rohmer too the late 1970s were in a real sense years of transition. After the ten-year effort involved in completing his series of six moral tales, Rohmer directed two films of a completely different kind in which the resources of cinema are used to present very varied literary texts, firstly Heinrich von Kleist's story *La Marquise d'O* (1976) and then Chrétien de Troyes's twelfth-century poem *Perceval le Gallois* (1978). These two films stand out among Rohmer's work in the cinema both for their use of period settings and their choice of visual styles derived directly from paintings contemporary with the works adapted. They also recall that a key period of Rohmer's career in the 1960s was spent working in educational television, where the application of images and sounds as a means of making literature more widely known was a crucial aspect of his work. In the early 1980s Rohmer began a new series of contemporary studies, entitled 'comedies and proverbs', dealing with the familiar problems of marriage and emotional relationships. The first of the new series, *La Femme de l'aviateur* (1981), is a highly formal work beneath the surface modernity of its seemingly casual shooting style, its direct-sound recording and use of little-known performers. The key element, as in the moral tales of the 1963–73 period, is the dialogue whose flow shapes the pattern of the film far more than the plot which, with its explicit exploration of the mechanics of passion, has some of the same anachronism as that explored by Robert Bresson as early as *Les Dames du Bois de Boulogne*.

For other survivors of the 1960s this was a difficult period. Jacques Rivette, for example, had experienced by far his most fruitful and creative time in the early 1970s with a succession of films which put him in the forefront of French cinema. In 1975 he was given the unique privilege of simultaneous advances for no less than four feature films, to be made quickly from largely improvised scripts and to comprise a set to be called 'Les Filles du feu'. Only two of these four planned films were actually shot. *Duelle* (1976) featured two of the stars of *Céline et Julie vont en bateau*, Juliet Berto and Bulle Ogier, but its curious mixture of fantasy and obscure allegory found few supporters and the film received almost universally bad reviews. As a result, *Noroît* (1976), the second completed film, did not receive any release at all and by this time the two remaining features – a love story to star Leslie Caron and Albert Finney and a musical with Anna Karina – had been abandoned, following Rivette's nervous breakdown. The director attempted a return to production with *Merry-Go-Round* (1978) starring Maria Schneider and Joe Dallesandro, but the two players proved totally unsuited to Rivette's personal style of production, and again the resulting work was judged unsuitable for commercial release by Gaumont, and was not seen until 1983.

Jacques Demy's career fared even worse. After the disastrous failure of his 1973 feature film ironically named *L'Evénement le plus important depuis que l'homme a marché sur la lune* Demy did not work again in French cinema for nine years. His only film shot for cinema release during this period was the Japanese-backed *Lady Oscar* (1980). This film, made in English and based on a popular Japanese strip cartoon called 'Rose of Versailles', proved to be no more than a dull and heavy period piece. Demy's only other work of the period was a version of Colette's *La Naissance du jour* (1980) made for French television with Danièle Delorme in the role of the novelist. The opportunities offered to Agnès Varda were also sparse. Her only French-made fictional feature after *Le Bonheur* (1963) and *Les Créatures* (1966) is *L'Une chante, l'autre pas* (1977), which traces the lives of two women over a period of some fifteen years. In characteristic fashion Varda moves lightly over the disasters and tragedies which they each experience and offers instead a celebration of their growth to maturity and liberation from imposed constraints. Affectionate and delicately shot, this film – like Varda's features of the 1960s – paints too idyllic a picture of its characters' lives to be wholly convincing. Earlier, in 1975, Varda had made an equally affectionate feature-length documentary study of the rue Daguerre, where she had been living for many years, *Daguerréotypes*, but this did not receive a commercial showing in France until 1979. Subsequently she worked in the United States on a pair of related films. *Murs murs* (1981) is naive and direct, a celebration of the visual exuberance of Los Angeles wall painting which invites the artists, subjects and patrons to present themselves in front of or alongside their work. Like its extrovert artists, the film asks itself no questions that do not have a simple answer. *Documenteur* (1981), by contrast, is a thinly disguised autobiographical fiction about a secretary working on the production of *Murs murs* and caring for a young son (played by Varda's own child). But in seeking to create a fiction, Varda here finds the obstacles overwhelming. Real faces communicate less humanity than those painted on the walls and the words string themselves together in associational puns, but never fill the threatening void or accede to communication. There are many compositions of great beauty, particularly the reiterated shots of the beach from the desk at which the woman works, but these are essentially still images, frozen moments that do not develop into a narrative flow. Potential narrative sequences occur only in the background, characters and conversations are barely sketched in, and within an hour or so the pseudo-narrative peters out inconclusively.

There were difficulties too for many of those who made their appearance in the aftermath of the New Wave. Maurice Pialat, for example, had to wait five years before he could complete a further feature film. *Passe ton bac d'abord* (1979), a clear-sighted but unfashionable study of provincial schoolchildren, uses non-professional players and a closely observed realistic style. It captures perfectly the dramas and contradictions of a group of young people at a crucial moment of transition in their lives (the baccalauréat). In contrast, *Loulou* (1980) uses star performers for its investigation of sexuality, showing without sentimentality the emotional entanglement of a working-class drifter and petty thief (Gérard Depardieu) and the well-brought-up middle-class girl (Isabelle Huppert) who falls in love with him. Pialat never patronises his characters and here uses a marvellously fluid camera style to depict at close range the physical interaction and mutual laceration of his two heroes. Pialat's world is far removed from the complacent conventionality of most French realist film making and he never offers abstract social analysis or studies of class structure. His cinema is rooted in his fascination for the ordinary human detail of life lived in banal surroundings and, through the gallery of portraits gradually built up in his work, he offers a unique insight into the workings of French society in areas which are elsewhere largely ignored. Equally impressive, in a very different style, is the career of René Allio, whose films constantly show the impact of his theatrical background. He too was able to make only two features in the eight years following *Rude journée pour la reine* (1973). If *Retour à Marseille* (1980) – a fictional account of a man's return to Marseilles which is also a return by the film maker to his native city – achieved only a limited success, *Moi, Pierre Rivière, ayant égorgé ma mère, ma soeur et mon frère* (1976) is a remarkable work. Based on the fifty-page confessional text discovered and published by Michel Foucault, the film combines an exemplary naturalism of detail (the actual locations of the crime, real peasants, precise period reconstruction) with a refusal to dramatise events. These latter are simply presented for our attention – to engage our emotions but at the same time to give rise to thought about the social conditions of the peasantry in 1935.

*

If the late 1970s were difficult years for those working within the mainstream of French cinema, they were by contrast very productive ones for those operating outside the conventional commercial constraints. In particular 1975 saw the return to full involvement with the cinema of Jean-Luc Godard whose *Numéro deux* (1979) is a kind of meditation on forty-five years spent getting to and then away from Paris. The new explicitness permitted in the mid-1970s merely allowed the old disillusion and clinical approach to sex to be presented more forcefully. *Numéro deux* is in many ways a bleak experience – the doubts and self-questionings of a man withdrawn into solitude, alone but for his shiny new video equipment. The film begins and ends with Godard himself, but whereas at the beginning he is talking incessantly in the old manner, by the end he is silent, almost asleep. Between these two moments, the fragments are deliberately not fused, but arranged in shifting, contrasting patterns. Godard sets brute reality (especially direct sound) against very structured images of video, man vs. woman, factory vs. landscape, politics vs. sex. Thanks to the use of video, the screen size and images are dynamic, but the film camera is leaden and immobile. The slogans are still there and Godard has widened his awareness to take in other age groups (the very young and the very old) and other classes (he is consciously struggling to escape from his bourgeois background). But the love of cinema has gone and it has not been replaced by a breakthrough to life; there is no longer any preaching of a collectivist political viewpoint (although the film was made, like all his late 1970s work, in collaboration with Anne-Marie Miéville), and no mature certainty either. In place of hope there is only the cold observation of human figures – the naked grandparents explaining their situation to the camera, the parents giving the children a lesson in sex and indulging in oral and anal intercourse. As Godard's commentary says at one point, 'things are complicated – only anguish is simple'.

In the one-hour 16 mm film *Ici et ailleurs* (1974–76) Godard and Miéville took footage shot and partially edited in 1970 about the Palestine liberation struggle (when the project was called *Victoire*) and submitted it to a rethinking and analysis in the light of the changed situation of the mid-1970s and Godard's own progressive questioning of the relation of film and the reality it captures. The same interrogative attitude marks *Comment ça va?* (1975–78) which similarly constitutes a questioning of both the role of the journalist in politics and the communication process as a whole. The issues raised here are further probed in two important video series – *Sur et sous la communication (6×2)* (1975–76) and *France tour détour deux enfants* (1978) – whose showing pre-dates the limited commercial release of the previously made films, thereby distorting the development of Godard's thinking. In *Comment ça va?* the possibilities of fiction are still in question, but with *Sauve qui peut (la vie)* (1980) there is a return both to narrative cinema and to an international audience. *Sauve qui peut (la vie)* opens with the director's alter ego, a film maker called Paul Godard (Jacques Dutronc) fighting off the amorous advances of a hotel liftboy and proceeds in four labelled sections to deal with aspects of the lives of the people he encounters. The view of human life and aspiration which emerges from this narrative is dispiriting in the extreme. As in the past Godard offers a few graffiti ('Cain + Abel = Cinema + Television') and uses prostitution as a metaphor for all commercial activity (as in the celebrated but ludicrously contrived foursome involving two prostitutes, a businessman and his male secretary). The film in fact offers little that is new in terms of its themes and no solutions to the perennial problems Godard raises. Its qualities reside largely in the performances of the two leading actresses and in Godard's response to landscape, captured with an agile camera and printed with a naively charming use of stop motion.

In contrast to Godard, another resolute independent in contemporary French cinema, Marcel Hanoun, was able to make only two films in the period – *Le Regard* (1976) and *La Nuit claire* (1978) – and remained a marginalised figure. But Jean-Marie Straub and Danièle Huillet were able to find funding and distribution for their films. In Italy they made two features, *Fortini-Cani* (1976), based on the book *The Dogs of Sinai* by Franco Fortini, and *Dalla nube alla resistenza* (1978), based on two novels by Cesare Pavese. In France, the short (ten-minute) film, *Toute la révolution est un coup de dés* – their first film ever to be made in their native country – offered a reading of Mallarmé's poem by actors located on the burial place of the victims of the Commune (although nothing in the film tells us this). It was followed in 1981 by the feature-length *Trop tôt, trop tard* in which the Straub taste for paradox is clearly apparent. It was Straub who described Chaplin, who had no interest in the relation of one shot to the next, as the 'master of film editing' and Kenji Mizoguchi (to his own amazement no doubt, had he lived to hear it) as the maker of 'the most Marxist films that exist'. It is not surprising therefore that the film which marks the return of Straub and Huillet should be impenetrable.

Most of Straub's films, though presented as explorations of the essence of cinema – editing, framing, sound and light – are based parasitically on pre-existing works: the music of Bach, an opera by Schoenberg, a play by Corneille. In *Trop tôt, trop tard* this support is reduced to just two fragmentary sources: a letter from Friedrich Engels (to whom the film is dedicated) to Kautsky and the postface of Mahmoud Hussein's *Class Conflict in Egypt*. Like its source, the film divides into two parts, one shot in France (beginning in the place de la Bastille and then moving out into the countryside) and the other in Egypt. Each part combines landscape shots with their original sound (an invariable Straub practice) and passages of voice-over commentary (the first read by Huillet, the second by Bhagat el Nadi). The problem facing the critic is how to relate these elements, since Straub affirms – and the film bears him out – that there is no connection between the two parts and no relation between the commentary and the simultaneous images/natural sounds. In this sense the film would seemingly seek to demonstrate the impossibility for documentary images to communicate the history of either France (poverty at the time of the Revolution is the theme of part one) or the Third World (in part two, a recital of the successive stages of the people's struggle in Egypt from Napoleon's invasion to the present day). This interpretation is reinforced by the strategy of creating distanciation (preventing the images being 'used up' by the documentary in the construction of a contrived and therefore falsified meaning) by holding the (literally) empty images until they become unwatchable. But since no one would imagine that one hundred and five minutes of incessant, slowly rotating circular or semi-circular pans of empty landscapes (360 degrees = a revolution?) could possibly communicate such concepts, one is left in some perplexity.

The work of Marguerite Duras in the 1970s is characterised by an intertextuality which links the films to novels, published texts, radio and stage plays. The key work is perhaps *India Song* (1975), but this forms only part of a vast cycle of variations on the same (or similar) themes and characters which begins with the novel *Le Ravissement de Lol V Stein* in 1964. In novel form the cycle continued with the two further books – *Le Vice-Consul* in 1966 and *L'Amour* in 1971 – and these in turn gave birth to three variously linked films: *La Femme du Gange* (1974), *India Song* (1975) and *Son non de Venise dans Calcutta désert* (1976). These filmic texts are closely related through reference and quotation to each other and have a complex and changing relation to the published texts bearing the same name. Thus, while the published text of *La Femme du Gange* is a reflection on the completed film (shot in 1972 but released, after the publication of the text, in 1974), *India Song: texte théâtre film*, which appeared in 1973, is an intermediate work, deriving from themes in *Le Vice-Consul* but conceived for stage performance. This text was itself subsequently adapted both for radio and for the film bearing the same title. Nor does the pattern of intertextuality end there, for the soundtrack of *India Song* was used, with only minor variations (at the end), as the basis for the subsequent film, *Son nom de Venise dans Calcutta désert*, where it was given a whole new set of images which eliminate the characters who are seen in *India Song*. In part these shifts and transition are possible because of the ways in which Duras largely ignores the possibilities of synchronised images and sounds, preferring to establish a dialectical interplay of image track and soundtrack. In Duras's films the narrative voices sometimes describe scenes which we see depicted and at others evoke events occurring at other times or in other locations, while the music and effects tracks constantly switch and intertwine.

The tensions set up by this method of creation are enormous. It is impossible to see, for example, the empty images of *Son nom de Venise dans Calcutta désert* without recalling the absent characters of *India Song*, and the combination of narrating voices describing India and images showing Paris or Versailles has a disconcerting effect on the spectator. Characteristically the key actions occur off-screen, the images are slow and ritualistic and, where actors appear, they conduct themselves with a formal dignity and elegance. In all three films the camera is generally immobile when depicting rooms, holding the shot before and after the action is complete, even after the characters have left the stage, but tracking and panning with solemn deliberation through gardens and corridors. And always the movement and stasis is subtly related to the various interwoven strands of the soundtrack. The themes of desire and death, loss and absence as well as the characteristic stylistic concerns of *India Song* and *Son nom de Venise dans Calcutta désert* are to be found again in the very varied series of films which follow in the late 1970s with a profusion which gives Marguerite Duras's work of this period an importance which is far in excess of the audience for her work and which is symbolised by the choice of *Le Camion* as one of the official French entries at the Cannes Film Festival in 1977. That year saw the release of three Duras films: a fairly straightforward adaptation of her stage play *Des Journées entières dans les arbres*, a meditation on woman and speech in *Baxter, Véra Baxter*, and a duologue between Duras herself and the actor Gérard Depardieu (playing a lorry driver) in *Le Camion*. They discuss the journey which will constitute the film but which the absence of Duras in the images of the lorry reveals to be a purely imaginary trajectory. With *Le Camion* the voice of Marguerite Duras becomes the key element in her film making and the task of narration is no longer delegated to actress intermediaries. This new pattern is followed in a whole series of works in which it forms the organising pivot: *Le Navire nuit* (1979), the four short texts of ten to thirty minutes which together make up *Aurélia Steiner* (1979) and the sombre meditation on incest, *Agatha et les lectures illimités* (1981).

With *L'Homme Atlantique* (1981), made from the out-takes of *Agatha*, Duras must have reached something approaching the end of this particular road. The voice is again her own – interrupted at just one point by the sound of waves breaking on the shore – and the images are reduced to just half-a-dozen shots: a seascape, an empty hotel lobby and four different shots of the sole player, Yann Andréa, The latter never speaks and represents, rather than embodies, an absent lover. The images occupy less than half of the film's running time of some forty-five minutes. At the start and for the whole latter half of the film we are offered only black spacing, a blank screen, while Duras's voice talks of images we do not see (a dog, a 'tragic' seagull, rain, a rose brushed by a bird's wing) and gives instructions to the now non-existent actor. At the end she gives him his name, which he will never know, L'Homme Atlantique.

*

In considering any area of interaction between French culture and society, the year 1981 – which forms the end point of this study – would seem, at first sight, a crucial turning point, since it saw a radical redrawing of the political map of France with the triumph of the parties of the left and the election of a Socialist President, François Mitterrand. But even allowing for the inevitable time lag in the reflection of new social forces in works which of necessity take months or years to reach an audience, it is clear that little or nothing produced in the cinema during the presidency of Giscard d'Estaing points to a radical change of the kind which actually occurred in France. Looking at the films of the late 1970s it would indeed be easier to argue that the trends in French society were quite the opposite – towards a greater conservatism and a reassertion of bourgeois values. The post-'68 surge of interest in a left-wing social and political cinema had long since subsided, leaving Chris Marker's *Le Fond de l'air est rouge* as its last monument in 1977. But this film is more of a memorial tablet than a programme for change, and none of the new film makers of the mid-1970s whose work we have considered – Tavernier and Téchiné, Miller and Corneau – offers hints of a changed society in the making. The popular film makers of the period who offer some kind of social depiction – such as Lelouch or Sautet – are celebrants of the status quo, and there is a retreat from the delineation of the contemporary face of France both on the part of directors like Truffaut, who retreat into increasingly hermetic private worlds or those, like Malle or Costa-Gavras, who turn to internationally funded, English-language productions. In this connection Marguerite Duras makes a fitting figure with whom to close, since her real debut as an independent film maker with *Détruire dit-elle* was very much in the aftermath of May '68. Then the need for an overt political stance (in the presentation of the film, if not in its style and texture) was self-evident. A new awareness of the fruitfulness of feminist perspectives was also apparent then, and the emerging structures of the film industry seemed able to accommodate radically new voices. But in ten years, all this has been lost: advocacy of revolution has been replaced by assertion of its impossibility, hope for change has given way to meditation on loss and absence. Duras has retreated, in *L'Homme Atlantique*, into a private world of personal reflection which confronts the anguished, but still eloquent, film maker with a blank screen. As so often in its history, the formally innovatory aspect of French film making has lost touch with a changing society.

Postscript
1981–84

The early years of François Mitterand's presidency brought no sign of the emergence of any radical new approach to cinema in France. The various measures undertaken by the new minister of culture, Jack Lang, failed to tackle the real problems, and instead of witnessing a reassertion of French cultural values, the early 1980s were marked in the cinema by the increasing adoption of Hollywood marketing methods, whereby thanks to a massive publicity campaign and simultaneous release in a large number of cinemas, a film would recoup its costs within a matter of weeks. In this climate of immediate consumption, a film needing time to find its audience would simply be annihilated. The resultant widening gulf between a dominant, purely commercial cinema and films with artistic pretensions – which the New Wave had once seemed to have bridged – was symbolised in 1982 by the differing release patterns and receptions of two films, the latest Jean-Paul Belmondo superproduction, Gérard Oury's *L'As des as*, and Jacques Demy's first French-language film for nine years, *Une Chambre en ville*. Despite the almost unanimous approval of the critics – who even went so far as to publish a collective letter of support at their own expense – *Une Chambre en ville* with its Paris total of seventy thousand spectators in its first five weeks was simply outclassed in commercial terms. Benefiting from a two-million-franc publicity campaign, *L'As des as* opened in fifty cinemas simultaneously, was seen by a million spectators in Paris alone within five weeks and had grossed some forty-five million francs by the end of the year. The whole financial operation was complete before the critics' impact and word-of-mouth comment on the film's inanity could make their impact felt.

The tightening commercial restraints are perhaps the principal cause of the growing move towards the imposition of a cinema based on traditional models, which was already apparent in the late 1970s. Increasingly, even films by the younger directors have come to echo the formulas of the 1950s or even the late 1930s. The stars – with

Belmondo and Alain Delon in the lead – have an even more important role in the obtaining of production finance. Supporting this centrality of the star has been the reappearance of the dialogue writer as a key figure – witness Jean Aurenche's contributions to the films of Bertrand Tavernier and Michel Audiard's work with Claude Miller. Even Michel Lang, who had shown a certain freshness of approach in his first comedies, was reduced in *L'Etincelle* (1984) to the pseudo-shocking situations of a certain brand of standard boulevard farce (here, a seven-months pregnant married woman falling in love with a man old enough to be her father). The work of Claude Sautet, to whose films the dialoguist Jean-Loup Dabadie has made a key contribution since 1969, exemplifies the trend. In the early 1970s Sautet's films were undeniably those of a director who maintained full command over all elements of his sentimentalised bourgeois world. But in *Garçon* (1983) everything is dominated by Yves Montand's mannered and overacted performance, with the unfortunate result that the contrivance of the situations and the calculation of the plot are all too cruelly revealed.

The recourse to well-tried stereotypes is particularly evident in the new importance of the thriller in French production, which has inevitably been accompanied by a shift away from a confrontation with actuality and towards studio filming, with variations on traditional Hollywood themes and displays of virtuoso *mise-en-scène* operating in a void. Not all new French cinema of the early 1980s is located within these constrictions, but it is becoming increasingly difficult to find evidence of viable alternatives. The thriller with its clear-cut formulas, its opportunities for star performance and its tangential relationship to social reality is the form *par excellence* for the re-establishment of a new 'tradition of quality' of the kind which had preceded the New Wave. Significantly, *Le Battant* (1983) – Alain Delon's sixty-seventh film as an actor and second as a director (after *Pour la peau d'un flic* in 1981) – was dedicated to a leading figure of that earlier cinema, René Clément. The film attempted the classic tale of a criminal emerging from prison after eight years and being confronted by both police and a rival gang as he attempts to collect the proceeds of his crime. But the limply written plot (co-scripted by Delon) never begins to create the requisite suspense and the wooden narcissism of the producer-star – like the performance of the ageing Belmondo in *L'As des as* – merely serves as a reminder of how much livelier French cinema was before its stars achieved their present predominance.

The *film noir* unites film makers of all ages. It was with a Georges Simenon adaptation, *Les Fantômes du chapelier* (1982), that Claude

Chabrol re-established his commercial reputation. The film brought little that was new, indeed its essence was the recreation of the Belgian author's timeless world, but the handling of actors and settings was assured and Chabrol succeeded in holding his sense of derision in check. The director was not, however, able to sustain this level of success when he returned to the world of international co-productions funded by an amalgam of film and television interests with an adaptation of a Simone de Beauvoir novel, *Le Sang des autres* (1984), starring Jodie Foster. The former New Wave directors' increasing closeness to precisely that *cinéma de papa* against which they had once rebelled so violently is even more fully typified by François Truffaut's *Vivement dimanche!* (1983). Like the later work of, say, Julien Duvivier, this is a film notable only for its director's name and past reputation, a comedy-thriller which is seldom comic and never thrilling. Taking a complicated American *série noire* plot and setting it in an anonymous and unconvincing French small town, the film generates none of the suspense or anguish essential to the genre. Truffaut's devotion to his star, the statuesque Fanny Ardent, is very evident, but the film's black-and-white photography and elaborate musical score are little more than pastiche. The principal qualities of *Vivement dimanche!* are indeed precisely those elements which had previously been the incidentals of the 'Truffaut touch'.

In similar fashion those newcomers of the mid-1970s – the post-New Wave generation – who tried to move away from such commercial constraints had only limited success. Alain Corneau's break with the *film noir* came with *Fort Saganne* (1984), an attempt to recapture the excitement, if not the ideology, of the colonial epic. But despite the resources poured into the production, it was neither a critical nor a popular success. Bertrand Tavernier fared better with the award-winning *Un Dimanche à la campagne* (1984). But in the absence of Jean Aurenche, the script lacked bite and though the film was exquisitely crafted, it remains a very minor work, unpretentious but essentially trivial. Particularly interesting is the case of Claude Miller, who had brought the thriller to a point of formal perfection with the widely seen *Garde à vue* in 1981. *Mortelle randonnée* (1983), with Michel Serrault and Isabèle Adjani, was again scripted by Michel Audiard. Made in reaction to the claustrophobic intensity of the earlier work as a picaresque, action-packed *série noire*, it begins when an ageing detective, still obsessed with his own daughter's death twenty years before, is set to investigate the girlfriend of a Belgian shoe manufacturer's son. He in fact witnesses the first of a whole series of murders committed by the young woman as she moves restlessly and in a dazzling array of identities across Europe. Her obsession with her lost father mirrors the detective's own most intimate concern, and a strange, unspoken complicity grows between the two. But his only positive steps towards her lead to the death of the man she loves and her own self-destruction. What is remarkable about *Mortelle randonnée* is the extent to which the lushly assured *mise-en-scène* and solid technical mastery are applied to a subject which is never remotely convincing or engaging. Unsurprisingly the French film industry's top awards for 1983 also went to a thriller. *La Balance*, directed by newcomer Bob Swaim, was a slick action film starring Nathalie Baye and Philippe Léotard. The most notable aspect of this violent tale of blackmailing cops and brutal criminals was that it was rooted not in the rich tradition of the Hollywood *film noir* but in the contrivance, superficial characterisation and gratuitous violence of the worst United States television series.

As so often in the past it is a film by Chris Marker which gives the clearest insight into the mood of the present. A key figure in French documentary film making, Marker had already summed up the achievements of the left in his massive four-hour compilation, *Le Fond de l'air est rouge*, in the mid-1970s. What is remarkable about his new film, significantly entitled *Sans soleil* (1983) (after a piece by Mussorgsky which forms the basis of its musical score), is its defensiveness. Where Marker's films were once noticeable for their optimism and exuberance, *Sans soleil* offers no vision of a future, beyond that of the video synthesiser, used not to create new images of reality but to decompose film documents into abstract patterns. This leads to a radical questioning of the documentarist's means of expression: what is the truth of a newsreel record when it has been turned into a barely recognisable set of shapes and colours on the video screen? Constantly, *Sans soleil* is seeking fusions from its welter of divergent images of Europe, Asia and Africa, but the synthesis it offers is never more than provisional, the result of an echoed gesture or a neat turn of phrase by the narrator. The film's unease is enhanced by the fact that it is not simply a personal work, but a collaborative effort involving, alongside Marker, the Japanese video artist Hayao Yamaneko, the Hungarian cameraman Sandor Krasna and his brother, Michel Krasna, the composer of the film's electronic score. Where the film touches on political issues – the liberation struggle in Guinea-Bissau once led by the Amilcar Cabral, or the fifteen-year struggle against a new Tokyo airport – the tone is hesitant, even apologetic, and the film's most positive commitment would seem to be directed towards an ill-comprehended Japanese religiosity. Marker's own personal comments are either backward-looking – a mass of filmic allusions including a retreat to the locations of Hitchcock's *Vertigo* – or negative – as in the account of a film project, on the loss of forgetful-ness, which the commentator's voice tells us will 'of course' never be made. Another documentary echo of the past is *Biquefarre* (1984), Georges Rouquier's sequel to his classic 1946 work, *Farrebique*. This new film by a largely forgotten documentarist treats the same setting and many of the same characters, but shows a world transformed by EEC regulations, new monetary approaches and the application of mechanisation and new technologies. Gone is the simple rhythm of the seasons so characteristic of *Farrebique*, but Rouquier remains observant, positive and totally individual.

There has always been an area of independent film making which ignores commercial constraints. The years since May '68 have seen film makers like Marguerite Duras, Marcel Hanoun and Jean-Marie Straub following their own personal paths, and each has created a totally independent *oeuvre*. In 1983 Straub and Danièlle Huillet filmed a seven-minute Duras text, *En rachâchant*, as a sort of trial for a more ambitious feature-length work, also in black and white, *Amerika/Rapports de classes* (1984). This contains all the character-istic features of the couple's style: a meticulous approach to image and sound, a literary source, a claustrophobic set of interior scenes and a mixture of scrupulous realism and deliberate anachronism. Filmed in the original German, Kafka's unfinished novel is stripped of its auto-biographical and psychoanalytic resonances but not – despite the title – given an explicitly Marxist reading. Instead the emphasis is on a simple dedramatisation, with non-professional players presenting the text rather than performing it.

Whereas twenty years or so ago there was a real interaction between avant-garde approaches and the commercial cinema, now the ex-perimental is clearly marked off from the commercial. This was borne out by the re-emergence in 1983 of Philippe Garrel, with a retro-spective at Studio 43 in Paris and the release of two new films. Though still in his mid-thirties, Garrel began his film work some twenty years earlier, as a precocious sixteen-year-old, and first came to prominence in 1967 with his first feature-length film, *Marie pour mémoire*. In the aftermath of May '68 he attracted considerable attention with *La Concentration* (1968) which featured Jean-Pierre Léaud, and two hour-long works, the silent *Le Révélateur* (1969) with Bernadette Lafont and Laurent Terzieff and *La Cicatrice intérieure* (1972). The half-dozen subsequent films made in the 1970s – some in colour, others silent and in black and white – remained largely unseen until the retrospective. *L'Enfant secret* (1983), awarded the 1982 Prix Jean Vigo, is a feature-length work made with Anne Wiazemsky. Shot in 1979, its release was delayed by production difficulties, but it emerges as a classic work of alternative cinema, though its likely impact on mainstream French production is nil. Shot, like all Garrel's work, on 35 mm, but in black and white with a meticulous concern for lighting and visual texture, *L'Enfant secret* could, in truth, have been made at any time in the last twenty years. Garrel's approach is resolutely personal and timeless. Concentrating on just a few characters and a handful of intimate settings, his film moves fluently and assuredly around its chosen themes of anguished solitude, the couple and the child, the temptations of drugs and suicide. Always presenting itself as a filmic representation and including the marks of its making (flashframes, refilmed sequences, freezing of the image, passages of silence), *L'Enfant secret* never builds into a narrative in a conventional sense, but pursues its personal path of investigation with a measured rhythm and chaste innocence. *Liberté, la nuit* (1984) traces the end of one love and the beginning of another against the barely sketched-in background of the Algerian war, which causes the death of the hero's wife and eventually his own death. In treating the film's theme of the difficulty of living and loving, Garrel's camera explores both the worn faces of experienced performers (such as Emmanuelle Riva and his father, Maurice Garrel) and a series of bleak, rainswept landscapes. Though music is used at times overemphatically, the film's principal concern is with the image: the texture and grain of the black-and-white photography and the spontaneity of performers limited to a single take of any given scene (Christine Boisson in particular is exceptional as the hero's second love).

It is against a background of commercial restrictions that the isolated attempts to maintain an innovative and truly personal French approach to the mainstream fictional feature film should be seen. Maurice Pialat has been one of the few to maintain the forceful originality of his work. *A nos amours* (1983) takes as its central theme a fifteen-year-old girl's doomed quest to find herself through a series of sexual encounters which bring a kind of sensual gratification but little else. Here, and indeed throughout the film, Pialat tackles extreme situations unflinchingly, remaining at the extreme level of intensity of his best work. But there is a change of emphasis. In the earlier films this central situation would have been set in a firmly contemporary world and used to widen the film's exploration of social issues. But here in *A nos amours* it is played against an equally intense, but more contrived and stagey depiction of the disintegration of the young girl's immigrant family, which could in fact have been set at any time in the past fifty years. Pialat's method of working with his actors (here he plays the key role of the girl's father) creates a powerful impact, but as scene follows scene there is no sense of actuality or of the passing of time and hence no possibility of development for the characters.

Jean-Luc Godard's *Passion* (1982) showed that he could still create something of the old controversy. The film is basically about its own making – a film maker shooting a film in the face of commercial pressures (here represented by a caricatured 'comic' Italian who is always asking for a 'story'). It seeks to combine in ways unexplained scenes shot in and around a factory with reconstructions of some of the most celebrated paintings in the history of western art. The tableaux which capture, vary and occasionally parody these works of Rembrandt, Goya, Delacroix et al. are lit and shot with great precision by Raoul Coutard (lighting only his second feature in ten years). But the precise status of these sequences and the undigested passages from Fauré, Mozart, Beethoven etc. which accompany them is very much in doubt, as is their relation to the rest of the film. This – the alleged plot concerning passion and power around the factory – seems to have been staged and shot out of sync in ways contrived to make the spectator's effort to comprehend as unrewarding as possible and to torment or ridicule the performers. Two distinguished foreign players, Hanna Schygulla (star of several Fassbinder films) and Jerzy Radzirvilowicz (the leading actor in Wajda's *Man of Iron*), are clearly at a loss as to what their roles are and what is expected of them. Isabelle Huppert as the representative of the working class is required to stutter (the proletariat's lack of access to speech?). And Michel Piccoli, as the factory owner, coughs incessantly while keeping a red rose between his lips (the decline of capitalism despite the trimmings of leftism?). Nowhere does the political or cultural insight rise above this 'gag' level, and the final sequences – as the actors/characters scatter to their respective homelands/next films – brings the film to a derisory ending. The award of the Venice Golden Lion to Godard's next film, *Prénom Carmen* (1983), was more a tribute to the loyal dedication of Bernardo Bertolucci (the jury chairman) to his erstwhile master, than a reflection of any real artistic novelty on the part of Godard. As with Truffaut's *Vivement dimanche!* one has the sense of a great director working at less than full power. The mixture is very much as before: the film-about-making-a-film structure, the inclusion of elements which have nothing to do with the ostensible plot (here a string quartet eternally rehearsing Beethoven), a mass of filmic allusions, a set of grotesquely parodied action sequences (including a farcical bankraid), a bleak, obsessively prurient view of human sexuality and an overall progression towards futility. What is perhaps most troubling about *Prénom Carmen* is the appearance of Godard himself as 'Uncle Jean', a one-time film director. This is very much a performance, not a direct confession, but its relentless self-parody does reinforce the impression of a talent turning in on itself in a void.

Though the 1980s have seen the emergence of few if any new directors of outstanding talent, they have continued to prove a difficult time for many of those who had achieved a world reputation in the 1960s. Alain Resnais had gained an unexpected popular success with *Mon oncle d'Amérique*, but was unable to repeat this with *La Vie est un roman* (1983), despite a seemingly promising filmic structure. The film combines – with carefully calculated overlaps and interpenetrations – three stories each with its own cinematic style: 1900s Méliès, 1920s L'Herbier and 1970s Rohmer. All have the same setting of a fantastic castle and all three focus in some way on the quest for happiness. But somehow the necessary fusions are never made, and *La Vie est un roman* remains as laboured as, say, René Clair's *Les Belles-de-nuit* or Resnais's own earlier *Je t'aime, je t'aime*. As so often in the early 1980s, one is left with a mere catalogue of characteristic directorial obsessions: the lyrical operatic style of performance, the filmic references and play with visual textures, the interaction of dream and reality, the hermetic world familiar since *Marienbad* etc. *L'Amour à mort* (1984) presents admirers of Resnais's work with similar problems, while indicating more clearly than the previous works the probable reason for the disquiet. The film explores a number of stylistic ideas and themes determined by Resnais at the very outset, before the scripting had begun: the use of the colours red and black, an alternation of depicted scenes and 'pauses' or gaps filled only by Henze's music, the concentration on just four characters and a beginning which features an apparent death and a subsequent (unexplained) resurrection. All of these are present in the finished film, but the script written by Jean Gruault (here writing his third successive Resnais film) lacks all the resonance of the texts provided earlier by Duras, Robbe-Grillet and Jean Cayrol. The script offers only a bare statement of the thematic material, without poetry, drama or real lyricism. As a result the contrivances of the film become all too clear and with its lush *mise-en-scène* this intended celebration of *amour fou* comes perilously close to the French 'tradition of quality'.

Among other veterans, Jacques Rivette showed great resilience in resuming directing after all the setbacks of the late 1970s with *Le Pont du nord* (1982). Unfortunately the approaches which had seemed so innovatory at the time of *L'Amour fou* – the involvement of the players in the scripting, the exploration of chance, the recurring theme of paranoia, the presentation of fiction as a game with truth and imagination – now seemed sadly tired and dated. Jacques Demy's *Une Chambre en ville* (1982) also showed the problems of renewal for the film makers of the 1960s. In contrast to *L'As des as*, the film could be seen by French critics to be full of desirable qualities, delicate cinematic allusions, a beautifully judged performance by Danielle Darrieux and a subtle evocation of Demy's personal world centred on the passage de Pommeraye in his native Nantes. But to an outsider uninvolved in the controversy, what is most remarkable about this dated project (it was first drafted in the 1950s) is its symptomatic quality as a product of the first years of a Socialist presidency. *Une Chambre en ville* reduces its working-class strikers who are confronting baton-wielding police and tear-gas assaults to stereotyped figures in a musical comedy which has as little political commitment as René Clair's 1931 *Le Million*. The hero's trade-union duties are here subordinated to his oneiric encounter with a luscious blonde bourgeois married woman (Dominique Sanda), who is whoring for kicks and naked beneath her expensive fur coat.

Alain Robbe-Grillet's *La Belle captive* plays somewhat subtler games with the collective erotic unconscious and has more than a touch of the asperity of Godard's *Passion*. Again acting performance is rejected in favour of a structure in which incoherence is crucial and deliberate, and a classical musical score (here a Schubert quartet) is both omnipresent and emptied of meaning. As with Godard, the play with aspects of cinematic representation looks back to the author's earlier work, which is present in a plethora of intertextual references to just about every previous Robbe-Grillet novel or film. Frequent reference is made too to Magritte's paintings, but Robbe-Grillet's imagery, much of it set in a studio-produced void, lacks the evocative precision of Magritte's work. Despites its constant dreamlike repetitions and deliberately unfathomable narrative, *La Belle captive* is, however, one of the author's more accessible fictions. The bleakness of Godard's *Passion* and Pialat's *A nos amours* is echoed too in Robert Bresson's first film for six years, *L'Argent* (1983). This is a film drained of psychological character-drawing and even normal dramatic plausibility. Basing his tale of a man's descent into hideous crime on a story by Tolstoi, Bresson has fashioned a work which is timeless despite its setting in a recognisably 1980s France. In *L'Argent*, which is totally personal in style, tone and moral ambiguity, hands play a role similar to that in *Pickpocket*, but here it is banknotes, real and forged, which pass from one hand to another. Setting out from a trivial incident of two schoolboys successfully passing a forged 500 franc note, the film reveals in its opening thirty minutes a whole network of treacheries, deceits and lies which this action triggers off. In this dark world the focus gradually sharpens and the film's implacable rhythm shows a man driven by wounded pride

54. Marguerite Duras: Détruire dit-elle (1969)

55. Costa-Gavras: L'Aveu (1970)

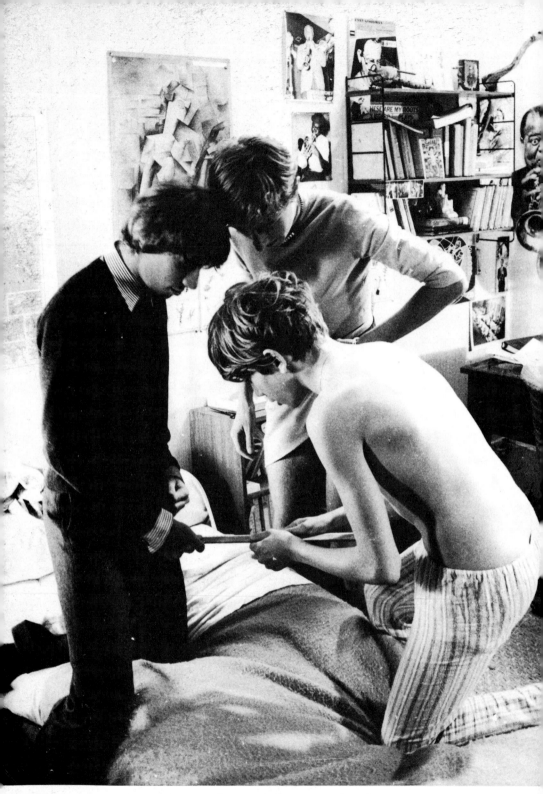

56. Louis Malle: Le Souffle au coeur (1971)

57. Claude Sautet: Les Choses de la vie (1970)

58. François Truffaut: Le Dernier métro (1980)

59. Bertrand Tavernier: Coup de torchon (1981)

60. Claude Miller: Garde à vue (1981)

into a spiritual void. As always with Bresson the moments of violence are only hinted at and indeed the whole film is dominated by images of emptiness, from the opening shot of a closed cash dispenser to the final image of a motionless crowd gazing off-screen at the empty scene of the final murder.

Perhaps the only leading film maker to forge seemingly effortlessly ahead in the difficult circumstances of the French film industry in the early 1980s was Eric Rohmer. His ability to work wonders with very limited means is a tribute to the harsh disciplines of 16 mm film making and educational television production which he endured for long years. His new series of 'comedies and proverbs', have a fluency which recalls the conversation pieces of Sacha Guitry in the 1930s and require only the slenderest of resources. While the first of the series, *La Femme de l'aviateur* (1981), featured a heroine who rejects all thoughts of marriage and told a story full of chance occurrences, coincidences and misunderstandings, *Le Beau mariage*, a year later, had a much tighter plot. It depicted a young woman arbitrarily intent on marrying a man whom she hardly knows and who is indifferent to her. In this sense the film recalled – with a change of sex for the protagonist – the underlying plot mechanics of the masterly *Ma nuit chez Maud*, but failed to achieve the same precise impact. The delightful *Pauline à la plage* (1983), the third of the series, was altogether more successful. It brings together just half-a-dozen characters in an end-of-season seaside resort and makes a positive virtue of its lack of extras or spectacular locations. The Pauline of the title is a fifteen-year-old holidaying with her cousin, the glamorous blonde divorcee, Marion. The film comprises no more than their encounters and involvements with a trio of men: Pierre, who is doggedly and dully in love with Marion; Henri, a free spirit who relishes his lack of attachments; and the young Sylvain, who is a little out of his depth in this adult company. Despite Henri's engaging attempts to go a little too far and sleep with Pauline as well as her cousin and a local girl, Rohmer's world emerges as a sunlit place unmarked by the shadows and traumas of emotional cruelty or perversion. There is little depth here, but the talk is always engaging, the plot very nicely contrived and the moralising which mars some of the director's work is happily absent. In the end Pauline is shown to be wiser than her more experienced but over-emotional cousin, and the film is remarkable for the freshness of its ability to capture unpatronisingly its young people's holiday entanglements.

In contrast *Les Nuits de la pleine lune* (1984) is a film of winter, marked by the image of the Parisian suburbs, where the heroine Louise (Pascale Ogier) cannot bear to live all the time. In this, the fourth of the series of 'Comedies and Proverbs', Rohmer offers one of his most successful portraits of a talker in the person of the verbal seducer Octave (Fabrice Luchini), who is more narcissistic than sensual and notes down those of his own phrases which appeal to him. But if Octave is quintessentially an inhabitant of Rohmer's customary world – someone for whom the lives of those around him are part of a construct, a novel waiting to be written – the central actions of *Les Nuits de la pleine lune* break this delicate balance. Louise's permanent boyfriend Rémi is too clumsy, brutal and ill-at-ease with words to fit easily into Rohmer's world: his simple passion and appetite destroy its delicate contours. And Louise herself, seeking space in too close a relationship with Rémi, finds that the risk so lightly accepted (if she falls in love with someone else she will tell Rémi and leave him) is turned against her. Shattered when Rémi announces his new love, Louise has nowhere to go. As she is crushed in this way, Rohmer's lack of tenderness for his characters is very apparent. Frail and butterflylike, even a little silly, Louise needs an indulgence that Rohmer's camera never allows her. Despite its flaws, however, *Les Nuits de la pleine lune* reaffirms Rohmer's unequalled skill as a director of dialogue scenes. Rohmer has never been an experimental film maker in the manner of Godard or Robbe-Grillet, and his particular classicism, rooted in a love of eighteenth-century literature, is clearly more in tune with the inward-looking unadventurous climate of current French film production procedures.

Bibliography

Abel, Richard: 'Jean Epstein's *La Chute de la Maison Usher* – Renewal and Liberation', *Wide Angle* 3/1, 1979
Afterimage 10, 1981: dossier on Jean Epstein, 'Myths of Total Cinema'
Agel, Geneviève: *Hulot parmi nous*, Paris: Cerf, 1955
Agel, Henri, et al.: *Sept ans de cinéma français*, Paris: Cerf, 1953
Agel, Henri: *Miroirs de l'insolite dans le cinéma français*, Paris: Cerf, 1958
——: *Les Grands cinéastes*, Paris: Ed. Universitaires, 1960
——: *Jean Grémillon*, Paris: Seghers, 1969
Ajame, Pierre: *Les Critiques de cinéma*, Paris: Flammarion, 1967
Allen, Don: *François Truffaut*, London: Secker & Warburg, 1974
Allen, Robert C.: 'Film History – The Narrow Discourse', *The 1977 Film Studies Annual*, 1977
——: 'Vitascope/Cinématographe – Initial Patterns of American Film Industry Practice', *Journal of the University Film Association* 31/2, 1979
Almendros, Nestor: *Un Homme à la caméra*, Paris: Hatier, 1980
Amengual, Barthélemy: *René Clair*, Paris: Seghers, 1960; new ed. 1969
——: 'Rapports entre le cinéma, la littérature et les arts en France dans les années vingt', *Cahiers de la cinémathèque* 33–34, 1981
Andrew, Dudley: *André Bazin*, New York: Oxford University Press, 1978
——: 'Sound in France – The Origins of a Native School', *Yale French Studies* 60, 1980
Annenkov, Georges: *Max Ophuls*, Paris: Terrain Vague, 1963
Aranda, Francisco: *Luis Buñuel – A Critical Biography*, London: Secker & Warburg, 1975
Arc, L' 31, 1967: 'Alain Resnais'
Armes, Roy: *French Cinema Since 1946*, 2 vols., London: Tantivy, 1966, 1970
——: *The Cinema of Alain Resnais*, London: Tantivy, 1968
——: *French Film*, London: Studio Vista, 1970
——: *The Ambiguous Image*, London: Secker & Warburg, 1976
——: *The Films of Alain Robbe-Grillet*, Amsterdam: John Benjamins, 1981
Arnoux, Alexandre: *Du muet au parlant*, Paris: Nouvelle Edition, 1946
Arroy, Jean: *En tournant 'Napoléon' avec Abel Gance*, Paris: Plon, 1927
Artaud, Antonin: *Oeuvres complètes*, Vol. III, Paris: Gaillimard, 1961; trans.: *Collected Works*, Vol. III, London: Calder & Boyars, 1972
Artsept 1–3, 1963
Astruc Alexandre: *La Tête la première*, Paris: Olivier Orban, 1975
Autant-Lara, Claude: *Télémafia*, Nice: Ed. Alain Lefeuvre, 1981
——: *La Rage dans le coeur*, Paris: Henri Veyrier, 1984
Avant-scène du cinéma, L': over 300 numbers since 1961 containing meticulously defined film scripts and two issues of stills: 279–80 and 299–300

Bachy, Victor: *Jacques Feyder*, Paris: Anthologie du cinéma, 1966
——: *Jacques Feyder – Artisan du cinéma*, Louvain: Librairie Universitaire, 1968

Badaire, Vincent: *Sacha Guitry*, Le Havre: SEDS-Editions, 1977

Bailblé, Claude, et al.: *Muriel*, Paris: Galilée, 1974

Bandy, Mary Lea (ed.): *Rediscovering French Film*, New York: Museum of Modern Art, 1983

Barsacq, Léon: *Le Décor de film*, Paris: Seghers, 1970; trans.: *Caligari's Cabinet and Other Grand Illusions*, Boston: Little, Brown, 1976

Bazin, André: *Qu'est-ce que le cinéma?*', 4 vols., Paris: Cerf, 1958–62; trans.: *What is Cinema?*, 2 vols., Berkeley: University of California, 1967–72

——: *Jean Renoir*, Paris: Champ Libre, 1971; trans.: London, W. H. Allen, 1974

——: *Le Cinéma de l'occupation et de la résistance*, Paris: UGE, 1975; trans.: *French Cinema of the Occupation and Resistance*, New York: Ungar, 1981

——: *Le Cinéma de la cruauté*, Paris: Flammarion, 1975

——: *Le Cinéma français de la Libération à la nouvelle vague*, Paris: Cahiers du cinéma/Ed. de l'Etoile, 1983

Bellour, Raymond: *Alexandre Astruc*, Paris: Seghers, 1963

Benayoun, Robert: *Alain Resnais – Arpenteur de l'imaginaire*, Paris: Stock, 1980

Bernheim, Nicole Lise: *Marguerite Duras tourne un film*, Paris: Albatros, 1975

Bertin-Maghit, Jean-Pierre: *Le Cinéma français sous Vichy*, Paris: Albatros, 1980

Bessy, Maurice: *Méliès*, Paris: Anthologie du cinéma, 1965

Bessy, Maurice and Lo Duca, Giuseppe Maria: *Georges Méliès, mage*, Paris: Prisma, 1945

——: *Louis Lumière, inventeur*, Paris: Prisma, 1948

Beylie, Claude: *Max Ophuls*, Paris, Seghers, 1963

——: *Ophuls*, Paris: Anthologie du cinéma, 1965

——: *Cocteau*, Paris: Anthologie du cinéma, 1966

——: *Marcel Pagnol*, Paris: Seghers, 1974

——: *Jean Renoir*, Paris: Lherminier, 1975

——: *Jean Renoir*, Paris: Anthologie du cinéma, 1980

Beylie, Claude and Lacassin, Francis: *Henri Fescourt*, Paris: Anthologie du cinéma, 1967

Billard, Pierre: *Jean Grémillon*, Paris: Anthologie du cinéma, 1966

Bion, Danièle: *Bertrand Tavernier – Cinéaste de l'émotion*, Paris: Hatier, 1984

Bonnaffons, Elisabeth: *François Truffaut*, Lausanne: L'Age d'Homme, 1982

Bonnell, René: *Le Cinéma exploité*, Paris: Seuil, 1978

Borde, Raymond, et al.: *Nouvelle vague*, Lyons: Serdoc, 1962

Borde, Raymond and Cadars, Pierre: 'La France des années trente', Paris: Avant-scène du cinéma 173, 1976

Bordwell, David: *Filmguide to La Passion de Jeanne D'Arc*, Bloomington: Indiana University Press, 1973

——: *The Films of Carl Theodor Dreyer*, Los Angeles: University of California Press, 1981

Boulanger, Pierre: *Le Cinéma colonial*, Paris: Seghers, 1975

Bounoure, Gaston: *Alain Resnais*, Paris: Seghers, 1962; 2nd ed.: 1974

Braucourt, Guy: *André Cayatte*, Paris: Seghers, 1969

——: *Claude Chabrol*, Paris: Seghers, 1971

Braudy, Leo: *Jean Renoir – The World of his Films*, New York: Doubleday, 1972

——: *Focus on Shoot the Piano Player*, Englewood Cliffs, N. J.: Prentice Hall, 1972

Bresson, Robert: *Notes sur le cinématographe*, Paris: Gallimard, 1975 trans.: *Notes on the Cinematograph*, New York: Urizen, 1977

Briot, Robert: *Robert Bresson*, Paris: Cerf, 1957

Brossard, Jean-Pierre: *Marcel L'Herbier et son temps*, La Chaux-de-Fonds: Ed. Cinédiff, 1980

Brown, Frederick: *An Impersonation of Angels*, London: Longmans, 1969

Brown, Royal S.: *Focus on Godard*, Englewood Cliffs, N. J.: Prentice Hall, 1972

Brownlow, Kevin: *The Parade's Gone By*, London: Secker & Warburg, 1968

Brumagne, M. M.: *Franju – Impressions et aveux*, Lausanne: L'Age d'Homme, 1977

Brunius, Jacques B.: *En marge du cinéma français*, Paris: Arcanes, 1954
Buache, Freddy: *Luis Buñuel*, Lyons: Serdoc, 1960; new ed.: Lausanne: L'Age d'Homme, 1970; trans.: *The Cinema of Luis Buñuel*, London: Tantivy, 1973
——: *Claude Autant-Lara*, Lausanne: L'Age d'Homme, 1982
Burch, Noël: *Praxis du cinéma*, Paris: Gallimard, 1969; trans.: *Theory of Film Practice*, London: Secker & Warburg, 1973
——: *Marcel L'Herbier*, Paris: Seghers, 1973

Cahiers de la cinémathèque 8 and 10–11 (1973) 'Le Cinéma de Vichy'; 23–24 (1977) 'Le Cinéma du Samedi soir'; 29 (1979) 'Le Cinéma des premiers temps'; 33–34 (1981) 'Le Cinéma des années folles'; 40 (1984) 'Dossier Feyder'
Cahiers du cinéma: over 360 issues since 1951
Cameron, Ian (ed.): *The Films of Jean-Luc Godard*, London: Studio Vista, 1967
——: *The Films of Robert Bresson*, London: Studio Vista, 1967
Carné, Marcel: *La Vie à belles dents*, Paris: Jean Vuarnet, 1979
Catelain, Jacque: *Jacque Catelain présente Marcel L'Herbier*, Paris: Jacques Vautrain, 1950
Cauliez, Armand-Jean: *Jean Renoir*, Paris: Ed. Universitaires, 1962
——: *Jacques Tati*, Paris: Seghers, 1962
Cayrol, Jean and Durand, Claude: *Le Droit de regard*, Paris: Seuil, 1963
Chabrol, Claude: *Et pourtant je tourne*, Paris: Robert Laffont, 1976
Chalais, François: *François Chalais présente H. G. Clouzot*, Paris: Jacques Vautrain, 1950
Chapier, Henry: *Louis Malle*, Paris: Seghers, 1964
Chardère, Bernard, ed.: *Jean Vigo*, Lyons: Serdoc, 1961
——: *Jean Renoir*, Lyons: Serdoc, 1962
Charensol, Georges: *René Clair et les Belles-de-nuit*, Paris: Cerf, 1953
Charensol, Georges and Régent, Roger: *Un Maître de cinéma – René Clair*. Paris: Table Ronde, 1952
——: *Cinquante ans avec René Clair*, Paris: Table Ronde, 1979
Chateau, Dominique and Jost, François: *Nouveau cinéma, nouvelle sémiologie*, Paris: UGE, 1979
Chateau, Dominique, et al.: *Cinémas de la modernité*, Paris: Klincksieck, 1981
Chazal, Robert: *Marcel Carné*, Paris: Seghers, 1965
Chirat, Raymond: *Duvivier*, Lyons: Serdoc, 1968
——: *Decoin*, Paris: Anthologie du cinéma, 1965
——: *Le Cinéma français des années 30*, Paris: Hatier, 1983
——: *Le Cinéma français des années de guerre*, Paris: Hatier, 1983
Chirat, Raymond and Barrot, Olivier: *Christian-Jaque*, Lausanne: *Travelling 47*, 1976
Chirat, Raymond and Beylie, Claude: 'Le Cinéma des années noires', Paris: L'Avant-scène du cinéma 127–8, 1972
Cinéma: over 300 issues since 1954
Cinéma s'insurge, Le 1–3, Paris: Terrain Vague, 1968
Clair, René: *Réflexion faite*, Paris: Gallimard, 1951; trans.: *Reflections on the Cinema*, London: William Kimber, 1953
——: *Comédies et commentaires*, Paris: Gallimard, 1959
——: *Cinéma d'hier, cinéma d'aujourd'hui*, Paris: Gallimard, 1970; trans.: *Cinema Yesterday and Today*, New York: Dover, 1972
Clouzot, Claire: *Le Cinéma français depuis la nouvelle vague*, Paris: Fernand Nathan, 1972
Cocteau, Jean: *La Belle et la bête – Journal d'un film*, Paris: J. B. Janin, 1946; trans.: *Diary of a Film – La Belle et la Bête*, London: Dobson, 1950
——: *Entretiens autour du cinématographe*, Paris: André Bonne, 1959; trans.: *Cocteau on the Film*, London: Dobson, 1954

——: *Entretiens sur le cinématographe*, Paris: Pierre Belfont, 1973
——: *Du Cinématographe*, Paris: Pierre Belfont, 1973
Collet, Jean: *Jean-Luc Godard*, Seghers, 1963; trans.: New York: Crown, 1970
——: *Le Cinéma en question*, Paris: Cerf, 1972
——: *Le Cinéma de François Truffaut*, Paris: Lherminier, 1977
Colpi, Henri: *Défense et illustration de la musique dans le film*, Lyons: Serdoc, 1963
Courant, Gérard (ed.): *Philippe Garrel*, Paris: Cinéma 43, 1983
Courtade, Francis: *Les Malédictions du cinéma français*, Paris: Alain Moreau, 1978
Crisp, C. G.: *François Truffaut*, London: November, 1972

Daquin, Louis: *Le Cinéma notre métier*, Paris: Editeurs Français Réunis, 1960
——: *On ne tait pas ses silences*, Paris: Editeurs Français Réunis, 1980
Daria, Sophie: *Abel Gance – Hier et Demain*, Paris and Geneva: La Palantine, 1959
De la Roche, Catherine: *René Clair – An Index*, London: BFI, 1958
Deslandes, Jacques: *Le Boulevard du cinéma à l'époque de Georges Méliès*, Paris: Cerf, 1963
——: *Jasset*, Paris: Anthologie du cinéma, 1975
——: *Histoire compareé du cinéma*, Vol. I, Paris: Castermann, 1966
Deslandes, Jacques and Richard, Jacques: *Histoire compareé du cinéma*, Vol. II, Paris: Castermann, 1968
Deutelbaum, Marshall: 'Structural Patterning in the Lumière Films', *Wide Angle* 3/1, 1979
Diamant-Berger, Henri: *Il était une fois le cinéma*, Paris: Jean-Claude Simoën, 1977
Dorzoretz, Wendy: 'Dulac versus Artaud', *Wide Angle* 3/1, 1979
Douin, Jean-Luc (ed.): *La Nouvelle vague 25 ans après*, Paris: Cerf, 1983
Droguet, Robert: *Robert Bresson*, Lyons: Serdoc, 1966
Drozuzy, Maurice: *Luis Buñuel – Architecte du rêve*, Paris: Lherminier, 1978
——: *Carl Th Dreyer né Nilsson*, Paris: Cerf, 1983
Duras, Marguerite and Gauthier, Xavière: *Les Parleuses*, Paris: Minuit, 1974
Duras, Marguerite, et al.: *Marguerite Duras*, Paris: Albatros, 1975
Duras, Marguerite and Porte, Michelle: *Les Lieux de Marguerite Duras*, Paris: Minuit, 1978
Duras, Marguerite: *Les Yeux verts*, Paris: Cahiers du cinéma 312–13, 1980
Durgnat, Raymond: *Luis Buñuel*, London: Studio Vista, 1962
——: *Nouvelle Vague – The First Decade*, London: Motion Pubs., 1963
——: *Franju*, London: Studio Vista, 1967
——: *Jean Renoir*, London: Studio Vista, 1975

Eaton, Mick: *Anthropology – Reality – Cinema: The Films of Jean Rouch*, London: BFI, 1979
Epstein, Jean: *Ecrits sur le cinéma*, 2 vols., Paris: Seghers, 1974–75
Estève, Michel: *Robert Bresson*, Paris: Seghers, 1962
—— (ed.): *Luis Buñuel*, Paris: Lettres modernes, 1963
—— (ed.): *Le Surréalisme au cinéma*, Paris: Lettres modernes, 1965
——: *Jean Vigo*, Paris: Lettres modernes, 1966
——: *Nouvelle histoire de Mouchette – De Bernanos à Bresson*, Paris: Lettres modernes, 1968
—— (ed.): *Alain Resnais et Alain Robbe-Grillet – Evolution d'une écriture*, Paris: Lettres modernes, 1974
——: *Robert Bresson*, Paris: Albatros, 1983

Fanne, Dominique: *L'Univers de François Truffaut*, Paris: Cerf, 1972
Farwagi, André: *René Clément*, Paris: Seghers, 1967
Faure, Michel: *Le Groupe Octobre*, Paris: Christian Bourgeois, 1977
Fescourt, Henri: *La Foi et les montagnes*, Paris: Paul Montel, 1959

Feyder, Jacques and Rosay, Françoise: *Le Cinéma notre métier*, Paris: Cailler, 1946
Film Dope 9, 1976: 'Louis Daquin'; 10, 1976: 'Jacques Demy'
Fisher, Lucy: *Jacques Tati: A Guide to References and Resources*, Boston: G. K. Hall, 1983
Fofi, Goffredo: 'The Cinema of the Popular Front in France (1934–38)', *Screen* 13/4, 1972–3
Ford Charles: *Max Linder*, Paris: Seghers, 1966
——: *Germaine Dulac*, Paris: Anthologie du cinéma, 1968
——: *Jacques Feyder*, Paris: Seghers, 1973
——: *Histoire du cinéma contemporain*, Paris: France-Empire, 1978
Fowler, Roy: *The Film in France*, London: Pendulum, 1948
Frank, Nino: *Petit cinéma sentimental*, Paris: Nouvelle Édition, 1950
Frazer, John: *Artificially Arranged Scenes*, Boston: G. K. Hall, 1979
Fryland, Maurice: *Roger Vadim*, Paris: Seghers, 1963

Gardies, André: *Alain Robbe-Grillet*, Paris: Seghers, 1972
——: *Approche du récit filmique*, Paris: Albatros, 1980
——: *Le Cinéma de Robbe-Grillet—Essai de sémiocritique*, Paris: Albatros, 1983
Gautheur, Claude: *Jean Renoir – La Double méprise*, Paris: Editeurs Français Réunis, 1980
Génard, Paul and Barret André: *Les Premières photographies en couleurs de Lumière*, Paris: André Barret, 1974
Gilson, René: *Jean Cocteau*, Paris: Seghers, 1964; trans.: New York: Crown, 1969
——: *Becker*, Paris: Anthologie du cinéma, 1966
Godard, Jean-Luc: *Introduction à une véritable histoire du cinéma*, Paris: Albatros, 1980
Goldman, Annie: *Cinéma et société moderne*, Paris: Anthropos, 1971
Gomery, Douglas: 'Economic Struggle and Hollywood Imperialism – Europe Converts to Sound', *Yale French Studies* 60, 1980
Gould, Michael: *Surrealism and Cinema*, Cranbury, New Jersey: A. S. Barnes, 1976
Graham, Peter (ed.): *The New Wave*, London: Secker & Warburg, 1968
Grange, Frédéric and Rebolledo, Charles: *Luis Buñuel*, Paris: Ed. Universitaires, 1964
Grangier, Gilles: *Flash-Back*, Paris: Presses de la Cité, 1977
Guérif, François: *Le Cinéma policier français*, Paris: Veyrier, 1981
Guidez, Guylaine: *Claude Lelouch*, Paris: Seghers, 1972
Guillot, Gérard: *Les Prévert*, Paris: Seghers, 1966
Guitry, Sacha: *Quatre ans d'occupation*, Paris: L'Elan, 1947
——: *Le Cinéma et moi*, Paris: Jean-Pierre Ramsay, 1977
Gunning, Tom: 'The Non-Continuous Style of Early Film', in Holman (1982)
Guth, Paul: *Autour des Dames du Bois de Boulogne*, Paris: Julliard, 1945
Guy, Alice: *Autobiographie d'une pionnière du cinéma*, Paris: Denoël/Gonthier, 1976
Guzzetti, Alfred: *One or Two Things I Know About Her*, Cambridge, Mass.: Harvard University Press, 1981

Halami, André: *Chantons sous l'occupation*, Paris: Olivier Orban, 1976
Hammond, Paul: *Marvellous Méliès*, London: Gordon Fraser, 1974
——: *The Shadow and its Shadow: Surrealist Writings on Cinema*, London: BFI, 1978
Harding, James: *Sacha Guitry*, London: Methuen, 1968
Harvey, Sylvia: *May '68 and Film Culture*, London: BFI, 1978
Haudiquet, Philippe: *Epstein*, Paris: Anthologie du cinéma, 1966
Hennebelle, Guy (ed.): *Cinémas d'avant-garde*, Paris: CinémAction 10–11, 1980
Higginbotham, Virginia: *Luis Buñuel*, Boston: Twayne, 1979
Holman, Roger (ed.): *Cinema 1900–1906*, 2 vols., Brussels, FIAF, 1982

Icart, Roger: *Abel Gance*, Toulouse: Institut Pédagogique National, 1960
——:'A la découverte de *la Roue*', Cahiers de la cinémathèque 33–44, 1981
——: *Abel Gance ou La Prométhée foudroyée*, Lausanne: L'Age d'Homme, 1984
Indsorf, Annette: *François Truffaut*, Boston: Twayne, 1978; new ed: London: Macmillan, 1982
Ishaghpour, Youssef: *D'une image à l'autre*, Paris: Denoël/Gonthier, 1982

Jacob, Guy: *Le Cinéma moderne*, Lyons: Serdoc, 1964
Jacob, Guy, et al.: *Jacques Prévert*, Lyons: Serdoc, 1960
Jeancolas, Jean-Pierre: *Le Cinéma des français – 1969–74*, Créteil: Art et Culture, 1974
——: *Le Cinéma des français – La Vᵉ République, 1958–78*, Paris: Stock, 1979
——: *Quinze ans d'années trente: Le Cinéma des français 1929–1944*, Paris: Stock, 1983
Jeanne, René: *Cinéma 1900*, Paris: Flammarion, 1965
Jeanne, René and Ford, Charles: *Histoire encyclopédique du cinéma*, Vol. I (Le Cinéma français 1895–1929), Paris: Robert Laffont, 1947; Vol. IV (Le Cinéma parlant 1929–1945), Paris: SEDE, 1958; Vol. V (Cinéma d'aujourd'hui 1945–1955), Paris: SEDE, 1962
——: *Abel Gance*, Paris: Seghers, 1963
Jenn, Pierre: *Georges Méliès cinéaste*, Paris: Albatros, 1984
Jost, François, (ed.): *Obliques/Robbe-Grillet*, Paris: Obliques, 1978

Kast, Pierre: *Jean Grémillon*, Paris: Anthologie du cinéma, 1966
King, Norman (ed.): *Abel Gance*, London: BFI, 1984
Kramer, Steven Philip and Welsh, James Michael: *Abel Gance*, Boston: Twayne, 1978
Kreidl, John: *Jean-Luc Godard*, Boston: Twayne, 1980
Kyrou, Ado: *Luis Buñuel*, Paris: Seghers, 1962; trans.: New York: Simon & Schuster, 1963

Labarthe, André S.: *Essai sur le jeune cinéma français*, Paris: Terrain Vague, 1960
Lacassin, Francis: *Louis Feuillade*, Paris: Seghers, 1964
——: *Feuillade*, Paris: Anthologie du cinéma, 1966
——: *Alfred Machin*, Paris: Anthologie du cinéma, 1968
——: *Pour une contre histoire du cinéma*, Paris: Union Génerále d'Editions, 1972
Lacassin, Francis and Bellour, Raymond: *Le Procès Clouzot*, Paris: Terrain Vague, 1964
Lacourbe, Roland: *Henri-Georges Clouzot*, Paris: Anthologie du cinéma, 1977
Landry, Bernard-G.: *Bernard-G. Landry présente Marcel Carné*, Paris: Vautrain, 1952
Lannes, Roger, *Jean Cocteau*, Paris: Seghers, 1968
Lapierre, Marcel: *Aux portes de la nuit*, Paris: Nouvelle Edition, 1946
Leenhardt, Roger: *Les Yeux ouverts*, Paris: Seuil, 1979
Lefèvre, Raymond: *Jean-Luc Godard*, Paris: Edilig, 1983
——: *Luis Buñuel*, Paris: Edilig, 1984
Léglise, Paul: *Histoire de la politique du cinéma français*, 2 vols., Paris: Lherminier, 1969 and 1977
Legrand, Gérard: *Edmond T. Greville*, Paris: Anthologie du cinéma, 1970
Leprohon, Pierre: *Présences contemporaines cinéma*, Paris: Nouvelles Editions Debresse, 1951
——: *Cinquante ans du cinéma français*, Paris: Cerf, 1954
——: *Jean Epstein*, Paris: Seghers, 1964

————: *Jean Renoir*, Paris: Seghers, 1967
————: *Julien Duvivier*, Paris: Anthologie du cinéma, 1968
————: *Marcel Pagnol*, Paris: Anthologie du cinéma, 1976
Lev, Peter: *Claude Lelouch: Film Director*, East Brunswick N.J.: Fairleigh Dickinson University Press, 1983
Levy Klein, Stéphane: 'Le Cinéma français des années 40–44': *Positif* 168 and 170, 1975
L'Herbier, Marcel: *Intelligence du cinématographe*, Paris: Corréa, 1946
————: *La Tête qui tourne*, Paris: Belfont, 1979
Lherminier, Pierre: *Jean Vigo*, Paris: Seghers, 1967
————: (ed.): *Le Cinéma français au présent*, Paris: Filméditions, 1977
Lorcey, Jacques: *Sacha Guitry par les témoins de sa vie*, Paris: Ed. France Empire, 1976

Macbean, James Roy: *Film and Revolution*, Bloomington: Indiana University Press, 1975
MacCabe, Colin: *Godard – Images, Sounds, Politics*, London: BFI/Macmillan, 1980
Maddock, Brent: *The Films of Jacques Tati*, Metuchen N. J.: Scarecrow, 1977
Maillet, Raymond: *Emile Cohl*, Paris: Anthologie du cinéma, 1978
Malle, Louis: *Louis Malle par Louis Malle*, Paris: Ed. de l'Athanor, 1978
Malthète-Méliès, Madeleine: *Méliès l'enchanteur*, Paris: Hachette, 1973
————: *Méliès et la naissance du spectâcle cinématographique*, Paris: Klinksieck, 1984
Marion, Denis: *André Malraux*, Paris: Seghers, 1970
Marker, Chris: *Commentaires*, 2 vols., Paris: Seuil, 1961 and 1967
————: *Le Fond de l'air est rouge*, Paris: François Maspéro, 1978
Martin, Marcel: *Jean Vigo*, Paris: Anthologie du cinéma, 1966
————: *France – An Illustrated Guide*, London: A. Zwemmer, 1971
————: *Le Cinéma français depuis la guerre*, Paris: Eidilig, 1984
Mast, Gerald: *Filmguide to The Rules of the Game*, Bloomington: Indiana University Press, 1972
Matthews, J. H.: *Surrealism and Film*, Ann Arbor: University of Michigan Press, 1971
McGerr, Celia: *René Clair*, Boston: Twayne, 1980
Mellen, Joan (ed.): *The World of Luis Buñuel*, New York: Oxford University Press, 1978
Mesguich, Félix: *Tours de manivelle*, Paris: Bernard Grasset, 1933
Micha, René (ed.): *Jacques Feyder ou Le Cinéma concret*, Brussels: Comité National Jacques Feyder, 1949
Michalczyk, John J.: *The French Literary Filmmakers*, Philadelphia: Art Alliance Press, 1980
————: *Costa Gavras: The Political Fiction Film*, Philadelphia: Art Alliance Press, 1984
Milne, Tom (ed.): *The Cinema of Carl Dreyer*, London: Tantivy, 1971
————: *Godard on Godard*, London: Secker & Warburg, 1972
Mitry, Jean: *René Clair*, Paris: Ed. Universitaires, 1960
————: *Esthétique et psychologie du cinéma*, 2 vols., Paris: Ed. Universitaires, 1963 and 1969
————: *Max Linder*, Paris: Anthologie du cinéma, 1966
————: *Histoire du cinéma*, 5 vols., Paris: Ed. Universitaires, 1967, 1969, 1973, 1980, 1980
————: *Maurice Tourneur*, Paris: Anthologie du cinéma, 1968
————: *Ivan Mosjoukine*, Paris: Anthologie du cinéma, 1969
————: *Louis Delluc*, Paris: Anthologie du cinéma, 1971
———— (ed.): *Le Cinéma des origines*, Paris: Cinéma d'aujourd'hui, 1976

Monaco, James: *The New Wave*, New York: Oxford University Press, 1976
——: *Alain Resnais*, London: Secker & Warburg, 1978
Monaco, Paul: *Cinema and Society – France and Germany During the Twenties*, New York: Elsevier, 1976
Mussman, Toby (ed.): *Jean-Luc Godard*, New York: Dutton, 1968

Narboni, Jean (ed.): *Jean-Luc Godard par Jean-Luc Godard*, Paris: Pierre Belfont, 1968
Noell, René: *Histoire du spectacle cinématographique à Perpignan de 1896 à 1944*, Perpignan: Cahiers de la cinémathèque, 1973
Nogueira, Rui (ed.): *Le Cinéma selon Melville*, Paris: Seghers, 1973; trans.: *Melville on Melville*, London: Secker & Warburg, 1971
Noguez, Dominique: *Le Cinéma, autrement*, Paris: Union Geńeŕale d'Editions, 1977
——: *Trente ans de cinéma expérimental en France*, Paris: Ed. ARCEF, 1982
Novik, William: 'Four Years in a Bottle', *Penguin Film Review* 2, 1947

Pagnol, Marcel: *Oeuvres complètes*, Vol. III, Paris: Ed. de Provence, 1967
Pathé, Charles: *Souvenirs et conseils d'un parvenu*, Paris: Pierre Latour, 1926
——: *De Pathé Frères à Pathé Cinéma*, Lyons: Serdoc, 1961
Perrin, Claude: *Carl Th Dreyer*, Paris: Seghers, 1979
Petrie, Graham: *The Cinema of François Truffaut*, London: A. Zwemmer, 1970
Pilard, Philippe: *Henri-Georges Clouzot*, Paris: Seghers, 1969
Pillaudin, Roger: *Jean Cocteau tourne son dernier film*, Paris: Table Ronde, 1960
Pinel, Vincent: *Louis Lumière*, Paris: Anthologie du cinéma, 1974
Pingaud, Bernard (ed.): *Alain Resnais*, Lyons: Serdoc, 1961
Point, Le 49, 1962: 'Constantes du cinéma français'
Porcile, François: *Défense du court métrage français*, Paris: Cerf, 1965
——: *Présence de la musique à l'écran*, Paris: Cerf, 1969
Positif: over 280 issues since 1952
Poulle, François: *Renoir 1938 ou Jean Renoir pour rien*, Paris: Cerf, 1969
Prédal, René: *La Société française 1914–45 à travers le cinéma*, Paris: Armand Colin, 1972
——: *Alain Resnais*, Paris: Lettres modernes, 1974
——: *Les Jeux de l'argent et du pouvoir dans le cinéma français*, Paris: CinémAction 13, 1981
——: *Jean Rouch – Un Griot gaulois*, Paris: CinémAction 17, 1982
——: *Le Cinéma français contemporain*, Paris: Cerf, 1984

Queneau, Raymond and Queval, Jean: *Rendez-vous de juillet*, Paris: Chavanne, 1949
Queval, Jean: *Marcel Carné*, London: BFI, 1950
——: *Jacques Prévert*, Paris: Mercure de France, 1955
——: *Jacques Becker*, Paris: Seghers, 1962

Régent, Roger: *Cinéma de France*, Paris: Bellefage, 1948; re-ed.: *Cinéma de France sous l'occupation*, Paris: Editions d'Aujourd'hui, 1975
Renoir, Jean: *Ma Vie et mes films*, Paris: Flammarion, 1974; trans.: *My Life and my Films*, London: Collins, 1974
——: *Ecrits 1926–1971*, Paris: Pierre Belfont, 1974
——: *Entretiens et propos*, Paris: Edition de l'Etoile/Cahiers du cinéma, 1979
——: *Ouevres de cinéma inédits*, Paris: Gallimard, 1981
Resnais, Alain: *Repérages*, Paris: Chêne, 1974
Richebé, Roger: *Au-delà de l'écran*, Monaco: Pastorelli, 1977

Rohmer, Eric: *L'Organisation de l'espace dans le Faust de Murnau*, Paris: UGE, 1977
——: *Le Goût de la beauté*, Paris: Cahiers du Cinéma/L'Etoile, 1984
Rosenbaum, Jonathan: *Rivette – Texts and Interviews*, London: BFI, 1977
Roud, Richard: *Max Ophuls*, London: BFI, 1958
——: *Jean-Luc Godard*, London: Secker & Warburg, 1967
——: *Jean-Marie Straub*, London: Secker & Warburg, 1971
Rousset-Rouard, Yves: *Histoire d'X*, Paris: J.-C. Lattes, 1976

Sadoul, Georges: *Histoire générale du cinéma*, Paris: Denoël, 5 vols. 1946–54; 6
   slightly different vols. in new edition 1973–75:
   1. *L'Invention du cinéma*, 1973 (and as Tome I, 1946, 1948)
   2. *Les Pionniers du cinéma*, 1973 (and as Tome II, 1947)
   3. *Le Cinéma devient un art: L'Avant-guerre*, 1973 (and as Tome III i, 1951)
   4. *Le Cinéma devient un art: La Première guerre mondiale*, 1975 (and as Tome III
      ii, 1952)
   5. *L'Art muet: L'Après-guerre en Europe*, 1975
   6. *L'Art muet: Hollywood, la fin du muet*, 1975
also: *Le Cinéma pendant la guerre* (only as Tome VI, 1954)
——: *French Film*, London: Falcon Press, 1953
——: *Georges Méliès*, Paris: Seghers, 1961
——: *Histoire du cinéma français*, Paris: Flammarion, 1962
——: *Louis Lumière*, Paris: Seghers, 1964
——: *Chroniques du cinéma français*, Paris: Union Générale d'Editions, 1979
Salès Gomès, P. E.: *Jean Vigo*, Paris: Seuil, 1957; trans.: Salles Gomes, P. E.: *Jean
   Vigo*, London: Secker & Warburg, 1972
Salles, Jacques: *Raymond Bernard*, Paris: Anthologie du cinéma, 1980
Salt, Barry: 'The Early Development of Film Form', *Film Form* 1/1, 1976
——: 'Film Form 1900–06', *Sight and Sound* 47/3, 1978
Screen 13/4, 1972–3: 'The Estates General of the French Cinema, May 1968'
Semolué, Jean: *Bresson*, Paris: Ed. Universitaires, 1959
——: *Dreyer*, Paris: Ed. Universitaires, 1962
——: *Carl Dreyer*, Paris: Anthologie du cinéma, 1970
Serceau, Daniel: *Jean Renoir l'insurgé*, Paris: Le Sycamore, 1981
Seskonske, Alexander: *Jean Renoir – The French Films 1924–1939*, Cambridge,
   Mass.: Harvard University Press, 1980
Siclier, Jacques: *La Nouvelle vague*, Paris: Cerf, 1961
——: *Guitry*, Paris: Anthologie du cinéma, 1966
——: *La France de Pétain et son cinéma*, Paris: Henri Veyrier, 1981
Simon, William G.: *The Films of Jean Vigo*, Ann Arbor: UMI Research Press, 1981
Sloan, Jane: *Robert Bresson: A Guide to References and Resources*, Boston: G. K.
   Hall, 1983
Smith, John M.: *Jean Vigo*, London: Movie, 1972
Stoneman, Rod: 'Perspective Correction: Early Film to Avant-garde', *Afterimage* 8–9,
   1978
Straw, Will: 'The Myth of Total Cinema History', *Ciné-Tracts* 9, 1980
Strebel, Elisabeth Grottle: 'French Cinema 1940–1944 and its Social Psychological
   Significance: A Preliminary Probe', *Historical Journal of Film, Radio and Tele-
   vision*, 1/1, 1981
Sweet, Freddy: *The Film Narratives of Alain Resnais*, Ann Arbor: UMI Research
   Press, 1980

Talon, Gérard: *Emile Reynaud*, Paris: Anthologie du cinéma, 1972
——: 'Le Cinéma du front populaire', *Cinéma* 194, 1975
Tariol, Marcel: *Louis Delluc*, Paris: Seghers, 1965

Thiher, Allen: *The Cinematic Muse*, Columbia: Missouri University Press, 1979
Thorel, Christian and Archie, Jean-Paul: *Les Films de Jean-Marie Straub et Danièle Huillet*, Paris: NEF Diffusion/Ombres, 1984
Tonnerre, Jerome: *Claude Lelouch filme 'Les Uns et les Autres'*, Paris: Plon, 1982
Truffaut, François: 'Une Certaine tendence du cinéma français', *Cahiers du cinéma* 31, January 1954
——: *Le Cinéma selon Hitchcock*, Paris: Seghers, 1975; trans.: *Hitchcock*, London: Panther, 1968
——: *Les Films de ma vie*, Paris: Flammarion, 1975; trans.: *The Films in my Life*, New York: Simon and Schuster 1978
Turatier, Jean-Marie and Busto, Daniel (ed.): *Jean-Luc Godard – Télévision/ Ecritures*, Paris: Galilée, 1979

Vadim, Roger: *Mémoires du diable*, Pairs: Sock, 1975; trans.: *Memoirs of the Devil*, London: Hutchinson, 1976
Vaughan, Dai: 'Let There be Lumière', *Sight and Sound* 50/2, 1981
Védrès, Nicole: *Images du cinéma français*, Paris: Chêne, 1945
Vialle, Gabriel: *Georges Franju*, Paris: Seghers, 1968
——: *Jean-Pierre Melville*, Paris: Anthologie du cinéma, 1974
Vianey, Michel: *En attendant Godard*, Paris: Grasset: 1967
Vidal, Marion: *Les Contes moraux d'Eric Rohmer*, Paris: Lherminier, 1977

Wagner, Jean: *Jean-Pierre Melville*, Paris: Seghers, 1963
Walz, Eugene P.: *François Truffaut*: A Guide to References and Resources, Boston: G. K. Hall, 1982
Ward, John: *Alain Resnais or the Theme of Time*, London: Secker & Warburg, 1968
Wide Angle 4/4, 1981: Special number on French cinema
Willemen, Paul (ed.): *Ophuls*, London: BFI, 1978
Willoughby, Dominique, et al.: *Les 200 films de Jean Painlevé*, Paris: Amis du Ciné – MBXA and Ciné-Doc, 1983
Wood, Robin and Walker, Michael: *Claude Chabrol*, London: Studio Vista, 1970

Yale French Studies 60, 'Cinema/Sound', 1980

Zimmer, Jacques and De Béchade, Claude: *Jean-Pierre Melville*, Paris: Edilig, 1984

Index

Abel, Alfred, 61
A bientôt, j'espère, 221
A bout de souffle, 179–180, 193, 201
Achard, Marcel, 88
Acres, Birt, 8
Adieu Léonard, 100, 117–118
Adieu Philippine, 171
Adjani, Isabèle, 272
A double tour, 177
Adrienne Lecouvreur, 87
Affaire des bijoux, L', 25
Affaire Dreyfus, L', 11
Affaire du courrier de Lyon, L', 118
Affaire est dans le sac, L', 78, 100
Afrique 1950, 146
Agatha et les lectures illimités, 268
Age d'or, L', 69–70, 77, 259
Agostini, Philippe, 116
Aigle à deux têtes, L', 143
Ailes de la colombe, Les, 250
Aimée, Anouk, 210, 211, 212
Aîné des Ferchaux, L', 195
Air de Paris, L', 160
Air pur, 76
Alcover, Pierre, 61
Ali-Baba et les quarante voleurs, 148, 152
Allégret, Marc, 72, 85
Allégret, Yves, 127, 128, 129–130, 149
Allio, René, 213, 233, 263–264
Almendros, Nestor, 228
Alphaville, 202
Amant de Lady Chatterley, L', 246
Amants, Les, 173–174
Amants de Vérone, Les, 128, 149
Amerika/Rapports de classes, 274
Ames de fous, 42, 43
Ames d'orient, 38

Ami viendra ce soir, Un, 126
Amour à mort, L', 277
Amour avec des si, L', 175, 212
Amour à vingt ans, L', 179
Amour en fuite, L', 255–256
Amour fou, L', 235, 236, 251, 277
Amour l'après-midi, L', 228, 229
Amours de la Reine Elisabeth, Les, 22
Andréa, Yann, 268
Andréani, André, 62
André Masson et les quatre éléments, 163
Andrew, Dudley, 77
Andreyor, Yvette, 26
Andriot, Josette, 26
Anémic Cinéma, 64
Angèle, 84, 95
Angelo, Jean, 58
Anges du péché, Les, 115–116
Angoissante aventure, L', 39
Annabella, 74, 76, 90, 99, 102
Anna Christie, 72
Anna Karenina, 137
Année dernière à Marienbad, L', 184–185, 207, 208, 277
Anouilh, Jean, 136
A nos amours, 275–276, 278
A nous la liberté, 75, 83, 190
A nous les petites anglaises, 249
Antoine, André, 39, 41, 51
Antoine et Antoinette, 131
Antoine et Colette, 179
Antonioni, Michelangelo, 176
Apollinaire, Guillaume, 4
Après le bal, 11
A propos de Nice, 78, 79
Ardent, Fanny, 272
Argent, L' (1929), 60–61, 64, 66
Argent, L' (1983), 278–279

Argent de poche, L', 255
Arlésienne, L', 39
Arletty, 85, 102, 113, 114, 125
Arme à gauche, L', 231
Armée des ombres, L', 238
Arnaudy, 94
Arnoul, Françoise, 166
Arnoux, Alexandre, 98
Arrivée d'un train à la Ciotat, 9, 200
Arrivistes, Les, 127
Arroseur arrosé, L', 9
Artaud, Antonin, 64, 65, 118
Arthur Honegger, 162
Ascenseur pour l'échafaud, L', 166, 174
As des as, L', 270, 271, 278
Assassinat du Duc de Guise, L', 21, 22, 31, 32
Assassinat du Père Noël, L', 111
Assassin habite au 21, L', 119
Assassins d'eau douce, 142
Assassins de l'ordre, Les, 238
Assommoir, L', 22
Astronautes, Les, 213
Astruc, Alexandre, 148, 165, 173, 175, 195, 198
Atalante, L', 80–81, 83, 85
Atget, Eugène, 3
Atlantic City, 261
Atlantide, L', 40, 45, 48, 54, 55
Aubert, Louis, 40, 68, 90
Auberge rouge, L' (1923), 61
Auberge rouge, L' (1951), 152, 153
Aubervilliers, 142
Au coeur de l'Ile de France, 163
Au coeur de l'orage, 125
Au-delà des grilles, 128, 134–135, 136
Audiard, Michel, 271, 272
Audran, Stéphane, 226
Audry, Colette, 134
Au hasard, Balthazar, 217–218, 241, 259
Aumont, Jean-Pierre, 102
Au pays du Roi Lépreux, 55
Au pays noir, 14
Aurélia Steiner, 268
Aurenche, Jean, 102, 119, 128, 129, 133, 135, 147, 152, 154, 271, 272
Auric, Georges, 70, 115
Au royaume des cieux, 137
Au secours!, 62

Aussi longue absence, Une, 185
Autant-Lara, Claude, 4, 44, 45, 51, 58, 59, 60, 118–119, 120, 127, 128, 129, 132–134, 144, 146, 147, 152–153, 165, 167, 189, 214, 259
Authentique procès de Carl Emmanuel Jung, L', 214
Automne, L', 237
Avant le déluge, 149
Aventure c'est l'aventure, L', 232
Aventures d'Arsène Lupin, Les, 148, 152
Aveu, L', 221, 224–225
Aymé, Jean, 37
Aznavour, Charles, 178

Baby-sitter, La, 238
Baie des anges, La, 211
Baisers volés, 200
Balance, La, 273
Balfour, Betty, 60
Balin, Mireille, 88, 114
Ballet méchanique, Le, 64
Bande à part, 201, 203
Bandéra, La, 90, 99
Bandits en noir, Les, 25
Barbarella, 195
Barbe bleue, 11
Barberis, René, 71
Barberousse, 46
Bardèche, Maurice, 86
Bardot, Brigitte, 166, 172, 174, 188, 196, 201
Barocco, 251–252
Barque sortant du port, 3, 9
Barrabas, 38
Barrage contre le Pacifique, 148, 188
Barrault, Jean-Louis, 100, 113, 188
Barrymore, Lionel, 72
Barsacq, André, 60
Barsacq, Léon, 138, 158
Bas-fonds, Les, 105
Bataille des dix millions, La, 221
Bataille du rail, La, 126, 128, 134, 135, 144, 154
Battant, Le, 271
Battle of Algiers, 225
Battleship Potemkin, The, 254
Baur, Harry, 100
Bayard, Hippolyte, 7

Baye, Nathalie, 273
Baxter, Véra Baxter, 267
Bazin, André, 167, 189
Beau mariage, Le, 279
Beau-père, 249
Beau Serge, Le, 176
Beauté du diable, La, 138, 158
Bébé, 27
Beccarie, Claudine, 248
Becker, Jacques, 27, 103, 104, 120,
  122–123, 127, 128, 129, 131–132,
  134, 145, 146, 148, 151–152, 165,
  170, 189–190, 195
Bel âge, Le, 173
Bel ami, 127
Bell, Marie, 96
Belle de jour, 215, 243
Belle équipe, La, 90, 99
Belle et la bête, La, 70, 134, 143, 190
Belle fille comme moi, Une, 230
Belle Nivernaise, La, 61
Belles-de-nuit, 157, 158, 159, 277
Bellon, Yannick, 142
Belmondo, Jean-Paul, 166, 172, 179,
  180, 195, 202, 232, 270, 271
Benoît-Lévy, Jean, 43
Bercail, Le, 44, 49
Bergen, Candice, 212
Berio, Luciano, 254
Bernard, Raymond, 41, 126
Bernard, Tristan, 40
Bernard-Aubert, Claude, 166
Bernède, Arthur, 37, 38
Bernhardt, Kurt (Curtis), 88
Bernhardt, Sarah, 22, 46
Berry, Jules, 102, 104, 113
Berthomieu, André, 170
Berto, Juliet, 236, 262
Bertolucci, Bernardo, 276
Bertrand, Paul, 117
Bête, La, 246, 247
Bête humaine, La, 106–107
Beylie, Claude, 96
Biches, Les, 198, 226
Big Sleep, The, 203
Bijoutiers du clair de lune, Les, 166
Bilitis, 246
Biquefarre, 274
Black Jack, 137
Black Moon, 260–261
Blain, Gérard, 166, 176

Blanc et le noir, Le, 85, 91
Blanchar, Pierre, 100, 111
Blanche, 234
Blavette, 95
Bled, Le, 58
Blé en herbe, Le, 152
Blier, Bertrand, 249
Bloch, Noé, 52
Blue Angel, The, 210
Bluwal, Marcel, 171
Bob le flambeur, 164–165, 172
Bogaert, Lucienne, 116
Bogarde, Dirk, 259
Bogart, Humphrey, 179, 203
Boisson, Christine, 275
Bonaparte et la révolution, 64
Bon dieu sans confession, Le, 152
Bonheur, Le, 197, 262
Bonne année, La, 232
Bonne chance, 92
Bonne femmes, Les, 177
Borde, Raymond, 144
Borowczyk, Walerian, 213–214,
  233–234, 244, 246–247
Bosetti, Roméo, 23, 31
Bost, Pierre, 119, 128, 129, 133, 135,
  147, 152, 154
Boucher, Le, 226, 227
Bouclette, 44
Boudu sauvé des eaux, 81, 83, 84
Bouise, Jean, 224
Boulangère de Monceau, La, 199,
  228
Boule de suif, 126
Bouquet, Michel, 226, 227
Bourgoin, Jean, 190
Bourvil, 153, 239
Bout-de-zan, 38
Bout-de-zan, 27
Brahmane et le papillon, Le, 11
Brakhage, Stan, 2, 12
Branice, Ligia, 234
Brasier ardent, Le, 52
Brasillach, Robert, 86
Brassens, Georges, 183
Brasseur, Pierre, 101, 114, 182
Brault, Michel, 187
Braunberger, Pierre, 81
Bräutigam, die Komödiantin und der
  Zuhalter, Der, 214
Break the News, 76

Bresson, Robert, 4, 46, 92, 112, 115–117, 139–140, 144, 148, 160, 161–162, 166, 167, 170, 172, 174, 190, 191–192, 193, 210, 215, 217–218, 230, 240–241, 244, 259, 261, 278–279
Brialy, Jean-Claude, 166, 176, 180
Bride sur le cou, La, 172
British Sounds, 222
Bronson, Charles, 238
Brown, Clarence, 72
Brownlow, Kevin, 63, 64
Brumes d'automne, 53
Brunius, Jacques, 104
Buffet froid, 249
Buñuel, Luis, 51, 65, 69, 215, 240, 243–244, 259
Burch, Noël, 60, 66
Burel, Léonce-Henry, 46, 62, 116, 140, 162

Cabinet of Doctor Caligari, The, 89
Calcutta, 223
Calef, Henri, 126
Calmettes, André, 21, 31, 34
Camion, Le, 267–268
Camisards, Les, 233
Cammage, Maurice, 89
Camus, Marcel, 166
Canonge, Maurice de, 89, 170
Canudo, Riciotto, 41
Capellani, Albert, 22, 31, 34, 39
Capitaine Fracasse, Le, 111
Caporal épinglé, Le, 189
Capra, Frank, 233
Carabiniers, Les, 200–201
Carambolages, 171
Carette, Julien, 106, 108
Carl, Renée, 28
Carmen, 55
Carmoy, Guy de, 100
Carnaval des vérités, Le, 44
Carné, Marcel, 1, 4, 65, 86, 87, 90, 91, 97, 98, 100–103, 104, 107, 112–114, 117, 120, 124, 127, 128, 129, 130, 135–136, 159–160, 170, 183, 211, 214, 238, 255
Carnet de bal, Un, 92, 99, 100
Carol, Martine, 156
Caron, Leslie, 262

Caron, Pierre, 89
Carrière, Jean-Claude, 216
Carrière de Suzanne, La, 199, 228
Carrosse d'or, Le, 156
Cartier-Bresson, Henri, 104
Casanova, 53
Casarès, Maria, 116, 143
Casque d'or, 151, 152
Castanier, Jean, 103, 104
Catelain, Jaque, 44, 45, 59, 60
Cavalcanti, Alberto, 51, 60, 65
Cavalier, Alain, 170
Cayatte, André, 88, 127, 128, 146, 149, 193
Cayrol, Jean, 164, 206, 208, 210, 277
Cazeneuve, Maurice, 171
Cecchi d'Amico, Suso, 134
Cela s'appelle l'aurore, 215
Céline et Julie vont en bateau, 236, 262
Cendrars, Blaise, 43
Cendrillon, 11
Cercle rouge, Le, 238
Cerval, Claude, 176
César, 94
César et Rosalie, 231
Cet obscur objet du désir, 259
Cette nuit-là, 171
Ceux de chez nous, 91
CGT en mai, La, 221
Chabrol, Claude, 169, 172, 175, 176–177, 178, 181, 197–198, 219, 220, 225, 226–227, 228, 244, 257–258, 261, 271–272
Chagrin et la pitié, Le, 223–224
Chambre en ville, Une, 270, 277–278
Chambre verte, La, 255
Champreux, Jacques, 239
Chant du styrène, Le, 164
Chapeau de paille d'Italie, Un, 56–57, 59, 64
Chaplin, Charles, 35, 43, 58, 160, 265
Chardans de Baragan, Les, 127
Charleston, 58, 64
Charlotte et son Jules, 166
Charme discret de la bourgeoisie, Le, 243
Charmes de l'existence, Les, 142
Charpin, 72–73, 94, 99
Charrette fantôme, La, 98
Charron, Le, 124

Chartres, 58
Château de verre, Le, 135
Chaudronnier, Le, 142
Cheat, The, 35, 41, 44
Chemin d'Ernoa, Le, 42
Cheminot, Le, 221
Chenal, Pierre, 89
Cheval d'orgueil, Le, 258
Chevalier, Maurice, 98, 138
Chevrier, Jean, 123
Chien andalou, Un, 1, 65, 69, 243
Chienne, La, 82, 85
Chiens perdus sans colliers, 129
Chinoise, La, 204
Choix des armes, Le, 249
Choses de la vie, Les, 231
Chotard et cie, 83
Chrétien, Henri, 118
Christian-Jaque, 89, 111, 122, 126,
    156
Christie, Julie, 199
Chronik der Anna Magdalena Bach,
    214
Chronique d'un été, 187
Chute de la maison Usher, La, 61
Ciboulette, 118
Cicatrice intérieure, La, 274
Ciel est à vous, Le, 121–122, 123
Cigalon, 94
Citizen Kane, 183
Civilisation, 35
Clair, René, 1, 51, 55, 56–57, 58, 64,
    65, 66, 73, 74–76, 78, 83, 84, 85,
    87, 100, 101, 111, 127, 128,
    137–138, 144, 145, 157–158, 170,
    189, 190, 191, 214, 255, 277,
    278
Clair de femme, 254
Classe tous risques, 231
Clément, René, 4, 126, 127, 128, 129,
    134–135, 136, 146, 148, 153–154,
    167, 188, 193, 214, 238, 271
Cléo et cinq à sept, 174, 196
Cléry, Corinne, 246
Climats, 171
Cloërec, René, 119
Cloquet, Ghislain, 211
Clouzot, Henri-Georges, 4, 119–120,
    124, 125, 127, 128, 129, 130–131,
    132, 137, 146, 148, 149–150, 162,
    167, 182, 214–215, 257

Cocteau, Jean, 65, 70, 114–115, 117,
    124, 129, 134, 142–144, 167, 190,
    193, 206
Coeur fidèle, 61
Cohl, Emile, 20, 31
Colette, 89
Collectionneuse, La, 199, 228
Collier de la reine, Le, 77
Colombier, Pierre, 89
Colpi, Henri, 185
Comité d'action, 221
Comment ça va?, 265
Communion solennelle, La, 250
Compartiment tueurs, 224
Comte de Monte-Cristo, Le, 189
Concentration, La, 274
Condamné à mort s'est échappé, Un,
    161–162
Constantine, Eddie, 202
Construire un feu, 118
Contes immoraux, 234, 247
Continsouza, Pierre Victor, 13, 24
Cooper, Gary, 210
Coppola, Francis Ford, 63
Coquille et le clergyman, La, 64
Corbeau, Le, 119–120, 124, 130,
    131
Corneau, Alain, 249–250, 268, 272
Corrupteurs, Les, 110
Costa-Gavras, 221, 224–225, 244,
    254, 269
Coup de grâce, Le, 208
Coup de torchon, 250
Coup de berger, Le, 166, 181
Course du lièvre à travers les champs,
    La, 238
Courtade, Francis, 5
Cousin Cousine, 249
Cousins, Les, 176, 177
Cousteau, Jacques-Yves, 166, 223, 230
Coutard, Raoul, 178, 179, 180, 187,
    201, 202, 210, 276
Crainquebille, 40, 54, 59
Créatures, Les, 197, 262
Crenna, Richard, 239
Cresté, René, 37
Crime de Monsieur Lange, Le, 90,
    103, 104, 105, 107
Cuba si!, 185–186
Cuny, Alain, 113
Cyrano et d'Artagnan, 45

Dabadie, Jean-Loup, 231, 271
Daguerre, Mandé, 7
Daguerréotypes, 262
D'Alcy, Jehanne, 11
Dali, Salvador, 65, 70
Dalio, Marcel, 105, 108
Dalla nube alla resistenza, 265
Dallesandro, Joe, 260, 262
Dames du Bois de Boulogne, Les, 115, 116, 117, 210, 261
Daquin, Louis, 73, 90, 120, 122, 123, 124, 126–127, 128, 146
Darrieux, Danielle, 111, 133, 152, 260, 278
Dary, René, 27
Dassin, Jules, 152, 165
Dasté, Jean, 80
Dauphin, Claude, 151
David Golder, 77
Davis, Miles, 166
Davy, Jean-François, 247–248
Déa, Marie, 113
Death Watch, 251
De Broca, Philippe, 170
Decaë, Henri, 142, 166, 172, 174, 176, 177, 178, 188, 196
De Chomon, Segundo, 20
Decoin, Henri, 111, 119
Dédée d'Anvers, 129
Deed, André, 21, 23
Déesse, La, 208
Déjeuner sur l'herbe, Le, 189, 197
Delair, Suzy, 119
Delamare, Lise, 106
Delannoy, Jean, 112, 114–115, 122, 124, 127, 128, 129, 145, 148, 165, 167, 193
Delerue, Georges, 196
Delluc, Louis, 32, 38, 41–42, 43, 50, 51, 59, 60
Delon, Alain, 188, 195, 238, 239, 271
Delorme, Danièle, 262
De Mayerling à Sarajevo, 89
Demazis, Orane, 73, 95, 96
Demenÿ, Georges, 8
De Mille, Cecil B., 35
Demoiselles de Rochefort, Les, 211
Demy, Jacques, 174, 175, 208, 210–211, 212, 213, 219, 233, 262, 270, 277–278

Deneuve, Catherine, 195, 211, 215, 231, 250
Denner, Charles, 255
Depardieu, Gérard, 263, 267
Deray, Jacques, 170
Dermit, Edouard, 190
Dernier atout, Le, 122
Dernier des six, Le, 119
Dernières vacances, Les, 141, 189
Dernier métro, Le, 256
Dernier milliardaire, Le, 76
Descente dans les mines de Fumay, 25
Description d'un combat, 185–186
Désiré, 91
Détective Dervieux, 27
Détruire dit-elle, 237, 269
Deutelbaum, Marshall, 10
Deux anglaises et le continent, Les, 231
Deux hommes dans Manhattan, 164, 172
Deuxième souffle, Le, 195
Deux ou trois choses que je sais d'elle, 203–204
Deux timides, Les, 57
Dévaliseurs de banque, Les, 25
Deville, Michel, 170, 171
Dewaere, Patrick, 250
Diable au coeur, Le, 60
Diable au corps, Le, 133–134, 144
Diable probablement, Le, 259
Diaboliques, Les, 150, 257
Diament-Berger, Henri, 170
Dickson, W. K. L., 8
Dietrich, Marlene, 55, 98, 136
Dieu a besoin des hommes, 129
Dieudonné, Albert, 63
Digua sul Pacifico, La, 148, 188
Dimanche à la campagne, Un, 272
Dimanche à Pekin, 164
Diptyque, 214
Disney, Walt, 20, 203
Dites-lui que je l'aime, 253
Divine, 89
Dixième symphone, La, 46, 48
Docteur Jekyll et les femmes, 246
Documenteur, 262, 263
Domicile conjugal, 231, 255
Doniol-Valcroze, Jacques, 167, 175
Don Juan et Faust, 45
Dorléac, Françoise, 211

Dossier noir, Le, 149
Douce, 118–119
Douchet, Jean, 198
Doulos, Le, 195
Douy, Max, 119
Drach, Michel, 170, 178
Drame au Château d'Acre, Un, 46
Drame chez les fantoches, Un, 20
Drame de Shanghai, Le, 88
Dreigroschenoper, Die, 82
Dreyer, Carl Theodor, 53–54, 62, 175, 181
Drôle de drame, 100, 117
Dubost, Paulette, 108
Duchamp, Marcel, 64
Du côté de la côte, 165
Duel, Le, 119
Duelle, 262
Dulac, Germaine, 4, 43, 59, 64–65
Dullin, Charles, 58
Du mouron chez les petits oiseaux, 214
Dunawaye, Faye, 238
Durand, Jean, 34
Duras, Marguerite, 5, 66, 183, 185, 208, 210, 237, 244, 266–268, 269, 274, 277
Du rififi chez les hommes, 152, 165
Dutronc, Jacques, 265
Duvivier, Julien, 40, 76, 77, 82, 85, 86, 89, 90, 92, 98–100, 101, 104, 107, 111, 127, 128, 137, 159, 160, 272
Dzieje Grzechu, 246

Eastman, George, 7, 24
Ecoute voir, 250
Eden et après, L', 234–235
Edgren, Gustav, 69
Edison, Thomas, 7, 11, 24
Edouard et Caroline, 132
Education sentimentale, L', 173
Eisler, Hanns, 164
El Dorado, 45
Elena et les hommes, 157
Emak Bakia, 64
Emmanuelle, 245–246
Empreintes, Les, 25
En cas de malheur, 189
Enfance nue, L', 225

Enfant de l'amour, L', 69
Enfant de Paris, L', 29
Enfant sauvage, L', 230, 255
Enfants du paradis, Les, 113–114, 135
Enfants du placard, Les, 250
Enfant secret, L', 274–275
Enfants gâtés, Des, 251
Enfants terribles, Les, 142–143, 206
En passant par la Lorraine, 142, 163
En rachâchant, 274
En rade, 65
Entr'acte, 56, 64, 78
Epstein, Jean, 43, 50, 52, 59, 61–62, 66, 69, 142
Equipage, L', 88
Ermoliev, Joseph, 39
Escamotage d'une dame chez Robert Houdin, 11
Esclave blanche, L', 88
Esmeralda, La, 15
Espions, Les, 150, 182
Espoir, L', 80, 91
Etaix, Pierre, 174, 175, 216–217
Etat de siège, 225
Et dieu créa la femme, 166
Eté, L', 237
Eternal retour, L', 114–115, 124, 129
Et mourir de plaisir, 172
Etincelle, L' (1918), 43
Etincelle, L' (1984), 271
Etoile de mer, L', 64
Etrange Madame X, L', 137
Etrange Monsieur Victor, L', 88
Eustache, Jean, 225
Evein, Bernard, 211
Evénément le plus important depuis que l'homme a marché sur la lune, L', 233, 262
Exhibition, 247–248
Exploits d'Elaine, Les, 24, 35
Exploits of Elaine, The, 35

Fabian, Françoise, 228
Fahrenheit 451, 199
Faisons un rêve, 91
Fait-divers, 59, 118
Faithfull, Marianne, 203
Falbalas, 122
Falconetti, Renée, 53
Fanny, 72–73, 93, 94

Fantasmagorie, 20
Fantômas, 21, 27–29, 33
Fantômas contre Fantômas, 28
Fantôme de la liberté, Le, 243–244
Fantômes du chapelier, Les, 271–272
Faraldo, Claude, 225
Farrebique, 124, 141–142, 162, 274
Fassbinder, Rainer Werner, 276
Faure, Renée, 115
Faute de l'abbé Mouret, La, 239
Faute d'orthographe, La, 40
Faux magistrat, Le, 28
Faux monnayeurs, Les, 25
Félins, Les, 214
Femme coquette, Une, 166
Femme d'à côté, La, 256–257
Femme de l'aviateur, La, 261, 279
Femme de nulle part, La, 42
Femme disparaît, Une, 98
Femme douce, Une, 240, 241
Femme du boulanger, La, 96
Femme du gange, La, 237, 266
Femme d'une nuit, La, 69
Femme est une femme, Une, 180
Femme infidèle, La, 226, 227
Femme mariée, Une, 201–202, 203
Femme spectacle, La, 212
Féraudy, Maurice de, 40
Feret, René, 250
Fernand, 250
Fernandel, 85, 89, 94, 103, 111, 112, 152, 160
Fescourt, Henri, 20, 31, 32, 34, 39, 52, 69
Fête à Henriette, La, 160
Fête espagnole, La, 42
Fêtes galantes, Les, 214
Feu follet, Le, 195–196, 229
Feuillade, Louis, 3, 5, 21, 23, 26–29, 31, 32, 33, 34, 35, 36–38, 39, 41, 51, 205, 206
Feuillère, Edwige, 152
Feu Mathias Pascal, 60
Feyder, Jacques, 40–41, 45, 48, 49, 54–55, 56, 57, 58, 59, 66, 71–72, 76, 84, 85, 87, 96–98, 99, 100, 101, 111
Fièvre monte à El Pao, La, 215
Fièvres, 42
Fille de l'eau, La, 57
Fille du puisatier, La, 96, 111–112, 124

Fille et des fusils, Une, 212
Film comme les autres, Un, 222
Film Esthétique, Le, 27
Fils de l'eau, Les, 186
Fin du jour, La, 99–100
Fin du monde, La, 69
Finis terrae, 62, 69
Finney, Albert, 262
Flamant, Georges, 82
Flammes sur l'Adriatique, 195
Fleur de l'âge, La, 136
Flic, Un, 239
Flins 68–69, 221
Florey, Robert, 91
Foire aux cancres, La, 127
Folie du Docteur Tube, La, 46
Fonda, Jane, 195, 223
Fond de l'air est rouge, Le, 254, 269, 273
Foolish Wives, 57, 79
Forces occultes, 110, 119
Forest, Jean, 40, 54
Forfaiture, 35
Fortini-Cani, 265
Fort Saganne, 272
Foster, Jodie, 272
Fradetal, Marcel, 163, 183, 206
Français si vous saviez, 224
France société anonyme, 249
France tour détour deux enfants, 265
Francen, Victor, 100
Francis, Eve, 42, 43, 45
François Mauriac, 162
Franju, Georges, 5, 33, 142, 163, 167, 171, 182–183, 205–206, 219, 239–240
French Cancan, 156–157
Frères Bouquinquant, Les, 126
Frères Boutdebois, Les, 20
Frères corses, Les, 39
Fresnay, Pierre, 73, 105, 119, 125
Fresson, Bernard, 224
Fric-Frac, 118
Fuller, Sam, 175, 202, 203
Fumée noire, 42
Funès, Louis de, 194

Gabin, Jean, 27, 88, 89, 90, 91, 100, 101, 102–103, 105, 106, 111, 129, 134, 136, 149, 153, 194, 238, 260

Gabrio, Gabriel, 96
Gaillard, Marius-François, 45
Gai savoir, Le, 222, 251
Galerie des monstres, La, 59
Gance, Abel, 1, 35, 41, 42, 43, 45–49,
    50, 51, 56, 59, 60, 61, 62–64, 65,
    66, 69, 85, 111, 140
Ganda, Oumarou, 186
Garbo, Greta, 55
Garçon, 271
Garde à vue, 253–254, 272
Gardiens de phare, 58
Garrel, Maurice, 274
Garrel, Philippe, 274–275
Gasnier, Louis, 35, 72, 94
Gauguin, 142
Gaumont, Léon, 3, 11, 13, 15–16, 17,
    19, 20, 23, 26–29, 30, 31, 32, 33,
    35, 40, 44, 45, 49, 50, 67
Gavotte, 214
Gaz mortels, Les, 46
Gégauff, Paul, 170, 177, 188, 226, 257
Gélin, Daniel, 132
Genou de Claire, Le, 228
Gens du voyage, Les, 87, 98
Germinal (1913), 22
Germinal (1962), 149
Gervaise, 148, 154
Ghost Goes West, The, 76
Giehse, Thérèse, 260
Gielgud, John, 259
Giraudoux, Jean, 115
Glace à trois faces, La, 61
Glenn, Pierre-William, 250
Glissements progressifs du plaisir, 235
Gloria, 259
Glory, Mary, 61
Godard, Jean-Luc, 1, 165–166, 167,
    169, 170, 175, 176, 178, 179–181,
    193, 198, 200–205, 219, 220,
    221–223, 241, 244, 251, 252,
    264–265, 276–277, 278, 280
Godeluraux, Les, 177
Goëmans, 142
Golden Coach, The, 156, 157, 196
Golem, Le, 98
Golgotha, 98, 99
Gorin, Jean-Pierre, 222–223
Goto l'île d'amour, 214, 234
Goupi-Mains-Rouges, 122
Gran Casino, 70

Grandais, Suzanne, 38
Grand amour, Le, 217
Grand amour de Beethoven, Un, 48
Grand illusion, La, 89, 105–106, 189
Grandes manoeuvres, Les, 158, 159
Grand jeu, Le, 84, 96–97, 99
Grand Méliès, Le, 163
Grands moments, Les, 212
Granger, Gilles, 170
Granier-Deferre, Pierre, 170
Great Waltz, The, 98
Greed, 49
Gregor, Nora, 108
Gréhan, René, 23
Grémillon, Jean, 51, 57, 58, 65, 73,
    77–78, 85, 87–88, 90, 120–122,
    123, 124, 127, 128, 135, 136–137,
    142, 162–163
Grève, La, 14
Gribiche, 54
Griffe, Maurice, 128
Griffith, D. W., 3, 23, 48, 59
Gruault, Jean, 260, 277
Guernica, 142, 185
Guerre est finie, La, 207, 224
Guet-apens, Le, 25
Gueule d'amour, 87
Gueule ouverte, La, 225
Gug, Madeleine, 119
Guitry, Lucien, 92
Guitry, Sacha, 38, 85, 91–93, 111,
    125, 279
Gunning, Tom, 18
Guy, Alice, 15, 19, 23, 25, 43, 67

Hamilton, David, 246
Hammond, Paul, 3
Hanoun, Marcel, 214, 237, 265, 274
Happiness, 221
Harald, Mary, 38
Harris, André, 223–224
Haute Lisse, 163
Hawks, Howard, 176
Hayakawa, Sessue, 35, 42
Heilbronn, Laurent, 14
Helm, Brigitte, 61
Henry, Pierre, 41
Héroines du mal, Les, 246
Herrand, Marcel, 114
Herrmann, Bernard, 199

Hervil, René, 44
Hessling, Catherine, 57, 58
Heureux anniversaire, 175
Heuzé, André, 23
Higgins, Johnny, 58
Hiroshima mon amour, 2, 61,
    183–184, 185, 207
His Glorious Night, 72
Histoire d'Adèle H, L', 254–255
Histoire de Paul, 250
Histoire d'O, 245–246, 249
Histoire d'un crime, L', 14, 18
Histoire simple, Une, 258
Hitchcock, Alfred, 176, 177, 198, 199,
    226, 251, 252, 253, 273
Hitler connais pas, 249
Hiver, L', 237
Holt, Jany, 115
Homme à la pipe, L', 162
Homme à la tête de caoutchouc, L',
    11
Homme Atlantique, L', 268, 269
Homme aux gants blancs, L', 22
Homme de trop, Un, 224
Homme du jour, L', 98
Homme du large, L', 44
Homme et une femme, Un, 209, 212,
    232
Homme orchestre, L', 11
Homme qui aimait les femmes, L', 255
Homme qui ment, L', 209–210, 219
Homme qui me plaît, L', 232
Hommes de la baleine, Les, 187
Honegger, Arthur, 93
Horloger de Saint Paul, L', 250
Hôtel de la plage, L', 249
Hôtel des Amériques, L', 252
Hôtel des Invalides, 163, 206, 239
Hôtel du nord, 91, 102, 111
Hubert, Roger, 115
Hugo, Jean, 53
Hugon, André, 77
Huillet, Danielle, 214, 265–266, 274
Huitième jour, Le, 214
Humain trop humain, 223
Huppert, Isabelle, 263, 276
Hurdes, Les, 65, 70

Icart, Roger, 48, 49
Ici et ailleurs, 264

Ignace, 89
Illery, Pola, 74, 76
Ils étaient neuf célibataires, 92
Image, L', 54
Immortelle, L', 208–209, 210
Ince, Thomas, 35, 43
Inconnus dans la maison, Les, 119
Inconnus de la terre, Les, 187
India Song, 266, 267
Inhumaine, L', 60
Innocents aux mains sales, Les, 257
Inondation, L', 42, 60
Intérieur d'un couvent, L', 246
Intolerance, 35
Ironie du destin, L', 53
Ivens, Joris, 207

J'accuse (1918), 47, 48
Jacquot, Benoît, 250
Jade, Claude, 200, 256
Jaeckin, Just, 245–246, 247, 249
Jancsó, Miklos, 246
Janssen, Jules, 7, 67
Jarre, Maurice, 182, 183
Jasset, Victorin, 5, 20, 21, 25–26, 27,
    31, 32, 34, 35
Jaubert, Maurice, 100, 255
Jaune le soleil, 237
Jazz Singer, The, 67
Jean-Jacques, 162
Jeanne, René, 41
Jeanson, Henri, 99–100, 102, 137
Jenny, 100
Jéricho, 126
Jessua, Alain, 213
Je t'aime, je t'aime, 207, 277
Jetée, La, 185
Jeu avec le feu, Le, 235, 246
Jeu de massacre, 213
Jeunes filles en détresse, 88
Jeunes loups, Les, 214
Jeux interdits, 153–154
Jeux sont faits, Les, 129
Joannon, Léo, 89
Jocelyn, 38
Jofroi, 85, 95
Joli mai, Le, 187, 219
Joly, Henri, 13
Joubé, Romuald, 47
Joueur, Le, 123

Jourdan, Catherine, 235
Jour de fête, 139, 145, 160, 161, 190
Jour et l'heure, Le, 214
Journal d'un curé de campagne, 117, 139–140, 145, 161, 162, 218
Journal d'une femme de chambre, Le, 215
Journal d'une femme en blanc, 133, 214
Journées entières dans les arbres, Des, 267
Jour se lève, Le, 4, 90, 102–103, 111, 112, 129, 130, 149, 170
Jouvet, Louis, 89, 94, 97, 100, 102, 105, 111, 130
Joyeux, Odette, 118, 132
Joyeux microbes, Les, 20
Judex (1917), 37, 38, 63
Judex (1963), 205–206, 239
Juge et l'assassin, Le, 250
Jules et Jim, 178–179, 199, 231
Juliette ou la clef des songes, 159
Juste avant la nuit, 226, 227
Justice est faite, 149
Juve contre Fantômas, 28

Kalfon, Jean-Pierre, 235
Kamenka, Alexandre, 39, 52, 53
Kameradschaft, 77
Kane, Robert, 71
Karina, Anna, 180, 181, 198, 202, 203, 262
Kast, Pierre, 143, 173
Kaufman, Boris, 78
Kazan, Elia, 78
Kean, 52
Keaton, Buster, 118
Kelly, Gene, 211
Kermesse héroique, La, 87, 96, 97–98
Kirsanoff, Dimitri, 51, 53
Kiss, The, 55, 72
Klein, William, 207
Knave of Hearts, 148, 154
Knight Without Armour, 55, 98
Komedie om Geld, 89
Korda, Alexander, 72, 76, 98, 137
Kosma, Joseph, 113
Krasna, Michael, 273
Krasna, Sandor, 273
Krauss, Henry, 62

Krauss, Werner, 58
Kristel, Sylvia, 246
Kruger, Jules, 60–61, 62
Kuhn, Thomas, 2–4

Labourdette, Elina, 116
Labourier, Dominique, 236
Lacassin, Francis, 15, 22, 27, 31
Lacombe, Georges, 65, 119
Lacombe Lucien, 229–230
Lady Oscar, 262
Lafont, Bernadette, 166, 231
Lagrange, M., 67
Lai, Francis, 212
Lamorisse, Albert, 168
Lamprecht, Gerhard, 123
Lancaster, Burt, 261
Lancelot du lac, 241
Landru, 197
Lang, Fritz, 77, 175, 182, 201, 239, 252
Lang, Michel, 249, 271
Langlois, Henri, 59, 63, 110, 167, 192, 220
Lapointe, Bob, 178
Laroche, Pierre, 112, 120
Laudenbach, Roland, 165
Laura, les ombres de l'été, 246
Laurent, Jacqueline, 102
Lauste, Eugène, 8
Lautner, Georges, 170
Laydu, Claude, 140
Léaud, Jean-Pierre, 178, 200, 203, 236, 256
Le Bargy, 21
Leblanc, Georgette, 60
Le Chanois, Jean-Paul, 125
Leclerc, Ginette, 96
Leçons d'histoire, 237
Lecoq, Jean, 93
Ledoux, Fernand, 106
Leenhardt, Roger, 140–141, 142, 162, 175, 189, 201
Lefèbvre, Louis, 80
Lefèvre, René, 74
Léger, Fernand, 60, 64
Legrand, Michel, 211
Lehmann, Maurice, 118
Lekain, Tony, 77

Lelouch, Claude, 175, 207, 209, 213,
    215, 219, 224, 232, 258, 269
Lemmon, Jack, 254
Léonce, 29
Léon Morin, prêtre, 172
Léotard, Philippe, 273
Leprince, Louis, 8
Le Somptier, René, 39
Leterrier, François, 162
Lettre à Jane, 223
Lettre de Sibérie, 164
Lettres d'amour, 118
Leubas, Louis, 37
Levesque, Marcel, 36, 37
Le Vigan, Robert, 113
L'Herbier, Marcel, 35, 41, 42, 43–45,
    49, 50, 51, 52, 56, 59–61, 65, 66,
    67, 69, 85, 87, 89, 90, 110, 111,
    118, 153
Liaisons dangereuses, Les, 172
Liberté, la nuit, 275
Ligne de démarcation, La, 198
Ligne de mire, La, 170
Limur, Jean de, 89
Linder, Max, 20, 22–24, 25, 34, 62
Lions Love, 233
Litvak, Anatole, 88, 89
Loi du nord, La, 98
Loin du Vietnam, 207, 212, 221
Lola, 174, 210–211, 212
Lola Montès, 156, 210
Longue marche, La, 195, 198
Lorenzi, Stellio, 171
Lost Horizons, 232
Lotar, Eli, 142
Loulou, 263
Lourdes et ses miracles, 162
Luchini, Fabrice, 280
Lucrèce Borgia, 48
Lulu, 246
Lumière, Antoine, 9
Lumière, Auguste, 10
Lumière, Louis, 3, 4, 8–10, 11, 12, 13,
    16, 17, 18, 32, 67, 200
Lumière d'été, 120–122
Luttes en Italie, 222
Lynn, Emmy, 46

Macao, l'enfer du jeu, 114
Machorka-Muff, 214

Madame Bovary, 83–84
Madame de . . ., 155
Made in USA, 203
Mademoiselle Docteur, 88
Mado, 258
Maison aux images, La, 163
Maison de la flèche, La, 69
Maison des bois, La, 225
Maison sous les arbres, La, 238
Maîtres fous, Les, 186
Maldone, 58
Malgovert, 162
Malle, Louis, 166, 172, 173–174, 175,
    178, 195–196, 200, 219, 223, 225,
    229–230, 244, 249, 260–261, 269
Mallet-Stevens, Robert, 60
Malraux, André, 80, 91
Manèges, 129
Manès, Gina, 55
Mann, Claude, 211
Man of Iron, 276
Manon, 130, 131, 188, 215
Manuel, Roland, 78
Ma nuit chez Maud, 228, 229, 279
Marais, Jean, 115, 143, 190, 260
Marchal, Arlette, 54
Marchand, Corinne, 196
Marchand, Léopold, 72, 94
Marchand de plaisir, Le, 59
Marey, Etienne, 7–8
Marèze, Janie, 82
Margaritis, Gilles, 81
Marge, La, 246
Marguerite de la nuit, 147, 153
Marie Chapdelaine, 77, 99
Mariage, 258
Mariage de Chiffon, Le, 118
Marie Chantal contre le Docteur Kah,
    198
Marie du port, La, 136
Mariée était en noir, La, 199–200
Marie pour mémoire, 274
Marius, 72–73, 94, 211
Marker, Chris, 146, 163, 164, 169,
    185–186, 187, 196, 207–208, 213,
    219, 221, 244, 254, 268, 273–274
Marnie, 199
Marquise d'O, La, 261
Marquitta, 58
Marret, Mario, 221
Marseillaise, La, 86, 106, 107, 122

Masculin féminin, 202–203
Maté, Rudolf, 53
Mater dolorosa (1917), 46
Mater dolorosa (1932), 69
Mathé, Edouard, 36
Maudits, Les, 134, 135
Mauriac, Claude, 183
Mauriac, François, 183
Mauvaises herbes, 10
Mauvaises rencontres, Les, 165
Mauvais fils, Un, 258
Max, Edouard de, 46
Max et les ferrailleurs, 231
Max pédicure, 23
Mayerling, 88
Mayniel, Juliette, 176
Medvedkine, Alexander, 221
Meerson, Lazare, 60, 74, 75, 85,
    96–97
Mégé, Clément, 23
Meilleur façon de marcher, La, 253
Méliès, Gaston, 11
Méliès, Georges, 3, 10–13, 14, 16, 17,
    18, 20, 30, 32, 46, 56
Meller, Raquel, 55
Mélomane, Le, 11, 18
Melville, Jean-Pierre, 92, 142–143,
    164–165, 172, 195, 219, 238–239,
    240, 244, 249
Menace, La, 249, 250
Ménegoz, Robert, 168
Ménilmontant, 53
Mépris, Le, 176, 201
Mercanton, Louis, 22, 38, 44
Mercer, David, 259
Merci Natercia, 173
Méril, Macha, 201
Merlusse, 94
Merry-Go-Round, 262
Merveilleuse visite, La, 238
Metropolis, 175, 182
Meurisse, Paul, 182, 238
Michel Strogoff, 53
Miéville, Anne-Marie, 264
Miller, Claude, 252–254, 268, 271,
    272–273
Million, Le, 74–75, 84, 137, 158, 278
Miquette et sa mère, 131
Misérables, Les, 22, 52
Misraki, Paul, 202
Missing, 254

Mistons, Les, 166, 177
Mitry, Jean, 32, 54, 82
Mizoguchi, Kenji, 265
Mocky, Jean-Pierre, 170, 171, 182
Model Shop, The, 233
Modot, Gaston, 74, 108
Moguy, Léonide, 170
Moi, Pierre Rivière, ayant égorgé ma
    mère, ma soeur et mon frère,
    263–264
Moïse et Aaron, 237
Moisson, Charles, 9
Moi un noir, 186
Molander, Gustav, 69
Molinaro, Edouard, 170
Monca, Georges, 23
Monde du silence, Le, 166, 223
Mon oncle, 175, 190–191, 216
Mon oncle d'Amérique, 260, 277
Mon père avait raison, 91
Monsieur et Madame Curie, 163
Monsieur Pinson, policier, 40
Monsieur Ripois, 148, 154, 188
Montagne infidèle, La, 61
Montand, Yves, 207, 212, 221, 223,
    224, 232, 250, 271
Monte-charge, Le, 171
Monte-Cristo, 38
Montparnasse 19, 152
Moreau, Jeanne, 166, 179, 196, 200,
    211, 215
Morgan, Michèle, 88, 98, 101, 111,
    158
Morin, Edgar, 187
Morris, Oswald, 154
Mortelle randonnée, 272–273
Mort en ce jardin, La, 215
Mort en direct, La, 251
Mort en fraude, 166
Morte saison des amours, La, 173
Mort qui tue, Le, 28
Mor Vran, 69
Mosjoukine, Ivan, 39, 52, 60
Mot de Cambronne, Le, 91
Mouchette, 218
Mundwiller, Jean-Paul, 62
Muriel, 164, 206–207, 219
Murs murs, 262, 263
Musica, La, 208
Musidora, 35, 36, 37
Muybridge, Eadweard, 7

My Dinner With André, 261
Mystère de la chambre jaune, Le, 69
Mystère Koumiko, Le, 207–208
Mystère Picasso, Le, 150–151
Mystères de New York, Les, 35, 36, 37

Nadi, Bhagat el, 266
Naissance du cinéma, La, 142
Naissance du jour, La, 262
Nalpas, Louis, 38, 42, 52
Nana, 57–58, 59, 64
Napierkowska, Stacia, 40, 43
Napoléon Bonaparte, 69
Napoléon vu par Abel Gance, 2, 60, 61, 62–64
Natan, Bernard, 68
Natan, Emile, 78
Nathalie Granger, 237
Natteau, Jacques, 133
Navarre, René, 28, 38
Navire nuit, Le, 268
Nicht versöhnt, 214
Nick Carter – Le Roi des détectives, 21, 25
Nièpce, Nicéphore, 7
Noailles, Vicomte de, 69–70
Noces rouges, Les, 257
Noël-Noël, 134
Nogent – Eldorado du dimanche, 65, 100
Nonguet, Lucien, 14, 23
Normandin, Ernest, 13
Noro, Line, 90
Noroît, 262
Notre-Dame de Paris (1911), 22
Notre-Dame de Paris (1956), 148
Nous les gosses, 123
Nous ne viellirons pas ensemble, 225
Nous sommes tous des assassins, 149
Nouveau testament, Le, 91
Nouveaux messieurs, Les, 55
Nouvelle mission de Judex, La, 38, 41
Novarro, Ramon, 96
Nuit américaine, La, 231, 255, 256
Nuit claire, La, 265
Nuit du carrefour, La, 82–83, 122
Nuit et brouillard, 164, 185, 202, 206
Nuit fantastique, La, 111, 112
Nuits de la pleine lune, Les, 279–280
Nuits rouges, 239

Numéro deux, 264
Nuytten, Bruno, 251, 252
Nykvist, Sven, 260

Occident, L', 69
Occupe-toi d'Amélie, 133
Octobre à Madrid, 214
Oeil du malin, L', 177
Oeuvre scientifique de Pasteur, L', 142
Ogier, Bulle, 235, 262
Ogier, Pascale, 279
Olivier, Paul, 56, 76
One plus one, 205, 221
On purge bébé, 81
On the Waterfront, 78
On vous parle, 208
Opéra Mouffe, 165
Opération béton, 165
Ophélia, 177
Ophuls, Marcel, 223, 224
Ophuls, Max, 77, 89, 146, 152, 155–156, 167, 210, 223
Or des mers, L', 69
Or du Cristobal, L', 122
Orgueilleux, Les, 149
Orphée, 117, 143–144, 145, 190
O saisons, ô châteaux, 165
Oser lutter, oser vaincre, 221
Ossessione, 103
Othon, 237
Oury, Gérard, 170, 270
Out one, 235
Out one spectre, 235–236

Pabst, G. W., 40, 77, 82, 88
Pagnol, Marcel, 72–73, 74, 84, 85, 87, 91, 83–96, 103, 111–112, 124, 211
Painlevé, Jean, 142
Panique, 128, 129, 137
Parade, 242–243
Parain, Brice, 181, 201
Parapluies de Cherbourg, Les, 208, 211
Parély, Mila, 108
Parents terribles, Les, 143
Parfum de la dame en noir, Le, 69
Paris 1900, 142
Paris brûle-t-il?, 214

Paris nous appartient, 175, 181–182, 198

Paris qui dort, 56

Paris vu par . . ., 198–199

Parlo, Dita, 80

Partie de campagne, 104–105

Partie d'écarté, 9

Partie de plaisir, Une, 257

Pasolini, Pier Paolo, 246

Passage du Rhin, Le, 149

Passager de la pluie, Le, 238

Passe ton bac d'abord, 263

Passion, 276, 278

Passion de Jeanne d'Arc, La, 53–54, 64, 175, 181

Pasteur (1922), 43, 61

Pasteur (1935), 85, 91, 92

Pathé, Charles, 3, 11, 13–15, 16, 17, 19, 22, 23, 24, 25, 26, 30, 31, 33, 47, 50, 248

Patrie, 126

Patrouille de choc, 166

Pattes blanches, 136

Pattes de mouche, 87

Paul, Robert William, 8, 10, 13

Paul Valéry, 162

Paulina s'en va, 251

Pauline à la plage, 279

Paviot, Paul, 168

Pays de cocagne, 217

Pays d'où je viens, Le, 160

Peau d'âne, 233

Peau douce, La, 199

Pension Mimosas, 97

Pépé-le-Moko, 88, 90, 99, 100, 129, 149

Perceval le Gallois, 261

Père tranquille, Le, 134

Périer, François, 154, 232

Perils of Pauline, The, 24, 35, 72

Périnal, Georges, 58, 70, 74

Perles de couronne, Les, 92

Perret, Léonce, 29

Petite Lise, La, 77, 85

Petite marchande d'allumettes, La, 58

Petit monde de Don Camillo, Le, 160

Petit soldat, Le, 180, 203

Petit théâtre de Jean Renoir, Le, 238

Phantasmes, 44

Philipe, Gérard, 133, 138, 152, 154, 158

Photogénie méchanique, La, 58

Pialat, Maurice, 225, 244, 263, 275–276, 278

Picabia, Francis, 56

Piccoli, Michel, 201, 232, 276

Pickpocket, 174, 191–192, 278

Pied Piper, The, 233

Piéral, 115

Pierre et Paul, 233

Pierrot le fou, 202

Pinel, Vincent, 10

Pisier, Marie-France, 256

Place de la République, 223

Plaisir, Le, 155

Play Time, 215–216, 219, 242

Pleins feux sur l'assassin, 182–183

Ploquin, Raoul, 87

Poil de carotte, 77

Point du jour, Le, 126–127, 128

Pointe Courte, La, 165

Poirier, Léon, 34, 38

Police Python 357, 249, 250

Pollet, Jean-Daniel, 170, 199

Pollock, Channing, 206

Pontcarral, colonel d'empire, 114, 124

Pont du nord, Le, 277

Pontecorvo, Gillo, 225

Porte des lilas, 158, 159

Portes de la nuit, Les, 128, 129, 135–136

Pot-Bouille, 160

Pouctal, Henri, 21, 38, 51

Poupon, Henri, 94, 95

Pour la peau d'un flic, 271

Pozner, Vladimir, 126

Pradot, Marcelle, 44

Pravda, 222

Préjean, Albert, 56, 74

Premier de cordée, 123, 124

Premier rendez-vous, 111

Prénom Carmen, 276–277

Préparez vos mouchoirs, 249

Presle, Micheline, 123

Pretty Baby, 261

Prévert, Jacques, 78, 88, 100–102, 104, 112–114, 117–118, 120–121, 128, 129, 130, 135–136, 149, 159, 211

Prévert, Pierre, 78, 104, 117–118

Prince, Charles, 23

Princesse de Clèves, La, 148

Printemps, Le, 237
Prisonnière, La, 214–215
Private Vices and Public Virtues, 246
Procès de Jeanne d'Arc, 192, 217
Proie pour l'ombre, La, 173
Prométhée . . . banquier, 44
Propre de l'homme, Le, 175, 212
Protéa, 26
Protozanov, Yakov, 39
Providence, 259–260
Pujol, René, 89
Punition, La, 187
Pyramide humaine, La, 186–187

Quadrille, 91
Quai des brumes, 87, 100, 101, 111,
    129
Quai des orfèvres, 128, 130, 150
Quand tu liras cette lettre, 164
Quatorze juillet, 85
Quatre cents coups, Les, 177–178,
    193, 199, 230, 231, 255
Quatre nuits d'un rêveur, 240–241
Quatre-vingt-treize, 34
Queen Elizabeth, 22, 38
Que la bête meure, 226–227
Que la fête commence, 250
Quelle joie de vivre, 188
Queneau, Raymond, 164

Rabier, Jean, 197, 211, 226
Rabinovitch, Gregor, 87
Radzirvilowicz, Jerzy, 276
Raimu, 72–73, 85, 88, 89, 94, 96,
    100, 103, 112, 119, 238
Ravel, Gaston, 40, 77
Ray, Aldo, 238
Ray, Man, 64
Ray, Michèle, 207
Ray, Nick, 203, 252
Rear Window, 199
Rebatet, Lucien, 121
Rebecca, 253
Reflux, Le, 170
Regain, 93, 95
Regard, Le, 265
Regard sur la folie, 187
Reggiani, Serge, 151, 232

Règle du jeu, La, 2, 58, 83, 84, 103,
    107–108, 120, 156
Reichenbach, François, 168, 221
Réjane, 38
Remontons les Champs-Elysées, 92
Remorques, 88
Renaissance, 213
Renaud, Madeleine, 88, 122
Rendez-vous de juillet, 131–132
Rendez-vous de minuit, Le, 189
Renoir, Claude, 173
Renoir, Jean, 1, 5, 51, 57–58, 76, 79,
    81–84, 85, 86, 89, 90, 93, 98, 100,
    103–108, 111, 122, 127, 128, 131,
    132, 146, 156–157, 167, 188–189,
    196, 197, 200, 238, 256
Renoir, Pierre, 82, 106
Repas de bébé, 9, 18, 200
Repos du guerrier, Le, 172–173
Resnais, Alain, 1, 5, 33, 61, 92, 142,
    146, 163, 164, 165, 167, 169, 171,
    178, 183–185, 193, 202, 206–207,
    208, 219, 224, 232–233, 259–60,
    261, 277
Retour à la raison, 64
Retour à Marseille, 263
Révélateur, Le, 274
Reynaud, Emile, 8
Richebé, Roger, 81
Rideau cramoisi, Le, 165, 173
Rien que les heures, 65
Rigaud, Georges, 76
Riva, Emmanuelle, 172, 207, 275
River, The, 156, 157
Rivette, Jacques, 63, 166, 175, 176,
    181–182, 198, 219, 235–236, 244,
    251, 261–262, 277
Robbe-Grillet, Alain, 5, 66, 184–185,
    208–210, 219, 234–235, 236, 244,
    246–247, 277, 278, 280
Robbe-Grillet, Catherine, 209
Robert, Yves, 170
Rohmer, Eric, 166, 167, 175, 176,
    177, 181, 193, 198–199, 225,
    227–229, 244, 261, 279–280
Romains, Jules, 54
Roman d'amour et d'aventures, Un, 38
Roman d'un mousse, Le, 29
Roman d'un tricheur, 92–93
Romans, Alain, 160
Ronde, La, 155

Ronet, Maurice, 132, 188, 195
Rosalie, 214
Rosay, Françoise, 54, 55, 97, 100
Rose France, 44
Rosier, Jacques, 171
Rossellini, Roberto, 86, 201
Rosza, Miklos, 259
Rouch, Jean, 186–187, 198
Roue, La, 35, 43, 47–49, 61, 85
Rouffe, Alida, 72–73
Rouge et le noir, Le, 152
Rouleau, Raymond, 123
Rouquier, Georges, 124, 141–142,
  162–163, 274
Route de Corinthe, La, 198
Rude journée pour la reine, 233, 263
Rue de l'Estrapade, 152
Ruisseau, Le, 118
Rupture, 175
Rupture, La, 227
Ruspoli, Mario, 187
Ryan, Robert, 238

Sadoul, Georges, 15, 114
Sagan, Françoise, 197
Saît-on jamais, 166
Salacrou, Armand, 138
Salaire de la peur, Le, 148, 149–150
Salou, Louis, 114
Salut les cubains, 196
Samouraï, Le, 195, 238
Sanda, Dominique, 241, 278
Sandberg, Serge, 92
Sang des autres, Le, 272
Sang des bêtes, Le, 142, 163
Sang d'un poète, Le, 65, 70, 115, 142,
  190
Sang et lumières, 162
Sans lendemain, 89
Sans soleil, 273–274
Santiago, Hugo, 250
Sapène, Jean, 38
Sassard, Jacqueline, 226
Sa tête, 62
Satie, Erik, 56
Sautet, Claude, 170, 231–232, 244,
  258, 269, 271
Sauve qui peut (la vie), 265
Scandale, Le, 198
Schell, Maria, 173

Schneider, Maria, 238, 262
Schneider, Romy, 232
Schpountz, Le, 94, 95
Schüfftan, Eugen, 182
Schwartz, Maurice, 23
Schygulla, Hanna, 276
Scob, Edith, 182–206
Scotto, Vincent, 93, 95
Séban, Paul, 221
Seberg, Jean, 179
Section spéciale, 254
Sedouy, Alain de, 223–224
Sel de la terre, Le, 142, 162
Selfish Yates, 43
Semaine de vacances, Une, 251
Semprun, Jorge, 207, 224, 232
Série noire, 249, 250
Serrault, Michel, 253, 272
Séverin-Mars, 46, 47, 48, 85
Seyrig, Delphine, 200, 206, 207
Shields, Brooke, 261
Sierra de Teruel, 91
Signe du lion, Le, 181, 193, 198, 228
Signora di tutta, La, 89
Signoret, Simone, 151, 238
Sigurd, Jacques, 128, 129–130, 188
Si j'avais quatre dromadaires, 208
Si j'étais un espion, 249
Si jolie petite plage, Une, 129, 144
Silence, Le, 42
Silence de la mer, Le, 142
Silence est d'or, Le, 128, 137–138,
  144, 159
Simon, Michel, 80, 82, 83, 100, 101,
  137, 138
Simon, Simone, 106
Siodmak, Robert, 88
Sirène du Mississippi, La, 230
Sixième face du pentagon, La, 221
Six juin à l'aube, Le, 122, 136
Sladanowsky, Max, 8
Smic, smac, smoc, 232
Soeurs Brontë, Les, 252
Soeurs ennemies, Les, 43
Solinas, Franco, 225
Solitude du chanteur de fond, La, 221
Sologne, Madeleine, 115
*Son nom de Venise dans Calcutta
  désert*, 266–267
Sortie des usines Lumière, La, 9, 10
S.O.S. Noronha, 162

Souffle au coeur, Le, 229, 249
Soupirant, Le, 216
Souriante Madame Beudet, La, 43, 59
Sous le ciel de Paris, 160
Sous les toits de Paris, 74, 76, 77, 85, 100
Souvenirs d'en France, 251
Spaak, Charles, 77–78, 88, 96–97, 99, 105, 121, 128, 137, 149, 159
Spacek, Sissy, 254
Specht, Georges, 40
Spielberg, Steven, 63
Spieler, Der, 123
Spirale, La, 254
Statues meurent aussi, Les, 146, 164
Stavisky, 232–233
Sternberg, Joseph von, 210
Stewart, Alexandra, 260
Story of Sin, The, 246
Stradling, Harry, 96–97
Straub, Jean-Marie, 214, 265–266, 274
Straus, Oscar, 155
Stroheim, Erich von, 49, 57, 78–79, 114
Subor, Michel, 180
Sur et sous la communication (6 × 2), 265
Suzanne Simonin, la religieuse de Diderot, 198
Swaim, Bob, 273
Sylvie, 116, 213
Sylvie et le fantôme, 132
Symphonie pastorale, La, 129

Tachella, Jean-Claude, 249
Talon, Gérard, 87
Tant qu'on a la santé, 217
Taris, 79
Tati, Jacques, 4, 13, 132, 139, 140, 144, 148, 160–161, 164, 167, 170, 190–191, 193, 215–216, 219, 240, 241–243, 244
Tavernier, Bertrand, 250–251, 268, 271, 272
Téchiné, André, 251–252, 268
Tempestaire, Le, 142
Tendre ennemie, La, 89
Terrain vague, 188
Terra trema, La, 141

Terreur des Batignolles, La, 119
Terzieff, Laurent, 274
Tessier, Valentine, 84
Testament d'Orphée, Le, 190, 193
Testament du Docteur Cordelier, Le, 188–189
Tête contre les murs, La, 182
Tête d'un homme, La, 82
Thérèse Desqueyroux, 183, 239
Thérèse Raquin (1928), 55, 59
Thérèse Raquin (1953), 159–160
Thiher, Allen, 2
Thomas l'imposteur, 206
Thon, Jean-Pierre, 221
Tigre aime la chair fraîche, Le, 198
Tigre se parfume à la dynamite, Le, 198
Tih Minh, 38
Tire au flanc, 58
Tirez sur le pianiste, 178, 203
Toni, 84, 93, 103, 107
Tonnelier, Le, 124
Tonnerre, Le, 42, 43
Topaze (1933), 72
Topaze (1936), 94
Torrent, Le, 44
Touchez pas au grisbi, 27, 152, 165, 195
Tour, La, 57, 65
Tour au large, 58, 65
Tourjansky, Viatcheslaw, 53, 62
Tournoi, Le, 58
Tous les garçons s'appellent Patrick, 166
Toute la mémoire du monde, 164
Toute révolution est un coup de dés, 265
Toute une vie, 232
Tout l'or du monde, 189
Tout va bien, 223
Trafic, 241–242
Tragédie de la mine, La, 77
Train en marche, Le, 221
Trans-Europ-Express, 209, 210
Trauner, Alexandre, 100, 102, 113
Travail, 38
Travailleurs émigrés, 221
Traversée de Paris, La, 153
Trenet, Charles, 117, 163
Tricheurs, Les, 188
Trintignant, Jean-Louis, 209, 212, 228

Tristana, 243
Trois chambres à Manhattan, 214
Trois masques, Les, 77
Trop tôt, trop tard, 265–266
Trou, Le, 189–190, 195
Trou dans le mur, Un, 71
Troye, Suzanne de, 93
Truffaut, François, 5, 147, 166, 167,
   169, 172, 175, 176, 177–178, 189,
   193, 199–200, 219, 225, 229,
   230–231, 244, 251, 252, 254–257,
   260, 269, 272, 276
Tu ne tueras point, 189

Ultimatum, 88
Une chante, l'autre pas, , L', 262
Une et l'autre, L', 213
Unholy Night, The, 72
Uns et les autres, Les, 258
Untel père et fils, 98
Urban, Charles, 11

Vacances de Monsieur Hulot, Les, 160,
   190, 216
Vadim, Roger, 166, 172–173, 195
Vailland, Roger, 126
Valentin, Albert, 121
Valse royale, La, 87
Valseuses, Les, 249
Vampire, Le, 142
Vampires, Les, 35, 36–37, 63
Vampyr, 62
Van Gogh, 142
Van Parys, Georges, 75, 158
Varda, Agnès, 148, 165, 174, 175,
   185, 196–197, 219, 233
Vauthier, René, 146
Vecchiali, Paul, 225
Védrès, Nicole, 142
Velle, Gaston 14, 20, 31, 34
Vendanges, 141
Vendémiaire, 36
Vent d'est, 222
Ventura, Lino, 195, 238, 253
Vénus aveugle, La, 111
Vénus d'or, La, 114
Vérité, La, 188
Vérité sur l'imaginaire passion d'un
   inconnu, La, 237

Verneuil, Henri, 170
Véronique et son cancre, 166
Vertige, Le, 60
Vertigo, 273
Vertov, Dziga, 78
Vice et la vertu, Le, 195
Victimes de l'alcoolisme, Les, 14
Victor Hugo, 162
Vie, Une, 173
Vie à l'envers, La, 213
Vie drôle, La, 27
Vie du Christ, La, 25
Vie d'un joueur, La, 14
Vieille dame indigne, La, 213
Vie est à nous, La, 90, 104
Vie est un roman, La, 277
Vie et passion de Notre Seigneur Jésus
   Christ, 14
Vie, l'amour et la mort, La, 232
Vie privée, 174
Vie sans joie, Une, 57
Vie telle qu'elle est, La, 27
Vigo, Jean, 76, 78–81, 83, 84, 85, 90,
   170, 183, 255
Vilardebo, Carlos, 168
Villa destin, 44
Vilmorin, Louise de, 173
Vincent, François, Paul . . . et les
   autres, 231
Vinneuil, François, 121
Violette Nozière, 257–258
Viot, Jacques, 102
Visages d'enfants, 54, 55, 59
Visconti, Luchino, 103, 141, 240
Visiteurs du soir, Les, 112–113, 124,
   135
Viva Maria, 196
Vivement dimanche!, 272, 276
Vivre pour vivre, 212
Vivre sa vie, 175, 180–181, 201
Vladimir et Rosa, 222
Voie lactée, La, 243
Voleur, Le, 196, 229
Volkov, Alexandre, 39, 52, 53, 62
Volonte, Gian Maria, 238
Voyage à la lune, 11
Voyage à travers l'impossible, 11
Voyou, Le, 232

Wademant, Annette, 128, 132

Wajda, Andrzej, 276
Wakhévitch, Georges, 115
Walbrook, Anton, 155
Warm, Hermann, 53
Weekend, 204–205, 241
Weingarten, Isabelle, 241
Welles, Orson, 183
Werther, 89
Wiazemsky, Anne, 205, 274
Wiene, Robert, 89
Willy, 93
Winnington, Richard, 115

Yameneko, Hayao, 273
Yanne, Jean, 225, 226
Yeux sans visages, Les, 182

Yoshiwara, 89
Yoyo, 216–217

Z, 224, 254
Zavattini, Cesare, 134
Zazie dans le métro, 174
Zecca, Ferdinand, 14, 16, 18, 19, 34
Zelnick, Friedrich, 55
Zéro de conduite, 79–80, 90
Zigomar, 25, 26, 32, 33
Zigomar contre Nick Carter, 26
Zigomar, peau d'anguille, 26
Zimmer, Bernard, 97, 100, 114
Zone, La, 65
Zukor, Adolph, 22